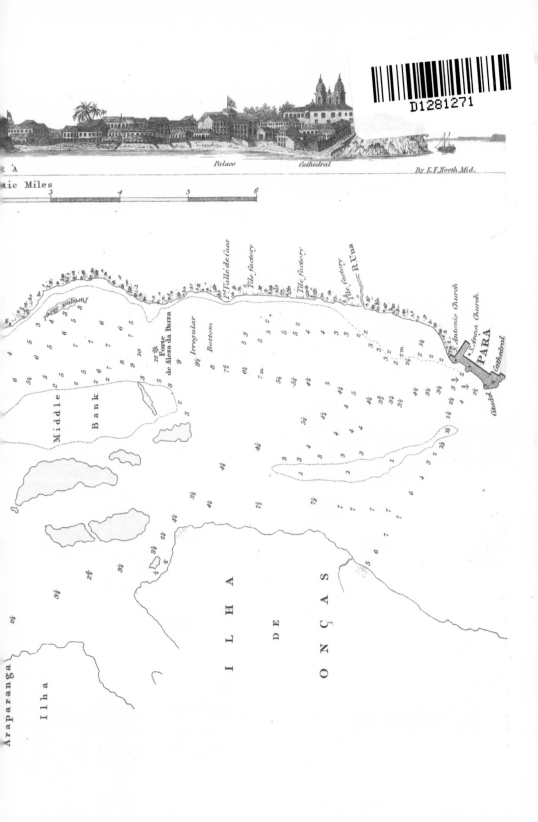

R A

Palace   Cathedral

By E.F.North Mid.

tic Miles

3   4   5   6

Ponta Sucuju

Middle   Bank

Forte de Aleza da Bara

Irregular   Bottom

Ft Folle de cias

Tile factory

Tile factory

The factory

The factory

R.Una

S.Antonio Church

S. Anna Church

PARÁ

Cidade Cathedral

Araparanga   Ilha

I L H A   D E   O N Ç A S

Rebellion on the Amazon

The Cabanagem, Race, and Popular Culture in the North of Brazil, 1798–1840

The Brazilian Amazon experienced, in the late 1830s, one of Brazil's largest peasant and urban-poor insurrections, known as the Cabanagem. Uniquely, rebels succeeded in controlling provincial government and town councils for more than a year. In this first book-length study in English, the rebellion is placed in the context of late colonial and early national society and economy. It compares the Cabanagem with contemporaneous Latin American peasant rebellions and challenges to centralized authority in Brazil. Using unpublished documentation, it reveals – contrary to other studies – that insurgents were not seeking revolutionary change or separation from the rest of Brazil. Rather, rebels wanted to promote their vision of a newly independent nation and an end to exploitation by a distant power. The Cabanagem is critical to understanding why the Amazon came to be perceived as a land without history.

Mark Harris is based at the University of St Andrews. He was awarded a British Academy postdoctoral fellowship, 1996–1999, and the Philip Leverhulme Prize in 2004. He is the author of *Life on the Amazon: The Anthropology of a Brazilian Peasant Village* (2000), editor of *Ways of Knowing* (2007), and coeditor (with Stephen Nugent) of *Some Other Amazonians* (2006). He has also taught at the Federal University of Pará in Belém, Brazil, and the London School of Economics.

CAMBRIDGE LATIN AMERICAN STUDIES

General Editor
Herbert S. Klein
Gouverneur Morris Emeritus Professor of History, Columbia University
Director of the Center of Latin American Studies, Professor of History,
and Hoover Senior Fellow, Stanford University

95
Rebellion on the Amazon: The Cabanagem, Race,
and Popular Culture in the North of Brazil, 1798–1840

Other Books in the Series

(Continued after the Index)

Rebellion on the Amazon

The Cabanagem, Race, and Popular Culture
in the North of Brazil, 1798–1840

MARK HARRIS

University of St Andrews

CAMBRIDGE
UNIVERSITY PRESS

CAMBRIDGE UNIVERSITY PRESS
Cambridge, New York, Melbourne, Madrid, Cape Town, Singapore,
São Paulo, Delhi, Dubai, Tokyo, Mexico City

Cambridge University Press
32 Avenue of the Americas, New York, NY 10013-2473, USA

www.cambridge.org
Information on this title: www.cambridge.org/9780521437233

© Mark Harris 2010

First published 2010

Printed in the United States of America

A catalog record for this publication is available from the British Library.

Library of Congress Cataloging in Publication Data
Harris, Mark, 1969–
Rebellion on the Amazon : the Cabanagem, race, and popular culture in the north of Brazil,
1798–1840 / Mark Harris.
p. cm. – (Cambridge Latin American studies ; 95)
ISBN 978-0-521-43723-3 (hardback)
1. Pará (Brazil : State) – History – 18th century. 2. Pará (Brazil : State) – History – Cabanagem,
1835–1840. 3. Amazon River Region – History – 18th century. 4. Social conflict – Brazil – Pará
(State) – History – 18th century. 5. Government, Resistance to – Brazil – Pará (State) – History –
19th century. I. Title. II. Series.
F2586.H37 2010
981'.15032–dc22 2010021221

ISBN 978-0-521-43723-3 Hardback

Endpapers: Profile of Belém, by E. F. North
[inset to River Pará, Image 8.1], 1835.
© British Library Board. All Rights Reserved, Maps SEC. 9 (1179).

Contents

List of Illustrations

Maps

Images

Figures

List of Tables

Abbreviations

ABAPP	*Annaes da Biblioteca e Archivo Publico do Pará* (a periodical)
ABNRJ	*Anais da Biblioteca Nacional, Rio de Janeiro* (a periodical)
AHI	Arquivo Histórico do Itamaraty, Rio de Janeiro
AHU	Arquivo Histórico Ultramarino, Lisbon
APEP	Arquivo Público do Estado do Pará, Belém
APOEP	Arquivo de Prelazia de Óbidos, Estado do Pará
APSEP	Arquivo de Prelazia de Santarém, Estado do Pará
BIHGB	Biblioteca do Instituto Histórico e Geográphico Brasileiro, Rio de Janeiro
BNRJ	Biblioteca Nacional, Rio de Janeiro
NAL	National Archives, London
RIHGB	*Revista do Instituto Histórico e Geográphico Brasileiro* (a periodical)

Preface and Acknowledgments

Most people will not associate the Amazon with what was arguably the largest peasant rebellion in the history of Brazil. The Amazon is known for reasons other than insurrections. Its indigenous people, lush forests, and profuse wildlife normally dominate popular and academic representations. This book tells another story. It seeks to recover the lives and demands of Amazonian rebels. Mostly peasants living near towns along the river, they sought to defend their livelihood from land-grabbing élites and their political exclusion from a newly independent nation. The defense of a way of life was as much about protecting their environment as advancing an ideological vision. The challenge of this book is to bring together these various histories in one study: the exotic and the mundane, the peasant and the Indian, the historical and the ethnographic, the political and the cultural. Known as the Cabanagem, the rebellion occurred during a time of general social upheaval in Brazil in the 1830s and affected much of the Brazilian Amazon.

The study is aimed at contributing to a new wave of scholarship on the region. Led by scholars who largely work and live in the Amazon, new understandings are emerging. The huge quantity of the material housed locally and nationally as well as in archives in Europe and North America is coming under greater scrutiny. More critical positions concerning the place of the Amazon in the context of the nation and Latin America are coming to the forefront. The hold of perceiving the region apart from, and yet dominated by, the rest of Brazil and as a land without a history of its own is loosening. I was fortunate to get to know some of these scholars while I taught anthropology in Belém at the Federal University of Pará, 2003–2004, and in a subsequent visit in 2006. Supported by the Leverhulme Trust, the British Academy, and the Arts and Humanities Research Council, I was able to steep my anthropological training in a thorough historical immersion.

In Belém, Manuel Dutra, Décio Gúzman, Magda Ricci, Aldrin Figueiredo, Geraldo Mártires Coelho, Heraldo Maués, Rafael Chambouleyron, Lúcio Flávio Pinto, and Wilma Leitão patiently answered my questions. They helped expand my understanding of Pará. Special thanks to Dutra and Rafael for their continuing generosity. The postgraduate students on my "500 anos do pensamento mestiço na Amazônia" ended up also teaching me a great deal, especially

Roseanne Pinto and Carmen Izabel. My transcribers in Belém were history students Leiticia Barriga, Alanna Souto Cardoso, and Paulo Barreto. They were prepared to spend uncountable hours in the archive and loyally sent transcribed documents to me across the Atlantic. The staff at the Arquivo Público do Pará, especially Guarete, provided invaluable assistance. In Rio, Otávio Vehlo, Claudia Barcellos Rezende, and Benjamin Buclet offered hospitality and good conversation. Back in Óbidos, Edson Gomes and Raimundo and Ana Côrrea wanted me to write about their histories. I hope this goes some way to addressing that request. Marta Amoroso and Leandro Mahalem de Lima, in São Paulo, shared their ideas and work with me. A brief meeting with André Machado was more than lucky. Conversations with David Cleary, mostly in Belém, were critical in developing my understanding of the material I was reading. His insights were always sharp and welcome.

Across the north Atlantic, Heather Flynn Roller and Barbara Sommer were invaluable interlocutors. Both pointed me toward numerous sources and made important observations that helped to contain some of my more far-flung interpretations. At St Andrews, Peter Clark generously supported the writing of this book by giving me time to think and write. Paloma Gay y Blasco, Will Fowler, James Harris, Tristan Platt, Nigel Rapport, and Huon Wardle have made comments (sometimes offhand) that, in various ways, found their way into the writing of this book. Tristan has constantly pushed forward my intellectual horizons. Graeme Sandeman drew the maps. In London, Stephen Nugent has helped me frame the pertinent questions and encouraged my interest in an historical anthropology of Amazonia.

Jim Hunter and Pat Stocker commented on a first draft of the manuscript. Their readings not only improved some of the poor expression but sharpened the argument. Herbert Klein and two reviewers for Cambridge University Press read a subsequent version and forced me to cast the net more widely. Without question, they have contributed to making this book better than it was. Any factual errors or misunderstandings are mine alone. All translations are mine unless stated otherwise.

My sincere gratitude goes to all these people. Lastly, and far from least, I thank my family. Their part in bringing this book to its conclusion is immeasurable – as is my appreciation.

Acervo da Fundação Biblioteca Nacional – Brazil:

Image 2.2 View of the riverside village of Monforte, c. 1785
Image 2.6 View of the Praça das Mercês with market, Belém, c. 1792
Image 4.1 Collecting expeditions and hunting for turtles, c. 1785
Image 5.1 A Mura Indian snorting tobacco (paricá), c. 1785
Image 5.2 The use of a trumpet by an Amazonian Indian [Mundurucu?], c. 1785

From Daniel Kidder and James Fletcher, *Brazil and the Brazilians*, 1865:

Image 2.3 Montaria, dugout canoe, c. 1840
Image 2.5 Amazonian canoe, river sailing vessel, c. 1840

Cyrillo Hercules Florence Collection – São Paulo, Brazil:

Image 2.4 A study of the sky, made from memory two or three months after seeing it. A view of the Amazon River is presented near Monte Alegre, in Portuguese Guyana (São Carlos, March 9, 1935), watercolor by Hercule Florence, c. 1828 [two igarités]

Portugal, Arquivo Histórico Ultramarino – PT, AHU:

Image 4.2 Topographic map of the land grant belonging to Francisco José de Faria, 1814

© British Library Board. All Rights Reserved, Maps SEC. 9 (1179):

Image 6.1 Profile of Belém, by E. F. North [inset to River Pará, Image 8.1], 1835
Image 8.1 River Pará surveyed by Captain Sir Everard Home, Baronet and Mr. Byron Drury, Mate of HMS Racehorse, 1835 (published 1836)

INTRODUCTION
Divergent Amazonia

At a major traffic intersection on the outskirts of Belém, one of the largest cities in the Amazon region, a striking monument can be seen. Slabs of concrete emerge from the ground in a diagonal fashion with a single break, like a hand rising from the earth, or perhaps a hand descending into water (what comes to my mind is Stevie Smith's poem, "Not waving but drowning"). Commissioned in 1985 by the state government and designed by Brazil's leading architect, Oscar Niemeyer, it is a memorial to the Cabanagem, the rebellion 150 years earlier by people of the Brazilian Amazon.

Even a backpacker could not mistake the modern regional government's appropriation of the rebellion. Yet the monument may be read in various ways. To some local residents it is an inconsequential piece of public art, while others gather there every year to mark the anniversary of the great assault on Belém on January 7. To the historian, it may represent the power of the masses to challenge how they are ruled, yet also the success of Brazil as a nation in quashing dissent and preventing its fragmentation shortly after independence from Portugal. The Cabanagem rebellion of 1835–1840 was not only a struggle by oppressed people analogous to many other such struggles around the world in the late eighteenth and early nineteenth centuries, it was also potentially separatist. It might have proved the turning point at which the Brazilian Amazon diverged from the rest of Portuguese-speaking America. Instead, the rebellion's ultimate failure forced the region back into convergence, subordinating its sociological and historical distinctness to a larger entity. An internal colonialism was achieved whose legacy lasts to this day. Ever since, the rulers of Pará (the name of the state in the eastern Amazon encompassing most of the rebellion) and Brazil have had to contend with the region's ambiguous identity; and the significance of the Cabanagem is as contested today as ever.

The present study goes back to the contemporary documents, though few of those that survived were written by the rebels. This book can be described as an historical ethnography written by an anthropologist. I hope that nothing intrinsically separates my methodology from that of someone trained in "history," but also that my anthropological fieldwork in Pará gives this study a distinctive strength. Since 1992 I have conducted fieldwork with peasant riverine dwellers in Pará (in a place upriver of Belém), and their oral histories are rich with references to the Cabanagem. They tell, for example, of the way the Portuguese hid their money and gold inside saints' icons, or buried it under the ground as they fled quickly to avoid the rebels. My experience of life in and on the Amazon gave me privileged access to the riverine world of these people and their bosses, and has allowed me to marry an ethnographically sharpened sensibility with R. G. Collingwood's method of imaginative reenactment of the 'inside' of human actions – people's thoughts and purposes.[1] I aim to paint an overall picture of the social and political conditions of life in the Amazon in the early nineteenth century: a shaped form in which to place rebel motivations. This approach is like creating a face from a mask.

The sources certainly exist for such an approach. Many have already been used by other scholars of the Cabanagem. Since the 1840s the rebellion has been the object of diverse examinations and commentaries. These examiners include visitors who came in the aftermath and heard anecdotes from those who had witnessed terrible scenes, military officials who wrote memoirs and a priest who collected stories.[2] Around the centenary of the Cabanagem, a series of books appeared that were based on a close reading of some of the extensive documentation in the archive in Belém.[3] The men who wrote these works were the first to address systematically such core problems as the conflict

1 My understanding of Collingwood and the method of reenactment has been coached by Tristan Platt. See, for example his "Knowing Silence and Merging Horizons: The Case of the Great Potosí Cover-Up" (with Pablo Quisbert), in Mark Harris (ed.), *Ways of Knowing*, Oxford: Berghahn Books, 2007. For Collingwood's statement on reenactment, see his Epilegomena in *The Idea of History*, Oxford: Oxford University Press, 1994, 282–302.

2 The visitors included the Protestant missionary Daniel Kidder (James Cooley Fletcher and Daniel Parish Kidder, *Brazil and the Brazilians: Portrayed in Historical and Descriptive Sketches*. Boston: Little, Brown, 1879), the Victorian naturalist Henry Walter Bates (*The Naturalist on the River Amazons*, 2 vols. London: John Murray, 1863), and the Prussian Prince Adalbert (Prince H. W. Adalbert, *Travels in the South of Europe and in Brazil with a Voyage up the Amazon and the Xingu*. London: 1849). The military officers were Felipe Leal (F. J. P. Leal, *Correções e Ampliações ao que Sobre a Revolução que Arrebantou na Cidade do Pará em Janeiro de 1835 publicou o Conselheiro João Manoel Pereira da Silva*. Bahia, 1879) and José Bettancourt (author of unpublished documents). The priest was Francisco Bernardino de Souza (F. de Bernardino de Souza, *Lembranças e Curiosidades do Valle do Amazonas*. Pará, Typografia do Futuro, 1873).

3 These main authors here are Jorge Hurley (*A Cabanagem*, Belém: Livraria Classica, 1936; and *Traços Cabanos*, Belém: Oficina Gráfica, 1936), João de Palma Muniz (*Adesão do Grão-Pará a Independência*, Belém: Conselho Estadual da Cultura, 1973, though strictly speaking this work is not on the Cabanagem it nevertheless is a substantial study of the independence period leading up to it), and Ernesto Cruz ("A Cabanagem," in *História do Pará*, vol. 1, Belém: Universidade Federal do Pará, 1963). Connected to this group but slightly later was Arthur Cesar Ferreira Reis, whose broad body of work covers all periods of Amazonian history, though he never wrote a study specifically on the Cabanagem. See especially his *História do Amazonas*, Belo Horizonte: Editora Itatiaia; and *A Política de Portugal no Valle Amazônico*, Belém: Secult, 1993.

between regional and national élites.[4] Subsequent analyses developed related themes, including the role of Afro-Brazilian slaves and Indians, the ideological bases of the rebellion and Pará's social networks with the transatlantic world.[5] Along with contemporary historians of Pará, I begin from the view that the insurrection cannot be portrayed as a conflict between two clearly marked enemies and that its origins are to be found in the colonial period.[6] Consistent with recent scholarship on most rebellions in post-independence Brazil, I also argue cabanos were not separatists. Rather, they were defenders of their way of life and motivated by their interpretation of liberalism. At the time, the rebels used the term *patria*, or homeland, to refer to the place they wanted to protect, which signified, according to Roderick Barman, "the visible, physical community in which an individual was born, brought up, married and pursued a living and raised a family"'[7]

4 However, the first examination of the Cabanagem was *Motins Políticos, ou Historia dos Principais Acontecimentos Políticos da Província do Pará, desde o ano de 1821 até 1835* (or literally "Political Revolts" for short, 3 vols, Belém: Universidade Federal do Pará, 1970) by Domingos Raiol. Originally comprising five volumes and published between 1865 and 1890, it remains foundational to understanding the turbulent period from independence to the Cabanagem. Raiol's father was murdered by rebels in a town in the interior; this fact seems to have committed him to a life of collecting material and then completing his study (while also serving in important political offices). Raiol, like anyone, has his prejudices; for example, the lack of interest in popular politics, but he treats the primary documents with respect. Given that documentary sources on the rebellion are extensive – difficult for any one researcher to command – the work of others becomes critically important. Whatever the biases of previous studies, I have found particularly useful those that have dealt reasonably with the documentation and permit new questions to be asked of it.

5 In the following chapter I review the secondary literature more fully. Some of the most recent authors who have written on those topics are Vicente Salles, for example, *Memorial da Cabanagem*, and "A Cabanagem, os Escravos, os Engenhos," 33–49; in his *O Negro na Formação da Sociedade Paraense*, Belém: Editora Paka-Tatu, 2004; Miguel Menendez, "A Área Madeira-Tapajós: Situação de Contato e Relações entre o Colonizador e Indígena," in Manuela Carneiro da Cunha (ed.), *História dos Índios do Brasil*. São Paulo: Companhia das Letras, 1992; Magda Ricci, "O Fim do Grão-Pará e o Nascimento do Brasil: Movimentos Sociais, Levantes e Deserções no Alvorecer do Novo Império, 1808–1840," in Mary Del Priore and Flávio dos Santos Gomes (eds,), *Os Senhores dos Rios: Amazônia, Margens e Histórias*, Rio de Janeiro: Elsevier, 2003; and "Cabanagem, Cidadania e Identidade Revolucionária: O Problema do Patriotismo na Amazônia entre 1835 e 1840," Tempo (Niterói), 2007, 11, 22, 5–30; John Chasteen, "Cautionary Tale: A Radical Priest, Nativist Agitation, and the Origin of Brazilian Civil Wars," in Rebecca Earle (ed.), *Rumours of Wars: Civil Conflict in Nineteenth-Century Latin America*. London: Institute of Latin American Studies, 2000.

6 See Carlos de Araujó Moreira Neto, *Índios da Amazônia, de Maioria a Minoria (1750–1850)*, Petropolis: Vozes, 1985; Vicente Salles, *Memorial da Cabanagem*, Belém: CEJUP, 1992; Pasquale di Paolo, *Cabanagem: A Revolução Popular da Amazônia*, Belém: Conselho de Cultura, 1985; Geraldo Mártires Coelho, *Anarquistas, Demagogos e Dissidentes: A Imprensa Liberal no Pará de 1822*, Belém: CEJUP, 1993; Magda Ricci, "O Fim do Grão-Pará e o Nascimento do Brasil;" David Cleary, "'Lost Altogether to the Civilized World': Race and the Cabanagem in Northern Brazil, 1750 to 1850," *Comparative Studies in Society and History*, 1998, 40, 1, 109–135.

7 Roderick Barman, *Brazil: The Forging of a Nation, 1798–1852*, Stanford: Stanford University Press, 1988, 26.

The Cabanagem is a well-known rebellion in the history of Brazil. It occurred during a time of rupture and uncertainty: the monarch who had led Brazil to independence had abdicated amid a rising tide of radical liberalism and virulent attacks on the Portuguese. His son was too young to rule, so a regency administration was created. Over the following four years, newly introduced laws gave more power to the regions. In the 1830s, significant uprisings took place not only in Pará but also in the northern provinces of Pernambuco (the Cabanada), Maranhão (the Balaiada) and Bahia (the Sabinada and the Muslim slave revolt of 1835), and in the far south of Brazil (the Farroupilha). Each one threatened the future existence of Brazil and challenged, in different measures, popular exclusion from politics, élite land grabbing, slavery, and monarchy. Ever since, historians have grappled with the national nature of the political breakdown during the regency period (1831–1840).[8] What interests kept Brazil together? Were the rebellions or, more accurately, their repression necessary for the assertion of national integrity and identity? If so, whose version?[9] How can popular participation in politics be understood? In what way, if at all, was each rebellion in line with the others? Given the large regional differences in Brazil at the time, might their contemporaneity hide local processes and relations that cannot be forced into a national perspective? These are ongoing questions to which this book makes a contribution.

In seeking answers, it becomes apparent that the Portuguese Amazon bears significant comparisons with Spanish-speaking areas of Latin America where concentrations of indigenous people were involved in the colonial regime (such as the Andes and Mexico). The rich literature on peasants, rural revolt, political consciousness, and agrarian structures in those places has helped to sharpen the questions emerging from the Amazon.[10] Across the continent in the nineteenth century there was mass engagement with

8 For example, see Henrique Handelmann, *História do Brasil*, Instituto Histórico e Geográphico Brasileiro, Rio de Janeiro 1931 [1860]; José Pereira da Silva, *História do Brazil na Menoridade do Pedro 2*, Rio de Janeiro: Havre, 1888; Caio Prado, *Evolução Política do Brasil*, São Paulo: Editora Brasiliense, 1976; Emilia Viotti da Costa, *The Brazilian Empire: Myths and Histories*, Chapel Hill: University of North Carolina Press, 2000; Boris Fausto, *História Concisa do Brasil*, São Paulo: EDUSP, 2001.

9 It should also be mentioned that the Institute of Brazilian History and Geography was inaugurated in October 1838. Intellectually, the moment was captured in the Institute's prize-winning essay by German naturalist Karl Martius on the topic of the identity of Brazil, namely, the combination of Indian, European, and African elements in a fusion unique to Brazil (Karl Martius, "How the History of Brazil Should be Written," in Bradford E. Burns, (ed.), *Perspectives on Brazilian History*. New York: Columbia University Press, 1967.).

10 In the following chapter, I review this literature more fully. See, for example, Steve Stern (ed.), *Resistance, Rebellion and Consciousness in the Andean Peasant World, 18th to 20th Centuries*, Madison: University of Wisconsin Press, 1987, for the Andes; and Friederich Katz, *Riot, Rebellion and Revolution: Rural Social Conflict in Mexico*, Princeton: Princeton University Press 1989, for Mexico.

liberalism and a factionalized élite mobilizing supporters in various kinds of alliances. Questions worth noting here: What were the peasants' and urban poor's motives in forming such connections? How did peasants engage with central state systems? What were the ethnic and class characteristics of the peasantry in the Amazon?

A note on the term Cabanagem: it means the activity of people who live in *cabanas*, the region's poorest housing – palm and wood huts. These inhabitants were called *cabanos*, the designation carrying associations of backwardness, poverty, and sedition. It is unlikely the rebels ever accepted the term *cabanos* for themselves; and they had no overall name for their rebellion. The leading participants described themselves as "defenders of the homeland and freedom." The term *Cabanagem* was applied retrospectively, later in the century.

Sources

This study relies chiefly on documents now housed in the Public Archive of Pará in Belém. These are mostly letters, military and municipal reports, and judicial investigations sent to the regional governor in Belém. Overwhelmingly, they were written by those who opposed the rebels. Some of the writers were Portuguese, but many were Paraenses of a few generations' standing. The local level documents have allowed me to get closer to life as it was experienced and to events on the ground as they were developing, while recognizing the possibilities of bias and deception. Church records from the older parishes of the region are variable and incomplete; yet it is possible to reconstruct some family relations from them. These books consist of baptism and marriage registers and are kept in church offices.

Not all letters were written by clerks; other educated people included priests, children of wealthy parents and Indian headmen sent to Belém to school.[11] The letters by these people tend to be more personal; sometimes they write to the governor to request charity. What has not survived is local correspondence between village officials, colleagues, or friends. One of the first acts of cabanos on taking a town was to burn the municipal archive, perhaps to start anew. For this reason and the lack of care, there are apparently no local collections of correspondence beyond Belém before the 1840s.

The enormity of the region has meant that for some topics, such as family and kinship, a more detailed picture has been sought. For this purpose I have focused on the Lower Amazon around Santarém, up to Manaus and

---

11 See Ângela Maria Vieira Domingues, "A Educação dos Meninos Índios do Norte do Brasil na Segunda Metade do Século XVIII," in Maria Beatriz Nizza da Silva (ed.), *A Cultura Portuguesa na Terra da Santa Cruz*, Lisboa: Editorial Estampa, 1995, 67–77.

down to Gurupá, and the tributaries in the vicinity, most importantly the Tapajós River. This conforms with my prior fieldwork experience. Furthermore, the rebellion ended in the Lower Amazon in a series of dramatic events that have hardly been written about. The Lower Amazon was traditionally a place between the capital and the great backlands of the Negro River, where most Indian slaves were captured during the seventeenth and eighteenth centuries. Most of the Lower Amazon's aboriginal inhabitants either died of disease, escaped up the tributaries, or were forcibly moved to Belém. Nevertheless, a number of missions had been established by the early eighteenth century. Over the rest of that century, Portuguese colonists and Brazilian migrants settled there and made it their home and brought in Africans. Santarém was the second-largest town in Pará, and after the capital, the Lower Amazon was the most important center, politically and economically. It is no coincidence that the political and social convulsions lasted longer there than in other places.

Another category of documentation that has almost completely disappeared is the newspapers and pamphlets, which were abundant at the time. The editions circulated by the liberal press in Pará in the 1820s are lost, save for a handful of numbers sent to Lisbon, Rio de Janeiro, London, and Paris. Original versions of the manifestos and proclamations printed during the Cabanagem exist only outside Belém, either in Rio or London. These absences are another indication of the severity of the repression.

These Pará-derived sources are complemented with a range of other archival material to cover the region, and Brazil more generally, some of which has been published in other accounts and is housed in Lisbon, Rio, and London. Generally, documents outside Belém are higher-level bureaucratic correspondence.

Another important source for details on popular culture and daily life are the travelogs, scientific and otherwise. Between the 1750s and the late 1810s Pará was not visited by foreign scientists or travelers. There were, however, a number of Portuguese and Brazilian expeditions, the most famous of which was led by Alexandre Rodrigues Ferreira and published as the *Viagem Filosófica* (1783–1792). The trip produced some of the finest drawings on colonial Amazonia as well as ethnographic and historical essays on the Indian populations. With the opening of the ports in 1808 and growing scientific, economic, and strategic interest in the Amazon, many travelers came. For my purposes, Johann Spix's and Karl Martius' humanistic ethnography and history of the eastern Amazon (1819–1820), Hercule Florence's ill-fated trip down the Tapajós River (1827), and Henry Bates's intimate and intelligent portraits of river life (1849–1860) are the most useful and important. In Chapter 6, I have used an extraordinary story of a young Scotsman's escape from rebels in late 1835 in order to build a picture of life during the rebellion outside of Belém.

Finally, a lively tradition of oral histories exists on the Cabanagem, including one book by another Scot: a priest who collected stories around the region outside of Belém in the 1970s where the rebellion was planned and where some of the protagonists lived. The various memories are seen as "dangerous" because they challenge the dominant version of those who defeated the rebels. Although we have the stories, there is no analysis of them. What comes through is the ongoing significance of locale-specific stories or memories of the events, such as one family's escape from rebels and the tactics of both the cabanos and the imperial troops. A particular place is associated with a story or person. This is confirmed in my work in the Lower Amazon. Villagers recount where a cabano lookout was, where and how a Portuguese trader was skinned alive, the ongoing search for buried treasure, and so forth. Also intriguing are stories about trickery. Men used to dress up as women to avoid being called up for military service. A village would fly the black flag to indicate loyalty to the Empire, but when imperial troops came ashore they would be attacked.[12] However, this book does not make use of these oral traditions. They are a separate study raising their own questions about the connection between memory, trauma, and landscape, and why deceit should be such a prominent theme. Instead, the context for the analysis here is Brazilian historiography.

The Structure of the Study

This book is about the emergence of a new political actor in the far north of Brazil. The period spans the late colonial and early imperial phases. Although the Cabanagem took place in the postindependence period, its origins are anticolonial. The opening chapter surveys the historical and historiographic framework for this study. It places the analysis in relation to peasant rebellions in Latin America and sets of questions emerging from other revolts in regency Brazil. The next three chapters provide background to the rebellion and indicate some of its social, economic and political context. Chapter 2 details the importance of the riverscape and the culture that grew up around it in the colonial period and its influence on Indian, mixed-blood (*mestiço*), and white dwellers and Portuguese settlement. Chapter 3 considers the patterns of kinship and social organization in the

---

12 Mutiny among imperial soldiers was common, as was side-changing. Red was the color of the rebels and black for "loyalists," as they were known. Needless to add, treachery was frequently involved. For oral histories of the Cabanagem from the Acará area see Thiago Thorlby, *A Cabanagem na Fala do Povo*, São Paulo: Paulinas, 1987. An excellent analysis of contemporary stories of the Balaiada rebellion is offered by Matthis Röhrig Assunção, *A Guerra dos Bem-Te-Vis, a Balaiada na Memória Oral*, São Luís: SIOGE, 1988.

region, focusing on godparenthood as a way to understand class and ethnicity. The fourth chapter examines the origins of the rebellion in terms of agrarian structures, economic factors, and international developments. The following chapter provides an overview of the various forms of opposition to colonial forms of domination involving Indians, slaves, and mestiços. These struggles and protests converged with the anti-Portuguese liberal sentiments around independence. This examination provides a bridge to the second part of the book, which focuses on the Cabanagem and the period immediately leading up to it.

Chapter 6 focuses on the changing nature of ethnic relations in the years of conflict, as various groups struggled to make their presence felt in Pará's postindependence era. In particular, the distinction between élite liberalism and peasant revolt in the Amazon is developed. One of the imbalances in the Brazilian historiography of Cabanagem is its concentration on the capital city, so Chapter 7 attends to the interior and especially the rebel camp of Ecuipiranga, which tried to coordinate resistance when Belém fell. The final chapter investigates the repression after the failure of the rebellion and its effect on the people of the region, and its significance as rubber production dominated regional life. The Conclusion compares the Cabanagem to the set of political and social revolutions in the Brazilian provinces during the regency period and places the events within the context of later Amazonian developments.

Following the rebellion, rubber came to dominate the Amazon. This phase (c.1850 to c. 1920) has been relatively better studied by historians such as Warren Dean, Roberto Santos, and Barbara Weinstein.[13] Rubber production brought great prosperity to the region. At first, the naturally occurring stands in Pará were exploited by laborers who lived near them. These were probably the same people who fought, or whose parents did, in the Cabanagem, for some of the areas of heaviest fighting and stands of rubber trees were close together. By the 1870s, thousands of people were engaged in rubber-tapping, which became well accommodated to the peasant way of life – relative freedom of the conditions of work and movement, the exploitation of a diverse set of economic activities, and family-based residential groups. The peasants of Pará may have been politically subordinated, but they were able to continue their semiautonomous livelihoods. This situation suited the expanding demand for rubber in the 1840s

---

13 See Warren Dean, *Brazil and The Struggle for Rubber Study in Environmental History*, Cambridge: Cambridge University Press, 1987; Roberto Santos, *História Econômica da Amazônia (1800–1920)*, São Paulo: Editora Queiroz, 1982; Barbara Weinstein, *The Amazon Rubber Boom 1850–1920*, Stanford: Stanford University Press, 1985; and "Persistence of Caboclo Culture in the Amazon: the Impact of the Rubber Trade, 1850–1920," in Eugene Parker (ed.), "The Amazon Caboclo: Historical and Contemporary Perspectives." *Studies in Third World Societies*, 1985, 32, 89–113.

and 1850s (that is, the early phase), for it meant a workforce was already on hand. For most historians of the rubber boom, the preceding period is precisely that – anterior and less significant. By exploring the connections between it and the earlier phase, my aim is to show how the success of the rubber economy was made possible both by the persistence of peasant values and the submission of the region.

I

Pará in the Age of Revolution: History and Historiography

The Amazon – or Grão-Pará and Maranhão, as it was known then – was administered directly from Lisbon until 1772.[1] The rest of lusophone (Portuguese-speaking) America, called the state of Brazil, was governed as a separate entity. This situation was practical as much as historical. Belém, the capital of Grão-Pará, and São Luis, the capital of Maranhão, were nearer to Lisbon than Salvador and Rio de Janeiro were, the main Atlantic seaports of Brazil. Travel between the southern and northern ports was slow. In the Amazon, missionaries – principally the Jesuits – had commanded most trade and the administration of Indians until their expulsion in 1759.[2] Portuguese America became united politically in 1772 under a viceroy based in the colonial capital of Rio. Although the change of colonial government had little effect on the surface, it signaled the end of the desire to recognize the Amazon as a different place and the beginning of concerted pressure to make it conform to a master command. Still, there were strong regional and environmental particularities in late colonial Brazil that undermined political integration.

This centralizing force was the reforms of the Portuguese empire for significant change and state-led development in the mid- to late eighteenth century. Directives were issued to regulate most aspects of social life, including the naming of towns and people, orthodoxy in marriage and family housing, and a ban on racist prejudice. Indians were forced to work

---

1 Grão Pará encompassed most of what today we recognize as the Amazon region; the term *Amazonia* was not used until the late nineteenth century. Grão Pará included the Upper Amazon (around the Solimões River) and Negro River right up to the border with the Viceroyalty of Peru. Administratively, Grão Pará was a captaincy with a governor until 1820. Between 1820 and 1824, it was ruled by regionally elected juntas and then, with the new constitution and independence, it became the Province of Pará, with an appointed president. The Upper Amazon and Negro River region remained a politically subordinate but separate legal entity until 1855. Then, Pará split with the creation of the Province of Amazonas, with Manaus as the capital.

2 Indeed, the overwhelming control of the Jesuits in the Amazon was the "spark" that led to their persecution in the Iberian colonies. See Kenneth Maxwell, "The Spark: Pombal, the Amazon and the Jesuits," *Portuguese Studies* 2001, 17, 1, 168–183.

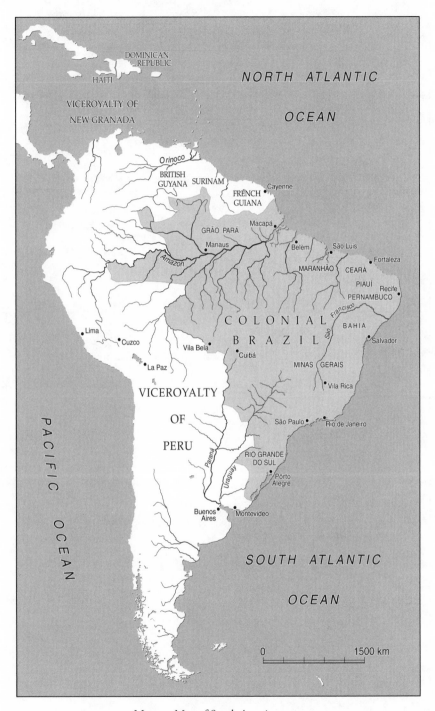

Map 1.1 Map of South America, 1799

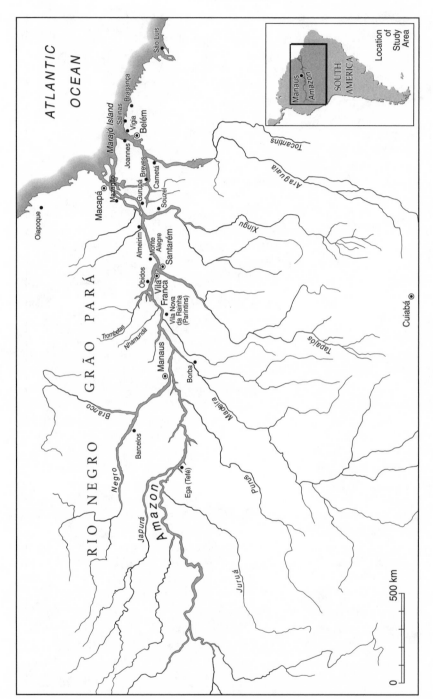

Map 1.2 Grão-Pará and the Rio Negro province, c. 1820

for the state, for a percentage of profits. Trade was monopolized by a publicly owned company, which also introduced slaves in tens of thousands: by the end of the eighteenth century they numbered about twenty percent of the population. Yet the slave presence did not significantly increase productivity, and attempts to recapture slaves after their frequent escapes were costly. The board of the Lisbon Inquisition was sent to Pará and spent seven years (1763–1769) there. The Italian architect, Antônio Landi, had built some fine baroque buildings in Belém, many of which stand today. Meanwhile, some tribally active Indian groups waged war on the Portuguese, successfully defending large areas of territory in the interior, preventing trade and the settling of colonists in frontier areas.

Despite these sweeping reforms, the region remained distinctive for its larger number of Indians, smaller number of whites, remoteness from the south of Brazil, relative proximity to Portugal, the lack of plantation agriculture, the success of long-distance riverine mercantile circuits, and the fact that most people did not speak Portuguese but *lingua geral* (derived from the Tupinambá language). The economy was based on the gathering of wild products (especially cacao), with some rice and coffee production. The lack of a monoculture (for example, sugar or cotton as elsewhere) or a developed pastoral base meant that colonist landholdings were small compared to the rest of Brazil. Landholdings often were located along the riverbanks in proximity to Indian villages to facilitate access to labor. Ethnic identities were extremely varied. The vocabulary for referring to the offspring of these people's sexual encounters was the most differentiated in Brazil.[3]

Metropolitan demands were in constant conflict with the requirements of both settlers and natives. This situation was worsened by further legislation, in 1799, designed to encourage Indians to become sedentary farmers. Indians of "good character" were promoted to locally important positions in the municipal administration and part-time military. This again antagonized Brazilian and Portuguese élites who could not accept an Indian as having a role in the colonial administration. In practice, the new policy left many Indians to their own devices and to the whims of the local élite. A semi-autonomous peasantry (a rural free population) emerged with a diverse economic base and a reluctance to sell their labor to others. Ironically, the new reforms of 1799 allowed a peasant mode of existence to become stronger.[4] At the same time, the wealthier landowners sought to expand their holdings to plant cacao trees – a crop that was increasingly significant

---

3 David Cleary "'Lost Altogether to the Civilized World': Race and the Cabanagem in Northern Brazil, 1750 to 1850." *Comparative Studies in Society and History* 40, no. 1 (1998): 109–135

4 On the theoretical analysis of peasants in the Brazilian Amazon, see Stephen Nugent, *Amazonian Caboclo Society: An Essay in Peasant Economy and Invisibility*, Berg, Oxford, 1993.

in the European market. This move led to pressure on land and labor in desirable areas, namely, high floodplain land near villages.

Pará also was not untouched by the flow of political ideas across the Atlantic and news of revolutions in America (1776), France (1789), and Haiti (1791). One event did draw Pará directly into this world of revolution. The control of the Amazon borders had always been of concern to provincial governors. Toward the end of the eighteenth century, the coast at the far northeast of the Amazon, known as the Cabo do Norte (now Amapá), saw an increase in smuggling to and from French Guyana. Some feared the French revolution would spread over the border. Plans were drawn up to invade Cayenne, French Guyana's capital, and put an end to these problems. Nothing was done until 1808, but then for nine years Cayenne was occupied by hundreds of Paraense (natives of Pará) troops, unchallenged by the French. Paradoxically, this actually strengthened the revolutionary connection. French prisoners, exiled to Guyana for being too radical, found their way to Pará. The Paraense soldiers themselves returned with new ideas and increased expectations.

The challenge to Portuguese rule was affected by the presence in Rio from 1808 of the Portuguese monarchy, who had moved to the New World after Napoleon's invasion of Lisbon. On one hand, the monarchy's presence calmed the situation by proving that Brazil was as worthy of royalty as Portugal. On the other, the Court's extravagance was in full view. A republican uprising in Recife in 1817, known as the Confederation of the Equator, was particularly damaging until it was repressed. Leaders sought dismemberment from the south and succeeded in gaining allies in neighboring provinces to the north. Yet it was the liberal constitutional revolution demanded by soldiers in Portugal in 1820 that persuaded King João VI to return to his country. João VI's son Pedro remained in Rio and declared independence in September 1822. Pará was the first Brazilian region to support demands for a constitution in 1821 and the last to join the independent nation of Brazil in August 1823.

Pará's allegiance was achieved only under duress from British mercenaries employed by the Brazilian court. The regional government was dominated by factions loyal to Portugal. They wished Pará to remain a province in the trans-Atlantic Portuguese nation, which it became in 1821, expressing its enduring ties of kinship and commerce. At the same time, Brazilians held a general expectation that the colonial bondage would be smashed. Liberal ideas were spreading, not just among the élite but among popular classes and the vast interior of the Amazon (mainly as a result of the activity of priests). Then, one event revealed the true colors of the newly independent nation. One of the British mercenaries put down a peaceful demonstration by 256 soldiers demanding Paraenses' election to the ruling junta and the president's resignation. The soldiers were rounded up and taken to a prison ship, the Brig *Palhaço*, at the harbor of Belém, where they were left without food, water, or circulating air in the ship's hull. By the next morning all but two had died. This tragedy reverberated in the actions of rebels in the years to come and was cited as a reason for suspicion of the new regime in Rio. Pedro I's representatives had imposed independence in the north, with majority support, yet ended up killing 252 Brazilians. The conflict, never simply split between Brazilians and Portuguese loyalists, continued for the next twelve years and engulfed the interior of Pará, as each town entered its own battle, involving Indian and mestiço peasants, slaves, urban artisans, priests, and traders.

During the regency period (1831–1840), liberals – themselves divided into radical and moderate groups – were dominant nationally and passed various decentralizing reforms. A revolutionary wave swept through the same provinces that had experienced a bloody and hesitant transition to independence. The period was characterized by urban riots, soldier mutinies, slave rebellions, lusophobic attacks (Portuguese hating), and destruction of property in rural areas, particularly in the north of Brazil. Independence had not brought peace and order.

In mid-1834 Pará reached a turning-point. Natives of the region remained excluded from government, and the urban free poor and peasants were being successfully mobilized by key regional figures. Frustrated, a prominent group of Paraenses planned a takeover for September 7, Brazil's Independence Day. Their plan was discovered and some leaders were arrested, while others escaped. Those who survived the attack regrouped and intended another assault for the evening of a major festival celebrating São Tomé, the patron saint of Indians. In the early morning of January 7, 1835, the rebels stormed the capital; murdered the president, his deputy, and some Portuguese traders; and opened the prisons. The Cabanagem proper had begun.

A prominent landowner was declared the new president. However, despite his proclamation of allegiance to the Empire of Brazil and Pedro II, the son of Pedro I, the administration in Rio refused to recognize him. Yet the rebels were in control of the provincial government and sought to continue its machinery. Soon factions opened up, bringing to the surface previous differences between local élites and their poorer counterparts. The soldiers of one group (allies of the urban and rural poor) fought with those of the president (an élite liberal). The president was captured. On his way to prison, he was shot and his body mutilated.

In the following month, February 1835, the dominant group elected another president. Again, Rio would not recognize him and appointed their own president, sending him to Pará with troops under the command of another British mercenary. These forces retook Belém easily in June 1835: the president had told cabanos to lay down their arms. However, the capital was once again taken by the rebels in late August, in full view of not just the Brazilian navy but also Portuguese, British, American, and French naval forces, whose presence had been requested by consuls to protect their countries' citizens and property.

The Cabanagem at this time was a broad and fragile alliance composed of different interests. For example, slaves often had pockets of resistance, and each town had its list of vengeances. The failure to end the rebellion swiftly prompted the regent to approach British, French, and Portuguese representatives in Rio secretly with a desperate proposition: to assemble a force and "deprive the insurgents of all hope of resistance."[5] This idea is remarkable for the inclusion of the Portuguese, as well as the fact that the action would have been illegal – foreign soldiers were permitted to land in Brazil only with the consent of the General Assembly in Rio. The plan was rejected; instead, a military general who had been forced into early retirement for the heavy-handed treatment of civilians was recalled and nominated by Rio as the next president of Pará.

On May 13, 1836, the capital reverted to imperial hands with hardly a shot fired. But the rebellion had not ended, for the rest of the region became embroiled in conflict. As it developed, ethnic and class alliances changed. The rivers were the conduit of information, supplies and personnel; the forests provided natural refuges. The advice from the Pará president in 1839 to the Minister of War in Rio was that the insurgency could never be eradicated for the rebels knew the country too well. Pedro II was prematurely proclaimed of age on July 23, 1840. Organized cabano attacks on property, soldiers, and military installations continued until the following month, when a general amnesty was granted to all rebels in the empire by Pedro II. There was no public execution of the surviving rebel presidents; instead, they were exiled. On the other hand, imperial military commanders in the interior were told to dispense with the formalities of justice when taking prisoners – the jails were full. The numbers killed are not accurately known; one commentator suggested losses of about 30,000 in a population of about 120,000, which is probably too high but not by much.

The repression was effective in racializing the largest rebel movement of nineteenth-century Brazil. The violent pacification of the region was justified by portraying the movement as a race war, dominated by "people of color" incapable of ruling themselves. At the time, the Rio administration argued that Brazil must be kept different from the rest of Latin America.[6] Yet the Cabanagem's characteristics do not fit neatly alongside the Brazilian

5 Henry Stephen Fox, British Minister in Rio to Lord Palmerston [Foreign Secretary], December 17, 1835, in David Cleary (ed.), *Cabanagem: Documentos Ingleses*, Belém: SECULT, 2003, 65.
6 For more on the general context of Brazilian dissimilarity, see Kenneth Maxwell, "Why was Brazil different: The Contexts of Independence," in his *Naked Tropics*, New York: Routledge, 2003, 145–170.

revolts in the same period. The provincial capital had been twice overcome, three presidents elected, the provincial government in the hands of rebels twice for a total of fifteen months. Municipal councils from all over Pará had backed the shift in power. A diverse and wide coexistence of people had joined the rebellion, which by then encompassed a large portion of Brazilian territory, rural and urban.[7] The Cabanagem's significance is only partially appreciated in terms of the other revolts of regency-era Brazil (1831–1840): liberal reforms and the lack of a strong monarch. The period leading up to Pará's independence and the Cabanagem was not a localized expression of a single national anticolonial movement. Rather, it was a complicated mix of a historical regional conflict misinterpreted by national politicians and the extension of liberal attitudes to all classes, which shaped political alliances through the appeal of violence to solve conflict.[8]

There is a danger, then, of interpreting local events as consequences of wider ones. In Pará, as in the other rebellious provinces, there was an evolving pattern of different interests, each with followers and patrons elsewhere. Liberalism and its demands for liberty, equality, and change had wide currency, finding common ground with values among peasants and Africans. But the radical liberal élite in Pará before the Cabanagem never offered decisive leadership to the masses. They mobilized when it suited their interests and never saw through their campaigns as they did in

7 See, for example, Caio Prado, who says the Cabanagem was one of the most remarkable popular movements in Brazil. His reasoning is that it was the only one where the lower and poorer classes participated and managed to take hold of political power (*Evolução Política do Brasil*, São Paulo: Editora Brasiliense, 1976, 69, first published in 1933).

8 Late-colonial Brazil was experiencing its own rebellions and then a bloody and unhappy independence, achieved in the northern provinces of Bahia, Maranhão, and Grão Pará with considerable military force supplied by British mercenaries, most famously Thomas Cochrane. Some of those in the northern parts called for a more federal organization to the Brazilian empire, which would give them more local powers, but the courts in Rio feared a breakup of the massive territory and responded aggressively to any threat. On Brazilian independence, see the work of Carlos Guilherme Mota (ed.), *1822: Dimensões*, São Paulo: Perspectiva, 1972; Fernando Henrique Cardoso, *O Brasil Monárquico. Vol. 4, Dispersão e Unidade* (Introdução geral, Sérgio Buarque de Holanda), Rio de Janeiro: Bertrand Brasil, 2004; José Honorio Rodrigues, *Independência: Revolução e Contra-revolução. As Forças Armadas. Vol. 3*, Rio de Janeiro: Livraria Francisco Alves Editora, 1975. For more recent reappraisals of independence, see István Jancsó (ed.), *Independência: História e Historiografia*, São Paulo: Hucitec, 2005 and István Jancsó (ed.) *Brasil: Formação do Estado e de Nação*, São Paulo: Hucitec, 2003. For regional studies of the struggle for independence, see Matthias Röhrig Assunção, "Élite Politics and Popular Rebellion in the Construction of Post-Colonial Order: The Case of Maranhão, Brazil, 1820–1841," *Journal of Latin American Studies*, vol. 31, 1, 1999, 1–38; Jeffrey Mosher, "Political Mobilization, Party Ideology, and Lusophobia in Nineteenth-Century Brazil: Pernambuco, 1822–1850," *Hispanic American Historical Review* 80, 2000, 881–912; Hendrik Kraay, "'As Terrifying as Unexpected': The Bahian Sabinada, 1837–1838," *The Hispanic American Historical Review*, 72, 4, 1992, 501–528. For Cochrane's version of events, which involved a number of tricks and skullduggery and the stealing of Portuguese property, see his autobiography, *The Autobiography of a Seaman*, 2 vols. London: Constable, 1996.

Pernambuco, Maranhão, and Bahia. Instead, they shifted their support to
the imperial forces with the opening of the rebellion and the murder of the
first cabano president. This was less a "selling out" than a rapid evolution of
their ideas in tune with liberals nationally and the conservative backlash
(*regresso*). This move decisively delivered Pará to the empire. In the confus-
ing and changing constellation of relations between Portuguese loyalists,
imperial representatives, Paraense élites, and the peasants and their regional,
national, and international connections lies the story of the Cabanagem.

Previous Studies

Although significant, the literature on the Cabanagem has limitations. As
political environments change, so have the motivations to which the revolt
was ascribed. In the second half of the nineteenth century, the revolt was
perceived as a justification to control the masses and assert central authority,
an interpretation associated with the most famous author on the period,
Domingos Raiol.[9] With the centenary of the rebellion in the midst of
Getúlio Vargas' populist nationalism, both its beginning and the ending
were celebrated. This was not a contradiction, rather, it was an attempt to
give voice to two kinds of patriotism: regional and national. This work is
associated with a dynamic group of lawyers, educators, and military officers
who formed the Historical and Geographical Institute of Pará. The studies
in these periods were careful to place the events within the context of
independence and the regency and to use primary sources. At a time of
regional decadence – the rubber economy had collapsed – these historians
gave content to Amazonia's culture and history. During the military dicta-
torship of Brazil (1964–1986), the Cabanagem was characterized in more
universal terms: a popular revolutionary movement of the masses against the
bosses. Pasquale di Paolo and Júlio Chiavenato, the principal writers in this
phase, mainly used secondary sources, perhaps thinking it would be impossible to work through the repressive apparatus of the documentary record.[10]
The result is that these authors bypassed the traditional questions of
Brazilian historiography, such as tensions between provincial and national
politics, regional identities, and popular culture. Nevertheless, these authors
contextualized the Cabanagem – correctly, I think – in a wider framework

---

9 Raiol's sources are various, though they do not seem to have survived together, and he occasionally
   lifts sentences or paragraphs from other work without citation. He must have been aware of Gottfried
   Heinrich Handelmann's *História do Brasil* (first published in Berlin in 1860, and translated into
   Portuguese by the IHGB in 1931, see especially 308–326, 383, 945–947). He also must have used
   Pereira Leal's *Correções e Ampliações ao que Sobre a Revolução que Arrebantou na Cidade do Pará*; and
   an unpublished manuscript by João Henrique Mattos now in the BNRJ.

10 José Júlio Chiavenato, *Cabanagem: O Povo no Poder*, São Paulo: Brasiliense, 1984; Pasquale di Paolo,
   Cabanagem: A Revolução Popular da Amazônia, Belém: Conselho de Cultura, 1985.

and on a longer timescale. More recently, scholarly studies have returned to some of the core historiographical questions. Making use of a wide set of documentation, they have broadened and advanced our understanding in ways that cannot be characterized simply. The rebellion has also been studied as part of a larger historical narrative to which its analysis contributes positively, namely, the history of the region from the Indian or mestiço point of view.[11]

Despite the various studies, there is no agreement on a core set of questions about the Cabanagem. Later studies have been more exploratory than conclusive. Should it be seen as an anti-Portuguese revolt by élite Brazilians who needed popular support? This interpretation would put the Cabanagem at the end of a series of uprisings dating from independence and is favored by the earlier generation of its students. Or should the Cabanagem be seen as a separatist, anticolonial rebellion where the colonizer switched from being based in Lisbon to being based in Rio? Moreover, was the Cabanagem one movement or many? Was the rebellion in the interior fundamentally different from the urban revolt? For early commentators, the Cabanagem proper took place in Belém; everything else was, at best, a messy, misguided, and gory offshoot. The move to the interior has not seen as part of the rebellion's core development; nor was the urban movement understood as being fed by rural interests, whether they were peasant small holders or Afro-Brazilian slaves. It was understood in terms of national regency politics. Surprisingly, the repression itself – how it was conducted and how it affected the political and cultural resolution – has commanded little attention.[12] Especially important here are the tactics used by imperial troops in preventing recruitment to the rebel side, such as summary executions, imprisonment, and torture.

A series of other questions also remain unresolved, some hardly debated. What did national politics mean to peasants, Indians, and slaves? How far back into the colonial period should we go to place the origins of the Cabanagem and who lived in Pará at that time? Magda Ricci has revealed the wide and diverse networks that embraced Pará during that period. These affected all levels of society, not just traders and the wealthy. In particular, she signals the invasion of Guyana in 1808 by Paraense forces as a key moment for the greater inclusion of the popular classes and their awareness

11 The review of the main literature has also been done by Magda Ricci, "Do Sentido aos Significados da Cabanagem: Percursos Historiográficos." *Anais da Arquivo Publico do Pará*, 2001, 4, 2, 241–271. See also John Hemming, *Amazon Frontier: The Defeat of the Brazilian Indians*, London: Macmillan, 1987, "The Cabanagem Rebellion," 211–237; Carlos Moreira Neto, *Índios da Amazônia, de Maioria a Minoria (1750–1850)*, Petropolis: Vozes, 1985; Robin Anderson, "The Caboclo as Revolutionary," in Eugene Parker (ed.), "The Amazon Caboclo," *Studies in Third World Societies*.

12 Jorge Hurley's *Traços Cabanos* and Lucas Alexandre Boiteaux's *Marinha Imperial versus Cabanagem*, Rio de Janeiro: Imprensa Naval, 1943 are exceptions.

of alternative political options. She has also drawn attention to the para-
doxes of patriotic feeling among the liberal élite: they were torn between
their loyalty to the emperor and their regional interests. In doing so, she
touches on the significance of popular culture, especially the Bible as a
source of knowledge and morality in shaping the rebellion. Yet we know
little about the formation of the élite and classes more generally. Though
John Chasteen has provided an analysis of the alliances across race and class
in the Cabanagem. Using prison entry books, he has shown that Blacks,
Indians, whites, and mestiços all participated as rebels. But we do not know
how these relate to racial categories as they were lived or social and economic
life, for his concern is with liberalism as a political force to unite different
interests.

What economic factors led to the rebellion? Only one study has discussed
the significance of the absence of large estates in Pará and the difficulties of
expanding production due to environmental and labor constraints.[13] Itala
Bezerra argues that the land situation in Pará was chaotic, with the state
unable to regulate the division of plots and the land-seizing strategies of the
powerful. At the end of the colonial period, as a consequence of the
strengthening of the peasantry and the rise of cacao as an export, the market
economy was growing. But these twin developments were at odds with each
other: the cacao growers required land and seasonal labor, and the peasantry
needed economic autonomy. Understanding this fault line and its political
ramifications in the countryside sheds light on why the rebellion covered
such a large area.

Other work has looked at the background of the rise of the rubber
economy but makes no mention of the circulation of counterfeit money
in the early independence period (which led to attacks on Portuguese
traders) or the growth of imports following the opening of ports to foreign
trade.[14] This information would feed into understanding the international
context in the buildup to the rebellion and the presence of consuls from
Britain, the United States, and France and traders from many more countries. What role did foreign trade have in bolstering local élites? Was there
any consular influence in determining regional politics? David Cleary has
studied the documents in Britain relating to the role of the British navy in
securing the province. Using this hitherto unknown material, Cleary has
forced a wide rethinking of the rebellion on such topics as racial and ethnic
categories, periodization, geographical extent, and the use of oral history. In

13 Itala Bezerra da Silveira, *Cabanagem, A Luta Perdida* ..., Belém: Secretaria de Estado da Cultura,
    1994. See also Ciro Flammarion Cardoso, *Economia e Sociedade em Areas Coloniais Periféricas: Guiana
    Francesa e Pará*, Rio de Janeiro: Graal, 1984, who focuses with late colonial Pará and its comparison
    with French Guyana.
14 Roberto Santos, *História Econômica da Amazônia (1800–1920)*, São Paulo: Editora Queiroz, 1982.

particular, he has pointed to the significance of British mediation between the main and last rebel president and the regency: while the imperial commander refused to talk to the rebels, the British did. Before, Raiol had claimed the British offered to support the rebel president if he wanted to break away from Brazil. It now seems this was a spurious claim, perhaps an attempt to discredit the British who were the targets of vilification when Raiol was writing. In any case, Raiol, Ricci, and Cleary – as do others – indicate that the Cabanagem was not an urban uprising that was relatively quickly put down by imperial troops.

Earlier, Raiol wrote a study of political Brazil (*O Brasil Político*), in which he condemned the liberal and conservative positions of the 1850s – which by then had been transformed into parties – for their lack of interest in promoting the welfare of the whole of humanity. Although in that book he does not mention Pará or its rebellion by name, it is clear that he has it in mind in the following reflections on the independence of Brazil.

After such a grievous subjection it was natural that the oppressed would want to breathe more freely and they would try little by little to throw off the domination that they had experienced for three centuries. . . . It was natural that the oppressed would want to gain the rights and franchises of free citizens. But it was natural that those oppressors want at all costs to hold on to their privileges and the same freedoms which they had enjoyed for a long time, and that they would disparage the sense of national honor, the patriotism, and the most pure aspirations of the oppressed.

The struggle, then, was inevitable and necessary.[15]

Although Raiol's volumes are basic, they nevertheless may have misled later studies. In the preceding quotation, the "oppressed" could seem to include all non-Portuguese Brazilians, Indians, mestiços, and locally born whites. However, in his writings overall, "the oppressed" turn out to be only a minority of educated and wealthy Brazilians; everyone else is excluded. There is some residual ambiguity, depending on the context, between an inclusive or exclusive understanding. This slippage was common at the time, for the masses were needed to realize political ambitions. Fiery rhetoric and powerful phrases were the order of the day for political men. It is important to understand the discrepancy between a way of speaking and ethnic and racial categories, as they were experienced. What about the exiled Portuguese criminals who made a home beside the river with Indian women and had little interest in their country of birth? Or Portuguese who, after independence, became "adopted Brazilians" and became the objects of

15 Domingos Antônio Raiol, *O Brasil Político*, (original 1858), reprinted in *Obras de Domingos Antônio Raiol, Barão de Guajará*, Belém: Conselho Estadual de Cultura, 1970, 158.

vilification? Or Indians who secured positions of authority in the colonial and early national systems of administration? Raiol never addressed the "ethnic question," since for him Indians and their offspring, mixed or otherwise, were not part of the political universe.[16] Yet this is a basic issue for our understanding of the rebellion.

In the absence of a systematic analysis of class formation, agrarian structure, family life, popular culture, ideological motivation, and ethnic and race relations, this book has had to cover some basic ground. I have begun from the premise that there was a complex dynamic of changing positions in which local and wider forces were thoroughly mixed up. After all, the Portuguese-speaking Amazon and even the most remote village had been part of a global empire since the seventeenth century. This realignment has allowed me to undercut distinctions between the rural (the sertão) and urban (Belém). The former did not represent the traditional, or backward, and the latter the modern and nationally oriented. The beginning point is situating the rebellion in this way of life and the tensions and alliances it induced. This forces a consideration of class relations and returns us to the connections across ethnic groups. Pará had a relatively flat social structure but considerable investment in colonially derived racial hierarchies. In the daily experience of that contradiction lies the emergence of a new political agent in the far north of Brazil in the early nineteenth century.

Peasant Rebellion in Latin America

Amazonian anthropological and ethnohistorical studies have traditionally investigated Indian and, less often, peasant societies.[17] While this work has

---

16 For further evidence of his perception of Indians, see Raiol, "A Catequese dos Índios do Pará," ABAPP, vol. 2, 1902, 117–183. There he openly views Indians as childlike creatures in need of patronage. These people were, however, ones still living in the forest and not the former mission residents.

17 Some recent and relevant monographs on Indians in Portuguese and English include Aparecida Vilaça, *Quem Somos Nós: Os Wari Encontram os Brancos*, Rio de Janeiro: Editora da UFRJ, 2006; Carlos Fausto, *Inimigos Fiéis: História, Guerra e Xamanismo na Amazônia*, São Paulo: EDUSP, 2001; Eduardo Viveiros de Castro, *From the Enemy's Point of View: Humanity and Divinity in an Amazonian Society*, Chicago: University of Chicago Press, 1992; and the collection by Manuela Carneiro da Cunha and Eduardo Viveiros de Castro (eds.), *Amazônia: Etnologia and História Indigena*, São Paulo: FAPESP, 1993. This body of work is significant for its general arguments showing that contemporary indigenous Amazonian symbolic and ritual worlds cannot be reduced to either resistance or submission to outsiders and their influences. Instead powerful and persistent cultural alternatives are created. The volumes by Anna Roosevelt (ed.), *Amazonian Indians from Prehistory to Present*, Tucson: University of Arizona Press, 1994; Alcida Ramos, *Indigenism: Ethnic Politics in Brazil*, Madison: University of Wisconsin Press, 1998; and Neil Whitehead, *The Lords of the Tiger Spirit: A History of the Caribs in Colonial Venezuela and Guyana, 1498–1820*, Dordrecht: Foris Publications, 1988, indicate another approach to the study of indigenous people, one that attempts to show the constructed

merit in itself, it has, on the whole, failed to capture the complex social landscape of the Brazilian Amazon. It has not accounted for the presence of the "new kinds of people" who live along the riverways – descendants of Indians, enslaved Afro-Brazilians, and poor Portuguese men – how they relate to each other, and attach themselves to the places they dwell in, or the political, religious, and intellectual frameworks in which they function.[18] By examining the "peasant" character of the rebellion, this work seeks to bridge some of these divisions.[19] As will be explained, the peasant at the time of the

nature of what and who is indigenous and in particular the discontinuous nature of some Amerindian histories. This is not to mention the material on indigenous people outside of Amazonia: see overviews in Manuela Carneiro da Cunha, *História dos Índios do Brasil*; and Frank Salomon and Stuart Schwartz (eds.), *The Cambridge History of the Native Peoples of the Americas, vol. 3, Part 2: South America*, Cambridge: Cambridge University Press, 1996. Work on Amazonian peasantries became established in the 1960s and the military plans for opening up of the Amazon. See, for example, Otávio Velho, *Frentes de Expansão e Estrutura Agrária*, Rio de Janeiro: Zahar Editores, 1972; José de Souza Martins, "The State and the Militarization of the Agrarian Question in Brazil," in Marianne Schmink and Charles Wood (eds.), *Frontier Expansion in Amazonia*, Gainesville: University of Florida Press, 1984, 463–490; Eugene Parker (ed.), "The Amazon Caboclo: Historical and Contemporary Perspectives," *Studies in Third World Societies*; Nugent, *Amazonian Caboclo Society*. For more recent work on Amazonian peasantries see Stephen Nugent and Mark Harris (eds.), *Some Other Amazonians: Modern Peasantries in History*. London: Institute for the Study of the Americas, 2005.

18 The phrase *new kinds of people* is from Stuart Schwartz and Frank Salomon, "New Peoples and New Kinds of People: Adaptation, Readjustment, and Ethnogenesis in South American Indigenous Societies (Colonial Era)," in Salomon and Schwartz (eds.), *The Cambridge History of the Native Peoples of the Americas*, 443–501. A sample quotation that fits well with my argument is: "The divided and subdivided typology of mixed peoples as painted did not, of course, actually restructure the fluid practice of mixed people. Mestizos, mulattoes, zambos and the rest continued to seek their life chances pragmatically." 494. Generally, however, studies in the Amazon have not been interested in the new kinds of people who played a central role in the colony. This neglect may also have been the result of a prejudice, in some quarters, which has little time for "degraded" or "illegitimate" Indians and mestiços – those who actively sought positions in the colonial hierarchy and became peasants. Yet the insurgents in the Cabanagem were from these groups, the reconstituted ethnicities of Pará.

19 Earlier historical studies of colonial Amazonia have investigated the specific character of Portuguese rule in the region, the political confrontations it created, and the impact of colonialism and missionary activities on Indians. Aside from the previously mentioned studies, see Arthur Reis, *A Amazônia que os Portugueses Revelaram*, Rio de Janeiro: Ministério da Educação e Cultura, Serviço de Documentação, 1957; and the two excellent collections by Mary Del Priore and Flávio dos Santos Gomes (eds.), *Os Senhores dos Rios: Amazônia, Margens e Histórias*, Rio de Janeiro: Elsevier, 2003; and José Bezerra Neto and Décio Guzmán (eds.), *Terra Matura: Historiografia e História Social na Amazônia*, Belém: Paka-Tatu, 2002. The ethnohistorical work includes Mathias Kiemen, *The Indian Policy of Portugal in the Amazon region, 1614–1693*, New York: Octagon, 1973; David Graham Sweet, "A Rich Realm of Nature Destroyed: the Middle Amazon Valley, 1640–1750," Ph.D. diss., University of Wisconsin, 1974; John Hemming, *Red Gold: The Conquest of the Brazilian Indians*, London: Macmillan, 1978; and *Amazon Frontier*; and Antônio Porro, *As Crônicas do Rio Amazonas*, Petrópolis: Vozes, 1993; and his *O Povo das Aguas: Ensaios de Etno-história Amazônica*, Petropolis: Vozes, 1996. David Davidson's unpublished Ph.D. dissertation, "Rivers and Empire: The Madeira Route and the Incorporation of the Brazilian Far West, 1737–1808," Yale University, 1970, is not ethnohistorical, and while concerned with colonial policy in the eighteenth century, it is attentive to the everyday reality of life at the time. Barbara Sommer has provided the most recent and relevant study in English, and has bridged not just anthropology and

Cabanagem should not be restricted to poor and free non-Indians. Here we can take our cue from the literature outside of Brazil.

Studies of peasant social protest have focused on the transition to capitalism in the countryside. On the whole, the negative impact of agricultural modernization on peasant access to land and other resources has guided research. This has led scholars to examine the ways peasants have sought to defend their interests from these outside forces. While analyses of peasant rebellion have treated a wide range of topics, Steve Stern has argued that a limited number of assumptions and assertions shape this literature. The most important concerns the supposed destruction of a peasant society or livelihood as the capitalist world economy encroaches. In the following paragraphs I will address this issue in the Amazon as it will link my study to this Latin American historiography. Another pertinent assumption is the major influence of agrarian conflict in shaping national political debate. Yet for all the scholarly interest in agrarian politics, Stern argues, peasants are frequently depicted as reactors to external forces. They are rarely interpreted to act independently and to articulate their own political consciousness. Each of these assumptions is not necessarily wrong, but we need to be explicit about how they operate in particular locations.[20]

First, the term *peasant* can be defined as "a subsistence-oriented agricultural producer subjected to the authority and economic exactions of a state or landed class of overlords, or both."[21] This designation is problematic in the Amazonian context because of the reduced significance of agriculture there and the extensive nature of livelihood making. Still, lives were tied to the land and people did plant staples such as manioc and maize. This definition is also awkward in the Amazon because of the nature of the peasantry's formation. It is generally assumed that aboriginal peasantries are only partially affected as the result of their contact with and subordination to Europeans. Even as they become integrated in a European-dominated

history but also the diverse societies of late colonial Pará: "Negotiated Settlements: Native Amazonians and Portuguese Policy in Pará, Brazil, 1758–1798," Ph.D. dissertation, University of New Mexico, 2000.

For ethnohistorical surveys apart from those in Carneiro da Cunha (ed.), *História dos Índios do Brasil*, see Robin Wright and Manuela Carneiro de Cunha, "Destruction, Resistance and Transformation: Southern, Coastal and Northern Brazil, 1580–1890," Salomon and Schwartz (eds.), *The Cambridge History of the Native Peoples of the Americas*. In addition, and important for my purposes, are local histories of towns and areas which follow through the development of a place from colonial to national times For example, the ones I have made much use of are Arthur Reis's *História de Óbidos*, Rio de Janeiro: Editora Civilização Brasileira, 1979; and *História de Santarém: Seu Desenvolvimento Histórico*, Rio de Janeiro: Editora Civilização Brasileira, 1979; João Santos, *Cabanagem em Santarém*, Livraria Atica, Santarém, 1986; and Paulo Rodrigues dos Santos, *Tupaiulândia*, Santarém, ICBS/CAN, 2000.

20 Steve Stern, *Resistance, Rebellion and Consciousness in the Andean Peasant World, 18th to 20th Centuries*. Madison: University of Wisconsin Press, 1987, 5.
21 Stern, *Resistance, Rebellion and Consciousness*, 4.

order, indigenous societies maintain some of the precapitalist features of their economic and social organization. The outcome is a peasant society and economy, though never final and always locally conditioned, with a mix of different values and practices. The engagement with national and international forces can either act to reinforce or undermine its foundations. The difficulty of applying this common portrayal to Brazilian Amazonia is that there were no societies left intact after conquest, or even partially so, to be transformed into a peasantry. Instead, with a few notable exceptions, there were many displaced and enslaved family groupings and individuals. Disease, war, and enslavement had depleted the riverbanks of indigenous societies.

In Spanish-speaking Latin America, scholars have used the terms *Indian* and *peasant* more or less synonymously. In the Andes, the two republics – of the Indians and the whites – allowed for different laws to regulate each sphere. Indian collective institutions were preserved, which meant group ethnic identity, access to land, and political organization continued to have legal status in structures of colonial domination.

This was not the case in Brazil. Indians incorporated into the Portuguese world were forced to shed their former identities, though informally they may well have kept them. In the large-scale reforms of the mid-eighteenth century, Indians of Brazil were given a separate collective economic and political position. Explicitly, all cultural affiliations were excluded. Moreover, while Indian agricultural plots, for example, were collectively farmed, they were state-owned. The collective institutions of Indian identity were imposed by Lisbon; they were not a continuation of pre-European forms. Indians who resisted colonial rule, such as the Mundurucu and Mura, were able to maintain their ethnic identity. The separation of Indians from the rest of the Amazon's inhabitants was abolished in 1799. At this point, Indians in the colonial sphere became "peasants" without formal collective recognition. So the term *peasant* in the Portuguese-speaking Amazon is justified on the basis that people were producing for a market and organizing their own subsistence and subject to the state or a local power holders.

The heterogeneous Amazonian peasantry at the end of the colonial period did not have a collective cultural baseline that went back before conquest, as was the case in some parts of Mexico and the Andes. The peasantry in Brazil, and especially the Amazon, comprised Indians, Portuguese exiles, and colonists as well as escaped and freed slaves. The peasantry, which faced agricultural modernization, such as the opening of markets to foreign goods and privatization of land holdings, was already familiar with externally induced transformation. In different ways, they had been swept up into war, violence, slavery, and long-distance travel. The viability of a livelihood was already contingent on the world economy and colonial domination. This is not to say that some people did not maintain older ethnic affiliations, craft activities and techniques, and religious practices and give them renewed significance in another context. New class and ethnic relations had overriding significance, as will be seen. Stephen Nugent puts the matter in the following way: "The emergence of peasantries in Lower Amazonia [Pará] did not depend on a forced transformation of indigenous societies ... the Santareno [from Santarém] peasantry emerged from the wreckage of colonial efforts to extract wealth from the region; the peasantry was, in short, constituted by default." Thus for Nugent contemporary peasant livelihoods do not represent a transition between precapitalism and capitalism but a suspended or blocked form, "a relic of a particular moment of capitalist transformation."[22] That "moment" can be located in the late colonial epoch, which this book treats as critical to the reasons for peasant rebellion in the Amazon.

The peculiar nature of the Amazonian peasantry leaves a problem with regard to peasant rebellions. If they were not defending collectively held traditional values, what were they resisting? If agricultural modernization had already had an impact, what was happening in the late colonial period? Taking the lead from the literature on peasant rebellions in the nineteenth century highlights patterns of land ownership, labor administration, the role of the élite, popular culture, interpretations of liberalism, and the ethnic and racial dimensions as valuable considerations. The transition to capitalism in the countryside is one factor among others, including élite factionalism, the failure or breakdown of the state, and commercial blocks, raising of taxes, and so forth.[23]

In these respects, Portuguese-controlled Amazonia bore greater similarity to Spanish America than to the rest of Brazil. These parallels are helpful to think about how and why the Amazonian revolt does not entirely fit the framework of contemporaneous coastal Brazilian ones in the independence and early national period. The first link is the character of land occupation and the labor regime. Throughout the colonial period, the state encouraged settlers to demarcate public land. Donations were made for military and administrative service so long as land would be used productively. But demarcating land was costly and time consuming, so most people occupied land by living from it. Although squatter rights were not legally recognized until the mid-nineteenth century, practically speaking, they represented the

---

22 Nugent, *Amazonian Caboclo Society*, 177, 178. Nugent's revisionist understanding and theoretical appreciation of the peasant issue in Brazilian Amazonia finds empirical confirmation in the present study.

23 There is no single cause to peasant activism and agrarian social revolt, as John Tutino argues in *From Insurrection to Revolution in Mexico: Social Bases of Agrarian Violence, 1750–1940*, Princeton: Princeton University Press, 1986.

chief means of acquiring land in the colonial Amazon, especially along the riverbanks. At the same time, reforms specific to the region at the end of the eighteenth century sought to promote increased availability of labor by introducing a threshold of economic production. Anyone below that level had to work for colonists or public institutions for most of the year. In turn, this freed up land occupied by poorer families unable to sustain themselves. This new labor policy bound workers to a town (rather than to estates, as in Mexico) and restricted their movement (to find new plots of land, for example). Undoubtedly, both these processes had a negative impact on Indian and mestiço small holders. They could not make a viable living or improve their prospects because they were forced to sell labor.

Thus labor policies and the pressure on land near towns are a major consideration in understanding the comparative significance of the Cabanagem. In the rest of Brazil, the combination of land and labor was not a source of conflict. Separately they were, however, in the interior of Maranhão (peasants against the military draft) and the interior of Pernambuco (peasants being evicted from land). Another crucial feature of wider discussions on early nineteenth-century revolts is the influence of the élite on peasant mobilization. How did the factions and political ideologies of the élite affect popular participation in the shaping of revolt?

Many scholars show that agrarian and urban revolts during the post-independence period involved cross-class and cross-ethnic alliances. For example, the image of the Latin America's most famous Caste War in Yucatán is of a fiercely divided situation. According to Terry Rugeley, in the first phase of the conflict (from 1800 to the late 1830s) ethnic and cultural identities did indeed exist; "the lines which separated the "'ladino' and 'macechual' worlds" (that is, Spanish and Maya) "were considerably less distinct than Nelson Reed or his academic successors have allowed." In the decades prior to the war in the 1840s, rural social conflict was multiethnic and shaped by networks of patronage extending from the Maya peasant leaders to urban "creole" (white) politicians and Church functionaries. The various intermediaries in these networks "were all Janus-faced individuals, addressing the highs and lows of their world."[24] The Maya élites (known as *batabs*) acted to control discontent in the countryside. As municipalities in Yucatán felt new pressures from the central authorities, these alliances became increasingly fragile. The Maya leadership lost the privileged status it enjoyed under colonial rule and were unable to contain widespread dissatisfaction with the failure of expectations to materialize, such as the elimination of taxes of church and state. Rugeley concludes that our under-standing of Mexico's early national period hinges on our ability to recognize

24 Terry Rugeley, *Yucatan Maya Peasantry and The Origins of the Caste War*, Austin: University of Texas Press, 1996, xiv, 183.

not only the peasant community, the Maya, and its unity and disunity, but also the multiple, shifting alliances between different groups.[25]

Similarly, the Cabanagem did not start as a caste war but became one as the repression got underway. Critical in Pará was the changing nature of the leadership. Radical white liberals, including priests, had introduced Indians and mestiços into the national political sphere. In the immediate aftermath of independence, with other local leaders they had directed popular violence against Portuguese traders and soldiers and conservative Brazilians, especially those who supported central control of the regions from the imperial capital. As it became clear the regency would not let the rebellion stand, white liberals redirected their efforts against the insurgents and formed their own tense alliance with imperial forces. In Pernambuco, for example, élites did not abandon their popular base of support. Jeffrey Mosher argues that liberal ideas were well received by the poor urban inhabitants. The quest for local autonomy united a large cross-section of population. As the effects of authoritarian centralization were felt after 1837 (during the *regresso*, Conservative comeback), Pernambucan liberals used Lusophobia to rouse popular resistance.[26] Why did white leaders in Pará act differently? One reason was the growing perception that the Amazon was different to the rest of Brazil. It needed to come into line for the sake of a stable nation. The murder of the first rebel president forced this group to consider their choices. Their decision was to exclude peasants from shaping the new Brazilian empire. Thus the Amazonian experience of nation building shares a family resemblance to the argument advanced by Florencia Mallon regarding Peru.[27]

Historians have also investigated peasants' understanding of central state systems.[28] In his study of the origins of the Chayanta rebellion (1780–1781), an important Aymara cultural zone in present-day Bolivia, Sergio Serulnikov argues that indigenous Andean communities tried to employ colonial frameworks, especially the legal system, to defend their

---

25 Rugeley, *Yucatan Maya Peasantry*, xvii, 184–185.

26 Jeffrey Mosher, "Political Mobilization, Party Ideology, and Lusophobia," 896.

27 Florencia Mallon, *Peasant and Nation: The Making of Postcolonial Mexico and Peru*, Berkeley: University of California Press, 1995. Peter Guardino argues that the Guerrero rebellions of the first part of nineteenth century were in part a reaction to centralism in the countryside. These revolts "facilitated alliances between peasant rebels and elite federalists," *Peasants, Politics and the Formation of Mexico's National State: Guerrero 1800–1857*, Stanford: Stanford University Press, 1996, 13.

28 In a comparative essay on patterns of rural rebellion in Latin America, John Coatsworth discusses the problems in addressing the complexity of multiclass and multiethnic revolts, namely the way peasants "frequently manage to insert their own objectives into these struggles [national and international]." He includes the Balaiada and Cabanada (both are misspelled at various points in the book) but fails to mention the Cabanagem, John Coatsworth, "Patterns of Rural Rebellion in Latin America: Mexico in Comparative Perspective," in Friederich Katz (ed.), *Riot, Rebellion and Revolution: Rural Social Conflict in Mexico*, Princeton: Princeton University Press, 1988, 30.

communities and livelihoods. In so doing, they dealt with all aspects of the colonial administration, experiencing gaps between norms and power, and testing the balance of forces between peasants and rural élites. In a similar manner to Pará, large-scale reforms were introduced in the mid-eighteenth century, which put more pressure on Indian labor and tribute to the state. In consequence, local power struggles escalated and the state became more involved in an attempt to resolve them. Serulnikov shows the village revolts were not localized or episodic instances of disquiet but the profound forays of indigenous communities to expand their ideological horizons beyond the community level. Their efforts were guided by the goal of overcoming entrenched tendencies toward ethnic fragmentation and widening collective entities.[29]

In common, then, with Mosher's example from Pernambuco, the Andes and Yucatan cases indicate that national politics and institutions as well as the political struggles of local élites be considered an important part of peasant revolt in Amazonia. These studies underlie the way peasants can be "very sophisticated interlocutors who dialogue and bargain with the powerful."[30] In defending their interests, they were not merely protesting about a material threat to their existence but expressing a fresh interpretation of political ideas of the time.

As part of their argument on the relationship between popular cultures and state formation, Gilbert Joseph and Daniel Nugent seek to explore the question of "peasant consciousness" and its appreciation of the day-to-day workings of the state. Their larger question, and how it applies to Brazil – how popular revolutionary movements acted upon the state and vice versa and how they influenced social change – is beyond the boundaries of this monograph. Yet the objective of bringing people back into an understanding of the state and the elaboration of popular culture is valuable in framing a sphere of relations where multiethnic and cross-class relations can develop. Joseph and Nugent insist on the recognition of "what was realized by those popular classes in historical practice, namely the articulation of distinctive forms of social consciousness and experience."[31] These forms are nourished by traditions of historical memory that reside in popular cultures of resistance.

---

29 Sergio Serulnikov, *Subverting Colonial Authority: Challenges to Spanish Rule in Eighteenth-Century Southern Andes*. Durham: Duke University Press, 2003, 3–5. In the Amazon, the only example of Indians using the colonial legal system for their own ends is provided in David G. Sweet's wonderful essay, "Francisca: Indian Slave," in David Graham Sweet and Gary Nash (eds.), *Struggle and Survival in Colonial America*. Berkeley: University of California Press, 1981, 274–291.

30 Peter Guardino, *The Time of Liberty: Popular Political Culture in Oaxaca, 1750–1850*, Durham: Duke University Press, 2005, 13.

31 Gilbert Joseph and Daniel Nugent (eds.), *Everyday Forms of State Formation: Revolution and the Negotiation of Rule in Modern Mexico*, Durham: Duke University Press, 1994, 11.

At the beginning of the nineteenth century, such "cultures of resistance" in the Amazon originated from a variety of symbols, values, practices, and meanings derived from the individuals who made it their home. There was no singular authentic popular culture. For Mexico, however, Joseph and Nugent argue that there was a continual interplay and borrowing between different traditions. In the Andes, *nativism* has been used to refer to this loose body of political consciousness and experience.[32] The term describes well the indigenous features of Andean rebellions and the protection of livelihoods. In the Brazilian context, the meaning is associated with radical nationalism and Lusophobia. Natives in Brazil, it would seem, were not Indians.[33]

The distinction is important to establish a comparative frame. In Amazonia the connection between a popular-class way of life and political motivations and interpretations generated a separate culture and its own forms of resistance to colonial and imperial authority. The opportunities provided by the state, such as collective judicial action, were not the same as in the Andes. Nor was the potential for peasants to influence and negotiate with the state as powerful as in Mexico. Yet in addressing popular partic-ipation in the Cabanagem we are dealing with comparative organizational features that structured peasant action as elsewhere in Latin America. In order to provide a new perspective on the Amazonian rebellion, the sphere of popular culture must be appreciated on its own terms, not as derivative of élite or high culture. Similarly, Amazonian peasants and the urban poor were partaking in wider political society and forming their own views on events experienced. Their revolt of 1835 was then a spectacular political realization of their consciousness and in particular of their demands on the center of power in Rio de Janeiro. In analyzing the Cabanagem using this continental framework, we find long and complex histories of alliances, betrayals, confrontations, and politicking that cannot be examined in a purely local context.

---

32 See, for example, Stern (ed.), *Resistance, Rebellion and Consciousness* and Sinclair Thomson, *We Alone Will Rule: Native Andean Politics in the Age of Insurgency*, Madison: University of Wisconsin Press, 2002.

33 For a recent discussion of the meaning of race, categories of the native, and outsider in the imperial period, see Gladys Sabina Ribeiro, *A Liberdade em Construção: Identidade Nacional e Conflitos Antilusitanos no Primeiro Reinado*, Rio de Janeiro: Relume-Dumará, 2002; and Ivan Stolze Lima, *Cores, Marcas e Falas: Sentidos da Mestiçagem no Império do Brasil*, Rio de Janeiro: Arquivo Nacional, 2003.

2

Life on the River

The land is everywhere covered with impenetrable forests; the houses and villages are all on the waterside, and nearly all communication is by water. This semi-aquatic life of the people is one of the most interesting features of the country . . . The natives are all boat builders. It is often remarked, by white residents, that an Indian is a carpenter and shipwright by intuition. It is astonishing to see in what crazy vessels these people will risk themselves . . . it is the custom of Brazilian and Portuguese travelers to leave the whole management to them [i.e., of river travel to the Indians].[1]

Central to any portrait of the Amazon is the river system itself.[2] Not only do rivers provide food and water, the fact of living alongside and with them

1 Henry Walter Bates, *The Naturalist on the River Amazons*, London: John Murray 1863, vol. 1, 75–76. Bates' thirteen years (1849–1852) in the Amazon were largely spent near or on rivers, dependent on local labor and goodwill for his procuring of botanical and zoological information. He never traveled to remote areas, preferring instead to remain close to small towns or homesteads and taking day trips into the forest. After being in the Amazon for only a few weeks he makes an important realization: "I had learnt by this time that the only way to attain the objects for which I had come to this country was to accustom myself to the ways of life of the humble classes of the inhabitants" (Henry Walter Bates, *The Naturalist on the River Amazons*, 1969, London: Everyman, viii, quoted in the introduction by Peter Fleming to the shortened version of the 1863 two volume publication). And so he did: he slept in a hammock, ate salted fish and manioc flour, and occasionally red meat, large amounts of fruit, and traveled by river on dodgy vessels loaded with cargo – though he avoided Mass and was critical of the idolatry of popular Catholicism. He also recorded conversations with some of the people he traveled with, and met the richest (e.g., the president of the province and many large landowners when in Belém) and the poorest as well as annoying bureaucratic administrators. He was disdainful of the treatment of women among the more wealthy classes, which was to shut them away and deny them education. In all, Bates offers a reliable and intimate portrait of a range of people who lived along the Amazon and the Solimões and aspects of their behavior in the middle of the nineteenth century. His book stands out among other travelers for his sympathy for the "humble classes," perhaps finding affinity with his own background in working-class Leicester of the British Midlands (see Hugh Raffles, *In Amazonia: A Natural History*, Princeton: Princeton University Press, 2002). For this reason, many insights into river life of the people of the Amazon can be drawn backwards to the first few decades of the nineteenth century.

2 In this chapter I have relied on published material in reconstructing the popular culture of the first part of the nineteenth century. In particular, I have mainly used the accounts of travelers and scientists who visited the region at this time. These chroniclers were an interesting mixed bag: an artist (Hercule

shapes life and excites the imagination of both residents and visitors. In the seventeenth century new practices, technologies, and perceptions associated with the network of rivers emerged as part of the colonial regime. The opening of Atlantic seaports to foreign trade in 1808 brought another set of influences, such as the fast-sailing schooner, foreign merchants, and their fine goods – though not the free movement of non-Brazilian vessels in Amazonian waters, which did not happen until 1867. Only with the building of roads, starting in the late 1950s with the Belém-Brasilia highway, would the dominance of the riverine way of life be challenged and, in turn, the forest threatened. However, today many rivers remain the most important source of nourishment, revenue, and means of transport. One fisherman from Óbidos told me in 1993 that his well-being was derived from drinking water straight from the Amazon River; whereas upper-class people in the town don't, and that is why they are weak and suffer from all kinds of diseases. Similarly, riverine dwellers prefer to travel by canoe rather than walk.[3] This chapter offers an overview of late colonial society focusing on relevant geographical characteristics, the flexibility of ethnic categories, and popular culture and language.

An Environmental Sketch

On a map the hydrographic system of the Amazon looks like a bewildering series of rivers, channels, outlets, tributaries, and lakes.[4] This representation fails to capture the seasonally dynamic and diverse forms of the natural environment. During the annual floods, the water level can rise by more

Florence c. 1828), naval officers (Henry Lister Maw c. 1827, Smyth and Lowe c. 1834), royalty (Prince Adalbert of Prussia c. 1845), a protestant missionary (Kidder c. 1836), natural scientists (Spix and Martius c. 1819; Bates c. 1850s). Like Bates, these visitors experienced firsthand the everyday life of the place and evoke these trials in their narratives. Their descriptions are written from their desks back in Europe, introducing the Amazon to a large audience for the first time, and their accounts are colored by their desire to sell copies with eccentric stories and adventure (Spix and Martius are an exception). Nevertheless, it is possible to sink into their narratives, flow with them, and with some imaginative effort regain something of what it was like to live at the time. In addition, important reports by Brazilian officials offer useful overviews of the time, such as the priest André Fernandes de Souza's piece on the Indians in the province of Rio Negro in early 1820s and José de Brito Ingles's account of the state of Pará in 1819.

3 See Mark Harris, "The Brazilian Floodplains: Where Cholera does not kill Caboclos," in Sophie Day, Akis Papataxiarchis, Michael Stewart (eds.), *Lilies of the Field: How Marginal People Live for the Moment*, Boulder: Westview Press, 1999, 196–211.

4 To my knowledge, there are no cartographic studies of the Amazon. This is not due to the absence of maps by the Portuguese; see, for example, the descriptive catalog of maps in different archives in Brazil and Portugal by Isa Adonias, *A Cartografia da Região Amazônica; Catálogo Descriptivo, 1500–1961*, Conselho Nacional de Pesquisas, Rio de Janeiro: Instituto Nacional de Pesquisas da Amazônia, 1963. On the Eastern sertão of Minas Gerais, see Hal Langfur, *The Forbidden Frontier: Colonial Identity, Frontier Violence, and the Persistence of Brazil's Eastern Indians, 1750–1830*, Stanford: Stanford University Press, 2006, 37–45.

than twelve meters and can redesign the riverside. Whole stretches of floodplain land can disappear overnight, ripped away by the tremendous force of the water. New land can also appear as the flood retreats and fertile sediments are deposited. People who live on the floodplain have to live with the insecurity of not being able to predict the height of the flood nor its effect on the land. One recent commentator has baptized the Amazon River "a great sculptor" that is forever shaping its course.[5]

Amazonia has three kinds of rivers, each with its own particular type of floodplain, depending on water chemistry. The first and largest is sediment-rich, or muddy (called whitewaters, even though the color is like milky coffee). These rivers all have their origins in the headwaters of the Andes and carry its eroded soils in their loads. In terms of this book the most important of these rivers is the Madeira, which begins in present-day Bolivia and enters the Amazon just below Manaus. The second group of rivers drain from the Brazilian Highlands in central Brazil, have clear water, and are nutrient poor, mostly acidic. The Tapajós, Xingu, and Tocantins are some of the largest examples. The third category is represented by rivers to the north of the Amazon River that drain from the Guiana Highlands and are known as the blackwaters. These have no heavy sediment load since millions of years of erosion have produced sandy soils with few nutrients. The Negro and Trombetas rivers are examples of these highly acidic waters. These three river types do not correspond to different ecosystems, but they do have consequences for the abundance and distribution of life.[6]

The dense network of watercourses is a result of the high precipitation rates over the whole basin (though peak rainfall differs across the Amazon). The northern blackwater tributaries rise from March or April and ebb in September or October. Those tributaries to the south begin to flood in November and recede in April. This uneven timing means the flood period of the main trunk is longer than if the two coincided. The main river itself starts to rise in November or December and falls away in May to June. The lower parts of the floodplain could be under water for more than half a year, enriched with fertile nutrients from the west. As Goulding, Smith, and Mahar explain, this extended flooding season is "the principal factor that makes the floodplain forests as much aquatic as terrestrial habitats."[7] It means that opportunities for human exploitation of the riverbanks are likely to involve a combination of strategies rather than a single focus.

5 See Nigel Smith, *The Amazon River Forest: A Natural History of Plants Animals and People*, Oxford: Oxford University Press, 1999, 5. The fluctuation of the height of the river varies along the course. It is highest at Tefé, about 12–15 meters, and about 6–7 meters around Santarém.

6 For an excellent overview on river ecology, see Michael Goulding, Nigel Smith, and Dennis Mahar, *Floods of Fortune: Ecology and Economy along the Amazon*, New York: Columbia University Press, 2000, 5–7.

7 Goulding, Smith, and Mahar, *Floods of Fortune*, 10.

Seasonal variations consist in changing precipitation levels and the ebb and flow of the river. Plants and animals do not follow the same periodical patterns as they do in temperate climates. Each species has its own season; flowering, shedding, molting, and breeding all occur at different stages in the year. For these reasons again, different environments – forest, river, lake, land – present diverse prospects at various times of the year for economic gain.

Along the rivers, the floodplains support dense forests. In some places the floodplain is high and in others it is low and more prone to longer periods under water. The flooded forests provide another rich environment for humans and animals. For example, fish swim into these darkened waters and gorge themselves on nuts and berries falling off trees. Special fishing techniques were developed to catch these fish.[8] This river–forest combination is specific to Amazonia. The floodplain accounts for only about two to three percent of land in the entire basin. This tiny amount, however, belies the economic and social importance of the floodplain in the late colonial and early national period, when it became a focus of conflict as incomers and Indians tried to establish themselves there. Part of the story of the Cabanagem is the struggle for the riverbanks.

The river may be powerful sculptor of land, but people have also shaped the environments in which they live. Watercourses have been altered through human intervention. Anthropologist Hugh Raffles has brought to light the ways in which communities rechanneled streams and connected rivers and lakes in tremendous acts of labor involving shifting tons of mud over a number of years. These are not recent practices but were taking place since before the conquest.[9] During the period covered by this book, for example, a canal was built connecting two rivers near the town of Cametá.[10] Water was, and still is, considered public property and rivers cannot be

8 The classic reference on fishing in Amazonia is José Veríssimo, *A Pesca na Amazonia*, Belém: Universidade Federal do Pará, 1970. Recent monographic studies include Lourdes Furtado, *Pescadores do Rio Amazonas: Um Estudo Antropológico da Pesca Ribeirinha numa Área Amazônica*, Belém: MPEG, CNPq, 1993; and Nigel Smith, *Man, Fishes, and the Amazon*, Gainesville: Florida University Press, 1982.

9 See Raffles, *In Amazonia* on "fluvial practice," 35, and "the ability of contemporary and historical Amazonian populations actively to produce new environments," 37. Raffles elegantly brings to light the ways the floodplain, and its rivers have been manipulated by multiple agencies of human and non-human actors. These "histories of creativity," as he calls them, help us understand the Amazonian environment as a place that both limits human life and enables it, offering potential and opportunity. There were in addition overland routes, known as *estradas* – literally roads – some of which may have been of considerable antiquity. The chronicler of the first European voyage down the Amazon, Gaspar de Carvajal, under the command of Francisco Orellana, observed wide roads leading away from the riverbanks into the forests. See *The Discovery of the Amazon*, José Toribio Medina (ed.), New York: Constable, 1988.

10 For more on the rechanneling and the tragedy involved in its construction, see Raffles, *In Amazonia*, 14–23.

redirected without legal permission. This suggests that such construction was probably undertaken illegally and by powerful, well-connected individuals who could defend themselves against the state. It was also a common, prohibited practice for riverbank dwellers to block off streams in order to trap fish. Municipal councils, since at least the early national period, have sought to introduce fines as a penalty against such activity.[11]

Henry Bates was also told in the late 1840s that Paraenses considered the Amazon the Mediterranean of South America.[12] In a sense, they had a point: it was a vast area internally connected by water, with a distinct environment and natural history. Indeed, the Amazon was known almost from the beginning of Portuguese colonization as the *rio-mar*, river-sea. Bates goes on to write that "the whole Amazons valley is thus covered by a network of navigable waters, forming a vast inland freshwater sea with endless ramifications, rather than a river."[13] Nevertheless, this river-sea was totally new to the Portuguese; they imposed their Mediterranean references as they strived to make themselves the lords of a new territory. In many ways the Amazon was not at all like the European ocean. Its endless ramifications, its peoples, its diverse environments and rivers, and its highland frontiers required a different casting.

In the colonial period, various geographic areas were recognized in Grão Pará. Those with significant population density included the tidal estuary around Belém; the island of Marajó; Macapá, and the Cabo do Norte area north of Marajó; the Atlantic coast around Bragança; the riverbank villages and towns on or near seasonally flooded land from Gurupá upwards to Manaus; the Negro River; and the Solimões River. In proximity to all environments was forested land that provided game and could be cleared to make way for agriculture, orchards and cattle. For the purposes of this book, I shall follow the official colonial regional distinctions: the capital (including Marajó island; producing principally cattle meat, rum, sugar, hides, fish, and agriculture, especially coffee), Macapá (gateway to Guyana, mainly military significance, cattle, and some agriculture, such as rice), Cametá (and the Tocantins; cacao, brazil nuts, cotton, sugar, and agriculture), Bragança (the Salgado area; sea fish, and rice), Santarém (the Lower Amazon; cacao, brazil nuts, fish, and wood for construction) and the Upper Amazon (known also as the Rio Negro captaincy, including the Negro, Branco, and Solimões Rivers; cacao and spices). The dominance of Belém meant each subregion sought its own links with the capital which, in effect, bypassed any intermediary.

---

11 For example, see Arthur Reis, *História de Óbidos*, Rio de Janeiro: Editora Civilização Brasileira, 1979, 58, where the town council of Óbidos publishes a series of instructions, one of which was a fine for closing off waterways.

12 Bates, *The Naturalist*, vol. 1, 33.

13 Bates, 39.

Colonization and Geographical Features

The novelty of the size and power of the rivers enabled, rather than hindered, the settlers in their pursuits.[14] During the 1660s and 1740s, missions were established well into Spanish territory along the Solimões, Negro, and Branco rivers.[15] Accompanying this expansion was a commercial push for both slaves and products, which linked the riverside missions under Portuguese control into a production and distribution network. The drive was achieved by the pioneering efforts of the pathfinders, or *bandeirantes* (or, as they were locally known, *cunhamenas*).[16] Once the Treaty of Madrid officially recognized colonial occupation of the immense territory in 1750, forts were built to protect the frontiers of the empire. The forts were largely symbolic, however; they had few soldiers and hardly any supplies and lay in chronic disrepair.

At first, the missions were the main kind of settlement along the rivers. Typically built on bluffs along the river, missionaries and cunhamenas forced Indians to participate in colonial life, often at some distance from their homeland. By the late seventeenth century, many Amerindian nations who had peopled the banks of Amazon River – such as the Tupinamba, Tapajós, and Conduris – had disappeared. Indians who resisted colonial inclusion were deemed enemies and therefore could be enslaved when captured. Most Indian slaves were taken straight to farms in and around Belém. The forts established at Gurupá, Óbidos, and Santarém in the 1690s started the establishment of colonist farmsteads, benefiting from the proximate natural resources.[17]

---

14 Charles Boxer, *The Golden Age of Brazil*, Berkeley: University of California Press, 1962, 271.

15 See, for example, the account by the Jesuit missionary Samuel Fritz, *Journal of the Travels and Labours of Father Samuel Fritz in the River of the Amazons between 1686 and 1723*, London: Haklyut Society, 1922; and the commentary by David Sweet on the establishment of the Carmelite missions on the Solimões River, "A Rich Realm of Nature Destroyed: The Middle Amazon Valley 1640–1750," Ph.D. dissertation, University of Wisconsin, 1974, 338–401.

16 Barbara Sommer, "Colony of the Sertão: Amazonian Expeditions and the Indian Slave Trade," *The Americas*, 2004, 61, 3, 401–428 and "Cracking Down on the Cunhamenas: Renegade Amazonian Traders under Pombaline Reform," *Journal of Latin American Studies*, 2006, 38, 4, 767–791. The rest of this chapter is concerned with the people who were a core part of colonial life – the workers, slaves, and planters.

17 Many of these original missions remain the location of towns today – it is not clear whether they were also settlements in the pre-European period. However, some, like Silves and Vila Franca, were among the largest colonial villages in the Amazon in the eighteenth century, but became much smaller in the late nineteenth century. Parintins and Juruti, on the other hand, were insignificant and grew with the growth of river traffic in the second half of the nineteenth century. Part of the explanation of the continued existence of places like Santarém was the ongoing presence of relatively wealthy cacao planters from the early to the late nineteenth century. These people managed to maintain their activity despite the horrific violence of the 1820s and 1830s.

Apart from the military and religious conquest, Portuguese colonization of the Amazon involved the occupation of land as its central strategy. The colonization of the riverbank bluffs and floodplain was intrinsic to Portuguese imperial domination. Outside the missions, Portuguese and Brazilian settlers established various kinds of farmsteads. These individuals were peasants, economically speaking, making a living from a diversity of activities, including fishing, livestock raising, hunting, and farming. They traded their goods by transporting them to Belém rather than local markets, which were little developed in the eighteenth century.

There was little deforestation in this phase of colonization as there was in the expansion into the interior along the Atlantic fringe of Brazil (though these regions had their rivers, too, but much smaller in scale). The relatively slow advance into the coastal interior in other areas of Portuguese America was not matched to the north of their colony. This speedy occupation also derived from the earlier colonial expeditions of the Spanish up and down river from the foothills of the Andes and the knowledge that communication was possible eastwards and westwards. In the late eighteenth century, connections were established into Spanish America via the Madeira and the Guaporé rivers and into Dutch America on the northern border, via the Trombetas and the Negro and Branco rivers.[18] Some of these were not new. In the mid-seventeenth century, the *bandeirante* Antônio Raposo Tavares blazed a trail from São Paulo overland and down the Madeira and Amazon to Belém, and in the late seventeenth century Dutch goods were being traded on the Negro and Trombetas.[19] The presence of Dutch products in Portuguese areas was exploited by indigenous groups such as the Manao people, who lived on the lower River Negro. Their chief, Ajuricaba, was accused of flying a Dutch flag on his canoe as he looked for Indian friends of the Portuguese in order to hand them over to the Dutch as slaves (for more on Ajuricaba see page 143). The river system made for an easy intermingling of interests and a visible confrontation of differences; in this sense there were no frontiers to be crossed or erected in the Amazon. The rivers offered ready-made pathways.

One recent commentator, Roberta Marx Delson, expresses well the connection between the web of rivers and colonial power: "a fluvial highway

18 David Davidson, "Rivers and Empire: The Madeira Route and the Incorporation of the Brazilian Far West, 1737–1808," Ph.D. dissertation, Yale University, 1970; also "How the Brazilian West was won: Freelance and state on the Mato Grosso frontier, 1737–1752," in Dauril Alden (ed.), *Colonial Roots of Modern Brazil*, Berkeley: University of California, 1973; Francisco José Rodrigues Barata, "Diário da Viagem que fez à Colônia Holandesa de Surinam, feito pelo Porta Bandeira da Sétima Companhia do Regimento da Cidade do Pará, pelos Sertões e rios deste Estado em Diligência do Real Serviço," RIHGB, 1846, 8, 1–53; Nadia Farage, *As Muralhas do Sertões: Os Povos Indígenas no Rio Branco e a Colonização*, Rio de Janeiro: Paz e Terra, 1991.
19 John Monteiro, *Negros da Terra*, São Paulo: Companhia das Letras, 1994.

link[ed] riches of the colony to the mother country. Via its often-turbulent waters the Portuguese envisioned the establishment of a vast maritime trade network over which would flow contraband Spanish silver, as well as more typical rainforest products, such as medicinals and lumber ... " and "riverine expansion thus occasioned a complete rethinking of the value of the interior [of the colony] and totally changed its appearance."[20] In the missionary-led phase of Portuguese expansionism in the Amazon, the Amazonas and the Negro rivers, leading to the region's northwest, were the principal conduits of commercial and slaving activity. Then, in the later Pombaline phase, the Madeira River and its tributaries, running up to the Mojos in the southwest of the Amazon, opened up a new route reaching the Spanish border in the far west of the Portuguese colony in the second half of the eighteenth century.

All rivers led to Belém. But by the beginning of the nineteenth century its grip on all interior commerce and interest had loosened somewhat. A Matto Grosso commercial route between Cuiabá and Santarém had started in the early part of nineteenth century. In turn, this route became important to the prosperity of Santarém; diamond miners from Matto Grosso came down river and spent money earned from the sale of the precious stone to traders.[21] With the move of the capital of the Upper Amazon region to Manaus from Barcellos in 1808, the population on the Negro River soon dropped and its villages tumbled into disrepair.[22] Manaus quickly established itself, becoming as big as Santarém in the decade before independence and as a military and commercial focus for the whole of the Upper Amazon, the Solimões, and the towns upriver from Óbidos. By the time of independence, the interior of the province was greatly strengthened by these internal developments upriver of Belém. Moving into the nineteenth century, the political and economic dominance constructed by the Portuguese for Belém in the seventeenth and eighteenth centuries was mutating into a more even regional distribution. These changes acted to accentuate the division between those (the colonial élite) whose vision of Pará and the Upper Amazon was transatlantic (with a route from Barcellos, or Manaus, or Vila Bella, to Lisbon, or

---

20 Roberta Marx Delson, "Inland Navigation in Colonial Brazil: Using Canoes on the Amazon," *The International Journal of Maritime History*, 1995, 7, 1, 1 and 6 respectively for each quotation.

21 Johann Baptist von Spix and Karl Martius, *Viagem pelo Brasil, 1817–1820*, Belo Horizonte: Editora Itatiaia, 1981, vol. 3, 100.

22 André Fernandes de Souza, "Notícias Geográphicas da Capitania do Rio Negro no Grande Rio Amazonas," RIHGB, 1848, 10, 411–503; João Henrique Mattos, "Relatório do Estado da Decadência em que se Acha o Alto Amazonas," RIHGB, 1979 [1845], 325, 143–180; Victor Leonardi, *Os Historiadores e os Rios*, Brasilia: Editora Universidade de Brasilia, 1999, on Airão on the Negro River. Many of these places were colonial administrative centers for Indian labor and with the ending of the Directorate their *raison d'être* was extinguished.

Oporto, via Belém), and those (everybody else) who saw the Portuguese Amazon as a distinct entity, in and of itself.

The convergence of the networks in the natural environment, the manner of conquest, the long distance of the interior trade routes, and the struggle for military domination all gave rise to a way of life closely bound up with the riverscape. As people's imaginations became embroiled with the river, new cultural and economic expressions developed around it. Each town had its own singular identity, depending on the kinds of people who lived there; some specialized in calabash making, others in canoe building; and so forth. Small holders, cattle ranchers, and larger-scale planters made use of the fertile floodplains, which had been the major locations for the pre-conquest settlements. Economic life followed not the climatic variations but the ebb and flow of the river. Boat travel was dictated by currents and winds and long-distance movement upriver was more common toward the end of the calendar year, when the river was at its lowest, a period which did not quite coincide with the drier months.[23] Religious processions with a saint's icon took place on land as well as on the river (see below). A folklore derived from Indian, African, and European traditions formed around fantastical creatures who lived in enchanted places and had a malignant effect on humans.[24] The riverine culture that accompanied Portuguese expansion into the interior was a multistranded way of life. It was "colonial," spawning its own culture and annual rhythm, but it was not Portuguese in character.

A few examples will provide some evidence. First, boats were needed to enjoy the riches and command the people on the river. Adapting the Indian large dugout canoe, the Portuguese administrators used local labor and timber to build suitable vessels.[25] João Daniel, a Jesuit, observed in the 1750s that Indians in Belém were superb craftspeople, compared with white artisans.[26] Some towns had their own boatyards using wood from nearby sawmills and were prodigious in their fulfillment of local needs; one private canoe factory had turned out eight hundred canoes over the owner's lifetime.[27] The most common boat was a *montaria*, a large canoe, outfitted with

23 The military officer Lourenço de Araujó e Amazonas, who wrote an invaluable dictionary of the Upper Amazon, writes that "The year is divided into two parts, winter or flood, summer or ebb, only in the last do they work … and with winter the villages start their round of *festas*, dances, banquets and their excursion. They do not work in the flood, they use up the gains from the summertime." *Dicionário Topográfico, Histórico, Descritivo da Comarca do Alto-Amazonas*, Recife, Typografia Comercial de Meira Henriques, 1852, 36.

24 See Candace Slater, *Dance of the Dolphin: Transformation and Disenchantment in the Amazonian Imagination*, Chicago: University of Chicago Press, 1994.

25 Delson Marx, "Inland navigation," 1995.

26 João Daniel, *O Tesouro Descoberto no Máximo Rio Amazonas*, Rio de Janeiro: Editora Contrapunto, vol. 1, 2003, 341.

27 These figures are from Colin Maclachlan, "The Indian Labor Structure in the Portuguese Amazon," in Dauril Alden (ed.), *Colonial Roots of Modern Brazil*, 211.

sails, that could carry up to about forty arrobas of produce (most could hold about twenty arrobas). As the word suggests, a montaria is a regular vessel for the movement of goods; it also means "pack horse" for carrying goods on land. Warships were also built in Belém at the end of the eighteenth century for export to the south of Brazil. Second, the relationship between the town and the country had a different configuration in this riverine environment. It was possible to travel between rural areas avoiding towns altogether. As elsewhere in Brazil, towns were primarily administrative and political centers. People visited their nearest urban center for mass and saints' festivals. Indeed, social life was punctuated by these occasions.[28] Even in Belém, Bates tells us that the "mode of living [in the mid-nineteenth century] was more like a large village than a city."[29] Third, as is clear in the opening quotation, the Portuguese came to rely on the Indians' superior knowledge of their environment as they acted as guides along rivers and into the forests. This dependence gave pilots, paddlers, and canoe men an important place in the colonial society. Indeed, their wages were higher than those of any other group of Indians.[30] Traces of this reliance can be seen in the *lingua geral*: derived names of many places, rivers, animals, and plants. The riverine form of life gave rise to a mobile, semiautonomous existence. Part of the flexibility associated with this mode of existence was the necessity of having diverse sources of livelihood.

Ethnoscapes of the Eastern Amazon

The connection between the river, ethnicity, and livelihood is fundamental in understanding the popular culture of the time. At the extremes of the "ethnoscape" were two groups of people with very different relationships to the river. A tiny group of white officials, judges, and administrators did not travel and exclusively stayed in Belém. At the other end of the spectrum were the Indian pilots, deserters, rower slaves, and mestiço traders whose very life was on the river. They traveled the river system, living on boats and temporary camps at the sides of the river. Between these extremes were the majority of people – broadly speaking, peasants – whose movements were seasonal and combined multiple economic identities, such as laborers, farmers, hunters, fishermen, administrators, and traders. Although ethnically diverse, they shared the dual connection to the river and a plot of land where their homes were situated.

The people living in the riverbank towns, villages, and hamlets were a diverse collection, hierarchically organized in terms of race and class. The

---

28 Bates, *The Naturalist*, vol. 1, 86–90.
29 Bates, 79.
30 Davidson, "Rivers and Empire," 465, 470.

stratification of social relations, however, was not fixed. The relatively small numbers of colonists and whites could not repress the aspirations of those they faced, and perhaps feared. Indians and mestiços achieved leading positions of authority in municipal, military, and judiciary offices in the interior's big towns. Some Portuguese men adapted by setting up a household with an Indian woman and performing the manual labor that some thought was supposed to be reserved for people of lower class. The neologism "ethnoscape," taken from the anthropologist Arjun Appadurai, indicates both the continuity between ethnic identities and their varying form. It characterizes the overlapping and heterogeneous nature of the people who lived along the riverbanks. What is at stake is the degree of social mobility across not only ethnic groups but also racial classifications.[31] Here we must not confuse race with the ascription of color. Race should be understood as a socially constructed system of ethnic classification. In the Amazonian context, it is linked to class, family, and marriage, and to power and authority.

Toward the end of the rebellion, the region became divided along lines of race. But race was not an organizing feature at the outset. Still racial categories as they were used at the time manifested a tension between the pragmatic and shifting needs of everyday life (which reshaped racial perceptions) and group expressions of loyalty (which reinforced them). One directed a person toward networks of reciprocity and the other pulled people together who shared a common identity construction, such as Portugueseness, but it could also be "luso-paraenseness" (Paraenses with strong links to Portugal) and many others. The question is, in what situations did an identity become pertinent, and to whom?

There was no single system for classifying the population in the late colonial period of Brazil. Three dimensions of official racial classification can be distinguished: legal, economic, and political.[32] The legal-ethnic axis was used in censuses; it distinguished between the free and the enslaved and also related to the right to vote. In the economic-ethnic dimension were

31 Appadurai uses the term *ethnoscape* to refer to shifting nature of identities in the contemporary world. In particular, he draws attention to the flow of people across boundaries and therefore emphasizes the transnational dimension and lack of territorial affirmation. This understanding fits well with the sense here, except that the connection to the land and river is a strong feature of Amazon peasant livelihoods at the time. Nevertheless the mobile and intercultural elements of the concept of ethnoscape are present. Arjun Appadurai, "Disjuncture and Difference in the Global Cultural Economy" in Michael Featherstone (ed.), *Global Culture: Nationalism, Globalization and Modernity*, London: Sage, 1990, 295–310.

32 I have borrowed these schemes from Assuncão's study of the social structure of Maranhão in the same period of this study. Matthias Röhrig Assunção, "Élite Politics and Popular Rebellion in the Construction of Post-Colonial Order: The Case of Maranhão, Brazil, 1820–1841," *Journal of Latin American Studies*, 1999, 31, 1, 1–38.

merchants and plantation owners at the top; administrators, poor whites, military officials, soldiers, farmers, and fishermen in the middle; and slaves at the bottom. The ideological-ethnic category was divided between whites (Brazilian and Portuguese), mestiços of all kinds, Indians, and Africans. In the 1820s a new category emerged to cover all nonwhite people: *gente de côr*, or people of color.

Although each dimension represented a different aspect of the configuration of race in colonial Pará, there was a degree of overlap between them and one axis influenced another. An Indian in the legal system might well have been appointed a judge in an interior town and acquired property. In turn, he may have been seen as white by poorer Indians. Indeed, racial terms are relative, revealing as much about the observer as the observed. Terms like *mameluco* or *índio* were often shorthand forms of dismissing the person or people being referred to, a way of saying they were the "rabble." *White* meant someone of high social ranking. Similar to elsewhere in the Americas, racial identity could be transformed by economic prestige, legal status, and family background.

The schemas outlined above were also complicated by internal hierarchies. Whites were far from a homogenous group by the end of the colonial period. They were divided by their political and national sympathies, which came to be expressed in factions radicalized by events and arguments. Another internal hierarchy existed between Indian headmen (*principais*) and their charges (see, for example, page 108). Headmen were granted much local power in the second half of the eighteenth century, with the power to organize labor and to extract a good share of the profits from collective production. Their children sometimes made important marriages to colonists. Another significant aspect is ethnic differentiation among village Indians – that is, Indians who were forced to participate and sought opportunities in the colonial sphere. Significant metropolitan reforms of the mid-eighteenth century had tried to extinguish tribal affiliations, but they remained an important element until at least the end of the eighteenth century. These differences manifested themselves in conflicts for colonial appointments and the control of labor.[33]

A good example of the complex nature of racial terms is found in the omnipresent "tapuya," or "tapuio." In the early nineteenth century it is used frequently in letters and reports from the Amazonian interior to refer generally to Indians within the colonial system. A term of abuse, similar to *caboclo*, it indicated the dispossessed of land and truculent laborers and their families. The tapuio was considered to have two Indian parents and to live not in the forest, as the *gentio*, or unconverted Indians, did. The contrast between gentile forest dweller and domesticated Christian Indian appears to

---

33 See Sommer, "Negotiated Settlements," 273–306.

be specific to the time and to the north of Brazil. When the Portuguese first colonized Brazil, the overriding distinction between natives was between those who were friends of the Portuguese (the Tupi) and those who were the enemies (tapuia), unwilling to submit to the colonial will. John Monteiro shows how in the early colonial period this generic division mapped onto others such as noble savage and heathen caste, the free worker, and the enslaved. As colonial knowledge of indigenous people grew, the term changed in meaning from "hated other" to "incorporated other," though precisely how and when is not clear. By the late nineteenth century the Paraense writer José Veríssimo, who was born in Óbidos, felt the term needed clarifying; he reckoned the tapuio should not indicate the pure Indian or the mixture of Indian and white. Instead, it was a catchall term for people who "live along the margins of rivers and contribute to *our* way of life and work in *our* industries" (my emphasis). The use of our (*nosso*) is typical of the élite post-Cabanagem view that rural poor were not just inferior but unwelcome outsiders. Implied in Veríssimo's clarification is that a person could be both a tapuio (defined by place of residence) and Indian or mameluco (a particular kind of racial ancestry). If the content of what is considered tapuio has changed and differs from region to region, it has consistently been used to refer to a nonspecific set of people who can be simultaneously included and excluded.[34]

Contemporary European observers were also perplexed by the perception of racial categories. The Bavarian scientists Johann Spix and Karl Martius observed that whites in the northern areas of Brazil jealously guarded their racial purity: at least, they said they did. But as far as scientists were concerned, "it was difficult for the impartial judgment of a foreigner to accept the claim."[35] The whites appeared just as mixed as all the other groups, despite their attempts to cover up the fact, for example, by not going out in the sun or by fabricating genealogies. The same sense of outsider bewilderment concerning local claims about ethnic categories is reproduced by Henry Bates: "these [racial terms such as mameluco or *cafuz*, and so on] are seldom, however, well-demarcated, and all the shades of color exist; the names are generally applied only approximately."[36] These foreigners' confusion is perhaps due to their own misunderstanding: racial terms are

---

34 References on tapuio are numerous. The Dutch painter Albert Eckhout produced wonderfully lively images of what he called "tapuya" Indians. See also John Monteiro, "The Heathen Castes of Sixteenth-Century Portuguese America: Unity, Diversity, and the Invention of the Brazilian Indians," *Hispanic American Historical Review*, 80, 4, November 2000, 697–719; Bates, *The Naturalist*, vol. 1, 77–78; José Veríssimo, "As Populações Indígenas e Mestiças da Amazônia: Sua Língua, suas Crenças, seus Costumes," in his *Estudos Amazônicos*, Belém: Editora da UFPA, 1970 [1878], 109.

35 The phrase is quoted in Caio Prado, *The Colonial Background of Modern Brazil*, Berkeley: University of California, 1969, 122. See also the German scientists' comment about a man they met in Belém who calls himself a white, but the authors did not think so: Spix and Martius, *Viagem pelo Brasil*, 28.

36 Bates, *The Naturalist*, vol. 1, 35, n. 1.

not descriptive of color but ascriptive of social status. Insider knowledge and the ability to read the clues of self-presentation were fundamental in arriving at such judgments. Nevertheless, their outsider perspective does reveal the somewhat arbitrary application of terms.

There is a point here about the changing nature of racial idioms and the composition of Amazonian society. Miscegenation and social and geographical mobility had blurred many of the differences between classes and ethnicities that marked the earlier conquest period. The colonial categories could no longer contain the flourishing of regional identities. Originally used to distinguish biological parentage and ancestry, the terms had come to be used to refer to assumed associated cultural characteristics loosely related to appearance. They had also become terms of abuse and control, and out of keeping with how the restless numbers of "cultural mestiços" (that is, village Indians and poor whites) wanted to see themselves. Put another way, it could not be assumed that because someone was called an Indian or a white, he or she would act in "Indian" or "white" ways, and vice versa.

Despite such difficulties in understanding the racial categories being used, the following broad picture can be constructed of the different kinds of people and their places of residence. At the time of independence, the region remained focused on Belém. Almost half the population of the whole Amazon lived in its district. Manaus, Santarém, and Cametá were the largest towns in the interior, though still small. Whites, including foreigners, lived in and around Belém, but there were a few in the interior also in administrative and military positions. Slaves were concentrated in the Belém area on the sugar cane plantations, though they were spread out in the whole region and had developed their own cultural forms (discussed below). Village Indians comprised the largest proportion of the population, living along the riverbanks near towns; in a few places they controlled town councils, especially on the Tapajós River, parts of Marajó, and the north bank areas of the Lower Amazon. Mestiços, freed slaves, and poor whites were hardly distinguishable in class terms from village Indians, though they may not always have recognized the similarities. They produced their own food on small holdings; they set up households together, traded their own produce, and sold their labor. Indian nations, such as the Mura and the Mundurucu in the Lower Amazon, were also part of this ethnoscape. They too earned piece wages, traded, and visited towns (sometime going under cover of darkness to conceal a raid). As a whole, these diverse groups comprised an interlocking and dynamic series of relations.

As mentioned earlier, there was considerable variation between each locality.[37] The make-up of people in each town and its countryside differed

---

37 Barbara Sommer, too, discusses the individual identity of each Directorate village, *Negotiated Settlements*, 95–98.

depending on the economic specialization, history of settlement, presence of military posts, ethnic composition, and numbers of migrants and settlers. Some had more élite and were therefore more likely to have more slaves, and others were almost entirely Indian and mestiço with very few whites and slaves. A good sense of this range is gained from reading the chronicles of scientists and travelers.

Spix and Martius reported that the town of Santarém had a mostly Indian population in 1819, and there were a few whites and slaves, both of whom were more numerous in cacao plantations in the neighborhood. The scientists described the relative wealth of the place following the increase in the diamond trade coming down the Tapajós. As a result, the town had a well-off appearance; walls were plastered with clay from the river and painted white or yellow; floors were either tiled or composed of hard-packed earth. People slept and rested on straw mats and hammocks. Animals were raised in the backyards and lighting came from burning on turtle oil in recycled tins.[38] The town had separate areas for the military, Indians, and whites, a legacy of the past century when the mission and town were segregated. In the Indian part of town, houses were made from wooden planks and thatch roofs (see Image 2.1 of Santarém by Hercule Florence dated 1828). Few towns in the interior were apparently as well turned-out as Santarém. Vila Franca, about a day's journey away, consisted virtually of all Indian and a few white administrators. Farther up river, the Bavarians caught up with a group of people from Silves who were out collecting turtle eggs. They all talked lingua geral and only a little Portuguese. Martius asked one of them what tribe he came from, but he did not know.[39] Another man was wearing around his neck a *pedra das Amazonas* (or a *muiraquitá*): a talisman made from green stone attached to a cotton string about an inch and half long, cylindrical and narrow, holding much symbolic value and very well polished.[40] The green stone is a form of jade, very rare, and was probably mined from near the source of the Trombetas River to the north. The amulet was associated with the Lower Amazon and, in particular, the Tapajós Indians at the time of conquest. The muiraquitá could also take the shape of a frog, a symbol of fertility and transformation.[41]

According to Spix and Martius, most people who lived along the banks of the Amazon were Indians.[42] They comment that it was rare that people

---

38 Spix and Martius, *Viagem pelo Brasil*, 99.

39 Spix and Martius, 130.

40 See note in Spix and Martius, 135.

41 According to Alexander von Humboldt, these stones were mined in the Orinoco but the French geographer Paul Le Cointe claimed they could be found near Mount Roraima in the upper reaches of Trombetas River and are made from jade nephrite. See Paul Le Cointe, "As Pedras Verdes das Amazonas," *Revista do Instituto Histórico e Geográphico do Pará*, 1932, 7, 170–172.

42 Spix and Martius, 97.

Image 2.1 A view of Santarém by Hercule Florence, 1828

of European origin reside in the rural settlements on the Amazon River and
its tributaries, which contradicts their observation that most of Santarém's
whites resided on their plantations and farms. Further down the tributaries
and in the unexplored forests was still the domain of Amerindian nations.
Some forest-dwelling Indians were interested in trade; others were the
declared enemy of the Portuguese and refused any contact. Of some of
the preconquest Indian people there were few traces, only a name on a map;
others had been reduced to a single family. The Indians in the colonial
villages, on the other hand, had left behind their language and cultures
and spoke lingua geral, and only in a few cases Portuguese. Few, however,
had assimilated either lingua geral or Portuguese well, and they adapted a
language any which way they wanted. The ones who lived among the whites
and adopted new identities called themselves *canicarus*, which meant "people with clothes, and who are civilized" and those further away "to the west
and upriver they call people from upriver, from the forest," indicating their
lack of civilization.[43] It would be wrong to read these comments as evidence
of a strong separation of the various kinds of people. Rather, Spix and
Martius were trying to sort out the dominant influences from the shifting
realities they were observing. Martius, after all, went on to write the foundational text for the study of Brazilian history and society. His prize-winning

43 Spix and Martius, 100.

Image 2.2 View of the riverside village of Monforte, c. 1785

essay argued that Brazil comprised three races and their convergence and fusion was what gave the country its distinctiveness.[44]

To return to the river: if "whites" traveled up the tributaries, it was for trade or scientific purposes. One such trader who visited Boim on the left bank of the Tapajós River in 1828, about two days travel up from Santarém, recalled the following story. He turned up at the town's port and was immediately met by a man who asked for help. He was taken to a room in a house that served as the chamber of the town council and was met by five Indians who were in a state of anxiety. One, sitting on a large chair, was the president of the council. They had received a letter from the governor but apparently had no idea what it said since they were illiterate, so they wanted the trader to tell them what was written and in turn to pen their response. He obliged and described his amusement at the display of pomp without competence in running their own affairs. Unable to do any more trading, he returned to Santarém, when a few days later he was showered with produce in thanks for his services.[45] Illiteracy was widespread

---

44 See Karl Martius, "How the History of Brazil Should be Written," in Bradford E. Burns, (ed.), *Perspectives on Brazilian History.* New York, Columbia University Press, 1967, 21–41.

45 Antônio Baena, *Ensaio Corographico Sobre a Província do Pará*, Brasilia: Senado Federal, 2004 [1839], 208; Arthur Reis, *História de Santarém: Seu Desenvolvimento Histórico*, Rio de Janeiro: Editora Civilização Brasileira, 1979, 103–104. The origin of this story is probably a report written on the

since there were few schools outside of Belém at the time. Nevertheless, most councils had a clerk who read and wrote official letters, and probably offered his services to other councils or individuals who needed his functions. It would seem that in the situation above there was a sense of urgency to the matter in hand, a key piece of information the trader does not reveal.

Relations between Indians and whites were frequently violent and abusive. The Brazilian priest André Fernandes de Souza was critical of whites of all kinds, whether traders or young exiles from Portugal, for their disdain of the Indian people. In the 1810s and 1820s, whites did not pay properly for services performed by Indians, worked them so hard they had no time to look after their own gardens, stole land from them, and punished them severely for minor infractions. The whites were "monsters of malice who infect everything with their pestilential and poisonous presence."[46] These were condemning words and their opinions were likely shared by other priests working the region in the 1820s, such as João Gonçalves Batista Campos and Antônio Manuel Sanches de Brito, whom we meet later on. Certainly the chroniclers noted the mutual enmity between whites and Indians during this time. Particularly those visitors who arrived at the height of the conflict in the 1830s and others who spent time in its aftermath in the 1840s and 1850s, wrote of the long history of exploitation and cruel treatment of Indians by whites as a reasonable explanations for the uprisings (see pages 282–285).[47]

All except the rich wore the same kind of clothes. Men's attire consisted of below-knee-length trousers and a shirt. Women were accustomed to wearing a long, dark skirt and tight shirt around the upper chest. Antônio Baena, a Portuguese military officer who wrote an encyclopedic essay on Pará in the late 1820s, could barely conceal his sexual appreciation of the women he describes when they put on their best clothes. They used to wear a shirt of the finest silk, which "reveals more than it covers of the two *semiglobos* . . . These clothes are almost a clear cloud whose outlines hug

state of the Lower Amazon, Anonymous, "Memória [of the Lower Amazon]," December 1, 1828, APEP cod. 851, doc. 74.

46 Fernandes de Souza, "Notícias Geográphicas," 501.

47 For example, one individual mentioned in reference to the abuse of Indians is an Italian migrant named Ricardo Zany. His biography needs further research but it is known he lived near current day Parintins and owned extensive pastures and cacao orchards in the late 1810s and 1820s. He met various travelers some of whom extol his generosity, for example Martius and Spix. Others readily condemn his illegal enslavement of Indians and general abuse of them, such the priest Fernandes de Souza, "Notícias Geográphicas," 475, 478, 490. Still, he sought in 1823 to set up villages in which freshly "found" forest Indians could be placed. This plan was a response to José Bonifácio's drive to integrate Indians in the future nation of Brazil, José Bonifácio de Andrada e Silva, *Projetos Para o Brasil*, ed. Miriam Dolmikoff, São Paulo: Companhia das Letras, 1998. Most condemning is a complaint by the governing junta of the Rio Negro in 1823. He was accused of falsifying papers, amassing Indians to work on his properties without reason, and enslaving them with no pay, Itala Bezerra da Silveira, *Cabanagem: Uma Luta Perdida* . . . , Belém: Secretaria de Estado da Cultura, 1994, 235–236.

the curves of the body."[48] Neither men nor women wore shoes frequently. Richer people were more likely to wear suits and uniforms. Most classes went to the river to bathe and wash clothes, possibly in segregated areas for men and women. Only the upper-class women did not bathe in the open, protecting their skin from the sun and their body from prying eyes. People stripped completely when they washed. A British navy officer on a reconnaissance expedition for a naval route across South America made a stop in Santarém in 1828. There he learned that the priest used to watch the spectacle of the women bathing at the end of each day through his telescope. Apparently, the women were perturbed only because they felt the priest was stealing their souls through the lens.[49]

Enslaved Africans

Slaves accounted for approximately twenty-five percent of the population, about 20,000 individuals, in the first part of the nineteenth century. Moreover, about three quarters of the slaves in Portuguese Amazonia were concentrated in and around Belém, working on sugar plantations (*engenhos*) and cattle farms (*fazendas*) and in the city itself. The Lower and Upper Amazon accounted for about fifteen percent of all slaves – about four thousand – and most of those in Santarém and Óbidos. Most masters had no more than a handful of slaves; only in rare cases did an individual own more than fifty.[50]

Slaves of African descent had always played an important role in the cultural life of the region, contributing music, songs, and dance as well as new forms of cuisine. In the early 1850s, Bates and Wallace, for example, were impressed by the slaves' animated street festivals and their choruses while working. But in the late colonial period, their rebelliousness was regarded as one of the major problems in the region (see page 165). Escape from slavery and formation of maroon communities was a constant headache for the authorities, especially those in the interior, where labor was scarce. Some slaves were granted considerable freedom of movement, especially if their master required them to work selling goods from place to place along the river.[51] An example of a rebellious slave who ridiculed the whites and defied capture in Santarém is presented in Chapter 5 (pages 172–175).

---

48 Baena, *Ensaio Corographico*, 109.
49 Henry Lister Maw, *Journal of a Passage from the Pacific to the Atlantic, Crossing the Andes in the Northern Provinces of Peru, and Descending the River Marañon, or Amazon*, London: 1829, 311.
50 See "Annual census tables," Governor of the Rio Negro, João Pereira Caldas, to Governor of Pará, Martinho de Melo e Castro, June 22, 1785, Barcelos, AHU Rio Negro, cx. 8, doc. 7509; also Appendix in José Maia Bezerra Neto, *Escravidão Negra no Grão-Pará (Séculos XVII–XIX)*. Belém: Editora Paka-Tatu, 2001, 122.
51 Vicente Salles, *O Negro no Pará sob o Regime da Escravidão*, Rio de Janeiro: Fundação Getúlio Vargas, 1971, 174–176.

Slaves were as much a part of the mobile world of Amazonia as their counterparts. They could earn their freedom by paying a fee to their masters, or their masters granting it to them. Twelve percent of the population in Belém in 1833 were freed slaves, though it was about four percent in the Lower Amazon in 1827.[52] Slaves could also be rented out for a short term, for example, as a wet nurse (*ama de leite*).[53] Mulattoes, the children of a slave mother and white father, could also be slaves. It was common, too for the children of slaves to be raised alongside the master's children. This practice continued until the slave children were old enough to work. In the baptismal records from Óbidos in the early nineteenth century, ethnic affiliations of newly arrived slaves were sometimes given, such as Guiné, Bissau or Angola; what these differences meant to either the masters or their captives is unknown. Given their cultural backgrounds, different experiences of work and punishment and varying periods of time in slavery, the human property of masters were no more a homogenous group than any of the others in the region.

As with most others, Africans worked and lived in both urban and rural environments. They excelled in artisanal activities, such as tailoring and woodwork in general. The inquisition records details their work as healers and diviners, bringing rituals from their homeland and applying them locally.[54] Most of all, in the early nineteenth century their cultural preeminence was down to their drumming and dance activities (*batuque*) in Belém. They processed through the streets with their drums. These were not the same as saints' festivals processions. The two ritual celebrations express the singular importance of the street for secular and religious celebrations, a potent mix that would eventually lead to the explosion of the Cabanagem.

Although slaves were set apart from the rest of the population as official property, they shared with Indians the experience – at least the traumatic memory – of enslavement. Indians helped slaves escape their masters, providing canoes, information, and safe places to move to in the forest. Sometimes the slaves were caught and punished severely, only to escape again, becoming multiple fugitives. In this way, they were like absentee Indians (see page 166) who would disappear from their employment for a while and then return. They also chose each other as godparents for their children (see Chapter 3). It is clear from the range of ethnic labels, cafuz and

52 Baena, *Ensaio Corographico*; "Memoria," January 8, 1828, APEP cod. 838, doc. 101–102.
53 Frei Francisco de N. S. dos Prazeres, "Poranduba Maranhense," RIHGB, 1891 [1820], 54, 134, 185–277.
54 Take, for example, José who lived in Belém and had a widespread reputation for healing with incantations and herbs in the 1760s, José Roberto Amaral Lapa (ed.) *Livro da Visitação do Santo Oficio da Inquisição ao Estado do Grão Pará (1763–1769)*, Petrópolis, Vozes, 1978, 137–139, 153. Another healer was Marçal, a Church slave, who used orations, see Lapa, *Livro da Visitação*, 157. Women also effected cures and divined answers to particular questions, such as the whereabouts of stolen money, using a straw basket and pieces of treasure; see Lapa, *Livro da Visitação*, 141–143.

curiboca, that the coupling of Indians and blacks was as common as other mixtures. This does not mean there was no hostility and confrontation between them, but that there was nothing intrinsic about their relative positions that disposed them to act any differently toward each other than they would to whites or mestiços.[55] However, some slaves did form their own rebel factions in the Cabanagem. Perhaps this separation was a consequence of the lack of ambition among some cabano leaders to abolish slavery. While slaves developed some distinct cultural characteristics and had their own political aspirations, they also shared much with the rest of the inhabitants.

Mobility, Vagrancy, and Desertion

An important aspect of the river-based life was the opportunity for a degree of geographical mobility, particularly for male adults. Many other residents of the interior visited Belém regularly. They may have stayed away for many weeks or even longer; certainly if they were coming from the Upper Amazon, for example, the trip itself was a big investment of time and effort. To Belém they took produce from their farms and, once there, made necessary purchases and participated in the political and religious life of the capital. All interior families needed their patrons at centers of power and to keep up with the news. Sometimes these people clubbed together to send their produce in one boat. Accompanying the larger vessels was a crew of paddlers, sometimes slaves, and workers acting as pilots, cooks, and deckhands. Poorer farmers and fishermen probably also made the trip to Belém each year, perhaps not trusting their richer counterparts to sell their produce for a good price.

It is likely then that many people had much experience of long-distance boat travel.[56] Some of the movements were part of well-established seasonal migratory patterns. During the flood, riverbank residents sometimes moved to upland areas, particularly if they had cattle, though raised platforms (*morumbas*) were, and still are, used to store the beasts out of harm's way. Typically in the riverine economy, the low water period (roughly from August to January and which does not quite coincide with the dry season) is marked by intense activity when the floodplain is available for agriculture and fish are more concentrated; the high water time (February to July) is

---

55 For analyses of the range of relation between Indians and Africans generally in Latin America, see Matthew Restall (ed.), *Beyond Black and Red: African-Native Relations in Colonial Latin America*, Albuquerque: University of New Mexico Press, 2005. The Amazon does not diverge from the general experience of the continent.

56 People in Belém were probably not as mobile as those from the interior; Bates said most Belenenses did not know their countryside. Bates, *The Naturalist*, vol. 2, 410.

characterized by recuperation. In terms of commercial activity, this meant that the produce tended to be delivered to Belém from January to August, when the winds and current were against upriver travel and the river covered the low-lying floodplain. It is no coincidence that the date of the takeover of the capital was in early January, a time when people were converging on Belém and a general movement could be directed to another purpose. In stories told today about the Cabanagem, the period when boats descended the river for Belém was known as the "time of the purchases" (*época das compras*). Indeed, the year is divided up, as it may have been then, into times coupled to a significant activity.

Apart from seasonal migration and commercial pursuits (and festival attendance), another important aspect of human movement on the river was vagrancy or desertion. This unorganized mobility was most vexatious to the local and national authorities, for they wanted a settled population working the land. In Brazilian historiography, this heterogeneous group of people has been characterized as an "immense floating population, without fixed social position, living parasitically at the margin of regular economic activities."[57] In this view, vagrants were everything that could not be included in the masters-and-slaves paradigm of colonial society, a model of the social structure that never fitted Amazonia well in the absence of large-scale plantations. Caio Prado adopted a more deprecatory view, regarding the poor and diverse assembly as the "unclassified individuals (*desclassificados*), the useless and the ill-adapted individuals whose occupations were more or less uncertain or shifting."[58] The people who made up the desclassificados were poor whites, those avoiding criminal charges, freed slaves, runaway slaves, army deserters, Indian fugitives forcibly transplanted from their native communities, and so on. *Contra* Prado, it could be argued, they were very well adapted to the economy of the colonial Amazon, which needed temporary or seasonal labor and those with the ability to mediate between different kinds of situations. Their shifting identity was what allowed them to cope with, and perhaps prosper in, the late colonial world.

Prado goes on: "[P]art of this category of the colonial population was made up of people who vegetated in obscurity in some remote and cut-off corner of civilization, living from hand to mouth, brutalized and morally degraded. This was true of a great part of the Amazonian population, of the *tapuyas*, who had ceased to be pure forest dwellers and had not become colonists. . . . "[59] However, it was these people, vegetating in the jungles,

---

57 See entry on "Vadios" [vagrants] in Ronaldo Vainfas (ed.), *Dicionário do Brasil Colonial*, Rio de Janeiro: Objetiva, 2000, 576.

58 Prado, *Colonial Background*, 328; see also 328–333.

59 Prado, 329. It would seem that Prado is here referring to tapuyas as Indians living within the colonial sphere, rather than non-Tupi speakers.

who were the participants in the rebellions of the 1820s and 1830s, according to Prado. So they could hardly have been unaware of the wider context of their lives and without ideas on how to improve their lot. Indeed, it was their extensive and varied experience of the colony that gave them the confidence to fight in the rebellion. It is difficult to exaggerate how wrong Prado's view is. Many of the leaders of the Cabanagem and the people they amassed to the cause can hardly be described as vagrants or landless poor (*vadios*). Some were poor wage-laborers, soldiers, and farmers, and a few were slave owners, municipal councilors, and a part of the provincial administration. These comments by Prado are even more surprising if they are tied to his judgment that Cabanagem was one of Brazil's most significant rebellions. It shows the lack of interest in connecting social and ethnic context with political analysis.

Prado's characterization does not work well for the Amazon, as it may not elsewhere.[60] For a start, the "tapuyas" above cannot be called part of the "vagrant poor" just because they had not settled down and farmed land. They may have been prevented from doing so because suitable land near towns may not have been available; or they were threatened if they tried to work well-placed plots (see Chapter 4 on land and the agrarian sector). Richer colonists may have not allowed them to establish themselves because their labor would have been lost to the élite. It is likely that some Indians' mobile way of life was an adaptation to the conditions they faced. Indian absenteeism from labor obligations to the state partly resulted from their movement between indigenous villages and colonial settlements, perhaps bringing goods backwards and forwards and attending to ritual obligations.[61] In this context, it makes more sense to narrow the definition of vagrants in the Amazon to those who had deserted from the army, or from abusive masters in the case of slaves, or fugitives from the law. By definition, they were from elsewhere. In other words, vagrants were people who were fully part of colonial life and sought new opportunities depending on their circumstances, perhaps shedding existing social relations each time; "travelers" might be a more suitable term. Indians, on the other hand, could rely on more extensive and intact social networks.

There were plenty of complaints in the late eighteenth and early nineteenth centuries about vagrancy. Various laws to address them were introduced in this period, which sought to restrict all movement beyond the

---

60 See Laura de Mello e Souza, *Desclassificados de Ouro*, 1983, Rio de Janeiro: Graal, on the unclassifieds in Province of Minas Gerais in the seventeenth century.

61 See Sommer, "Neogotiated Settlements," 174–180. Baena, writing in 1833, reports that in ten years the population of the Rio Negro halved from 34,690 in 1821 to 16,213 in 1831, *Ensaio Corographico*, 19–21. The reasons for the decrease, according to Baena, are the desertions of Indians from the towns, death from disease, and Mura attacks. It is also possible that they chose not to be identified as Indians.

municipal district. Only those with permission and papers to travel could do so and anyone who was not on the municipal rolls could be arrested. These laws addressed not just Indian absenteeism but also the growing numbers of exiles (*degredados*) being brought in from Portugal.[62] In the attempt to increase the Amazon population, the Portuguese sent their own prisoners and criminals to settle in Pará. In an otherwise upbeat report on Pará in 1819, José Brito Inglês, a Brazilian-born military official, says this about the exiles: "In changing the climate they live in, they do not change their condition. The General takes them to their final destinations [to work on a farm]. However they all escape easily – *because of the nature of the country* – and wandering about in the Captaincy they often go to the Island of Joannes [Marajó] which then becomes subject to their banditry." He was probably referring to the stealing of cattle, a long-term problem on Marajó.[63]

Deserters from work parties or the army were another category of the mobile poor. The narratives and reports of scientists and administrators, who traveled the region on boats, are replete with comments about escaped crew members – that so and so, who was the cook, just disappeared as they landed in such and such a town. In replacement they had to pick up someone else who in turn left them with no warning. It is impossible to know whether these people deliberately made off at a point when they knew they could be reunited with friends who would help them or because they could not suffer their working conditions anymore. Sometimes the fugitives did not go far before being tracked down. A few made it only to the next town before being reported and arrested.[64] As the region became increasingly militarized during the 1820s and 1830s, participation in patrols was compulsory for many adult men. Then, desertion was sometimes a synonym for defection to the rebel side. In early 1821, a group of so-called "vagrants" attacked a number of farms in the region of Santarém. They killed slaves, stole cattle, and "threatened the whites." They were eventually caught by soldiers; sixteen vagrants were arrested and a few killed. Their numbers suggested a degree of organization and preparation.[65] As the conflicts over independence and political reforms grew, these occurrences became commonplace.

Last, the stereotypical image of vagrancy was of a single man moving from place to place. Some "vagrants," however, moved in couples. For

---

62 José de Brito Inglês, "Memória sobre a Capitania do Pará," RIHGB, 1949, 203, 147.

63 My italics, Brito Inglês, "Memória," 149.

64 For example, Manoel Costa Vidal, president of the town council, to Governor of Pará, July 4, 1804, Monte Alegre, APEP cod. 610, doc. 86; Leonardo José Goncalves to Amazonas military commander José Bernardes Barralho, September 12, 1804, Óbidos, doc. 103.

65 Town judge José Cavalcante de Albuquerque to Governor of Pará, April 26, 1821, Óbidos, APEP cod. 717, doc. 40.

example, João Pedro, who was from Maranhão, traveled with his wife in search of short-term work. They moved from one farm to another along the Amazon River. They apparently caused no trouble and were peaceful people but they did not have permission to travel around so they were arrested. Presumably they had survived by performing seasonal labor duties for some time; the people they worked for had not turned them in. This suggests that employers benefited from such an arrangement. Workers turned up at seasonal "crunch times" of the year when extra labor was needed.[66] In other words, both parties gained advantage from this arrangement. The couple could continue on their travels and the employer knew there was a source of cheap labor. A man and a woman also complemented each other's labor, according to the gendered division of tasks. This pair's movements may also have been about finding "a good boss," someone who would give them work and be obliged to look after them.

The Portuguese had always tried to control the movement of people and river craft in Amazonian waters. But the seasonal nature of the economy, the long-distance trade networks, and the facility of desertion made the restriction of mobility impossible. A contradiction was unwittingly created between the territorially expansive occupation of Amazonia and the demands of the élite for a sedentary populace of laborers. Vagrancy was only a problem for those who wanted a reliable labor force (and to control the political aspirations of the masses). Yet the earlier example of João Pedro and his wife shows that labor may not need to have been fixed down for it to be available. The control of movement, however, became a top priority for political rather than economic reasons, for municipal and provincial authorities in the 1820s and 1830s.

River Craft

In the early nineteenth century, three types of vessels saw everyday usage on the Amazon waterways: the *ubá*, the *montaria*, and the *igarité* or *canoa coberta*.[67] In addition, there was the *bote*, or *batelão*, which was used to transport cattle and other animals; *jangada* (a raft), and brigs (for naval movements). There seemed to be little difference between those boats that moved predominantly around the delta of the Amazon, where the river could be choppier, and those that worked the interior. Given the need for boats

---

66 Manoel Costa Vidal, president of the town council, to Governor of Pará, July 4, 1804, Monte Alegre, APEP cod. 610, doc. 86.

67 The term *igarité* is lingua geral and means good or large canoe; it is the superlative form of *igara*, a canoe. The common term for a stream is *igarapé*, also derived from igara, and signifies the path of the canoe. See Alfred R. Wallace, *A Narrative of Travels on the Amazon and Rio Negro with an Account of the Native Tribes and Observations on the Climate, Geology, and Natural History of the Amazon Valley*, London: Reeve, 1853, Appendix on "Vocabularies of Amazonian Languages," 523.

THE MONTARIA.

Image 2.3 Montaria, dugout canoe, c. 1840

that could move long distances and through different environments, a more flexible design was used. Small sailing vessels, typically the igarité, were commonest for moving along the river, but these do not appear to have been common until the second decade of the nineteenth century. For important dignitaries, long covered canoes were employed with many paddlers.

Regardless of size or structure, canoes in the eighteenth century had a long bow with a pronounced flare for shore landing and hauling up the beach for safekeeping. This design was modified as harbors were constructed in the early nineteenth century, which obviated the need for landing some boats. Boats then became shorter and fatter, with a more pronounced keel.[68]

The ubá, a small dugout, and the montaria were omnipresent in the region and an essential part of daily life, both used for short trips and fishing in still water. The ubá was made from a single trunk and about fifteen feet long, whereas the montaria could be forty to sixty feet in length, and therefore excavated from a much larger tree, with a layer of planks to make a

68 Delson Marx, "Inland Navigation," 1995.

Image 2.4 A study of the sky, made from memory two or three months after seeing it. A view of the Amazon River is presented near Monte Alegre, in Portuguese Guyana (São Carlos, March 9, 1935), watercolor by Hercule Florence, c. 1828 [two igarités]

AMAZONIAN CANOA.

Image 2.5 Amazonian canoe, river sailing vessel, c. 1840

hold for cargo. Later in the nineteenth century, the montaria was built from a series of planks rather than one tree. It had no rudder or keel, but made use of a paddle to steer and to propel.[69] It had a round prow and some had a poop with a cabin for protection from sun and rain; a few large ones could take a jib and main mast with round sails.

The igarité was a more substantial canoe, fitted with two masts, a rudder and keel, an arched awning, and a cabin near the stern, made from a palm leaf covering. They could range in size from forty to seventy feet. Prince Adalbert describes an igarité as having a short jib attached to a front bench and rigged with a big sail, without a keel and a flat bow and stern.[70] The pilot looked over the cabins when he stood at the helm. Under the roof of the cabin were benches that also served as beds and tables. Rowers were positioned in the middle of the boat and used paddles, not oars. An igarité could also be turned into a military vessel and would then have cannon at the rear and the front.

The time it would take to travel from Belém to Santarém depended on the season, currents and, critical for sailing vessels, the winds. The *vento geral* or "Amazons trade wind" is an easterly that blows from August to December, making that period the most convenient for upriver travel. Also at this time of the year, the river is ebbing and currents slack due to the diminishing volume of water. Outside of these periods, progress upriver could be very slow and sometimes only possible by pulling the boat with a cable along the shore. Therefore, most movement downriver took place in the first half of the calendar year and the traffic came into the interior in the second half.[71] During the low-water season, an igarité would take about ten days to get from Belém to Santarém, two more days to reach Óbidos, and another fourteen days to Manaus, for a total of twenty-six days from Belém to Manaus (forty days in smaller vessels). In the high-water season, with little wind and increased water flow, the times were much extended: thirty-one days from Belém to Santarém, an extra four days to struggle to Óbidos and a slog of thirty-three days to Manaus – sixty-eight days in all from Belém to Manaus. Going downstream, a typical journey from Manaus to Belém was about thirty days and about fifteen to twenty days from Santarém. All times varied depending on squalls (common in the dry season) and the wind strength, paddlers' effort, and the type of craft. It took a brig about twenty days to sail from Belém to Lisbon, about six days to reach São Luis, and

---

69 Bates, *A Naturalist*, vol. 1, 75; James C. Fletcher and Daniel P. Kidder, *Brazil and the Brazilians. Portrayed in Historical and Descriptive Sketches*, Boston, Little, Brown 1879; Delson Marx, "Inland Navigation."
70 Prince Henry William Adalbert, *Travels in the South of Europe and in Brazil with a Voyage up the Amazon and the Xingu*, London, 1849, 170–171.
71 Bates, *A Naturalist*, vol. 1, 212–213.

Table 2.1 *Population of Monte Alegre, Óbidos, and Santarém, 1827–1828*

Town	Free	Slaves	Total
Óbidos	3,500	1,295	4,795
Monte Alegre	2,789	291	3,080
Santarém	5,361	2,095	7,456

Source: "Memoria," January 8, 1828, APEP cod. 838, doc. 101–102; Anonymous, "Memória" [of the Lower Amazon], December 1, 1828, APEP cod. 851, doc. 74.

Table 2.2 *Numbers of boat owners in Óbidos and Monte Alegre, 1827*

	Owners of igarités	Owners of montarias (i.e., 1–3 per owner)
Óbidos	75	228
Monte Alegre	57	176

Note: Igarité owners also had montarias but have been excluded from the total in order to highlight the difference in economic position.

another thirty to reach Rio de Janeiro. The relatively longer length of time to sail from Belém to southerly cities could be attributed to the unfavorable winds and currents coming up the Atlantic coast.

The numbers of boats and the kinds of labor engaged on board can be seen in the tables above. The information was taken in 1827 from two detailed censuses of towns in the Lower Amazon.[72] The smallest kind of canoes are left out of the census, perhaps because they were ubiquitous, but the more valued ones were recorded, offering a unique insight into the riverine world. In order to put this in a demographic context, the population of the two relevant municipalities with Santarém as a comparison is presented.

The figures above are designed to show the economic and class differences between the residents of the two towns. The igarité was a boat that allowed for long-distance travel and the storage of many tons of cargo. The figure shows that seventy-five men in Óbidos and fifty-seven in Monte Alegre owned an igarité (they also owned montarias, but those in the second

---

72 "Relação das embarcações existentes nos portos dos districtos da vila Monte Alegre, suas qualidades, estação, numero dos individuos da sua tripulação, suas condiçõens, nomes dos seus proprietarios e seus empregos," Monte Alegre, APEP cod. 828, docs 39, 40; "Mapa geral de todas as canoas que existem em os portos dos districtos desta vila," March 27, 1826, Óbidos, APEP cod. 828, docs 41 and 42, March 1826. There is a much shorter and less informative census for Santarém, which I have not used. APEP cod. 828, doc. 44.

Table 2.3 *Main use of boats in Óbidos and Monte Alegre, 1827*

	Fishing	Commerce	Transport
Óbidos	50	11	200
Monte Alegre	231	10	49

Table 2.4 *Types of labor on boats in Óbidos and Monte Alegre, 1827*

	Total no. of owners in census	People working on boats	Boat owners using one or more slaves	Slaves on boats	Free people (family and paid) on boats	Boats with combined slave and free labor
Óbidos	293	764	126	450	167	100
Monte Alegre	223	507	30	93	414	17

column did not own an igarité). In other words, these numbers reflected the men who were relatively well-off and with commercial power; they were, in short, the local bosses and amounted to just over two percent of the free population. If we take into account their families, calculating six people per family, the number of elites amounted to about thirteen percent of the total population for both towns. The names of the igarité owners were those who served at one time or another as judges and on the town councils, whereas montaria owners were the rest of the population: poorer and with more restricted access to resources. About six to eight percent of the total population were registered boat owners in each place. Most owners from both towns had one montaria, which is suggestive of an important characteristic of peasant societies, namely, the pooling of resources and labor among kinspeople and neighbors.

The tables allow the relative differences in the economic activity of each town to be seen. One was predominantly fishing-based and the other was primarily engaged in the transport of produce, in this case, mainly cacao and cattle. Individual boat owners used their boats for the movement of their goods. Only a few vessels were involved in itinerant commerce.

In both places, about a third of the slave population worked on boats. Their work consisted of fishing, maintaining the vessel, cooking, and transporting goods and animals. Thus, slaves were as much a part of the mobile population as anybody else, and the numbers suggest that both male and female slaves were involved in river craft labor. Monte Alegre, however, had a different demographic structure, with many fewer slaves compared to Óbidos. Monte Alegre engaged more free labor in fishing activities than did Óbidos. This can be explained by the fact that fishing was a more important commercial activity in Monte Alegre than in Óbidos and was associated with Indians and mestiços. Although there were some interesting similarities across the town and their class structure, they had their singularities. In this case, the different numbers of slaves and the economic profile meant each place had its own identity and networks reaching out to other towns.

Popular Religious Activity

There were four main reasons for social movement: desertion or escape, search for seasonal work, commerce, and participation in religious festivals. The last is a large topic that could lead into discussions on cultural mixing of different religious and folkloric traditions. Although this is important, it is not strictly relevant to the current focus. By way of brief introduction I want to recall the description by Laura de Mello e Souza of religious life in eighteenth-century Brazil, which fits Pará well. She writes about a "coexistence and interpenetration of populations from different places of origin and of different creeds. A diversity of cultural traditions thus flowed into sorcery and popular religiosity. Accounting for this complexity means understanding it as the place where multiple cultural levels intersected and were reconfigured, as agents in a long process of concretization."[73] She stresses that in the colonial period there was "a yawning gap" that separated popular religious belief and practice from official, particularly inquisitorial, Catholicism.[74] However, at some times, hybrid forms were tolerated and perhaps even actively fostered on a local level; the early nineteenth century appears to be one of those times.

During the Pombaline period in the Amazon, official Catholicism attempted to control local manifestations and mixtures. Inquisitor Geraldo José de Abranches headed the visitation of the Inquisition of Lisbon to Pará between 1763–1769. It remained in the capital, tried forty-six cases, and meted out relatively weak punishments.[75] On either side of this period, individuals were denounced and their cases sent to Lisbon, including some "whites" who had upset the church or élite administrators. At this time, the Inquisition was a rather toothless beast but it could still cause trouble, a fact in evidence in the reciprocal nature of denunciations. Almost all cases came from Belém, the towns of Cametá and Vigia, and from a small group of people who acted interchangeably as accused,

73 Laura de Mello e Souza, *The Devil and the Land of the Holy Cross*, Austin: University of Texas, 2003, xvi.
74 Souza, 87.
75 Amaral Lapa (ed.), *Livro da Visitação*, 69.

denouncer, and witness.[76] Before and after the visitation, *comissários* acting on behalf of the Inquisition traveled to Pará and some of the larger villages in the interior.

By the end of the eighteenth century there appeared to be little official attempt to manage popular religious life.[77] Indeed, in the mid-1790s governor Francisco de Souza Coutinho promoted the Our Lady of Nazareth celebration in early September to include both commercial and profane elements.[78] One could speculate that there was a toleration of the saints' festivals, shamanic forms of curing, and sorcery and folklore that were emerging as a result of the creative confrontation between different religious traditions. Certainly, *pajés*, the shamans who healed and blessed with the help of their special cigars and a glass of rum, were ridiculed by the so-called educated men writing in the period, but there was never the implication they were being persecuted.[79] Religious festivals where songs were sung to a saint in lingua geral (see the following paragraphs) were still openly taking place in the early nineteenth century and continued to do so for many decades. For example, Bates said he heard Christmas hymns sung in lingua geral in Parintins (then Vila Nova da Rainha) in 1853.

It is the connection between the ritual calendar and rebellious activity, already noted in the Brazilian and the Andean context, that needs special

---

76 The records of the trials are located in the Arquivo Nacional da Torre do Tombo in Lisbon. The *Livro da Visitação* contains the initial process of the Inquisition team, the confessions, and denunciations. Each one is followed up and, if necessary, the confessor or accused is imprisoned during the calling of further witnesses, questioning, and final verdict. The cases occurring outside the Visitation were sent to Lisbon, along with the accused. The last such trial I have located took place in the early 1780s. Some of the Paraense material has been analyzed by Mello e Souza and Barbara Sommer, "Cupid on the Amazon: Sexual Witchcraft and Society in Late Colonial Pará, Brazil," *Colonial Latin American Historical Review*, 2003, 12, 4, 415–446.

77 In addition to the Inquisition trials, two bishops of Pará, João de São José Queiróz (early 1760s) and Caetano Brandão (1780s), visited the interior and left diaries of observations of the religious behavior of not just Indians but of whites, priests, and official administrators as well. See João de São José Queirós, "Viagem e Visita do Sertão em o Bispado do Gram Pará em 1762 e 1763," RIHGB, 9, 43–107, 179–237, 328–375 and 476–527, 1847; Camillo Castello-Branco, ed. *Memórias de Fr. João de São José Queiroz (Bispo do Pará)*, Porto: Typographia da Livraria Nacional, 1868; and Luis de Oliveira Ramos (ed.), *Diários das Visitas Pastorais no Pará de Caetano Brandão*, Porto: Universidade do Porto, 1991.

78 On the building of the chapel and the creation of the Our Lady of Nazareth festival see Raiol, *Motins Políticos*, 835. The excellent book by Geraldo Mártires Coelho, *Uma Crônica do Marivilhoso: Legenda, Tempo e Memória no Culto da Virgem de Nazaré*, Belém: Imprensa Oficial do Estado, 1998, provides a thorough history of the cult.

79 Ignácio Accioli de Cerqueira e Silva, *Corographia Paraense, ou Descripção Física, Histórica, e Política, da Província do Gram-Pará*, Bahia, 1833, 114, 136; Fernandes de Souza, "Notícias Geográphicas," 487; Veríssimo, "As Populações Indigenas e Mestiças," 351; APEP cod. 732, doc 67, 1822 on pajés on the Tapajós River; and see also Francisco Bernardino de Souza, *Pará e Amazonas, Comissão da Madeira*, Rio de Janeiro: Typographia Nacional, 1874–1875. One explanation for the toleration is that the whites are just as much involved as everybody else in aspects of the religious life of the region.

mention.[80] The ritual calendar in the late colonial and early independence period was dominated by Catholic festivals, regional and local. Aside from Christmas and Easter, each town had a patron saint, which was honored annually with a two-week long celebration. During these times, people came from their rural homesteads to attend the festivities, meeting friends and family and eating and drinking. The town was decorated and processions, music, and fireworks occurred most days. The saint's icon was carried through the streets with banners, and sometimes along the river, people wishing to kiss and touch it. Contributions were requested to finance the events and to maintain the cult and its brotherhood. In all such festivities, commentators noted that they appeared more about having fun than anything else, even though participants were most devoted to their religion.

Aside from the local town *festas*, others of larger regional significance were attended by large numbers of people from the whole area. At least three such festivals took place in Belém during the early nineteenth century. It was no coincidence that they took place at significant moments in the river's rhythms. São Tomé occurred in early January when the river started to rise, the vento geral stopped blowing, and people started bringing their produce to Belém after the dry season. The feast of the Holy Spirit (Espírito Santo) took place in early June when the river level was at its peak, the capital's population was at its highest, and its stores were stocked full of produce from the interior. Our Lady of Nazareth occurred in early September just when the vento geral started and boats used to set off up river for the low water period.

São Tome was the extremely popular saint of Indians and mestiços of the time in Belém and his anniversary was January 6.[81] Two weeks before the celebration, people carried his image through the streets begging for money so as to honor him. At the beginning of the fortnight, the icon would be brought from its chapel on the outskirts of Belém to the cathedral, stopping along the way. Once at the cathedral, it spent a few days for all to see before being returned to its home, where the main festivities would be held. On some special days, a large banner known as *sairé* or *toriua* – a wooden semicircle atop a large pole – was carried in the procession. Measuring about one meter in width, the *sairé* was divided into four parts. Each section had a mirror and a cross; another cross stood at the top of the banner. The *sairé*'s wooden frame was wrapped in cotton; ribbons dangled from it, with six small cotton-covered sticks attached. Three Indian women held these sticks,

---

80 The connection is made and analyzed in France by Emmanuel Le Roy Ladurie, *Carnival: A People's Uprising at Romans 1579–1580*, London: Scholar Press, 1980. In Brazil, see João José Reis, *Death is a Festival: Funeral Rites and Rebellion in Nineteenth-Century Brazil*, Chapel Hill: University of North Carolina Press, 2006; and in the Andes, see Tristan Platt, "The Andean Experience of Bolivian Liberalism," in Steve Stern (ed.), *Resistance, Rebellion and Consciousness in the Andean Peasant World*, Madison: University of Wisconsin Press, 1987.

81 Baena, *Ensaio Corographico*, 110.

while a fourth held a ribbon tied to the cross at the top. As they marched, they sang in lingua geral:

In a stone basin was baptized the child of God. Santa Maria is a beautiful woman; her child is like her; in the heavens with a great cross to protect our souls.[82]

In the early morning of January 7, 1835, rebels stormed Belém. Already congregated for the festival in Belém, the crowds found another focus – for their anger.[83] In later years, chroniclers fail to mention the commemoration of São Tomé in Belém, perhaps because the day was no longer observed due to repression and a process known as Romanization, an effort initiated by a reforming bishop during the 1860s to standardize saints' festivals and other religious practices.[84] The commemoration did continue, however, in the interior of Pará.

The other two large festivals in early nineteenth-century Amazonia involved significant commercial elements. Large markets (*festas do arraial*) were temporarily installed outside the relevant place of worship, either at the church dedicated to Our Lady of Nazareth or the main cathedral for the Holy Spirit. These markets, designed to take advantage of the animated spirits during the festivals, offered the "agricultural and industrial products of the state" and present were "Indians of all races, mestiços of all types of mixtures, all in ecstasy in the streets of the capital."[85] Souza Coutinho wanted these markets to be showcases for such regional specialties as Indian crafts, and to sell food and drink. The commercial and the religious were tightly bound together.

In the very early part of the nineteenth century, the feast of the Holy Spirit was probably bigger than that of Our Lady of Nazareth (despite the state's promotion of that festival). As mentioned, June was the month when the flood was at its highest and people amassed in Belém to buy and sell goods while they waited for the river to lower and for the start of the new seasonal year. However, by the 1860s, the Bishop of Pará deemed the Feast of the Holy Spirit too profane, and suppressed it by refusing to allow the cathedral to be used for the festivities and banning market stalls from the cathedral

---

82 Baena, 110. The Portuguese version is *Em uma pia de pedra foi batizado o menino de Deus. Santa Maria é uma mulher bonita; o seu filho é como ela; no alto ceu numa cruz grande para guardar a nossa alma.*

83 Raiol, *Motins Políticos*, 542, for the day of rebellion, see 961–966.

84 The bishop was Antônio de Macedo Costa see Antônio de Almeida Lustosa, *Dom Macedo Costa, Bispo do Pará*, Belém: Cruzada da Boa Imprensa, 1993; for an anthropological commentary, see Raymundo Heraldo Maués, *Pajés, Padres, Festas e Santos: Catolicismo Popular e Controle Eclesiástico. Um Estudo Antropológico numa Área do Interior da Amazônia*, Belém: CEJUP, 1995. For a general overview of the religious history of the Amazon see Eduardo Hooneart (ed.), *História da Igreja na Amazônia*. Petropolis: Vozes, 1991.

85 Arthur Vianna, "As Festas Populares," ABAPP, 1968, 3, 234.

Image 2.6 View of the Praça das Mercês with market, Belém, c. 1792

square. As a consequence, one of Belém's most popular festivals was weakened and withered away by the end of the nineteenth century.[86]

Saints' festivals provided a ritual and a social focus for large numbers of people; they were a natural meeting point and required coordination to organize. We cannot know if the concurrence of rebellious activity and ritual calendars was a matter of planning, a coincidence, or a mixture of both at different times. There would certainly seem to be a degree of forethought, and the general excitement and solidarity of collective ritual life would have aided rebel leaders in mobilizing others. In 1829, the municipal authorities of Óbidos banned all religious celebrations within its borders, threatening participants with severe punishment if they took a saint's icon – or a crown, in the case of the Holy Spirit – on a procession from house to house. They also prohibited the circulation of pamphlets. Even though the councilors in

---

86 Vianna, "As Festas"; Maués, *Pajés, Padres, Festas e Santos*, on the "romanization" of the church in the Amazon. The festival of the Holy Spirit in Rio de Janeiro in the mid- to late eighteenth century was also very popular. Attempts to control the celebration were also implemented by the ecclesiastical and city authorities. According to Martha Abreu during the 1830s, the élites were especially frightened by the gathering of large groups of people and sought to limit the festival to three days only. Marta Abreu, "Popular Culture, Power Relations and Urban Discipline: The Festival of the Holy Spirit in Nineteenth Century Rio de Janeiro," *Bulletin of Latin American Research*, 2005, 24, 2, 175.

Óbidos were largely "liberals," they feared the collective potential of Indians and slaves.[87]

Languages

Although Portuguese was the official language of correspondence and was spoken among whites, it was probably not the dominant language at the beginning of the nineteenth century. The Tupinamba-derived *lingua vernácula* (or *vulgar*) was widely used until the second half of the nineteenth century.[88] More usually known as the lingua geral, the common language of the colony was not Portuguese, despite the stringent efforts of many peninsular administrators, especially with the Pombaline reforms. Only with increased European migration in the early nineteenth century and, more significantly, northeastern Brazil settlement in the 1870s did the everyday language of the *sertão* come to diminish in prominence. By this time it had also attracted the interest of scientists – such as geologist Charles Hartt, who wanted to understand geographical names – and scholars like the writer Couto de Magalhães, who introduced the term *nheengatu*, the "good language," in 1876.[89] Nowadays, a form of lingua geral, also called nheengatu, is spoken only on the upper Negro River.

The significance of language to the rebellion is critical, though little can be concluded for certain. Was lingua geral the language of the Amazonian way of life? What was the attitude of early nineteenth-century liberals toward it (later in the century, it became a popular topic)? Was lingua geral the preferred language of the rebellion? Clearly, it was widely spoken but this does not mean it was a written language. There is hardly any evidence to suggest it was the language of choice of the rebellion, but this may be because all that has survived from this period are written proclamations from Belém and official letters by cabano presidents, all in Portuguese. The role of lingua geral would have been oral, not textual. Moreover, other languages may also have had a place in the region – Amerindian ones, for example, which were in use between kinsfolk. Nevertheless, the

---

87 Reis, *História de Óbidos*, 50.
88 Discussions of lingua geral in the Brazilian Amazon include Sweet, "A Rich Realm of Nature," 75; Charles Hartt, "Notes on the Lingoa Geral or Modern Tupi of the Amazonas," *Transactions of the American Philological Association*, 1872, 3:58–76; Aryon Dall'Igna Rodrigues, "As Linguas Gerais Sul-americanas," http://vsites.unb.br/il/lablind/lingerais.htm, 1996; Maria Candida Drumond Mendes Barros and Antônio Luis Salim Lessa, "Um Dicionário Tupi de 1771 como Crônica da Situação Linguística na Amazônia Pombalina," In "Anais do Seminário Landi e o século XVIII na Amazônia," Belém: http://www.filologia.org.br/soletras/8sup/4.htm, 2003; José Bessa Freire, "Da 'Fala Boa' ao Portugues na Amazônia Brasileira," *Amerindia* (Paris), 1983, Paris, 39–84, 8; Wallace, *A Narrative of Travels*, Appendix on "Vocabularies of Amazonian Languages," 521–541.
89 José Vieira Couto de Magalhaes, *O Selvagem*, São Paulo: Companhia Editora Nacional, [1876] 1935.

reconstituted nature of Amazonian livelihoods would have matched well the creolized characteristic of lingua geral and its extension.

The lingua geral of Brazilian Amazonia was different from the one spoken in São Paulo and the version used in the far south of Portuguese America known as the Guarani criollo[90]. All three were mestiço languages and originated in the miscegenation of European and Tupi Amerindians. They became the new language of a new people, including a significant contingent of slaves and other indigenous groups. Over time, lingua geral has came to refer to different kinds of "general languages": (1) one promoted by the Jesuits using a Latin grammar in the sixteenth century and (2) a creole of Tupinamba of the seventeenth and eighteenth centuries that grew especially strongly among the children of mixed ethnic unions. The Jesuits thus did not create the lingua geral but systematized and formalized regional variations. Even after their expulsion, at least one priest challenged the use of Portuguese in catechism. The priest argued that doctrinal observation was much easier to maintain in a language understood by the Indians than in one they had to learn anew.[91]

Tupinamba was generally spoken in the northern coastal areas and in the lower part of the Amazon River as far as Tocantins River at the time of conquest. As the Portuguese extended their dominion over the rest of the basin, so did a creolized version of the language spread. The preference for the lingua geral over Portuguese was pragmatic since it was the language of labor and trade between mission Indians, Africans, mestiços, and whites. Even some white children did not learn Portuguese as their first language, and recently arrived slaves picked up lingua geral quickly.[92]

Charles Hartt helps give some historical specificity to the ethnic use of lingua geral. "In its modern form," he wrote in 1872, " . . . it is still in use on the Amazonas from Peru to the sea, not only by Indians of Tupi origin, but also many tribes of different stock . . . Along the main river, and in towns, the Portuguese is fast superseding it, and with the rapid process of civilization, the Tupi must soon die out. But the lingua geral of the Amazonas is not the old Tupi of the Jesuits. In the pronunciation and structure the two differ even more than Spanish and Italian."[93] The irony in Hartt's view was that two hundred years earlier, lingua geral was the harbinger of civilization,

90 Rodrigues, "As Linguas Gerais Sul-americanas."

91 Manuel da Penha do Rosário, "Lingua Vulgar versus Lingua Portuguesa: A Defesa do Padre Manuel da Penha do Rosário Contra a Imposição da Língua Portuguesa aos índios por meio de Missionários e Párocos," *ABNRJ*, 111, 7–62 [original dated 1773], 1993. See also the derogatory remarks on lingua geral by Baena, who says that it is an extremely monotonous language to listen to and has an impoverished grammar, *Ensaio Corográfico*, 28.

92 Sweet, "A Rich Realm," 77; Arthur Reis, *A Política de Portugal no Valle Amazônico*, Belém: Secult, 1993, 79.

93 Charles Hartt, "Notes on the Lingoa Geral," 59.

actively promoted by the colonial administration, the Church, and missionaries. The living lingua geral differed so greatly from its earlier missionary form because of its transformation through continued use, a fact well documented by Hartt.[94]

Clearly, in the early nineteenth century, Portuguese and lingua geral coexist. Words and phrases, Hartt says, move between the languages, with Amazonian Portuguese being as influenced by lingua geral-derived words as it is by Portuguese.[95] This interweaving makes it difficult to claim continuity of cultural action between a word, a concept, and an ethnic identity. Take a word like *panema*, for example: the lingua geral word for "bad luck in hunting." The term is still used among riverine dwellers, but one cannot assume that it is referring to an aboriginal Amerindian belief and practice. Whatever the word's original meaning, it has become infused with newer senses that may have little to do with the past. The same could be said of Portuguese terms like *quebranto*, which means "evil eye" and surfaced in some trials of the Inquisition. This may have linked with Indian perceptions, making it different, subtler, or otherwise, from its European terminological equivalents. In other words, there is no simple correspondence between any cultural practices, identities, categories, and terms. We cannot assume either that an Indian or a white would act according to some predetermined cultural schema or that conquest caused a rupture so great that all cultural meanings were dislodged from their mooring.

Most frustratingly, documents of the pre-Cabanagem period, published or not, hardly mention the continued use of lingua geral. Even chroniclers do not make systematic observations. Martius wrote a small dictionary of Tupi words but, according to Hartt, it is small and inaccurate. Throughout Spix and Martius' narrative, lingua geral words (and their translations) are provided for certain objects, places, or towns indicating what Indians called it. Some thirty years later, Bates picked up lingua geral piecemeal, though the impression is that it is much less spoken in the Lower Amazon of the early 1850s than in the upper Amazonian towns. That change was likely to have been the result of the repression following the Cabanagem rather than migration of nonlingua geral speakers and any dilution.

Overall, before the late 1830s, "the lingua geral was the universal means of communication between and with the 'civilized,' detribalized, nominally Christian Indians and mamelucos who formed the vast majority of the settled population of the Amazon basin."[96] It may not have unified politically such a heterogeneous series of people, but its persistence and

---

94 Denis Moore, Sidney Facundes, and Nadia Pires, "Nheengatu, (Lingua Geral Amazônica)," *Proceedings of the Meeting of the Society for the Study of the Indigenous Languages*, July 1993, 93–118.
95 Hartt, 72; and Moore et al., "Nheengatu."
96 Sweet, "A Rich Realm."

pervasiveness "served both to blend together and to preserve for the modern *caboclo* [a person of mixed ancestry] population of that region a more diverse and comprehensive heritage of indigenous folk beliefs, usages and traditions than exist for mestiço populations elsewhere in Brazil, and very possibly anywhere outside of 'Indo-America.'"[97] The rise and fall of the lingua geral parallels, more or less, the most innovative and resilient kinds of characters of the last four hundred years of Brazilian Amazonian history. The contemporary riverine peasantry today may have inherited some of the culture created in the first two hundred years of modern Amazonia's existence but it is much impoverished one without the lingua geral. This suggests the peasantry of riverine Amazonia in the twentieth and twenty-first centuries are not the outcome of successive transformations of past inhabitants. They are, instead, quite different beings and persons to the region's predecessors of the early nineteenth century. The Cabanagem was a turning point in breaking up the dominant Indian culture in the colonial period.

Was there a connection between the politics of Amazonian peasants and lingua geral? Given the prevalence of lingua geral and its omnipresence and popularity with mestiços and natives, it might have become the language of choice for a rebel movement. In the early 1830s, for example, many place names were returned to the neo-indigenous original in an attempt to move away from Portuguese domination. As far as can be said, this was not accompanied by a shift to conducting municipal affairs in the lingua geral. Enlightened liberal leaders in Belém, such as Batista Campos, did not apparently call for its more widespread use in building opposition to rule from the South of Brazil and Portuguese control, or in unifying a mixed bag of a movement. There could be two reasons for this. It was possible the intellectual leaders of the rebellion could not speak lingua geral, even though they were Paraense and probably brought up by maids and nannies who used it. Another possibility was that the radical liberalism the leaders were promoting was of a certain kind, one acceptable to local élites. It could be speculated that the absence of references to lingua geral in the documents is evidence of the disdain in which it was regarded by the higher echelons, whatever their allegiance. Their liberalism was an urban metropolitan phenomenon, essentially concerned with having locally elected leaders, not Portuguese or those imposed from the south of the country.

There is only a sliver of a story told to the Victorian botanist, Richard Spruce, some fifteen years after the rebellion about the significance of language. He was informed that if a person could not speak lingua geral, or had a beard, then he or she was liable to be slaughtered by rebels.[98] This statement exists on its own, and in a period when antirebellion propaganda

97 Sweet, 78.
98 Richard Spruce, *Notes of a Botanist on the Amazon and Andes*, London: Macmillan, 1908, 61.

was in full swing. While it cannot be taken at face value, it is nevertheless likely that parts of the rebel movement may have articulated such a position and saw the promotion of lingua geral as part of their political project without seeking the support of leadership in Belém.

Despite the size of the region, the peoples of the Amazon were regionally integrated by the commercial, military, and political hold of Belém. Yet imposing a central authority on these fluid and diffuse forms of life was the Portuguese predicament. Centralization was characteristic of colonial relations generally and would come to be a major source of political conflict in the 1820s and 1830s. On a cultural level, however, there was a unique regional complex associated with the rivers. It gave Indians an advantage and provided them with opportunities. Rather than an amalgamation of the European, Indian, and African, it was a definite historical creation of the various protagonists who reconstituted the influences in a new form following their experiences and aspirations.

Importantly, colonial and early imperial relations cannot be reduced to a duality of colonized and colonizer: rather, there were many fault lines between kinds of people, only some of which were predictable or inevitable. But new social associations were also emerging. In the case of laboring people in eighteenth-century England, E. P. Thompson notes the existence of wider solidarities and a "horizontal consciousness" that existed between different craftsmen, that is, individuals from different guilds.[99] Aside from the few Portuguese patriarchs closely linked to Lisbon, the same could be said of Paraense society. Festivals, healers, diviners, a new language, and river craft provided some of the common references for these people, even if ethnic groups had their own dances, music, and rituals. A lingua franca gave them a means of communication, and the mobile world of the rivers connected them across great distances. In this chapter, some of the foundations have been laid for understanding these diverse interests and what happened when they came together.

99 Edward P. Thompson, "Patrician Society, Plebian Culture," *Journal of Social History*, 7, 4, 1974, 396.

3

The Family and Its Means in the Lower Amazon

João Felipe Bettendorff was a Jesuit missionary from Luxembourg and friend of the much-esteemed fellow Jesuit Antônio Vieira. Bettendorff lived in Pará in the second half of the seventeenth century and traveled extensively and frequently, setting up new missions and supervising established ones. His lengthy, and at times charming, chronicle of his work in the Amazon was one of the first nonconquest pieces of writing. It described a world, if not at peace, functioning as a colony and a mission. In the early 1660s, he went on a return journey to Santarém (then called Tapajós) with a military escort, João Corrêa, who had also been to the place before. After a particular grueling journey upriver in which his canoe almost capsized during a storm, he arrived at dawn in Santarém to be greeted by the Tapajós Indians. They were very pleased to see him again, he related, "all the more so for being accompanied by a white who was already known and loved for his compassion in curing their diseases and for this reason they all called him *atoassanã*, which means *compadre* [coparent]."[1]

Nothing is said about what this relationship meant to either party. (Bettendorff later recounted the marriage of two white men, one an ex-missionary, to women who were part of the native Tapajós Indian nobility.) The chronicler implies that there was no actual link created by baptism between the persons. Instead, the use of the term compadre seemed to be a friendly way of incorporating strangers within the realm of kinship. This act connected with instances dating from the first days of conquest, when chroniclers recorded the significance of the compadre-like relationship for indigenous peoples from all over South America, particularly those from the Tupi language group. For Tupi people, the person designated as an

---

1 João Felipe Bettendorff, *Crônica dos Padres da Companhia de Jesus no Estado do Maranhão*, Belém: Cejup, 1990, 164. João Corrêa was the son of the captain-general of Ceará, the next captaincy to the south of Pará and Maranhão. For histories of Jesuit missions in the Amazon, see Serafim Leite, *História da Companhia de Jesus no Brasil*, (vols 3 and 4 on the Amazon), Rio de Janeiro: Instituto Nacional do Livro, 1943; João Lúcio d'Acevedo, *Os Jesuitas no Grão Pará: Suas Missões e Colonização*, Belém: Secult, 1991 (first published in 1901).

atoassanã played a similar role to a brother-in-law in their kinship system, but both these relations were more than just coparents or affines. People from different groups – who were probably related as cross-cousins – would seek to establish wider and more lasting relations between their kinsfolk. In this way, the indigenous relation was a political one that worked to ensure reciprocal links over time. According to Claude Lévi-Strauss, European observers latched onto the relationship because of its resemblance to Iberian coparenthood constructed through baptism. Both sought to establish a new, special, and artificial connection. Lévi-Strauss argues that the formal parallel is "a striking example of a convergence in which the native and the Latin-Mediterranean institutions show numerous apparent similarities overlying important structural differences."[2]

The social significance of the utterance of *atoassanã* (roughly meaning coparent) in Santarém in the 1660s is the recognition of a common future, whether the parties knew it or not. Whatever the general cultural and political differences, the moment represented a bridge between two partners, albeit unequally associated. It revealed the basic importance of kinship to the conduct of affairs on the ground in the colony, almost as a spontaneous expression. (We should not forget the marriages in this regard.) Of course, kinship lay at one end of the scale, with war at the other; and in between were all kinds of other reciprocal ties, which characterized society in Pará. The point is that these intimate relations grew up in spite of the encouragement of, or restrictions by, the state and the church. Local interests and standards were nowhere more evident than in the workings of family life, so its study is a good way of understanding an important aspect of historical peasantries and how local political expressions diverged from metropolitan demands. Kinship connects individuals though locally meaningful idioms of relatedness. It also provides the basis of attachment to a place as residential groups work together. Although the state controlled temporarily the labor of some individuals through conscription and so on, it did not of the majority. Therefore, by reconstructing what kinship meant at the time, we are coming closer to an understanding of power in the early nineteenth century, and thus also of Indian peasant life.

About one hundred and forty years on from the *atoassanã* moment, family relations had adapted to the demands placed on critical resources such as labor. "Towns," Barbara Sommer writes, "were not random aggregates of individuals, but communities built through deeply-rooted kinship

---

2 Claude Lévi-Strauss, "The Social Use of Kin Terms," in Paul Bohannon and John Middleton (eds.), *Marriage, Family and Residence*, New York: The Natural History Press, 1968, 169. Note that one of the Tupi terms mentioned in Lévi-Strauss article is "atour-assap," and a Tupi dictionary translates *atuasaba* as *compadre* or *comadre*, Antônio Geraldo da Cunha, *Dicionário Histórico das Palavras Portuguesas de Origem Tupi*, São Paulo: Melhoramentos, 1999. The similarity between the words suggests the Tapajós were part of the Tupi language group.

ties."[3] The centrality of family life in Pará does not support the generalized and stereotypical view expounded by Caio Prado for colonial Brazil: "Slavery, economic instability – everything contributed to the weakness of the family unit, to the failure to establish family relations on a solid and more durable basis."[4] Rather, it was the opposite: the peculiar nature of the family enabled mobility and fluidity in social organization. This understanding follows Maria Beatriz Nizza da Silva's study of importance of property and its transmission to all types of people in the colony not just the wealthy.[5] In Pará, the economy was based on access to free natural resources. "Property" amounted to land for planting crops and raising livestock and technology (boats and tools); for a few, it included Africans who were slaves. Labor meant one's kinsfolk and neighbors. By maintaining control of these resources, a family would ensure its reproduction.

Given the absence of documentation, it is impossible to tell precisely how the ties of kinship influenced Paraense society, especially appointment to political office. However, given the importance of family ties to the mercantile and peasant economy and political life, it seems safe to assume the influence of the family was considerable. Whether through patronage or kinship links, networks of families across social classes and ethnic groups were brought together in a vertically organized arrangement; and one network set itself up in competition to others. The rivalry affected accession to and functioning of political office, administration of justice, and use of labor and supply to goods.

One manner in which individuals pursued their own, or their family's, interests was through the selective and arbitrary implementation of the law. This experience was deeply felt by those on the receiving end of law enforcement and sometimes had terrible implications, as the following example will show. A year or so before he died in 1800, the governor of the Rio Negro (Upper Amazon) captaincy, Manuel da Gama Lobo de Almada took a lover. Apparently, she brought him much happiness. She soon became pregnant and went to a convent to give birth, as was the custom of well-connected women. There, midwives would take care of everything, only in this case they did not, for the woman died in childbirth. As a result, the midwives were imprisoned in separate locations. Then, on the orders of the governor, Mother Valeria and two other midwives were taken at night to the edge of the river, adorned with a stone necklace, and

3 Barbara Sommer, "Negotiated Settlements: Native Amazonians and Portuguese Policy in Pará, Brazil, 1758–1798." Ph.D. dissertation, University of New Mexico, 2000, 242.

4 Caio Prado, *The Colonial Background of Modern Brazil*, Berkeley: University of California Press, 1969, 409.

5 Maria Beatriz Nizza da Silva, *História da Família no Brasil Colonial*, Rio de Janeiro: Editora Nova Fronteira, 1998.

"thrown to perpetual immersion under the waves." Antônio Baena, who recounted this story, revealed that the real reason behind his lover's death was her "jealous curiosity" over Almada's interest in another woman. She had driven herself to despair and either died of natural causes or committed suicide shortly after childbirth. Nevertheless, Almada was so saddened by her death that he was unable to hide his grief and blamed the midwives. Even though the dead woman "could not compare to a Countess of Salisbury or a Madame Pompadour" his personal honor, Baena relates, had been offended and someone had to pay. There was no trial and the act appeared to take place at the whim of one person. Such were the experiences of many others, and if a governor was unfair, all those under him could be as well.[6] On a large scale, whatever the justification sought by élites for their own actions, apparently undeserved or excessive punishments stood as prime examples of arbitrary justice.

Most frequently, the injustice was felt when another family benefited for no other reason than their connection to someone in power. So in this chapter I will ask how the society at the time fitted together. It will draw out the complicated mix of loyalties and rivalries that were crosscut by kinship – itself a compound of relations involving ethnicity and class – and discuss the continuity of some families from the second half of the eighteenth century to the Cabanagem rebellion.

A special note on sources is required for this chapter. I have made use of Parish records for two towns in the Lower Amazon (no others were available). Santarém has one book of marriages for the second half of the eighteenth century, but that is all for the colonial and early imperial period. Óbidos has baptismal books dating from 1805. In both, information is given on parentage, ethnic status (and whether a slave), residence, birthplace, and godparents. These records provide data not available elsewhere and have enabled me to compile genealogical charts for some families in the Óbidos region at least.[7] As with the other chapters, correspondence from individuals and town councils to the provincial governor has also been used. This reveals local factions and rivalries, as well as key flashpoints. When writing these letters of complaints, authors often exaggerated others' misdemeanors and completely ignored their own. Another invaluable local source helping

---

6 Antônio Ladislau Monteiro Baena, *Compêndio das Eras do Pará*, Belém, UFPa, 1969, 242. Of course, taking lovers was nothing new. For men of an élite background, though, there were different rules and values, and we do not know all circumstances in the case to make a full evaluation of Lobo de Almada's actions. See Arthur Reis, *História do Amazonas*, Belo Horizonte, Editora Itatiaia, 1989, 141–148, on Almada's governorship in the Rio Negro captaincy.

7 At least in 2004 there were no records in other towns that church workers were willing to show me. In the Lower Xingu, the area studied by Arlene Kelly, records for baptisms start in 1824, "Family, Church and Crown: A Social and Demographic History of the Lower Xingu Valley and the Municipality of Gurupá, 1623–1889." Ph.D dissertation, University of Florida, 1984.

track families were three comprehensive census lists – for all non-Indian domestic households in 1778, the militia in 1799, and the National Guards in 1832. Lastly, there is a useful set of documentation concerning the recognition of children born out of wedlock, which was sent to the Overseas Council in Lisbon. Such requests permit us to see the kinds of relationships relatively wealthy white men engaged in.

One methodological point should be stressed. A particular constraint is the nonstandard nature of naming practices, which makes it almost impossible to establish with total certainty consanguineal relations (unless backed up by another source, such as the baptismal records). The civil code dictating how surnames (*apelidos* in European Portuguese and *sobrenomes* in Brazilian Portuguese) should be passed down was not fixed until the early twentieth century. Therefore, siblings did not always share the same surnames and were named after different parts of the family (this included elite Portuguese families). If the child was born to unmarried parents, which was very common, the link between a father and son might also not be evident in the child's name. Moreover, in the period here, surnames were interchangeable with or additional to nicknames and profession (a practice that Mendonça Furtado tried to stop unsuccessfully in the 1750s). Similar names were not always a reliable indicator of shared relatedness unless corroborated elsewhere. A possible reason for the confusion is that baptismal names were only for use by the state; individuals were more commonly known by their nicknames, which gave a person a unique identity. To these various difficulties should be added the inconsistent transcribing practices of municipal officials, who spelled names differently and did not write out the full name every time.[8]

The Family: Dispersal and Networks

How, then, can the family be understood and what was its role? An answer can be begun by considering the language used to refer to the values of the inhabitants of Pará. As in other parts of Brazil, priests and administrators would write about the "bad customs" (*maus costumes*), meaning the lack of observation of Christian morals. Thus couples who lived together but were not married were living "scandalously," or women who went about without company in the street were acting "lasciviously" (in higher class families, this

---

8 The same kind of problems affects the identification of ethnicity; the accusations against a person for being an *indio* cannot be taken at face value. On Portuguese naming practices generally, see the special issue of *Etnográfica*, 12, 1, 2008, "Outros Nomes, Historias Cruzados: Os Nomes de Pessoa em Português," João de Pina Cabral (ed.), and on the Amazon in that issue, see Mark Harris, "Uma História dos Nomes: A Alcunha, o Primeiro Nome, e o Apelido no Pará, Norte do Brasil," *Etnográfica* (Lisbon), 2008, 12, 1, 215–236.

was considered exceptionally bad conduct). One commentator wrote that "whites or traders who live in Indian villages are frequently the worst, the most scandalous and insolent, putting women in their houses and living with them publicly without fear of God."[9] It is not clear from this quotation whether the writer meant that the whites lived with many Indian women or just one. Worse still were traders who went from place to place engaging in "not just mercantile activities but in sordid obscenities and thus pass their lives much satisfied."[10] So common were such judgments that these few examples can be taken as illustrative of a general pattern. The application of strong language did not indicate terrible crimes, *per se*, but rather aberration from Christian morals, which was, of course, a serious matter.

In order to achieve conformity to a common value system, the state regulated a series of aspects of family life. As part of his extensive reforms, the governor of the Amazon in the 1750s, Francisco Xavier Mendonça Furtado (see pages 107–108) ruled that village Indians should live in single-family households. We can assume he wanted to outlaw the multiple-family *maloca* (large Indian house), which was the residential norm in the Lower and Upper Amazon among Indian nations. From the early nineteenth century, and possibly earlier, it seems that malocas were rare in the main colonial areas.

In terms of the household, the evidence points to large households composed of unmarried children, adopted children, grandchildren, elderly parents, and visitors (short and long term). In richer households, slaves probably slept in separate accommodations. Without data on the composition or the development cycle of households, we cannot know the precise arrangements.[11] In the context of a peasant economy, the desire for domestic independence probably drove couples, when resources allowed, to set up their own house close to one set of parents on the same plot of land. The numbers of people present depended on seasonal activities. Labor, food, and technology were probably shared and controlled by the head parental couple. The family should be understood in the extended sense, the *parentela*, the network of related people in frequent contact, including consanguines, affines, and adopted kin. If slaves were working for the family, they were seen as part of it.[12] The relevant unit of domestic reproduction then

---

9 André Fernandes de Souza, "Notícias Geográficas da Capitania do Rio Negro," RIHGB, 1848, 10, 500.

10 Fernandes de Souza, "Notícias Geográficas," 503.

11 The censuses do contain information on the number of *fogos* (household hearths) and it would be possible to set this against the total population for a district. These data fluctuate between censuses so only speculative conclusions can be reached.

12 Vicente Salles, O *Negro do Pará*, 113. In the 1778 census, slaves are listed as composing part of the family. In that census it is not clear whether *família* is synonymous with *fogo*. "Annual Census Tables," Governor of the Rio Negro, João Pereira Caldas, to Governor of Pará, Martinho de Melo e Castro, June 22, 1785, Barcelos, AHU Rio Negro, cx. 8, doc. 7509.

was not the household itself but the cluster of families in one site (*sítio* or farmstead).

The militia censuses for the Lower Amazon (such as the one in 1799) listed soldiers by area of residence.[13] Each town had a patrol and was supported by divisions in the nearby countryside, typically five to ten men in each area. Similar surnames were not always an indicator of shared family identity, yet in the censuses of the part-time militia, men in one geographical area often shared the same name. Although it is not stated how many houses there were in each cluster, it is likely that there was more than one. The richer the family, the larger the house. From the river, these dwellings appeared to be spaced at irregular intervals. In one place, one might see a small hamlet consisting of many small houses built from cheap materials and in another there would be an imposing house on stilts with a large veranda with clay tiles and wooden planks. In between there were cacao stands; cattle grazing; fields of manioc, tobacco, and maize; and forest.

In other words, we can distinguish between two ideal types of domestic organization: the "peasant" and the "plantation." However, the uneven nature of economic development in colonial Amazonia meant that the differences between classes were less than elsewhere and not consistent. The peasant was by far the predominant type. The plantation family with a handful slaves or so was not much better off or different from a peasant family with none.[14] Both lived with few luxuries and there was little productive advantage gained by owning only a small number of slaves. This relative class flatness does not mean there was no heterogeneity between families; rather, it has much to do with the control of labor. The plantation family depended on slave labor; the peasant family, on its own kin and residential networks. The former was precariously dependent on unreliable labor, more costly than the mutually cooperative forms in which the latter engaged. In an economy so limited by access to labor, how it was called upon was a central factor in relative wealth and status. A patron could mobilize nonslave workers with either forced public service (that is abusing it for private ends) or persuasion. In turn the peasant landholding required constant attention if it were to maintain subsistence levels and its members avoid selling their labor. The development of these ideal types was held in check by this squeeze on both slave and nonslave workers (slaves were allowed one day a week to attend to their own plots of land).

13 "Relação dos Novos Alistados," Captain Joaquim Francisco Printes to Governador Francisco de Souza Coutinho, Santarém, April 24, 1799, APEP cod. 561, doc. 34.
14 Data published by Itala Bezerra da Silveira shows that 105 property owners in the rural districts near to Belém in 1823 held an average of six Africans, *Cabanagem: Uma Luta Perdida* ..., 131. She uses this information to claim that the land situation in Pará was very different from that of the rest of Brazil.

The 1778 census gives the economic position of each family and its number of slaves. The largest family by far in the Lower Amazon was headed by Manuel Corrêa Picanço, a widower with three married children (working in the local army and living at home) and thirty-nine slaves. While he had a cacao plantation, he was only *remediado*: that is, able to provide just enough to survive and slightly above poor on the scale used. This same economic value was accorded families with no slaves and similar numbers of children. On the other hand, most slave-owning families (a third of the non-Indian population) possessed a slave or two and were listed as poor. Nobody was described as rich.[15] Still, when the nineteenth century dawned, cacao became ever more dominant, and slaves were introduced in greater numbers, these distinctions became stronger.

In political terms, there were large differences, particularly when it came to influence in the capital, Belém. The plantation families considered it their right to control local politics and resented the clamoring of others for equality. In turn, élites imagined their position would be strengthened and general economic development occur as a result of their conduct. Instead, arrogance and exclusion led to increased rivalry and antagonism between high-status families and marginalized poorer peasants and laborers from the political process, and opened the way for violent confrontation.

The plantation and peasant paradigm is complicated by an observation of a bishop of Pará on his pastoral visits in the early 1760s. Typically, an itinerant bishop traveled in a canoe powered by slaves or Indians and stopped off at significant locations. At one such break, the bishop spent the night at a house near the town of Gurupá on the Amazon River. There he found a man who was married but not living with his wife, who occupied another house nearby – and who must have been reasonably wealthy and important to have attracted the bishop. Apparently, the pair found this a convenient seasonal arrangement given their different kinds of work: fishing and gardening, respectively. They saw each other regularly and exchanged food.[16] Similar conjugal residence patterns were mentioned in the Inquisition and are noted by Barbara Sommer in her study of sexuality and witchcraft in Pará, so this was not a unique occurrence.[17] Although we do not know what kind of labor each spouse engaged to help (slave or family), the seasonally based two-house family would appear to be an

15 See Santarém, 151–153, in the "Annual Census Tables," Governor of the Rio Negro, João Pereira Caldas, to Governor of Pará, Martinho de Melo e Castro, June 22, 1785, Barcelos, AHU Pará Avulsos, Rio Negro, cx. 8, doc. 7509.

16 Camillo Castello-Branco, *Memórias de Fr. João de São José Queiroz (Bispo do Pará)*. Porto, Typographia de Livraria Nacional, 1868, 206.

17 Barbara Sommer, "Cupid on the Amazon: Sexual Witchcraft and Society in Late Colonial Pará, Brazil." *Colonial Latin American Historical Review*, 12, 4, 2003, 433.

adaptation that fitted well with gendered work regimes and the need to maximize time spent in complementary economic activities. This example also suggests that women had a large degree of independence.

Female-headed households were relatively numerous, especially in urban locations. In the central area of Belém in 1778 there were 824 households, 183 of them (twenty-two percent) headed by women. Of the total, 105 were listed as occupied by specifically white women who were either married, widowed, or single.[18] This high number could be a reflection of the dual residence strategy outlined above; or else the husband was stationed at a military post in the interior or worked as an itinerant trader regatão. Alternatively, some of these women could have been single or widowed, relatively well-off on their own, able to command the labor of slaves and to call on a network of men for favors. The significant numbers of households controlled by women is in keeping with observations made elsewhere for late colonial Brazil.[19] The high proportion of white women as household heads is not replicated in the interior, where manual labor was at a premium. In such rural locations as the Lower Amazon, female-headed households were less common, accounting for about five percent of the total in 1778 and occurring only where the woman was a widow.[20] From the urban center a women could nevertheless take hold of the reins of authority, raise and educate children, and manage estates and properties. All in all, women made a significant contribution to Pará's society and economy (see page 132).[21]

Although Portuguese men did migrate individually, plenty came with partners and families and subsequently set up households together.[22] The well-known examples in Pará were of families transplanted from the Azores in 1754 and from Mazagão, a Portuguese military outpost in the north of Africa, during the 1770s.[23] In both cases, hundreds of families were shipped

18 "Annual Census Tables," Governor of the Rio Negro, João Pereira Caldas, to Governor of Pará, Martinho de Melo e Castro, June 22, 1785, Barcelos, AHU Rio Negro, cx. 8, doc. 7509.

19 Elizabeth Kuznesof, "Sexual Politics, Race and Bastard Bearing in Nineteenth Century Brazil: A Question of Culture or Power?" *Journal of Family History*, 16, 3, 2005, 241–260.

20 "Annual Census Tables," Governor of the Rio Negro, João Pereira Caldas, to Governor of Pará, Martinho de Melo e Castro, 22nd June, 1785, Barcelos, AHU Rio Negro, cx. 8, doc. 7509.

21 Alfred J. R. Russell-Wood, "Women and Society in Colonial Brazil," *Journal of Latin American Studies*, 9, 1, 1977, 33.

22 Most colonists from Portugal were "poor and lowly if able-bodied and enterprising young bachelors," Charles Boxer, *The Golden Age of Brazil, 1695–1750: Growing Pains of a Colonial Society*, Berkeley: University of California Press, 1962, 164.

23 The majority of the men were soldiers who were stationed to defend the region from Moorish attacks. See especially Laurent Vidal, *Mazagão, La Ville Qui Traversa l'Atlantique: Du Maroc a l'Amazonie, (1769–1783)*, Paris, Aubier, 2005; and also Ângela Maria Vieira Domingues, "Fámilias Portugueses na Colonização do Norte Brasileiro," in Maria Beatriz Nizza da Silva (ed.), *Sexualidade, Familia e Religião na Colonização do Brasil*, Lisboa: Livros Horizonte, 2001, 215–221; Nizza da Silva, *História da*

across the Atlantic. The Mazagão lot was relocated together in a new town in order to develop autonomously. Another phenomenon was where men, exiled as punishment for crimes committed in Portugal, were joined by their spouses and children in Brazil.[24] These examples demonstrate the force of family ties not just for the state but also for those who were coming to the Amazon.

Even when families were not together, they would actively maintain their ties by travel and communication. Nizza da Silva argues that "dispersal" was not just a characteristic of families in colonial Brazil but a deliberately developed strategy to maximize access to labor and property.[25] Families sometimes had to spread themselves out over long distances as they kept open their connections to allow movement between kinspeople and facilitate new opportunities. Some of these extensions may have been necessary due to compulsory labor service or military postings. Or couples had to adjust to seasonally dynamic residential changes. In these features, there was a merging of obligation and strategy.

By the beginning of the nineteenth century there were many large, powerful, well-established families in Pará. These were Portuguese and Brazilian families and would have counted whites, mestiços, and perhaps Indians and Africans among their numbers. Many had widespread networks over the whole region. Some families' wealth and status derived from their plantations (cacao or sugar) and the holding of political office. Other families specialized in military commissions or commerce. Such specialization was also related to family histories.

One of the main contentions of the rebel peasants during the years of violent upheaval in the Amazon from 1820 to 1840 was that judges, slave owners, landowners, and municipal officials were tyrants and imposed the law arbitrarily. The élite ruled for themselves and not for all the people. They made sure their family members got important salaried positions and applied the law according to personal preference. Family influence was almost everything. Whatever the concerns of liberalism, such as sovereignty, citizenship, inclusion, and legitimacy of rule, people's experience of the state was in terms of their local encounter with the élite. Debates about legitimacy and authority were channeled into these antagonisms and perceptions of despotism and injustice.

Família, 166; Sommer, "Cupid on the Amazon," 442. Vidal's book offers a fascinating account of this extraordinary story and the culture of colonization, the objects considered essential, the process of building a new town out of the forest with Indian labor, and the social impact of the transplanting people to an unfamiliar environment.

24 See, for example, "Requisition of José Antônio de Souza to be accompanied by his wife during his exile in Pará to Prince Regent," AHU Pará Avulsos, cx. 119, doc. 9132, written after 1800 [probably 1801].

25 Nizza da Silva, *História da Família*, 145.

Some Family Histories

Some examples will demonstrate the influence of the family over an extended area. Antônio José Malcher was an administrator in an Indian village in the Lower Amazon in the late eighteenth century. He was white and Brazilian-born (probably in Pará) but, unlike some administrators, he did not come from a military background. His wife was from a well-to-do family from Belém, but they lived and had land near Monte Alegre. Malcher's sister Anna Micaela was married to João da Gama Lobo (de Anveres), another civil official who had official positions in the Lower Amazon.[26] Lobo's older brother was Manuel, the aforementioned governor of the Rio Negro region at the end of the eighteenth century.[27] Brothers Manuel and João were soldiers and had been among the families to come to Pará from Mazagão in Africa in order to populate the region in 1770s.[28] João Lobo was given a land grant near Santarém in 1796. He sent his eldest son to Coimbra University, who graduated in 1807 and became a priest elsewhere.[29] His other children remained in the Lower Amazon and entered military, judicial, and municipal positions in the region, marrying locally. Both families had cacao plantations, slaves, and probably some livestock. They were examples of the plantation-type family, though as the families developed over the early nineteenth century they may have become more peasantlike, as resources were shared out.

The lives of Malcher's children were more clearly forged by the political situation. One daughter married Lobo's son Nicolau, who defended Monte Alegre against Indians in the unrest surrounding independence (see Chapter 6) but was killed by cabano rebels in 1836. Yet it was a son, Felix Clemente Malcher, born in Monte Alegre in 1772, who occupied a significant place in the history of the Amazon. He married a rich land-owner's daughter from the Acará River, near Belém, and was elected to the first provincial junta government of Pará following independence in August 1823.[30] His liberal views against absolutism were too threatening

---

26 For example, Malcher was a director in Vila Franca before he was caught trying to sell off Indian produce as his own. Governor Coutinho sacked him, lieutenant Pedro Miguel Ayres Perreira to Governor, Santarém, August 3, 1790, APEP cod. 470, doc. 3.

27 See Fernandes de Souza, "Notícias Geográphicas," 472–474; Arthur Reis, *História do Amazonas*, 145–148.

28 Carlos Rocque, *Grande Enciclopédia da Amazônia*, Belém: Amazônia Editora, 1968, 604.

29 Francisco Morais, "Estudantes Brasileiros na Universidade de Coimbra (1772–1872)," *ABNRJ*, LXII, 1940, 137–335, entry 605.

30 Baena, *Ensaio Corográfico*, 421. This collective form of government was in line with the Portuguese constitution of 1821 and was composed of men elected by popular vote. It was first elected in Pará on January 1, 1821 and lasted until October 1823.

to the Portuguese, so he was imprisoned a number of times; he was once strapped against a mouth of a cannon. In late 1834, he led a conspiracy to overthrow the government, but was found out and arrested with his brother Aniceto.[31] When the rebels entered Belém on January 7, 1835, he was released from prison in one of their first acts and proclaimed the legitimate president of Pará. However, within a few weeks the rebels considered him too reactionary and he was killed. Felix's son emerged unscathed from the Cabanagem and served frequently on Belém's town council in the later imperial period. While the Lobos and the Malchers were not the most powerful families in the Amazon, they were able to command significant influence through marriage, friendship, and political office.

The coupling of dispersal and connection is seen in the example of a family of military distinction. One of the more colorful literary characters to emerge from Portuguese Amazonia is Henrique João Wilckens, the author of a schoolboyish poem about the declaration of peace by the Mura in the 1785. The poem's main character is an angel sent to persuade the Mura out of their state of savagery.[32] Wilckens' origins are obscure, but he may have been of German and Portuguese parentage. He came to the Amazon in the 1750s, served on the boundary commission in the Upper Amazon, and came to occupy an important military position while living in Barcellos, a relatively remote town on the Negro River. Working in the Upper Amazon, Wilckens met and married an Indian woman.[33] One of his daughters married a military officer from Belém and also settled in Barcellos, where they had at least one son, João Henrique de Mattos, born in 1784. This son worked as a military officer and was elected to the same provincial junta as Felix Malcher in 1823. He was on the liberal side (though no friend of Malcher), yet fought against the rebels in the Lower Amazon in the 1830s.

---

31 "Correio Official Paraense No. 33 de 1834," *Fundo Cabanagem, Revolta de Vinagre*, BNRJ II-32, 4, 1, 003.

32 For discussions of the Muhraida, see David Sweet, "Native Resistance in Eighteenth-Century Amazonia: The 'Abominable Muras' in War and Peace'," *Radical History Review*, 1992, 53, 49–80; Carlos de Araújo Moreira Neto, "Henrique João Wilkens e os Índios Mura," *ABNRJ*, 109, 1989 , 227–301; Marta Amoroso and Nadia Farage (eds.), *Relatos da Fronteira Amazônica no Século XVIII. Documentos de Henrique João Wilckens e Alexandre Rodrigues Ferreira*, São Paulo: NHII/USP, FAPESP, 1994. Perhaps the most incisive literary and national political discussion is David Treece, *Exiles, Allies, Rebels: Brazil's Indianist Movement, Indigenist Politics, and the Imperial Nation-State*, Westport: Greenwood Press, 2000, 66–74. Also excellent is Marta Amoroso, "The Portrayal of Indians in the Colonial Epic," in Bernard MacQuirk and Solange Ribeiro de Oliveira (eds.), *Brazil and the Discovery of America: Narrative, History, Fiction, 1492–1992*, Lewiston: Edward Mellon Press, 1996, 113–124, who argues that Wilckens' poem permits a reevaluation of the archival documentation on the Mura's peace accord.

33 I am grateful to Barbara Sommer (personal communication) for providing some details of Wilckens' life.

His immediate family lived in Manaus, but he continued to travel and write reports until his death in 1857. Although his family did not have established plantations (they depended on his salary as a high-ranking commissioned officer), his networks were widespread.[34]

Although these examples involve relatively well-off families, there is no reason to think that poorer ones would not have had similar long-distance connections. In the absence of other connective institutions, the family was at the center of social life. In this way, it surpassed the dividing lines of class and ethnicity and contributed positively to reconstituting people's identities. However, the price of the supreme significance of kinship to society was its interference in the political realm: "[f]amily connections overrode considerations of official duty."[35]

This feature of colonial life explains the constant accusations of injustice and authoritarianism, which express not just the sense of outrage as one of losing out. It would be reasonable to assume that people perceived the political influence of the family and despotism and injustice when they did not get their way, and not when they benefited themselves. For example, local legal processes were enmeshed in social and family relations in a way that is difficult for the contemporary reader to appreciate. There is a particular good insight into a land dispute in the novel by Inglês de Souza, *O Cacaulista*, first published in 1876 but set in the Lower Amazon of the early 1850s. Two wealthy men, claiming the same parcel of land, decided to resolve the matter by requesting that a town judge adjudicate on the basis of witness statements. Both men knew they had to offer huge sums of money to get respectable witnesses connected to each family to testify, regardless of the respective merits of the claim. Money changed hands and the reader is led to believe this was entirely commonplace. The young hero of the book loses the case because his key witness betrays him, as he is offered more money by his adversary. Behind the land dispute was a long-standing rivalry between the families, centering on ethnicity and class. The hero perceived his adversary to be an impostor whose status came from his military commission, not from his possession of property or hard work. The captain, identified as a mulatto, in turn exploited his links to important liberal politicians in Belém in order to win his case. Given Souza's realism the story provides a reliable and important portrait of the workings of justice and daily life.[36]

34 See Manoel Cardoso Barata, *Formação Histórica do Pará*, Belém: Universidade Federal do Pará, 1973, 114–5; John Hemming, *Amazon Frontier: The Defeat of the Brazilian Indians*, London: Macmillan, 1987, 493. Neither gives the sources for their information.

35 Sommer, "Negotiated Settlements," 241.

36 Inglês de Souza, *O Cacaulista: Cenas da Vida de Amazonas*, Belém: Universidade Federal do Pará, 2003 [1876].

The Continuity of Families

As noted earlier, there was a fluid form of social organization, yet the most important mission villages and population centers in the early eighteenth century continued to be so into the early nineteenth century. Sommer explains this continuity with reference to the Indian nobles whose strong connections and networks "maintained stability."[37] Throughout the eighteenth century, the headmen provided the core around which colonial society developed and provided new recruits from the "forests." The questions are then (1) whether this locally significant power persisted into the nineteenth century, and (2) whether Indian leadership fed into the positions on councils, or in the judiciary, or into the Cabanagem.[38] In fact, it was not just Indians who endured. Many others succeeded in surviving from one period to another.

In the key areas outside Belém and in the larger towns (Santarém, Gurupá, Macapá, Cametá, and Bragança), some Indians participated in town councils (see the story on pages 47–48) and held military and legal positions. Just as pertinent is how local élites used these public offices to pursue and strengthen their interests, which were just like those of the village Indians. If this is the case, as I believe from the available evidence presented below, did the noble Indians, who lost some of the privileges and power they gained in the second part of the eighteenth century, become disgruntled and emboldened by anticolonial and revolutionary movements taking place in the Atlantic world and organize their own uprising?

As mentioned in Chapter 2, no two towns were alike at this point in the colonial period and families were spread across places. The networks that resulted gave a unity to the region or, more accurately, various unities. There were principally two ways in which these networks were achieved and maintained: (1) the descendants of one couple remain close to their family origins, or (2) siblings migrate together and settle in neighboring locations, then build up their own families. Such extended family connections in this period appear reasonably common as an idiom to organize labor and distribute limited resources.[39]

Map 3.1 denotes the land grants (known as *sesmarias*) ceded to inhabitants and settlers of the Lower Amazon between 1740 and 1821. In total, it was

---

37 Sommer, "Negotiated Settlements," 317.

38 Sommer offers limited evidence of the "enduring nobility" and suggests that in some cases there was some overlap with local officials in the Directorate and the post-Directorate period: "Negotiated Settlements," 230–235.

39 See, for example, Deborah Lima-Ayres, "The Social Category Caboclo: History, Social Organization, Identity and Outsider's Social Classification of the Rural Population of an Amazonian Region (The Middle Solimões)," Ph.D. dissertation, University of Cambridge, 1992; Mark Harris, *Life on the Amazon: The Anthropology of a Brazilian Peasant Village*, Oxford: Oxford University Press, 2000.

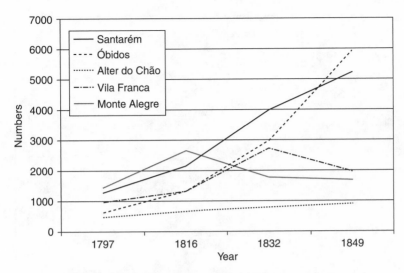

Figure 3.1 Comparison of the free population of selected towns in the Lower Amazon

possible to identify six land grants to between forty and fifty individuals (with some persons receiving more than one; see Table 3.1). This group represented the local élite: some had slaves, large plots, diverse economic activities, including cacao plantations, and served on the local council. Some were white, though Indians were also granted land in Pará. Many other people were mentioned in letters and petitions as living in the region, being slaveholders, and serving on councils but did not have sesmarias. This could have been because they were too poor to demarcate the land and employ a lawyer to draw up the request (see Chapter 4 for land acquisition, for example pages 137–138).

Some of the settlement patterns mentioned above can be viewed in the list of people with land grants. The Souza e Silva siblings (João Caetano and Lourenço Xavier) had plots in Santarém granted in 1746 and 1747 and half a century later were given more land in Faro in 1794 and Vila Franca in 1805.[40] João Caetano served as a soldier in Santarém in the fort in the 1740s and was made a tenant sometime afterwards. He had four children by two Indian women and married neither but sought to recognize his offspring as his legal heirs so they could acquire his property on his death.[41] In addition,

40 Biblioteca e Archivo Público do Pará. "Catálogo Nominal dos Posseiros de Sesmarias," ABAPP, 3. 1904, 5–149.

41 "Requisition of Tenente João Caetano de Souza e Silva to Prince Regent" (with "Auto de justificação"), Santarém, before October 14, 1786, AHU Pará Avulsos, cx. 96, doc. 7597; and "Requisition of tenente João Caetano de Souza e Silva to Prince Regent," before October 14, 1796, AHU Pará Avulsos, cx. 108, doc. 8500.

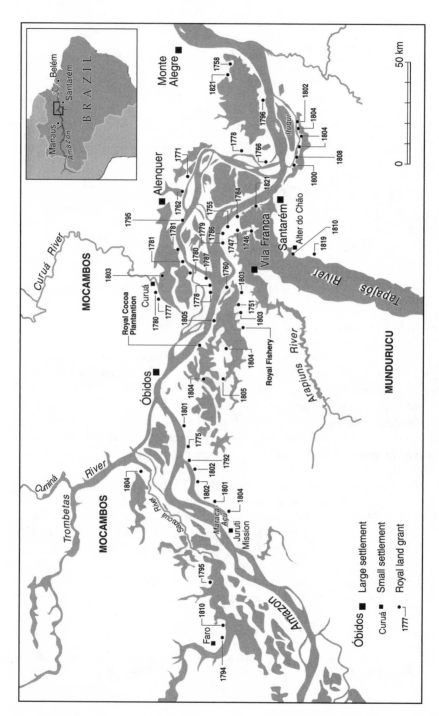

Map 3.1 Land grants in the Lower Amazon, 1740 and 1821

João and Ignácio de Souza e Silva were present in Santarém in the second half of the eighteenth century, serving on councils there in the 1750s and 1760s.[42] The actual relations between these people is not clear but the exact coincidence of the family names is likely to indicate kinship ties. Another example of continuity from the mission period (that is, pre-1757) to the Directorate is the Miguel Ayres family. André, a captain in Santarém in 1749, must have been related to Antônio, who was given a land grant in 1758 in Monte Alegre. At the end of the Directorate, Pedro Miguel Ayres Perreira was a captain in Santarém but what happened to the Monte Alegre connection is obscure.[43]

The crossover of some of the élite from the Directorate to the end of the colony and the Independence period is especially strong. Many of the names of those who gained land grants in the second half of the eighteenth century or who were directors or soldiers appear on council elections lists and boards. Some regularly recurring names include Picanço, Marinho, Faria, Printes, Rabello, Pimentel, Baptista, Lobo, Bentes, Gama, Malcher, and Tavares.[44] An example will elaborate the extent of residential stability from one period to another. The two Picanço brothers, one of whom has already been mentioned, had land in Vila Franca (Manoel Corrêa, 1760) and Alenquer (Domingos Corrêa, 1777). Manoel was elected to Santarém's council in the 1760s. Domingos also planted cacao: in 1766 he sent 120 arrobas (1,770 kg) of the dried seeds to Belém, which was a large amount, indicating he had about 5,000 trees (see pages 133–140 for a discussion of economic aspects of cacao orchards).[45] The son of Domingos, who had the same name, was appointed a judge in Alenquer and then moved to Santarém where he sat on councils up to the 1840s though, despite being an elected representative, he was not a signatory to the session that gave support to Angelim's presidency in March 1836. He may have been the brother, however, of Antônio Corrêa Picanço, one of the rebel leaders at the fort of Ecuipiranga at the time. Antônio was listed as a soldier in the Alenquer section of the National Guards in 1832, an army made of civilians who could be called upon to maintain order (see page 119).[46]

42 João de Palma Muniz, "Limites Municipais do Estado do Pará," ABAPP, vol. 9, 1916, 666. All the Souza e Silva individuals are listed as living in Santarém in the "Annual Census Tables," Governor of the Rio Negro, João Pereira Caldas, to Governor of Pará, Martinho de Melo e Castro, June 22, 1785, Barcelos: AHU Rio Negro, cx. 8, doc. 7509.

43 Lieutenant Pedro Miguel Ayres Perreira to Governor, Santarém, August 3, 1790, APEP cod. 470, doc. 3.

44 Biblioteca e Archivo Público do Pará, "Catálogo Nominal dos Posseiros de Sesmarias," ABAPP vol. 3. 1904; Carlos Rocque, *Grande Enciclopédia da Amazônia*, Belém: Amazônia Editora, 1968; Barata, *Formação Histórica do Pará*, 107; Morais, "Estudantes Brasileiros."

45 Director Henrique [José] de Vasconcelos to Governor, Santarém, August 20, 1766, APEP cod. 73, doc. 49.

46 "Relação Nominal dos Guardas Nacionais do Municipio desta Vila de Alenquer," Judge Nicolão Nunes to President of Province of Pará, November 30, 1832, APEP cod. 915, unnumbered doc., before 89.

Table 3.1 *Land grant holders* (sesmeiros) *in the Lower Amazon, 1740–1821*

Name	Year	Region
João Caetano de Souza	1746	Igarapé Uaripira, Tapajós River
Lourenço Xavier de Souza	1747	Igarapé Uarapixuna, Tapajós River
Manoel João Baptista	1751	Igarapé Pucá, Arapiuns River
Joaquim de Costa	1755	Amazon River [Santarém]
Antônio Miguel Ayres Pereira	1758	[Monte Alegre]
Manoel Corrêa Picanço	1760	Ilha no Igarapé Arapary, R. Amazonas
Victorino Antônio Pimentel	1762	Santarém
Domingos Rebello	1766	Amazon River [Santarém]
[Constantino] Manoel Marinho	1771	Mouth of Surubiu River [Alenquer]
Domingos Corrêa Picanço	1777	Curuamanema Lake [Alenquer]
José Goncalves Marques	1778	Igarapé Itamaraca [Santarém]
José Goncalves Marques	1778	Tapará Farm [Santarém]
José Pereira Ribeiro	1778	Igarapé Itamaraca [Santarém]
Manoel Antônio de Oliveira Pantoja	1779	Amazon River [Santarém]
Vincente Marinho de Vasconcellos	1780	Igarapé Boca da Curua, [Alenquer]
Manuel Rodrigues Pinto	1780	Santarém
Joaquim Francisco Printes	1781	Amazon River [Alenquer]
José Ricardo Printes	1781	Amazon River [Alenquer]
Manoel Gomes Monteiro	1784	Amazon River [Santarém]
Mauricio José de Souza	1786	Igarapé Itanduba [Óbidos]
Manoel Baptista	1787	Igarapé Cuticanga [Óbidos]
Constantino Manoel Marinho	1792	Igarapé Parana-mirim [Óbidos]
João Caotano de Souza e Silva	1794	Faro
Ana Xavier Freire da Fonseca	1795	Amazon River [Monte Alegre]
Constantino Manoel Marinho	1795	Faro
João de Gama Lobo	1796	Cueiras coast, [Óbidos], Amazon River
José Cavalcante de Albuquerque	1801	Amazon River [Óbidos]
Policarpio Antoino da Silva	1801	Juruti lake
Francisco José de Faria	1802	Óbidos
Francisco José de Faria	1802	Maraca-assu River [Óbidos]
Thomaz Luiz Coelho	1802	Ituqui island [Santarém]
Luiz Angello Baptista	1803	Vila Franca
Luiz de Miranda	1803	Santarém
Mauricio José Valadão	1803	Surubiu River [Alenquer]
João Baptista da Silva	1804	Lago Grande [Vila Franca]
João Pedro de Andrade	1804	Igarapé Curumumcury [Óbidos]
José Ricardo Picanço	1804	Sapucua River [Óbidos]
José Joaquim Pereira do Lago	1804	Ituqui [Santarém]
Lourenço Goncalves Chaves	1804	Ituqui [Santarém]
Miguel Antônio Pinto Guimaraes	1804	Ituqui [Santarém]
José Cavalcante de Albuquerque	1805	Igarapé do Salé, Lago Grande, [Vila Franca]
Lourenço Xavier de Souza e Silva	1805	Lago Grande, [Vila Franca]
João Gomes Pereira	1808	Ituqui [Santarém]
Jacinto Caetano Faria	1810	Faro

Table 3.1 (cont.)

Name	Year	Region
José Joaquim Pereira do Lago	1810	Amupy Lake [Santarém]
João Duarte Lobo	1819	Tapajos River
Anna Micaela Malcher	1821	Aijo [Monte Alegre]
Francisco José Pereira	1821	Amazon River [Santarém]

Source: ABAPP vol. 3. Catálogo Nominal dos Posseiros de Sesmarias, 1904.

A branch of the same Picanço family was also prominent in the north bank towns of Alenquer, Óbidos, and Faro, where José Ricardo, Raimundo Ricardo, and Antônio Ricardo worked as judges and councilors, shifting from one town to another once they completed a term of office. None of these people was listed as losing their lives in the Cabanagem, so they were not targeted by one side or the other. They probably fought on the imperial side (those loyal to Rio and against the rebels), since they would have been arrested if they had not; certainly when the leader of the repression came he was welcomed by Raimundo.[47]

Other local leaders at the rebel fort known as Ecuipiranga (see Chapter 7) also had family listed in the census of militia soldiers dating from 1799, such as Apolinário, Vianna, Bras, and Baptista, though the exact natures of the relationships are not known. There are some other intriguing possible linkages between the rebels from Santarém and an earlier colonial period. One of the "First Commanders of the Trenches" at Ecuipiranga was a João Pais Pedroso, whose name cannot have been common; there was one other Pedroso man, Thomas Caetano Pedroso Pereira, in Alenquer in the 1830s. A João Pais Pedroso arrived in Santarém from São Paulo sometime before 1762 (when he was a councilor there) and sought to legitimize children he had outside marriage. He may have brought (or followed) his sister Rita Pedroso, who married a military commander in Santarém, Henrique José de Vasconcellos, in the late eighteenth century (when the priest was Leandro Pedroso).[48] This connection would make the *cabano* from Ecuipiranga a grandson or great-grandson of the migrant from the south of Brazil.

47 President of council Raimundo Ricardo Picanço to General Andréa, December 23, 1836, Pauxis [Óbidos], APEP cod. 1010, doc. 202.
48 João de Palma Muniz, "Limites Municipais do Estado do Pará," ABAPP, vol. 9, 1916, 666; *Livro de Termos de Casamentos da Freguesia de Santarém 1764–1798* (APSEP); "Requisition of João Pais Pedroso to the Queen," before February 25, 1785, AHU Pará Avulsos, cx. 93, doc. 7481. In the census of 1799, a João Pais Pedroso (a son or grandson?) was registered as a military official in Alenquer. The same name appears in the list of the National Guards in 1832. "Relação Nominal dos Guardas Nacionais do Municipio desta Vila de Alenquer," Judge Nicolão Nunes to President of Province of Pará, November 30, 1832, APEP cod. 915, unnumbered doc., before 89.

These examples reveal that the differences between enemies in the rebellion were far from distinct and predictable. Many rebel leaders from the Lower Amazon were fully integrated within the familial, legal, and military organization of Paraense society.[49] They were not rabble or a mass of individuals bent on revenge with no political consciousness. As will be also seen, there was a good deal of side swapping as the rebellion progressed, not to mention violent factions developing within a general common position.[50]

While there was continuity for non-Indian families, did the Indian nobility in the Lower Amazon continue to maintain stability? The Indian headman in Santarém in 1778 was Santiago de Fonseca and Matheus de Fonseca was part of the council during the 1760s.[51] By the end of the Directorate, the headman was still a Fonseca, named Antônio. The military census of 1799 listed many Fonsecas for the districts of Santarém, Alter do Chão, and Vila Franca, but a generation later their family name occurred only in Alter do Chão and in no official capacity. Unless they had changed their names, it would seem they had stopped playing a significant role in local political life.

A similar story surrounds the name Silva e Mello. At the end of the eighteenth century in Óbidos, Vila Franca, and Alenquer, the headmen were Bras Antônio de Silva, Pedro de Mello, and Marcos de Silva e Mello, respectively. Marcos had been in place since at least 1784, and shared the

49 Other signatories from Ecuipiranga were also from the National Guards: Antônio Corrêa Vianna in Alter do Chão ("Lista dos Efetivos da Guarda Nacional," Alter do Chão, July 6, 1832, APEP cod. 915 doc. 60), Antônio Manuel Brancher, and Miguel Apolinário both in Santarém ("Lista Geral dos Jurados que forão apurados no Termo daquelles Cabeças da Vila de Tapajós," Antônio Marcolino Marinho Gamboa, September 3, 1833, Tapajós [Santarém], APEP cod. 947 [Number 85]).

50 Other examples could be cited as evidence of the continuity from one stage to another. Of importance to the rest of this book is the following. The origin of the four Sanches de Brito brothers is not known; they were Brazilian-born and appear in the Lower Amazon at the end of the eighteenth century. Raimundo, possibly the eldest, was a director in Alter do Chão on the Tapajós River in 1792. Following the end of the Directorate he must have trained as a priest, perhaps in the northeast of Brazil, and returned to the Lower Amazon in 1816 to take up the vacant position in Óbidos. He owned slaves and was "liberal" in his political positioning. During the Cabanagem, he was instrumental in negotiating with the surrender of rebels in some towns and he also maintained Óbidos' opposition to joining the side of Angelim, the third and most important rebel president in Belém. When the English naturalist Henry Bates met him in 1851, Raimundo was described as very old with white hair and good morals. His brother Padre Antônio Manoel was a missionary (and apparently without trade interests, see the following discussion) in Juruti with Mundurucu and Maués Indians in the second decade of nineteenth century and was closely linked to João Gonçalves Batista Campos, the fiery priest from Belém. Vicente and Bento lived in Monte Alegre and were also listed as slave owners and farmers.

51 Director João da Gama Lobo to Governor, February 6, 1778, Santarém, APEP cod. 277, doc. 74, also written as Fonceca and Thiago in some codices; Muniz, "Limites Municipaes," ABAPP, vol. 9, 1916, 666–667; "Relação dos Novos Alistados," Captain Joaquim Francisco Printes to Governor Francisco de Souza Coutinho, April 24, 1799, Santarém, APEP cod. 561, doc. 34.

same name as a 1764 headman from Óbidos, Antônio de Silva e Mello.[52] It is probable that these men belonged to the same extended family given their shared names and position in the colonial hierarchy; the different writing of the names could reflect different scripts of the council scriveners who wrote out the census. If this were the case, it would indicate that one large Indian noble family occupied a powerful position across a wide area. They all but disappeared in the nineteenth century, though a Mello sat as a councilor in Santarém in 1829–1832, a Silva e Mello was military official in Alenquer in 1832, and another Mello (Bernardo de Mello Genipapo) was the last rebel leader of Ecuipiranga in July 1837.[53]

Even though their names were absent from the documentary record, it cannot be assumed this means the Indian nobility stopped being an active presence in the region. Moreover, other Indian officials and headmen from the Tapajós region named in the military census gained places in councils at the time, such as Alfonso de Souza in Vila Franca (who would defend Indians against the abuse of labor in the royal cacao plantation and fishery – see pages 160–164) and José Florindo in Pinhel (who would help relocate many Mundurucu). Nevertheless, in the villages with more whites, the Indians did lose out and were displaced from locally important offices. One could cynically say that one of the aims of Coutinho's large-scale reforms of 1799 (as described in the next chapter) was to dislodge the headmen from their locally strong role, making it easier for mestiços and whites to take over.

Why is all of this important? First, the purpose here is to demonstrate the strength of some families in the Lower Amazon across periods. In other words, a "society" was operating and reproducing effectively, even if it was contested by different interests. Despite the fluidity and mobility of social relations, there existed a sense of belonging to a place, which was expressed in continuous residence. Second, each town from the region reacted differently to independence and to the requests to join Angelim's rebel government. These diverse reactions can be understood only by attending to the make-up of a place and how residents were linked to others.

Marriage, Concubinage, and Legitimacy

Marriage was a central thrust of colonial policy in the Amazon, especially in the late eighteenth and early nineteenth centuries.[54] The goal was to

---

52 "Relação dos Novos Alistados," Captain Joaquim Francisco Printes to Governor Francisco de Souza Coutinho, April 24, 1799, Santarém, APEP cod. 561, doc. 34; Sommer, "Negotiated Settlements," 200–201.

53 Muniz, "Limites Municipaes," ABAPP, vol. 9, 1916, 668; "Relação Nominal dos Guardas Nacionais do Municipio desta Vila de Alenquer," Judge Nicolão Nunes to President of Province of Pará, November 30, 1832, Alenquer, APEP cod. 915, unnumbered doc., before 89.

54 See Sommer, "Negotiated Settlements," Chapter 2.

establish Portuguese-style patriarchal peasant families by encouraging Portuguese colonists to marry Indian women, to live as a family with a hearth (*fogo*) on their own in a separate house, and produce goods for the export market. This aim was both pragmatic – few white women – and idealistic, to establish the dominance of Portuguese values (in the form of the man) over Indian ones. A package of fiscal, material, and legal incentives were offered to encourage the Portuguese into such stable unions. Sometimes the efforts took concrete form. Daughters of Indian headmen were advised by village administrators to marry Portuguese soldiers and colonists. This convergence was clearly significant to cementing alliances and promoting local interests. Indeed, Sommer stresses the vitality of the noble Indian family, with headmen strategizing to incorporate outsiders to achieve their political ends.[55]

In the main, however, these policy measures did not sufficiently consider the difference between sex and marriage, nor the fact that migrants and exiles may already be married and arrived with their own norms and values. If marriage for Mendonça Furtado was one of the chief ways to lead a quiet conquest of the Amazon, then the reality was a form of marriage different to his ideal. Yet we do not know the relative percentages of the different kinds of unions entered into. Some may have fitted the white man/Indian woman ideal and may have benefited from the incentives, but as I have stressed, "the white man" or "the Indian woman" was only a stereotype, for each person was by varying degrees adapted to life in the colony. The fact they were marked out differently in colonial law was not reflected in real life. In Monte Alegre, a predominantly Indian town with few whites in the eighteenth century, a local official informed the Pará government that there had been no white/Indian marriages in the last four years.[56] This does not necessarily mean that "whites" and "Indians" were not setting up households.

Most of the cases heard in front of the visitation of the Lisbon Inquisition to Pará concerned neither sexual practices nor lack of family morals but witchcraft, magic, and blasphemy – forty out of the forty-six trials.[57] Of the remaining six cases, five were accusations of bigamy, where a Portuguese colonist was said to have married twice, in Portugal and Belém; the last one was brought by a slave who accused her master of excessive punishment. Outside the visitation but still part of the Inquisition, a handful of Indian men and women from the Upper Amazon were accused of bigamy. In these cases there was evidence of both false matrimony (as in a second marriage) and living in a household with a partner as a spouse. Confusion could have arisen from the native belief that a marriage was annulled if a person was no

---

55 Sommer, "Negotiated Settlements," 240.
56 Town councillors to [unnamed] Governor, November 1803, Monte Alegre, APEP cod. 601, doc. 31.
57 José Roberto do Amaral Lapa (ed.), *Livro da Visitação do Santo Ofício da Inquisição ao Estado do Grão Pará (1763–1769)*, Petrópolis: Vozes, 1978, 32.

longer living with a spouse.[58] While the church condemned concubinage, it could do little about it. Indeed, the church was acutely aware of the divergence of local practices from advocated doctrines and state laws. In this regard, it is worth noting that baptism was more important than marriage as an observed rite of passage, perhaps because of its convergence with native custom as outlined above.

About six hundred people were baptized in the town of Óbidos between 1805 and 1816. Of these, the priest listed five children as legitimate (*legítimo*), which meant the parents were married. It is possible the priest did not record all marriages in these baptisms, but then why did he register the fact for some and not for others? In a few cases considered below, the children (often those born to prominent white men) sought recognition of paternity or a father requested his illegitimate children be made his legitimate heirs. The recent study by Linda Lewin of Brazilian of the categories of birth of *legítimo*, *natural*, and *bastardo* shows, among other arguments, that Anglo-American understandings were very different to Luso-Brazilian traditions. While Luso-Brazilian law considered natural and bastardo as illegitimate it did not bifurcate between individuals as legitimate or illegitimate and then impose legal identities as permanent conditions: "individual born outside of wedlock occupied a continuum ranging from quasi-legitimacy to bastardy, while the law generously offered several ways for them to be legitimized."[59] Once recognized, natural children enjoyed equal rights in inheritance law. The high numbers of children born out of wedlock in Óbidos was in line with the rest of Brazil at the opening of the nineteenth century. What we do not possess is a fuller appreciation in the Pará context of the ways parents and children elicited "specific strategies for heirship."[60] Given the relative paucity of immovable and movable resources in the region as well as the tradition of land ownership based on continued use and the stronger presence of Amerindian customary practices, the Paraense situation is likely to offer a significant variant to the social history told by Lewin. For example, one customary tradition in the Amazon of today is of ultimogeniture: the last born has precedence in inheritance over elder siblings.

One explanation for the lack of interest in legal marriage is given by Muriel Nazarri in her study of concubinage in colonial Brazil, which for her can be attributed to class.[61] Despite the promotion of white and Indian

---

58 Amaral Lapa, *Livro da Visitação*, for example, 126–129 and 270–274.

59 Linda Lewin, *Surprise Heirs: Illegitimacy, Patrimonial Rights, and Legal Nationalism in Luso-Brazilian Inheritance, 1750–1821*, Stanford: Stanford University Press, 2003, xiv.

60 Lewin, *Surprise Heirs*, xxii.

61 Muriel Nazarri, "Concubinage in Colonial Brazil," *Journal of Family History*, 1996, 21, 2, 107–118; Alida Metcalf, *Family and Frontier in Colonial Brazil*, Berkeley: University of California Press, 1992; Sommer, "Cupid on the Amazon," 439. See also Boxer, *The Golden Age of Brazil*, 164–165.

marriage in the Amazon, there was a general tendency in Portugal to understand marriage as an endogamous union, that is, a partnership between people of more or less equal class status. Rarely would a man marry down. Given the lack of white women in the colony, white men's sexual relationships were with women considered a lower class (and just as regulated by customs as much as any relation, as we saw in the examples at the beginning of this chapter).[62] If no property or dowry was to be passed from the woman's family to the man, there appeared to be little interest in legalizing a long-term union.

In this respect, a priest writing in the later 1820s about the upper Amazon said that the "white men [of the region] are a mixture of Brazilians (*nacionaes*), Paraenses, and other Europeans. The Brazilians, who are the sons of the Portuguese, ally themselves with native women (*mulheres naturaes do pais*) and procreate. And the daughters continue to marry with whites, they are in the fourth and fifth generation, and as a result they have become much whitened."[63] The sense is here of a deliberate strategy on behalf of native women, also emphasized by Sommer, seeking unions with certain kinds of men. Over time the children became white not because of their skin color *per se*, but because of their parentage. These well-placed intermarriages allowed the children to be seen as white because their parents were considered white.

White men also sought Indian women as wives. José Cavalcante de Albuquerque was born at the Atlantic seaport and old capital of Brazil, Bahia, in 1760, and went on to study at Coimbra University in Portugal in the 1780s. For some reason, he decided to pursue his life in Pará, and was offered various administrative and military positions there; he also had a cacao plantation in the Lower Amazon, run by about a dozen slaves. The pinnacle of his life was probably his election to the Portuguese Cortes in 1823 as representative of the Rio Negro region. However, he never sat in the chamber because he resigned over Portuguese mistreatment of Brazilian deputies. In his various letters to the governor of Pará in the 1790s, he comes across as a defender of Indians against the abuse of colonists and demanded reforms to end the tyranny of the whites. In the early 1820s he devised a plan to "civilize" Indians in the Rio Negro but it never received backing. Sometime after 1792, he set up a household with Rita Vitória do Carmo. They had at least three children baptized in Óbidos. In the baptismal records the children were not listed as being "legitimate" and no ethnic identity was attributed to Rita. Cavalcante appeared in a few contemporary chronicles by visitors to the region. For example, Henry Lister Maw, a British naval officer, for no other reason than curiosity stopped his boat at

62 Nazarri, "Concubinage in Colonial Brazil," 107.
63 Fernandes de Souza, "Notícias Geográphicas," 501.

a house on the river margin near Óbidos town; the house may have been quite grand, hence Maw's interest in the plantation-type residence. He had a very brief drink of coffee and took his leave. As he did so, he looked back and saw the family together on the veranda: a couple and their son and two daughters. He said the daughters were pretty but not fair, with long dark hair, dark eyes, and good figures. Cavalcante was a "white" of relatively high status, but to Maw his family were dark-skinned. We should add here that the prevailing treatment of well-to-do women, especially unmarried daughters, was to keep them inside the house out of the sun and away from visiting men.[64] Thus their skin color was natural rather than from the sun. This suggests that a high-status man from the upper classes had made a family with a woman who was more than likely an Indian.[65]

Another element can be added here concerning the nature of peasant marriage and the build up of resources in the family group. "Farmsteads" large and small, not using slave labor, were organized around the family and a neighborly network. Parents put their children to work and production was coordinated across the extended web of relations. Apart from scale, there may have been little economic difference between the plantation and peasant family enterprises. The incentive for a man to set up a homestead, find a "wife," and have children was powerful, since without a family he would not have been integrated in a network of mutual and reciprocal solidarity. Typical of peasant societies, these forces were conservative in the sense that they promoted private rather than collective or common interests of the peasant class. (This is not to discount the significance of mobility, particularly of a mobile unregulated workforce.) In the more general context of peasant societies, "marriage" creates a domestic environment in which material resources can be consolidated and labor organized, where labor was a form of wealth and power.

If peasant unions tend to be endogamous and aimed at conserving family resources, it follows people will seek partners within a network of neighbors, friends, and family, particularly those people who live nearby. This strategy prevents outsiders from acquiring land in the vicinity and the fission of kin groups. When outsiders were brought in, this may have been part of a design to strengthen local relations and alliances. In other words, nonlegal marriages would have been connected to other strategies, such as the passing down resources to children and choice of godparents. Subsequent partnerships

64 See Frei Francisco de Nossa Senhora dos Prazeres, "Poranduba Maranhense, ou Relação Histórica da Província do Maranhão," RIHGB, 54, 185–277, 1891 [1820], 134.

65 Sources for the life of Cavalcante include APOEP Livros de Baptismos, 1805–1816 and 1816–1830; José Cavalcante de Albuquerque to Governor Francisco de Souza Coutinho, March 1793, Vila Franca, APEP cod. 501, doc. 06; Henry Lister Maw, *Journal of a passage from the Pacific to the Atlantic, crossing the Andes in the Northern Provinces of Peru, and Descending the River Marañon, or Amazon*, London, 1829, 340.

built on previous ones, such as marrying an in-law (that is, a sibling's spouse's sibling or a cousin). These sibling set marriages are common today in rural communities and are a way of relinking networks and making them stronger.

An important value, then, in kinship relations was placed on sibling sets remaining close. The Marinho family "started off" in the mid-eighteenth century in Óbidos with Constantino Manoel Marinho, who was the pilot (*cabo*) of the town's canoe in the 1760s. He had a number of children, including Vicente and Bernardo Marinho dos Vasconcellos. Both Manoel Marinho and his son Vicente obtained royal land grants. From this time, individuals with the name of Marinho appeared regularly in the military and municipal letters from Óbidos, Alenquer, and Faro. It would seem that from being relatively humble – as indicated by Manoel Marinho's job, typically held by a poor white with much knowledge of boats and the environment – the Marinho family was able to work its way to the center of local society. The fact that the sibling sets remained together was critical to this achievement, for it meant not only loyalty but solidarity. Although it is not possible to reconstruct marriages between the various cousin groups or sibling sets, it is logical to assume that existing unions would have been made stronger by further endogamous ones.

What about children born without a listed father in the parish records? From the six hundred entries from 1806 to 1817 in Óbidos, a total of sixty-five children were born to unknown fathers. This number excludes two adults who were recently arrived slaves, where the priest wrote "unknown parents," perhaps because he could not see the point of writing them down. Most of the total were children born to slave mothers (sixty-two percent). The rest were children born to Indian and ethnically unspecified mothers. The proportion of children born to slave mothers is explained by the fact that the priest may have been under an obligation not to write down the name. The unknown father can be seen more as a father who does not want to admit paternity. So, in a sense, the father's name appears elsewhere on the register, as the slave's owner. The other thirty-eight percent of absent fathers could be seen in the same light. Another explanation is that the mother is trying to "negotiate" the father's identity so as to advance the child's interests. Thus the mother was trying to get a man of high social status to accept his responsibility or persuade others of the connection. This practice was common in the Andes, where Indian mothers would try to attain mestiço status for their children, which in turn might allow for "social betterment and make new choices available in the colonial order."[66] Whatever

---

66 Thérèse Bouysse-Cassagne, "In Praise of Bastards: The Uncertainties of Mestizo Identity in the Sixteenth and Seventeenth Century Andes," in Olivia Harris (ed.), *Inside and Outside the Law*, London: Routledge, 1996, 98.

prejudices mestiços may have suffered, they were outweighed by the potential advantages.

Social advancement may have been secured if a high-status father recognized the child as his own. This legitimization gave some of the father's status to the child or children, and guaranteed that the father's inheritable wealth was passed down. Indeed, the two were hardly distinct. This fitted neatly with the marriage strategies outlined above – keep children and property close. From the late eighteenth and early nineteenth centuries, there were petitions from Pará to the monarch seeking recognition of a child's identity. Some of these requests were sent by the father, and at least two from the Lower Amazon involved the sets of children from two different mothers.[67] Others were sent by the children and included witness statements from elite men testifying to the veracity of the claim (these were called *requerimentos de perfilhação*, rather than *legitimação*). As mentioned above, the second lieutenant in Santarém in 1785 was João Pais Pedroso, whose sister Rita was married to another soldier, lieutenant Henrique José de Vasconcellos. In 1785 João sought to have his daughter with a local woman made legitimate. Another soldier in Santarém at the time, João Caetano de Souza, sought the legitimization of his four children with two women, one listed as an Indian and the other the sister of his colleague.[68] The explicit justification was to make them his heirs (*herdeiros universais*).

Similarly in 1818, a petition seeking the right to inherit the goods of their father came from half-brothers Manuel and Serafim Printes, slave owners active in municipal politics and married to two sisters.[69] Born to different mothers, they made their case after their father's death. Their father came from a relatively wealthy Portuguese family. Joaquim Francisco Printes was born in Lisbon in 1743 and had been in the army since 1777, eventually promoted to captain in 1794 of the ninth company of the fourth militia regiment based in Macapá. His father, José Agostinho Printes, had been the chief doctor for Pará and Maranhão in 1770s and 1780s; having also treated parts of the royal family in Portugal, he was granted one of the highest colonial honors, the *Hábito da ordem do Christo*.[70] While in Belém, a sister and brother were born to Joaquim, the latter following him to the Lower

---

67 "Requisition of João Pais Pedroso to the Queen," before February 25, 1785, Santarém, AHU Pará Avulsos, cx. 93, doc. 7481; "Requisition of Manoel Joaquim Printz and Serafim Angelico Printz to the King," Óbidos, AHU Pará Avulsos, cx. 149, doc. 11447, December 2, 1818.

68 "Requisition of João Caetano de Souza e Silva to the Queen," Santarém, October 24, 1796, AHU Pará Avulsos, cx. 108, doc. 8500.

69 *Printes* is also spelled *Printz*. See, for example, "Requisition of Manoel Joaquim Printz and Serafim Angelico Printz to the King," Óbidos, AHU Pará Avulsos, cx. 149, doc. 11447, December 2, 1818.

70 See the entry on the decoration in *Dicionário do Brasil Colonial*, Ronaldo Vainfas (ed.), 437–439.

Amazon (it is not clear if they shared the same mother). Joaquim Printes also applied for a prestigious award (*Hábito da ordem de Avis*) for services to the Crown in 1803. However, he was less concerned with sorting out the future of his children and lovers. The mothers of the two children applying for recognition were described as "single and destitute." Manuel and Serafim wanted not only the connection to a family of distinction but also the material goods and better conditions for their mothers. Their participation during the decades of violent conflict (1820 and 1830) appeared to be have been neutral, since their names appear in council documents before and after. As so neatly argued by Elizabeth Kuznesof, legitimization in Brazil was a process, not a single event.[71]

Though significant, it would be a mistake to exaggerate the effect of social betterment in the Amazon at the time. The political divisions were more relevant, since they were linked to the control of local administrative and legal functions. In other words, the interest in upward mobility was tempered by the relatively few advantages in specifically local terms. This was a time of growing consolidation of achievements on a local level, and alarm that others might take away what had been gained. Such anxieties were made worse by newer lines of antagonism being drawn within and between the Portuguese and Brazilian élites during the 1820s and 1830s. The assertion of social boundaries using kinship in its various forms is confirmed in the following section.

Lastly, what were the connections between family, gender, and Indian peasant ways of life. Women in Pará were active participants in economic and social life. Their lives were less mobile than men's and were centered on the household, but this does not make them any less pertinent. The stability of domestic organization was provided by women, as men were more likely to carry out seasonal or temporary work away from the village or town. It follows that households were governed by women's values and these were either a modification of Portuguese mores or had some continuity with Indian or African ones. Certainly, there would have been no direct transplantation of European standards. In other words, women were central to the development of peasant livelihoods, for their relations of kinship between households provided its connective tissue and reproductive potential.[72] The broad ethnic alliances of the rebellion then had their origins in both men's mobility and women's networks.

---

71 Kuznesof, "Sexual Politics, Race and Bastard Bearing," 249.

72 It is unclear what role these networks played in the Cabanagem, since there exists little material on their participation in the rebellion. Oral histories told by contemporary residents of the Lower Tapajós River attest to the presence of women in the towns during the rebellion, while men went to fight or were forced to, but whether women bore arms is not known. In one story from Pinhel, the mistreatment of a maid in a wealthy person's employment sparked a local attack.

The Political Choice of Godparents

In the colonial period in Pará, godparenthood was as important as it was elsewhere in Brazil. Missionaries' accounts, such as Bettendorff's, tell of their pleasure in baptizing whole groups of children at a time, and adults receiving basic teachings to prepare for their baptism. Sometimes, the baptism of an Indian headman persuaded his people to become baptized. This happened with some Mundurucu groups settling near Santarém in the first decade of the nineteenth century.[73] In fact, these large-scale baptisms are still common today, owing to the irregular visits of priests to rural villages; often they are preceded by the parents' marriage. Two hundred years ago, many rural areas had only private chapels, which the priest visited as often as he wished or could be persuaded to. The parish church, however, was the main site for such rituals, especially during festival periods.

Although the Church sanctions the spiritual relationships involved, the popular expression of godparenthood and coparentage is more social and political than religious. Thus anthropological interest in the institution has been directed to understanding how such ties reinforce previous links or create new ones. Although the focus of this research has been on the establishment of vertical relations between people of unequal status, studies show that godparenthood varies in Latin America from place to place and over time in one place.[74] Moreover, elsewhere in Brazil (but not as far as I know in Pará at the time), godparenthood relations were not just derived from baptism but also from marriage witnesses, confirmation, and at festivals such as St John's day, when coparents would be created by leaping over a fire together.[75] We know little of the meaning of the relations to participants, but if contemporary ethnography is an indication a critical element of such relations is respect. Coparents, godparents, and godchildren should avoid sex and social conflict. Thus, coparents address each other as Mr. or Mrs. so-and-so, and godchildren request blessing from their godparents, as they would their parents. Asking for a blessing from an elder involves proffering one's hand to be kissed, and is a ritual that can be performed many times a day, often between the same people.

---

73 See, for example, priest Pedro Alexandre de Nazareth, Santa Cruz to Captain Barralho [in Santarém], Santa Cruz, January 12, 1805, APEP cod. 610, doc. 124.

74 Stuart Schwartz, *Slaves, Peasants and Rebels*, Champaign-Urbana: University of Illinois Press, 1992. The classic anthropological studies on godparenthood include Sidney Mintz and Eric Wolf, "An Analysis of Ritual Co-parenthood (Compadrazgo)," *South Western Journal of Anthropology*, 6, 4, 1950, 341–368; and Stephen Gudeman, "Compadrazgo as a Reflection of the Natural and Spiritual Person," *Proceedings of the Royal Anthropological Institute*, 1971, 45–71.

75 Schwartz, *Slaves, Peasants and Rebels*, 139; for twentieth-century variations in the Amazon, see Charles Wagley, *Amazon Town*, New York: Macmillan, 1976.

With baptisms being performed in groups on the same day, there was no segregation between people; all were baptized together and there were relatively long fallow periods between mass events. Each entry in the baptismal records for Óbidos contains the name of the child (first name only), the names of the parents (or just the mother if the father was not known), and the names of godparents. Surnames were written neither consistently nor in full, especially when the person was a woman, a slave, or an Indian. The entries refer to ethnic status only when the person was a slave or an Indian; when the person was a slave, the owner was mentioned, as well. There is a small bias toward males in the choice of godparents. One person baptized during the period between 1805 and 1835 has two men as godparents (on April 16, 1814); and in several instances, a child was given a local godfather and as godmother, the town's patron saint, Saint Anna (Mary's mother). The assigning of the patron saint had been outlawed by the Council of Trent but was still a frequent practice, at least to the 1830s, and apparently came about as the result of a promise made to the saint.

It is the choice of godparents that concerns us here. We know nothing of the conditions in which such choices were made or the reasons for them. Nevertheless, godparents were indicative of the kinds of relations a couple – or person, in the case of a single parent – wished to strengthen in the future, for the relationship was, above all, oriented to what was to come. For example, although it was the slave owner's responsibility to baptize the children of slaves, it was the parents' responsibility to select the godparent(s) and they never chose their master – their own or anyone else's. Given the extra information available for slaves, most of the following discussion is devoted to them.

Most baptisms took place between people of unspecified ethnicity. When such data is given, we know that slaves invited fellow slaves, Indians, and other folk as their coparents. In three cases, the slaves were newly introduced, and their "nation" in Africa is specified. The rest were first- or later-generation slaves. When slaves chose other slaves as coparents, they sometimes lived in neighboring farmsteads. This feature may have applied to Indians as well who wanted to affirm existing friendly relations. For example, in the "Livro dos Baptismos 1805–1816" from Óbidos, on December 27, 1815, Thereza was baptized by priest Raimundo Antônio Martins in the church of Santa Anna in the town. She was born to Francisca Xavier and an unknown father (*pai ignorado*); her mother was the property of José Ricardo Printes. Thereza's godparents were the *preto* Apolinário, a slave also belonging to Printes, and Thereza de Jesus, a slave of Dona Anna Xavier. Printes had land concession at the mouth of the river Curuá for a cacao plantation.[76] The land concession document for Anna

---

76 Biblioteca e Archivo Público do Pará, "Catálogo Nominal dos Posseiros de Sesmarias," ABAPP vol. 3.
     1904, no. 1377, 97.

Xavier Freire de Fonseca reports that her plot borders Printes.[77] It would seem that neighboring slaves referred to each other in order to build on existing ties. The absent father could, of course, be any man, but the fact it was not written down by the priest suggests that someone might not have wanted the paternity registered at that point. Many other cases follow the same pattern.

Thereza was baptized with two other people. Two days before, on Christmas Day 1815, five children had been baptized together. One imagines the town filled up with people from the countryside for the festivities. Felipe was one of those baptized on December 25, 1815. His parents were the Indian Damião and the cafuza Joanna, the slave of João Pinheiro. The godparents were "Felipe," listed neither as a slave nor an Indian, and "Catarina," a slave of Bernardo Marinho. The parents were not married or the record would have stated *filho legítimo*. The network of relations in this case was not limited to a single ethnic category, revealing a small incidence of the mixtures of relations that could be found in many other instances. In these two examples, the child has the same name as the same-sex godparent, which is not an infrequent occurrence.

However, some combinations were not present at baptisms. The children of slave owners and town officials were never offered to individuals named as slaves or Indians, and vice versa. The "wealthy" and those who owned slaves invariably chose their godparents from people close to them, such as brothers or sisters, and affines. The overwhelming majority of godparents were residents of the parish; the parish of residence was always given when not Óbidos, which was listed in only a handful of cases. José Cavalcante de Albuquerque designated the Crown-appointed judge of Pará (*juiz de fora de Grão-Pará*), João Martins Pena, as the godfather of his daughter Joanna in April 1812. Though the judge was not present at the baptism, a local man, Guilherme de Seixas, acted as his proxy. The child's godmother was listed simply as "Joanna Perpétua" and does not appear elsewhere in the records. On the same day, Guilherme de Seixas and his wife Maria dos Prazeres baptized their son Leonoro. The godparents were Cavalcante and his wife Rita Vitória do Carmo. Cavalcante and his wife were also the godparents of many Indian children, much more than other whites.[78]

---

77 Biblioteca e Archivo Público do Pará, "Catálogo Nominal dos Posseiros de Sesmarias," ABAPP vol. 3. 1904, no. 102, 12.

78 When Cavalcante resigned from the Cortes, he was more or less destitute in Lisbon. Without funds for his return journey, he concocted a plan to civilize the Indians of the Upper Amazon. He did not get approval or the money to realize his ambition, not least because of Independence. Somehow he found his way back to the Lower Amazon. "Report by Overseas Council on Cavalcante's plan for the catechism of Indians," Lisboa, March 24, 1823, AHU Pará Avulsos, cx. 159, doc. 12129. The national

In about ten cases over the period in question, a female slave was emancipated on the baptism of her child. Some of these occur where the father was not another slave, so it is possible he paid the money for her release. In the others it is stated that the mother was liberated by the wife of the slave owner. The coincidence of liberation and baptism suggests the special significance of the event, not just within an individual's lifecycle but also the family's development.

This brief examination shows that most godparents came from within a circle of geographically proximate friends and family. Rather than select godparents from a higher status than oneself, the predominant pattern was for reaffirming existing ties. Over the period of this study, there does not appear to be significant change in this claim; the features outlined above applied for the whole time. How can we understand these characteristics?

Many studies of godparenthood show that it is connected to wider political and economic processes. Since the relationship in Pará was one of election, this should not be controversial. The selection of godparents was an expression of other social concerns as well as the protection and support sought by parents for their children. In other words, the economic and political divisions of the region were bound up with the choice. The fault lines of a hierarchical society were likely to define the group of people elected. This was reinforced by the sentiments of respect, friendship, and trust characteristic of egalitarian-type relations, which encompassed the triangle of *compadrio* (between parents, godparents, and children) relations. The period was, above all, characterized by a development of local identities, which in turn led to different interests grouping themselves around their core economic and political strengths. For "whites," these interests were land, control of army positions (so as to access Indian labor), and holding local office, which grew into rivalry between competing élite families. For Indians and mestiços, their concerns were controlling their labor, skill, and knowledge of the environment. Slaves had their labor, too, but were also working to make sense of the world they had been thrown into. What united these last two groups most critically was their resistance to what they saw as the despotism and tyranny of the élite. Thus conflict and violence found easy expression in the maintenance of the boundaries between different identities. By rejecting godparents from outside a relatively safe network, a boundary was created, attaching value to potential of same status relations. As such, godparenthood was about protection and support, and the people to whom one turned were those with whom a person had a more or less equal relationship. Lower status individuals did not seek patronage through godparenthood.

context for the revival in liberal attitudes to Indian politics came from José Bonifacio's plan for the civilisation of Indians. See José Bonifácio de Andrada e Silva, *Projetos para o Brasil*, ed. Miriam Dolmikoff, São Paulo: Companhia das Letras, 1998; George Boehrer, "Variant Versions of José Bonifácio's 'Plan for the Civilization of the Brazilian Indians,'" *The Americas*, 14, 3, 1958, 301–312.

In terms of the argument of this book, I have highlighted the way in which godparenthood in the Lower Amazon is connected to a complex of wider relations. That is, group affirmation through the selection of godparents was a central feature. In his study of godparenthood in colonial and imperial Brazil, Stuart Schwartz provides an example from a parish in the Bahian Recôncavo. He finds that the predominant choice of godparents among slaves from within their own midst indicated "a growing sense of community among the slave population and a decreasing sense of dependency on the part of the slaves or of paternalism on the part of the free."[79] The reason, he suggests, was the context in which such choices were being made in Bahia. There were numerous slave revolts at the time, not to mention the struggle for independence, which heightened the distrust and divisions between people. "It is not surprising," he concludes, "to find a lessening of the bonds between the free and the slave or across the color lines as reflected in the choice of godparents."[80] The correlation between the interiors of Bahia and Pará, despite the different demographic and economic structures, is striking. This parallel might indicate that political conditions at times of crisis and ongoing social turmoil overrode other facts in the choice of godparents.

This chapter has shown how the relations surrounding the family were intrinsic to the creation of regional identities. Through the establishment of kinship and its strengthening by the overlaying ties of marriage and godparenthood, individuals developed networks that embedded them in Amazonian society. The family made outsiders natives of the region and reconstituted insiders in the new colonial world. At the same time, each family had their allegiances that determined how they implemented their official obligations.

The domestic realm was observed and regulated by the Church and the state but these institutions did not have control over the family. Indeed, their peculiar nature in Pará allowed kinship relations to flourish. This applied equally to the two loosely different kinds of families, peasant- and plantation-based. For whatever regulations were imposed or diverse traditions inherited, the family adapted to the prevailing mercantile economy oriented to export. In so doing, it was shaped by local pressures, such as the need to assert loyalty, protect livelihoods, maintain resources, and keep production above a certain level to avoid state obligations. Overall, the reproduction of the peasant family was the central way in which people could sustain the value of working for oneself and not a boss or the state. That combination formed the basis for the peasant way of life, a feature that will become clearer in the following chapter.

79 Schwartz, *Slaves, Peasants and Rebels*, 152.
80 Ibid.

4

Some of the Origins of Peasant Rebellion in Pará and the Agrarian Sector

The rivers enabled the Portuguese occupation of a massive expanse of territory. Initially, however, the colonizers wanted land less than they wanted products and people. The kinds of commodities they sought were those in the river or close to the water's edge: cacao, clove, nuts, a medicinal oil called *drogas do sertão*, turtle and manatee oil, fish and, in the days of Indian slavery before 1755, human beings. These collecting expeditions, using specially adapted canoes, took place following a seasonal pattern: they would leave their towns after the beginning of the ebb of the river in September and return to Belém to sell the goods, when the water started to rise in February. Fortune and misfortune was an intrinsic part of this river-based life for anyone who followed it, whether Amerindian, slave, mestiço, missionary, crown employee, or settler. The river was not just the theatre on which life was conducted, it also wrote the play and acted in the performance. This is not to say that social and economic life was determined by the constraints of nature, but the river was a living part of everyday experience of individuals in Amazonia. There was a rhythm to all social and economic activity, and it was punctuated by religious festivals. Each locality maintained its own calendar arising from local ecological conditions, production and marketing preferences, and residence patterns as well as parameters imposed by the state, such as when produce should be delivered.

One Pará governor Francisco de Souza Coutinho, understood better than most the link between river, empire, and commerce. The younger brother of two extremely well-placed Portuguese politicians, he served from 1790 to 1803. One of his grand proposals for reform was the redevelopment of an inland waterway stretching from Belém to Vila Bela on the Madeira River some 1,500 miles away. Private traders had already opened up the route to the west in the early eighteenth century, but had been thwarted by the creation in 1757 of a state-owned monopoly company in the region. Coutinho wanted to offer concessions to traders and encourage the free market in goods. The proposal failed because of lack of external interest in the scheme.[1]

---

1 David Davidson, "Rivers and Empire: The Madeira Route and the Incorporation of the Brazilian Far West, 1737–1808," Ph.D. dissertation, Yale University, 1970, 204.

Coutinho stands out for other reasons: his thirteen-year tenure on the Amazon was marked by a series of reforms in most areas of colonial life concerning the civilization of Indians, an increase in slaves, stimulus of shipbuilding, and the modernization of the military. His zeal to address the region's problems matches that of Francisco Mendonça Xavier Furtado, the governor of the Amazon from 1751 to 1759. Furtado was the younger brother of Sebastião José de Carvalho, the Marquis of Pombal, chief minister of Portugal from 1750 to 1777. Both governors were well-connected through family ties to the heart of colonial policy and implemented extensive legislation to develop the region and bring it into the Enlightened world. Given Pará's greater proximity to Lisbon, the access to a vast hinterland, and the apparent richness of the Amazon's environment, the governors probably thought it would be easy to augment commerce and fill the royal coffers with taxes. What was needed was a system of production that brought out the best efforts of the region's inhabitants. Furtado's one major plan, the Directorate, was abolished by Coutinho, who then devised another. The problem was always labor or, more accurately, the people who were to work the system, namely, the Indians who had been brought into the colonial world by missionaries or slave traffickers in the early eighteenth century. Later on, the crises would also apply to enslaved Africans as they escaped from their masters. The problem was not just that the labor force was truculent, liable to desert, and small, but that it had a different relationship to the river than the governors'. For these people, the river was a way of life, sustaining it with its produce and directing actions in accord with the rhythm of the river's movements. But for the others, the river was a means to an end, it was about conquest; whatever the local conditions were, they must be made to conform to Portuguese policy.

In other words, there were divergent notions of society at the heart of Portuguese Amazonia. The cultural momentum behind the rebel movement was an alliance among the self-identified natives of Pará. The common identity arose from the livelihoods associated with those who lived on or close to the river: pilots, canoe paddlers, fishermen, farmers, riverbank dwellers, river bandits, pirates, artisans, and so on. The small numbers of élites, traders, military officers, cacao planters, administrators, and cattle ranchers also had an intimate connection to this watery colonial world. These were people of property and while they may have been attracted to liberal ideas, they would find their implementation very difficult. Unlike other provinces, such as neighboring Maranhão, Pará's profits never generated enough capital to reinvest in production or to buy many more slaves. If the revenues had been greater, the ability to make Pará conform would have been made easier. Instead, the region remained stubbornly different, local, and heterogeneous.

This chapter charts the political and economic characteristics of the region as it emerges into the nineteenth century. In many ways, this means understanding the legacy of Pombal and Furtado as seen from the Amazon at the time. The most significant aspect here is the creation of a multiethnic – if predominantly Indian – peasantry tied to a commercial network. For it was this peasantry that played an important role in Brazilian shipments of cacao, which represented more than half the value of Pará's exports from 1776 to 1822. The story of the Amazon in the late eighteenth and early nineteenth century has cacao at its center.[2] To understand how that was achieved, we need to return to the region's reforms.

The Directorate

"The brutal devastation and the suffering in those remote districts [Pará] between the years of 1820 to 1836 are rooted in the ill-starred brainchild of Francisco Xavier Mendonça Furtado." Capistrano de Abreu[3]

The *Directório que devem observer nas povoações dos índios do Pará e Maranhão* (Directorate) legislation was written by Francisco Xavier Mendonça Furtado in 1755, but came into effect only in 1758, a delay caused by local Jesuit opposition. Their hostility toward Furtado's reforms was the Amazonian dimension of a more general phenomenon and a factor that contributed to their expulsion from the Portuguese empire in 1759.[4] Among the Directorate's more important aspects were the creation of an Indian élite to run the villages in conjunction with a "director," the secularization of daily life, the promotion of marriage between settler and Indians by providing economic incentives, the provision of schools in each village, the sole use of the Portuguese language, and the allocation of profit incentives to Indians in the economic production of a village.[5] These were the heady days of the Iberian Enlightenment; development of the Amazon was considered central to the geopolitical strategies of the Portuguese empire. Above all, the Directorate was designed to restructure the economy to meet the needs of

---

2 Dauril Alden, "The Significance of Cacao Production in the Amazon Region during the Late Colonial Period: an Essay in Comparative Economic History," *Proceedings of the American Philosophical Society*, vol. 120, 2, April 1976, 127.

3 Capistrano de Abreu, *Chapters of Brazilian History*, Oxford: Oxford University Press, 1997, 156.

4 For discussions on the Directorate other than Barbara Sommer, see Colin Maclachlan, "The Indian Directorate: Forced Acculturation in Portuguese America (1757–1799)," *The Americas*, 1972, 28, 357–387; John Hemming, *Amazon Frontier: The Defeat of the Brazilian Indians*, London: Macmillan, 1987; Rita Almeida, *O Diretório dos Índios*, Brasília: Editora Universidade de Brasília, 1997; Ângela Maria Vieira Domingues, *Quando os Índios eram Vassalos: Colonização e Relações de Poder no Norte do Brasil na Segunda Metade do Século XVIII*, Lisboa: Commissão Nacional para as Comerações dos Descobrimentos Portugueses, 2000.

5 A facsimile of the Directorate is in Carlos de Araújo Moreira Neto, *Índios da Amazônia, da maioria a Minoria, 1750–1850*. Petrópolis: Vozes, 1988, 170–206.

the state and to convert the missionary Indians into proper vassals of the Crown.[6]

This particular package was part of a bundle of other reforms also instituted by Mendonça Furtado in the mid-1750s. It became illegal to enslave Indians and to use the term *caboclo* (the child of an Indian and a white person) because it was deemed pejorative. The missions were secularized in 1757. The Crown established a monopoly trading company, the *Companhia Geral do Grão Pará e Maranhão*, whose main goal was to advance economic development by supplying slave labor from Africa and provide regular transatlantic shipping. A number of private investors contributed to founding the company and, despite the state's support, it was disbanded twenty years later.[7]

Although the Directorate was an enlightened and progressive piece of legislation heralding a new phase in the colony and bringing the region ever closer to the metropolis, it was written also with local conditions in mind. By the time it was completed, Mendonça Furtado had spent four years in the Amazon, traveled widely and spent a significant part of that time in a relatively remote part of the country – halfway up the Negro River in Barcellos (then called Mariuá) – as part of his work with the boundary commission. He had a good sense of what the missions had done successfully, which was creating an extensive "missionary-mercantile complex" with the Jesuits at the center.[8] Like the missions, the Directorate villages were to be collectively organized. Previously, Indians had worked under the tutelage of missionaries and were kept physically separate from colonists.

6　See Kenneth Maxwell, "The Spark: Pombal, the Amazon and the Jesuits," *Portuguese Studies* 17, 1, 2001, 168–183, for colonial Portuguese thinking of the geopolitical importance of the Amazon.

7　On the General Company, see Davidson, "Rivers and Empire," especially 140–227, and Manuel Nunes Dias, *Fomento e Mercantilismo: A Companhia Geral do Grão Para e Maranhao (1755–1778)*, 2 vols. Belém: Universidade Federal do Pará, 1970.

8　The phrase is Kenneth Maxwell's in *Conflicts and Conspiracies: Brazil and Portugal 1750–1808*, Cambridge: Cambridge University Press, 2004, 17. Mendonça Furtado was a keen letter writer even when he was on the River Negro, so the development of his knowledge and thinking towards Amazonia is extremely well documented, see Marcos Carneiro de Mendonça, *A Amazônia na era Pombalina: Correspondência Inédita do Governador e Captião-General do Estado do Grão-Pará e Maranhão Francisco Xavier De Mendonça Furtado*. Rio de Janeiro: IHGB, 1963. There nevertheless remains very little written on this outstanding figure, though see Isabel Vieira Rodrigues, "A Política de Francisco Xavier Mendonça Furtado no Norte do Brasil (1751–1759)," *Oceanos* 40, 1999, 94–111, October/November, special issue on "A Formação Territorial do Brasil," and Kenneth Maxwell, *Pombal: Paradox of the Enlightenment*, New York: Cambridge University Press, 1995. Perhaps some have been put off by Dauril Alden's evaluation of his personality: "A one-time naval officer, Mendonça Furtado was imperious, hard-driving, crude, violent tempered, ambitious though completely loyal to his elder brother, pious in an Old Testament sense, gullible but suspicious of the motives of anyone, particularly one whom he regarded as an inferior, who held views contrary to his own; he was therefore entirely uncompromising," Alden, "Economic Aspects of the Expulsion of the Jesuits from Brazil: A Preliminary Report," in Henry Keith and S. F. Edwards (eds.), *Conflict and Continuity in Brazilian Society*, Columbia: University of South Carolina Press, 1969, 41–42.

The reforms would continue to keep Indians separate through the regula-
tion of their labor, but villages were now open to all.

The promise of the legislation was never fulfilled. Few if any schools were
set up outside of Belém and some Indians continued to be abused. For these
reasons, historians who have written on this period in the Amazon have
emphasized the combined aspects of the absolute power of Portuguese
administrators and the miserable state of the Indian population. The
directors' brutal treatment of Indians went unchecked and they personally
benefited from their economic exploitation of village laborers.[9] However,
new research modifies this binary opposition. Barbara Sommer has argued
convincingly that "indigenous inhabitants of the Directorate towns were
not simply victims of Portuguese oppression, but contenders in the events,
conflicts, and changes during the colonial period."[10] Through a reading
of the documentation from the villages (rather than from the governors or
relatively high-up officials), Sommer shows that Directorate Indians determined much of the daily running of the villages. They were able to control
their own labor (in consultation with headmen) and win special privileges
for themselves, and had access to heathen Indians (*gentios*) in remote forest
areas. In some villages they sometimes also maintained their ethnic identity,
a process that caused conflict among competing groups. On the whole,
these were important gains for village Indians and undermine the view
that they had no power or were not significant participants in the colonial
world.

Moreover, Sommer reveals that the "village Indians" were not homogenous but differentiated by family membership, social status, and ethnicity.
Of particular importance, Sommer demonstrates, were the Indian nobles,
principais, who were entrusted with much power in each village. In other
words, Indians maintained an active interest in the colonial system and
adapted aspects of the policy to their own advantage, seeking appointments
and promotion, for example, from the governor. At the same time, they
absented themselves from village labor and "fle[d] into the forest," a
euphemism that could have had many different meanings. It might have
indicated the person had decided to go (back) to his or her Indian nation
up a tributary (only to reappear at a later date) or wanted to visit family
elsewhere. Everybody had to be accounted for in Directorate lists and
reports, so precious were labor and its products. Indeed, the amount and
quality of documentation is a key reason why the period has been relatively

---

9 For example, Robin Anderson, "Following Curupira: Colonization and Migration in Pará 1758–1930
   as a Study in Settlement of the Humid Tropics," Ph.D. dissertation, University of California, 1976;
   John Hemming, *Amazon Frontier: The Defeat of the Brazilian Indians*, London: Macmillan, 1987.
10 Sommer, "Negotiated Settlements: Native Amazonians and Portuguese Policy in Pará, Brazil, 1758–
   1798." Ph.D. dissertation, University of New Mexico," 2000, 315.

well studied by scholars (as compared with the lesser amounts of locally produced material before and after).

The Abolition of the Directorate and the Emancipation of Indians

By the end of the eighteenth century, Coutinho proposed a revision of the Pombaline policy for the Indians in Pará. This was entirely in keeping with the spirit of the times for colonial Brazil and its 1790s generation of liberal reformers, of whom Coutinho's brother Rodrigo de Souza Coutinho was one of the most outstanding.[11] Although the "Directorate" for administering Indian villages was presented as corrupt, outdated, and easily abused by whites, the new regulations were very much in the same spirit and tone.[12] Both policies identified a group of people responsible for much of the ills of the province (the Jesuits in Furtado's case, and the directors, the Indian villages administrators, in Coutinho's). They were concerned with Indian welfare and the promotion of marriage between whites and Indians, offering concessions to those men who did set up with Indian women, strategies generally intended to develop the captaincy. Most critically, both programs were about the organization of labor and the stimulation of economic production by agricultural means. As Sommer notes, there was a "historic pattern," to the problems recognized and solutions offered in the colonial period.[13] In the Indian villages, *"The emancipation and civilization of Indians"* occasioned an important rupture whose effects would eventually lead to the Cabanagem rebellion.[14] One of its aims was to bring people together without prejudice – that "Indians would be treated without difference to the [Queen's] other vassals."[15] Yet, in practice, it divided even further the different and diverse interests at play in the region. In some respects there was continuity of policy and in others there was a developing chasm between the people who lived in Pará.

The key reform of the 1799 legislation was to remove the Crown from involvement in the organization of Indian labor. Indians were now free to

---

11 See Kenneth Maxwell, "The Generation of the 1790s and the Idea of a Luso-Brazilian Empire," in Dauril Alden (ed.), *The Colonial Roots of Modern Brazil*, Berkeley: University of California Press, 1973, 107–144; and see Kenneth Maxwell, *Conflicts and Conspiracies*, 206.

12 Governor Francisco de Souza Coutinho to Rodrigo Souza Coutinho, Belém, August 3, 1797, "Informação Sobre a Civilização dos Índios," AHU Pará Avulsos, cx. 109, doc. 8610. The plan was sent with a proposal to develop shipping from Belém to Matto Grosso along the Madeira.

13 Sommer, "Negotiated Settlements," 308.

14 The royal letter was signed May 12, 1798, Prince Regent to Francisco Coutinho de Souza, "Carta Régia ao Capitão-Geral do Pará Acerca da Emancipação e Civilisação dos Índios; e Resposta do Mesmo Acerca da Sua Execução," RIHGB, vol. 20, 1857, 433–450. The instructions for its implementation were sent out in January 1799.

15 "Carta Régia," RIHGB, 434.

work for themselves so long as they established their own homesteads and farms. If they did not, or were unmarried, they would be recruited for a royal labor corps (*corpos do real servício*) that permanently engaged workers on various projects. All Indians as well as mestiços and those without property and slaves were to be registered in militia units (*corpos de milicias*) administered by district. For part of the year these people would have to work on whatever it was the officers demanded, such as building a church, cutting wood, tracking down runaway slaves, and so on.[16] For performing this service they would be paid a daily salary, which was a portion of salt and some rum (*aguardente*). Funds for these payments would be raised from town councils, which were able to collect some taxes and oversaw the appointment of officers (though the governor would still approve them). Coutinho was very concerned that this work not be too burdensome to the militia soldiers so as to detract from their own domestic economy. So he left the precise details of the length of obligatory labor service to officers; presumably because he believed they would be sensitive to local needs.

Coutinho also granted various people exemptions from annual labor service. If a man enlisted in the militia paid more in his tithe payment than a soldier's salary, he would not have to leave his family. A private employer could also take on a man ready for service if he could be paid the equivalent of a soldier. Whites who married Indians were exempt from all public service, such as serving as military officers, judges, and councilors. These individuals would be allowed to build on their success and act as examples to others.[17] However, at the other end of the spectrum, those who refused to settle down or work for others would be forced to join the royal labor corps.[18] To this end, the activity of each man listed in the town's militia regiments would be reviewed every six months.

The Crown would also auction off state-owned property and some of the royal firms, though it would keep the most lucrative ones such as the Royal Cacao plantation near Santarém, the various fisheries, and the boatyard in Belém. In this way, the state was removed from overseeing the day-to-day running of the interior, where the Indian villages were, though it would continue to demand a tithe from all producers when they sold their produce in Belém. Politically, this absence was filled by the rise of local councils (*câmaras*, see the following discussion).

16 Some projects are listed in "Carta Régia," RIHGB, 456.

17 Also exempt from militia work were those paddlers and pilots who went to Belém to sell the produce annually and those who worked on the royal firms, the fishery, and cacao plantation.

18 About fifty came from villages in the Lower Amazon; they were based in Belém, "Relação dos Novos Alistados," captain Joaquim Francisco Printes to Governador Francisco de Souza Coutinho, Santarém, April 24, 1799, APEP cod. 561, doc. 34 and Captain Manoel Antônio da Costa Souto Maior to Governor Francisco de Souza Coutinho, Santarém, July 19, 1800, APEP cod. 575, doc. 31.

As noted, the availability of labor had always been a problem: a constant shortage of labor and what laborers there were tended to desert, slack off, or mutiny. Coutinho was acutely aware of this background as well as the abuse of those who commanded labor. To end this state of affairs, his proposal was that each man enlisted in the militia would work for themselves for part of the year (or for an employer) and then for the local militia unit for the rest. This strategy would encourage people to settle down in their own establishments. (It might also encourage employers to compete for labor by paying well.) So the incentive was to move out of annual labor service – work hard to produce more. The interests of the peasant family became those of the state. If the Mendonça Furtado's reforms were essentially mercantilist in spirit, Coutinho's were an Amazonian implementation of the physiocratic approach to economic life.[19]

In summary, the Amazon region had been only tentatively part of the Portuguese empire before the arrival of Mendonça Furtado as governor in 1750. From this time onwards, there was an aggressive implementation of state-led plans for development. The state not only enforced royal law and collected revenue, it protected the frontiers of the northern part of the colony and became "an influential employer, entrepreneur and director of the economy."[20] The public sector was greatly expanded in the eighteenth century and compared well with other regions of Portuguese America; the involvement of the state in the region was "probably of a greater magnitude" than private interests.[21] The end of the century saw a development of these state-led initiatives and engagement, this time retreating from the direct employment of Indians in villages and the handing over of control of labor to military officers and strengthening the power of town councils. The

---

19 Before the ending of the Directorate, Indians were employed in four ways. The first was the village-organized collecting expeditions, which accounted for about thirty percent of men and were mostly profitable. The directors were allowed a sixth of total profits, and since they were already subsidized by the state by the supply of provisions, it is not surprising that Coutinho identified the directors, on paper and with some evidence, as the villains of the piece. The second kind of work was village-based, such as boat building, agriculture, and craft manufacture and accounted for about thirty percent. The third form of engagement was in the royal companies, which consisted of about twenty-two percent of the work force. And the fourth form was to private individuals, arranged through a license from local officials. The number of Indians involved in this kind of service is unknown but likely to have been about twenty percent. All figures on the breakup of the working population are from Anderson, "Following Curupira," 125. For different figures, see also Colin MacLachlan, "The Indian Labor Structure in the Portuguese Amazon," in Dauril Alden (ed.), *The Colonial Roots of Modern Brazil*, Berkeley: University of California Press, 1973, 221; see also Sommer, "Negotiated Settlements," 324. At the beginning of the Directorate an estimated 3,375 male Indians were available for work; MacLachlan, "The Indian Labour Structure," 208. By the end of the period, the number had dropped to 2,249 males and 722 Indian women, Souza Coutinho, "Informação," paragraph 20.
20 Davidson, "Rivers and Empire," 229.
21 Ibid.

region remained somewhat separate but the market and production stimulating reforms initiated by Coutinho would consolidate its position in the Luso-Brazilian empire envisaged by the liberal reformers. The Indians who had gained a measure of local political dominance during the Directorate were now marginalized from the larger towns' political life and forced to retreat to the countryside and juggle the competing demands of domestic needs and obligations to the militias. The rest of this chapter will elaborate on these points.

The Impact of the New Policies for the Nineteenth Century

The "Royal letter" to Coutinho advising him on the emancipation and civilization of Indians (May 1798) was an amended and slightly expanded version of his own "Plan" (August 1797). The instructions for bringing the charter into law were then rewritten by Coutinho and circulated to the Directorate villages in January 1799, once key individuals had been identified to implement the changes. The dissolution of the Directorate consisted of a coherent series of reforms designed to encourage production, intermarriage, and the fair functioning of the law. According to Coutinho, the directors were tyrants who gave no tutelage to the Indians; as a result, the Indians had no reason to stay in the villages.[22] One Indian had told the governor that "Pará was good for whites but terrible for Indians," offering an Amazonian variation on the theme that Brazil was "a hell for Blacks, a purgatory for whites, and a paradise for mulattos."[23]

The economic stimulation sought by Coutinho never became a reality. Employers could not get Indians to work for them, more than likely because Indians disliked the annual draft and being forced away from their affairs. The withdrawal of the state as the protector, monitor, and organizer of Indians in the villages permitted a return to the abusive and discriminatory practices of military officers and employers, who themselves had few resources. The negative consequences of the plan were far-reaching despite the good intentions of its author. Coutinho's proposal still envisaged Indians as victims of white corruption, just as the missionaries had done, and in need of protection. For this reason, somewhat paradoxically, he wanted to free them from special legislation. Inevitably this would mean they would mix with the other inhabitations of Pará. In truth, Coutinho favored the mestiço over the other kinds of people in Pará, since he reckoned

---

22 Coutinho, "Informação," paragraph 16.

23 Coutinho, "Informação," paragraph 19; see Charles Boxer, *The Golden Age of Brazil, 1695–1750: Growing Pains of a Colonial Society*, Berkeley: University of California Press, 1969, 1, quoting André João Antonil's *Cultura and Opulência do Brasil por suas Drogas e Minas*, first published in 1711.

they worked the hardest and embodied the best qualities of the Indian and the white.[24] The result was that those Indians living in the colonial system no longer enjoyed collective recognition. Individually they may have continued to be labeled Indian, as a term of abuse perhaps, but the term had no official status. Only those Indians defined as wild, indigenous, and unchristian remained a legal entity.

On a different note, Coutinho's vilification of directors was a matter of convenience for his government rather than a comprehensive analysis of the problems of the region. There was no strong evidence of crisis at the provincial level, since the economy and population were growing steadily and, in many Directorate villages, the Indian headmen were able to keep the directors in check. Coutinho surely must have been aware that the historical record showed that the forms of labor service he sought would be bad for the Indians: they would never be paid properly and officers would abuse their soldiers/workers. Furthermore, how easy would it be to judge whether someone should be exempt from labor service? Who would monitor payments to the militia? Internally and on paper, the region was in a better state than it had been since the coming of the Portuguese.[25] Admittedly, Pombal's and Mendonça Furtado's modernization of Amazonia as a colony was ongoing. Certainly, some Indians were in a "sad condition" and the economy could be more dynamic, but there was nothing new about those features.[26] Instead, what was at issue, as always, was labor and Coutinho's conviction that more revenue could be raised if people worked for themselves or for good salaries. Besides, the Amazon was being inserted into a new context.

Coutinho was the longest serving governor of the region in the colonial period (June 1790 – September 1803) – though unlike Mendonça Furtado he did not travel into the interior of the Amazon (at least there is no evidence of his doing so). His father, a close friend of Pombal, had been a governor of Angola and his elder brothers, during his time in the Amazon, were preparing their ascent to two of the highest positions in the empire. Rodrigo, Pombal's godson and the future Conde de Linhares, was the secretary for colonial affairs in Lisbon from 1796–1801 and would be the Brazilian minister for home affairs at the end of the colonial period in Rio. Domingos, the future Conde do Funchal, was the ambassador to Britain in this period.[27] By the time Francisco de Souza Coutinho had written the

---

24 Coutinho, "Informação," paragraph 14.
25 See Roberto Santos, *História Econômica da Amazônia, (1800–1920)*, São Paulo: Editora Queiroz, 1982.
26 Coutinho, "Informação," paragraphs 1, 20.
27 See Manoel Barata, *Formação Histórica do Pará*, Belem: Universidade Federal do Pará, 1973, 153–154, for Francisco de Souza Coutinho's obituary written in 1820; and Reis' entry for "Francisco de Souza Coutinho" in Joel Serrão's (ed.) *Dicionário de História do Portugal*, 1963–71, Lisbon: Iniciativas, 736–737.

Plan, he had already devised many solutions to regional problems, such as the setting up of a royal boatyard using hard Paraense timber to build ships of war, reformed the navy and army (which included outlawing color or class as criteria for organization of the regiments and promotion), initiated the policing of the Atlantic coast to stop contraband traffic, increased slave imports, promoted trade with Matto Grosso, and gave state support to a religious festival.[28] He also was fearful of a French invasion from Guyana and, aside from the Atlantic patrols, put troops on the northernmost border.[29]

As mentioned, the reforms also included the auction (*arrematação*) of much of the state's assets, which proved hard in some places because of the lack of private capital. A *mameluco* from Alter do Chão was the only person interested in buying a communal coffee plantation; he offered a fraction of its value and obtained it in 1801. In one town, communal lands were still to be auctioned off eleven years later, though this was because a group of Indians managed to hold on to them.[30] In general, the Indians were in no position to buy the land for they lacked finance.

One policy that sought to augment the labor force did have a measure of success. The Amerindians currently in peace agreements with the Portuguese included the Mundurucu and the Mura in the Lower Amazon and Madeira River region, and, in a more remote region, the Carajás on the Xingú River. Much of the text of both the Plan and the Royal letter is concerned with the encouragement of these groups to establish themselves near towns and make new settlements. The Amerindians should be treated properly, and offered trade goods, except for arms and munitions. For those who disregarded Indian rights, the gravest penalties ensued (separate legislation covered "heathen Indians," *gentios*). Missionaries should accompany the traders and soldiers who sought to bring the Indians near the settlers' establishments. By 1805 there were a number of newly created hamlets on the Tapajós River (Santa Cruz) and in between Óbidos and Manaus on the

---

28 Antônio L. M. Baena, *Compêndio das Eras do Pará*, Belém: Universidade Federal do Pará, 1969, 251; Davidson, "Rivers and Empire," 204–227.

29 Of the many letters in the 1790s see, for example, Governor Francisco de Souza Coutinho to Dom Rodrigo de Souza Coutinho, Belém, April 15, 1797, AHU Pará Avulsos, cx. 109, doc. 8566; Baena, *Compêndio das Eras*, 252. Discussions can be found in Flávio dos Santos Gomes, "A 'Safe Haven': Runaway Slaves, Mocambos, and Borders in Colonial Amazonia, Brazil," *Hispanic American Historical Review*, 82, 3, 2002, 469–498; Jonas Queiroz and Flavio Gomes, "Amazônia, Fronteiras e Identidades: Reconfigurações Coloniais e Pos-coloniais (Guianas- Séculos xviii-xix)," *Lusotopie*, 2002, 1, 25–49; Flavio dos Santos Gomes, "Etnicidade e Fronteiras Cruzadas nas Guianas (secs xviii-xx)," *Estudos Afroamericanos Virtual*, May 2004, 30–59.

30 Judge José Joaquim Pereira do Lago to Governor Francisco de Souza Coutinho, Alter do Chão, December 10, 1799, APEP cod. 575, doc. 48; Autos de demarcação da terra, Óbidos, March 19, 1812, APEP "Documento do Judiciário" – Comarca de Óbidos.

south side of the river (Juruti, Parintins, and Maués) containing a couple of thousand people altogether. Three men were principally responsible for the "resettlements": José Rodrigues Preto (from São Paulo), João Pedro Cordovil, and Angello Francisco Gatto. They no doubt benefited financially. In early 1800 Gatto informed the governor of his intention to enter into trade with the *gentio* Maués, using Silvestre José, an Indian who was "from that nation" and currently living in Óbidos, registered with the militia.[31] In the next decade, Cordovil was accused of theft and the exploitation of Indians, and Gatto of gun-running for the Mundurucu.[32] The Mura were portrayed as the Indian group in the worst condition by traveling scientists Spix and Martius and the priest André Fernandes de Souza. The rest of the story is taken up in later chapters.[33]

The new legislation was not only a continuation of the modernization plans but a quiet official celebration of the mixtures of Portuguese and Indian at a biological and cultural level. Of course, the recognized fusions omitted some subjects, such as religion. Nothing was said of the ubiquity of lingua geral, which apparently some slaves learned before Portuguese. Nothing was mentioned of well-established folk traditions of shamanic curing and witchcraft; health and medicine could reasonably be said to be a part of any plan for the civilization of Indians. Perhaps the assumption was that the Indian would die out if mixed with the Portuguese. Why then did the Prince regent and Coutinho both condemn the influence of white directors and praise the working capacity of mestiços? The Prince's words here were quite precise: "You [governor Coutinho] should be the instrument of the total civilization of these Indians, to the point of mixing up (*confundirem*) the two castes of Indians and whites into only one kind of useful vassal for the state and the church."[34] The plan sought to remove all barriers between Indians and others in the Amazon. The reality was that the Indians were thrown into the same world as the whites and mestiços and had to compete with them for the same kinds of resources: labor, land, and capital on one hand and local positions of power in the council on the other. At the same time they were also required to do part-time "military service."

31 Manoel Antônio da Costa Souto Maior to Governor Francisco de Souza Coutinho, Santarém, January 19, 1800, APEP cod. 572, doc. 01. The suggestion that Gatto would use an Indian who retains a specific ethnic identity is very important since it supports Sommer's claim that the Directorate had not effaced indigenous ethnicity.

32 *Autos e devassas* [against João Pedro Cordovil], Silves, n.d. [various witness statements taken over a number of years ending c. 1829, APEP cod. 607; judge Romão Jozé to Sargeant Major [the general commander of forces in the Lower Amazon] in Santarém, Pinhel [before July], 1805, APEP cod. 610, doc. 151.

33 See Governor Marcos de Noronha e Brito to Secretary of State João Rodrigues de Sá e Melo, Belém, October 27, 1803, AHU Pará Avulsos, cx. 127, doc. 9773; José Rodrigues Preto to Prince Regent, Silves, before June 15, 1804, AHU Pará Avulsos, cx. 129, doc. 9951; Baena, *Compêndio das Eras do Pará*, 257.

34 "Carta régia," RIHGB, 437.

Not only did the measure continue to separate them from others, it placed an impossible burden on them. This meant following the orders of commissioned officers to work on public and private projects. This obligation was detested by Indians and abused by officers, as will be discussed in the next section.

The Militarization of Labor

Up to the end of eighteenth century, the military presence in Pará was probably one of the smallest in Brazil. All non-Indians were enlisted in the militia, but this meant a large portion of the population – that is, the Indians – were not engaged in either full- or part-time military service. In 1798 Coutinho transformed this situation. Every man, regardless of race or class, was required to be counted in some military unit. This growing militarization was as much about having the personnel to keep order as being able to control the men in the ranks. Once again, another area of the region's life was being brought into line with the rest of the colony. More to the point, the reforms meant that it became increasingly impossible to separate civilian and military interests. Not only did the army embody race and class divisions, key political choices were rarely free of a militaristic element.[35]

The regular army was known as the *tropa da linha* and was composed at the time of two infantry regiments, one based in Belém and the other in Macapá.[36] From Macapá detachments were sent to the rest of the region, including policing the frontiers and manning the forts with small detachments. The majority of soldiers in these regiments came from Portugal. In the early nineteenth century new cavalry and artillery regiments were added, principally with Paraense recruits (some were probably forcibly enlisted). Regular troops traveled up and down the Amazon frequently in armed canoes; they could requisition food and labor from any town, potentially depleting stores. It is not difficult to imagine the disorder such a visitation might make.

---

35 Hendrik Kraay, *Race, State and the Armed Forces in Independence-Era Brazil: Bahia, 1790s–1840s,* Stanford: Stanford University Press, 2001, 2. Surprisingly, Kraay's excellent and readable study offers one of the few book-length analyses of the Brazilian military. See also Roberta Marx Delson, "The Beginnings of Professionalization in the Brazilian Military: The Eighteenth Century Corps of Engineers," *The Americas,* April 1995, 555–574, for a specific aspect of the Brazilian case. General summaries on military organization can be found in Vainfas, *Dicionário do Brasil Colonial,* 395–396, and Caio Prado, *The Colonial Background,* 361–364. The history of Pará's military is given by Baena, *Ensaio Corográphico Sobre a Província do Pará,* Brasilia: Senado Federal, 2004 [1839], 131–135 and 149–156.

36 Baena, *Ensaio Corográphico,* 133.

Recruitment to the regular troops would sometimes happen under duress. Indeed, this was common practice in colonial Brazil (and in the Empire) when an army needed to be raised. Special officers were charged with recruitment and it seems it did not matter much who was selected. In particular, those people who fell afoul of the law, such as "vagabonds," were sent to Belém and conscripted to the army. Money to pay these troops in the early nineteenth was raised by the government but frequently salaries were not paid, a constant source of disquiet.[37]

The second level of the military body was the *milicias*, militia or auxiliary forces. These were divided into regiments according to neighborhood (there were nine in the Amazon). The purpose of the new militia was for organizing labor and maintaining order. Coutinho stipulated that militia soldiers wear a black cotton uniform consisting of a shirt and shorts. Officers should be marked out but it was left to them to decide what to wear. Since militia activities and their duration were locally administered, little information was sent to the governor. Nevertheless, Antônio Baena, himself an outstanding military officer as well as writer, came to speak highly of Pará's soldiers and especially the militia which, he reckoned, attained the same level of competence as the regular troops.[38]

The third military body was known as the *corpos das ordenanças*, or territorial units. In colonial Brazil, this level was designed to include all who fell outside of the previous two: that is, those whose jobs prevented them from being called up (for example, priests), the injured, and nobles. However, in times of emergency, such as a rebellion, they could be required to help suppress disorder. In Pará and the Rio Negro, these territorial units were never very strong. Coutinho decided to disband them, rename them the *corpos dos ligeiros*, and put them under the same command as the corpos das milicias. It would include the same people as the *ordenanças* and also those exempt from labor service. They could be called upon for local action at a moment's notice, which is probably the origin of their name.

The 1799 instructions ordered that the officials in charge of these units be interchangeably Indians and whites (*serão promiscuamente brancos e índios*) and be chosen from the same district as the men they commanded.[39] The choice of officers should be by election; candidates should be selected from the Indian nobility (and Indians in authorized positions) and any "whites." This practice may have been employed in the first few years of the nineteenth century but Indians were pushed quickly out of officer roles. The names of the most officers in the Lower Amazon were self-identified whites

---

37 Ronaldo Braga Charlet, "Construção da Hierarquia Militar no Pará: Contestações e Negociações Dentro da Ordem, 1808–1822," master's thesis, Belém: Federal University of Pará, 2000, 48, 74–75.
38 Baena, *Ensaio Corográphico*, 154–156
39 "Carta Régia," RIHGB, 451.

and many had property and slaves. This development introduced a new hierarchy along racial and class lines.

As stated, the objective was for the militias not to be racial segregated. All posts and units should have been mixed up, which was a radical difference to the rest of Brazil where regiments were organized according to class and race.[40] However, the intention was short-lived. Soon "whites" were able to control the councils and military positions (see the following discussion). We should remember that those people who were whites were those who were in an influential position in local society. A promotion to an officer rank might contribute to being seen as white. In other words, whites sought to distinguish themselves from Indians, freed blacks, and mestiços by controlling these positions of authority. It is not surprising some families spent much of their time squabbling among themselves.

The militia lists for Pará do not contain consistent information on the kind of engagement of each person. For example, some town rolls do not have complete details of the service of each man. Nevertheless, for the Lower Amazon some important information can be discerned (data on other areas could not be found). Without complete figures, no general conclusions can be drawn, but the data does reveal some patterns worth noting (see Table 4.1). The largest category is men who were ready for service (*prompto*) for either the militia or an employer (294, 42 percent) in the towns on the Tapajós River. In some villages the second category (royal service) is not much smaller than the first. These men (207, 29 percent) worked on special Crown projects such as boat building in Belém (the number of those in such work was not higher in Vila Franca because of the royal fishery). The third and last significant category is that of the men who were earning enough from their domestic group to exempt them from militia duty. These numbers are small, however: only 60 male heads of households, or 9 percent, and most of them lived in Santarém. The reason for the higher figure in that place could be its better general economic situation, the greater circulation of products and people. The more upstream and isolated the town, the fewer the numbers of exempt soldiers. Yet Vila Franca does not fit this pattern since it has no one in the category and is relatively near Santarém. The town certainly did present a special situation: the largest number of Indians and the royal fishery. Moreover, during the Cabanagem it was the nearest town to the rebel fort of Ecuipiranga. Overall, the figures reveal that significant numbers (77 percent) of poor men who lived in the Tapajós region were engaged in part-time service either to the Crown to local council-controlled activities or to private employers. While not conclusive, this data suggests that the

40 Kraay, *Race, State and Armed Forces*, 82–83.

nearer to congregations of whites, such as Santarém, the higher the numbers of militia men not doing part-time duty (a corollary might have been the greater number of militia involved in employment to private individuals).

The establishment of the militias then had the effect of creating new fault lines in Amazonian colonial society. It pitted officers and council men against the soldiers and peasants. It also offered a way out. By developing a rural-based livelihood, they might escape the draft. Nevertheless, the reforms meant that rural areas became militarized in a way they had not been; a process that also gave a new lease of life to popular participation in political movements for it linked people directly with order and disorder, and political decisions. The militias survived independence and were only abolished in 1831 when they were replaced by the National Guards, a new institution based on the concept of the armed citizen. Recruits were expected to maintain order and put down rebellions and mutinies. They were subordinate to officers who were eligible to vote in council elections and hold local positions (that is, those who had an income above 100 mil réis). In other words, the formation of the National Guards reinforced extant social divisions and the oligarchical hold on local institutions.

Labor and the Peasantry

The militia never worked as Coutinho intended it: the Indians had little interest in working for it and the officers had no incentive to lead the groups of workers (unless they could be deployed on private business). Undoubtedly this failure was due to the emphasis on leaving the militia and setting up an independent farmstead. In his royal letter the Prince Regent wrote that the "Indians should not suddenly, but gradually and successively [be removed from compulsory service]" and he recommended the policy be reviewed in six months' time to find out how many have settled into their own "establishments," that is, farmsteads.[41] Aside from freeing up the market in labor, the Prince Regent wanted to create a peasantry.

In 1797 there were 900 working Indian men on the village rolls in the Lower Amazon.[42] In the first list of militia there were 1014, an increase mainly experienced in the areas on the Tapajós (Aveiros, Boim, Pinhel, and Alter do Chão), which could be due to the influx of Mundurucu and Maués Indians. In addition, there was a massive drop in the number of absentees (runaways) from villages (3 in 1799 compared to 75 in 1792), which implies that Indians thought something was to be gained from the reforms and allowing themselves to be listed.[43] Within four months of the circular

41 "Carta Régia," RIHGB, 439.
42 Sommer, "Negotiated Settlements," 324.
43 The figure of 75 absentees in 1792 for the Tapajós region is from Sommer, "Negotiated Settlements," 328.

Table 4.1 *Employment of militia in selected towns in the Lower Amazon, 1799*[44]

	Officers Ψ	Available for militia	Royal service	Private service	Contracted to council	Absent	Royal fishery	Royal Cacao plantation	Trading in Belém	Total
Santarém	17 [12%]	39 [27%]	35 [24%]	46 [31%]	4 [3%]	4 [3%]	1 [0.5%]	0	2 [2%]	147
Alter do Chão	11 [11%]	40 [40%]	34 [34%]	7 [7%]	3	0	2	0	3	100
Aveiros	13 [12%]	43 [41%]	40 [38%]	7 [6%]	0	0	2	0	0	105
Pinhel	10 [10%]	53 [55%]	30 [31%]	0	3 [4%]	0	0	0	0	96
Boim	9 [11%]	31 [39%]	36 [46%]	0	1 [1%]	0	2 [3%]	0	0	79
Vila Franca	12 [7%]	88 [49%]	32 [18%]	0	0	0	35 [20%]	3	8	178
Faro	8	42?	?	?	?	?	?	?	?	50
Óbidos	10	71?	?	?	?	?	?	?	?	81
Alenquer	8	69?	?	?	?	0	?	?	?	77
Monte Alegre	12	90?	?	?	?	0	?	?	?	101
Total	110	294* [42%]	207* [29%]	60* [9%]	11*	4*	42 [6%]*	3*	13*	1014

*Totals exclude Faro, Óbidos, Alenquer, and Monte Alegre, for which information was not available (705 people in all: that is, 70 percent of the total militia list, 1014).
Ψ Officers are those who are given titles; for example, sergeant listed at the outset of each place and Indian officials listed at end of each roll.

44 The data in Table 4.1 was compiled from "Relação dos Novos Alistados," Captain Joaquim Francisco Printes to Governador Francisco de Souza Coutinho, Santarém, April 24, 1799, APEP cod. 561, doc. 34. The compiler of the list did not have complete information for all towns. Given the militia were under local control, future lists were not sent to the governor so there can be no longitudinal view of those who managed to escape the draft.

announcing the end of the Directorate, the captain of Santarém informed the governor that "Indians are enthused with their new freedom but they now do not respect authority and obey orders. They have left the houses of the residents and stopped doing their services and cannot be made to fulfil their obligations. For this reason we no longer have agriculture and commerce and the goods have not been transported to Belém. The Indians are on occasions drunk, which has led to disorder, and deaths. We need a military detachment to keep control of the district." This letter was written in April, the key time of the seasonal year for reaping crops, returning from collecting expeditions, and taking cargo down river to Belém.[45]

A year later, the same captain provided another update from the Lower Amazon. He was at a loss to know the remedy for the ills of the towns, for the Indians had deserted them. They went to their homesteads for months on end and never returned. Moreover, they had no respect for the officials who supervised them and did not work for those who wanted to buy their labor (or for the militia). Instead, prospective employers had to go the hamlets in search of people and rarely had success.[46]

Nine percent of peasants from the Tapajós region had indeed bought themselves out of service to others (a figure that would be higher if information were available on the north bank towns for reasons mentioned above). Whether they already had small plots of land and enlarged them or their existing land was sufficient to produce enough to exceed their daily salary in the militia as required is difficult to know. So the old Indian villages were emptied and residents set up farms and houses in neighboring riverbank hamlets, made up of an extended family.[47] Further down river in Almeirim, local Indians immediately started to plant larger gardens and "enjoy her Majesty's honours."[48] No longer were they forced to work away from their families at the whim of others. Indians interpreted the new legislation in their own terms, as a freeing of their labor power – now they could work for themselves – and adapted their behavior accordingly.[49] Some of the Indian élite also retreated to the countryside, perhaps disgruntled with their diminishing position. Towns were not places that many people wanted to be because it meant one could be called upon by the local élite for service.

45 Captain Manuel Antônio da Costa de Souto Maior to Governor Francisco de Souza Coutinho, Santarém, April 24, 1799, APEP cod. 561, doc. 39.

46 Captain Manoel Antônio da Costa Souto Maior to Governor Francisco de Souza Coutinho, Santarém, July 19, 1800, APEP cod. 575, doc. 31.

47 The list of new militia recruits was by location of residence, so it is possible to see groupings of people according to locally recognized places. In fact, there was nothing new about towns being empty of people. This was a common complaint during the second half of the eighteenth century; see discussion in Sommer, "Negotiated Settlements," for example, 127.

48 Sommer, "Negotiated Settlements," 311–312.

49 Sommer, "Negotiated Settlements," 312.

From the point of view of the employers, the policy, which was supposed to help them, was disastrous. Too numerous to mention are complaints of the lack of workers as the new century dawned.[50] The situation threw prospective employers into competition with each other, with accusations of "theft" of Indian women from farms and men scouting the riverbanks for "willing" labor. The most common argument was about who had the right to call on the labor of another; for instance, the judge in Óbidos wanted his illegitimate son to be exempt from militia because he needed his labor at home but could not pay him enough.[51] One result was that greater numbers of slaves were introduced. Besides, the kind of labor needed for cacao production was seasonal and extensive, not ongoing and intensive as in sugar production. Outside the cacao harvest, one slave could look after two thousand trees (see below).

The post-Directorate legislation created the conditions in which a semi-autonomous peasantry could establish a strong social and economic standing in Paraense society at the beginning of the nineteenth century. This peasantry was ethnically heterogeneous, composed of Indians who moved away from their compulsory labor obligations in the villages, and poor whites, freed blacks, and mestiços who were probably already in the countryside. In addition, there was a sizeable mobile section of people who were either escaping justice or the army or who survived by doing odd jobs at farms along the river. Both these groups became the core fighters of the Cabanagem. The companies of the militia were still operating at the end of the colonial period in Pará, though with only a handful of individuals per town.[52] In the words of Alfonso de Souza, a town official in Vila Franca in 1818, the emancipation of Indians had meant that the town "has progressively diminished in the number of its people."[53] The Indians had fled and the people who were left recognized no authority and "respond with indecency when ordered to complete a task." On the other hand, Souza told the governor that "many are the Indians who are dispersed" in these districts. It is precisely these people who were recasting their political consciousness as they achieved a level of material security and ability to control their own labor. Their move to the countryside was not a withdrawal

---

50 Manuel Antônio da Costa de Souto Maior to Governor Francisco de Souza Coutinho, September 12, 1799, Santarém, for example, APEP cod. 561, doc. 65; Óbidos; Judge José Joaquim Perreira do Lago, Alter do Chão, August 15, 1800, cod 575, doc. 41; Judge Alfonso de Souza to Governor, Vila Franca, January 25, 1802, APEP cod. 597, doc. 12; Judge José Placido Pagones to Governor Conde dos Arcos, July 29, 1805, Óbidos, APEP cod. 623, doc. 152.

51 Pedro Estanistão Ferreira to Governor Francisco de Souza Coutinho, Obidos, October 8, 1799, APEP cod. 575, doc. 43.

52 For example, see town council of Óbidos to Governor, Óbidos, August 3, 1819, APEP cod. 636, doc. 124.

53 APEP cod. 684, doc. 77, Alfonso de Souza, March 2, 1818, Vila Franca.

from society but a development of their awareness of their position and value and relationship to the state. They were flourishing in the space in between Indian nations and white controlled colonial society.

Local Élite and Town Councils

The other set of people, who were not distinct from this new peasantry, were the élite who sought positions on the town councils. It will be recalled that these individuals were also a diverse bunch of slave owners, cacao planters, military officers, and full-time administrators. They also combined many jobs. The term *élite* is strictly inaccurate for they were not much better off than their poorer counterparts and did not occupy really powerful political offices. Nevertheless, they were able to control public resources and strategically place themselves on, or near those who were on, municipal boards. Even though they were small fish in a big river, the influence they could wield on a local level was considerable. A select few were wealthy enough to send their children to attend Coimbra University. The only people who voted were those who had a certain amount of property, which meant that the most influential families were elected. The result was that town councils "advocated, articulated and protected the interests of local élites."[54]

In his circular letter to the military captains ending the Directorate, Coutinho said that the system had to be abolished because of the despotism, tyrannical rule, and insolence of the directors.[55] He instructed each captain to entrust the town council with the responsibility to implement the new rules. There would be elections, and the governor recommended that councils incorporate the headmen, if they were not already in place, by putting them up for election to the council posts if they were suitably qualified.[56] The elections that followed were not universal; the only individuals who could vote were those considered *homens bons*, defined by an income of more than 100 mil-réis.[57] In the absence of other state representatives, the municipal council became the most important local form of government linked to the state administration. If members of the council were elected, "the popular vote would recognize those people who are

54 Alfred Russell Wood, "Centers and Peripheries in the Luso-Brazilian World 1500–1808," in Christine Daniels and Michael Kennedy (eds.), *Negotiated Empires: Centers and Peripheries in the Americas, 1500–1820*, New York: Routledge, 2002, 117. I counted 35 Paraense graduates of Coimbra between 1772 and 1823, Francisco Morais, "Estudantes Brasileiros na Universidade de Coimbra (1772–1872)." *ABNRJ*, 62 (1940): 137–335.

55 Francisco de Souza Coutinho to military commanders in Pará, January 22, 1799, in "Carta régia," RIHGB, 458.

56 "Instruções Circular sobre a Formatura de Novos Corpos de Milicias," Francisco de Souza Coutinho, Pará, January 22, 1799, in "Carta régia," RIHGB, 451.

57 100 mil-réis was about the cost of a good slave; see also Prado, *Colonial Background*, 367.

competent to carry out the governor's orders" and put an end to the "monstrous acts" of a few tyrants.[58]

One feature of the absolutist state was the direct access those in remote regions of the empire had to the monarch. A slave, for example, could write complaining of abuse by a master and expect to receive a letter back on behalf of the highest authority. Similarly, councils in Brazil, according to Caio Prado, were not the lowest layer of colonial power; rather, they functioned as special departments of central government.[59] They were meant to implement new legislation and fulfill the demands of the regional governor, rather than act independently within their own enclave. There was a seamless connection between the various bodies of colonial rule. This characteristic of absolutism had the effect of integrating towns in the same political world and smothering local differences, at least on paper. However, the apparent homogeneity in the administration of Pará concealed deep intra and inter regional differences, which emerged in the early nineteenth century.[60]

Although Coutinho's vision for Pará gave special new responsibilities to the councils, they had come into existence following Mendonça Furtado's elevation of the old missions into towns in the 1750s. Yet the Paraense councils of the second half of the eighteenth century were limited, given the paucity of people outside of the Directorate. Belém had had a *câmara* since its origins in the early seventeenth century and it had played an important role in representing the colonists' point of view as distinct from the missionaries' and the Crown's. Each câmara was elected for three years and consisted of a judge-president (*juiz presidente*, who was in practice the same as the alderman, *juiz ordinário*), three councillors (*vereadores*), and a procurator (*procurador*). The council was required to nominate a scrivener (*escrivão*) and a tax collector (*almotacé or contratador da câmara*). The Prince Regent recommended in his royal letter of 1798 that the position of the judge alternate between whites and Indians; high hopes indeed! All these offices, except for the councillors, could start work only once they had received confirmation of their election by the governor. In other words, he could veto a particular person or delay his installation.[61] Councils were supposed to meet twice a week and members had to live in town rather than the interior; they raised taxes from local contracts, had the ability to make by-laws (which

58 "Instruções," in "Carta régia," RIHGB, 451.

59 Prado, *Colonial Background*, 372.

60 Alfred Russell-Wood, "Local Government in Portuguese America: A Study in Cultural Divergence," in his *Society and Government in Colonial Brazil*, Aldershot: Variorum, 1992. See also Charles Boxer, *Portuguese Society in the Tropics: The Municipal Councils of Goa, Macao, Bahia, and Luanda, 1510–1800*, Madison: University of Wisconsin, 1965; Prado, *Colonial Background*, 366–378.

61 See Prado, *Colonial Background*, 368, for details on the indirect and arcane form of voting involving small wax balls in the Portuguese empire. See also Baena, *Ensaio Corográfico*, 139, for Pará.

they did, particularly repressive measures to prevent congregations of rebels) and the handing out of contracts for the pottery, abattoir, sawmill, and cloth manufacture (for a fixed period giving a monopoly to the contractor).

Aside from their integrating function, councils were an important conduit of information from the "people" to the governor. According to Prado, the São Paulo council called itself the "head of the people" and informed the governor of complaints: "this was the source of their strength, and what empowered them to intervene – as they did intervene – and to take effective action in the successful implementation of independence, the drafting of the constitution and the founding of the Empire. The municipal council was the only administrative body that survived the wholesale destruction of all the colonial institutions."[62] Pará was no exception; each council expressed their support for independence by acclaiming the monarch.[63]

The running of councils underlays much of what happened in the buildup to the rebellion. Although corruption and favoritism were rife, they were conducted through official channels, as was the nature of an absolutist state. Two matters became very significant in the new lease of life given to Paraense town councils in the early 1800s: whether whites accepted the sharing of local power with Indians and mestiços, and whether there was conflict between élite families. In essence, both questions were about the character of social relations and how they were divided by race and class. In some instances, the conflict took on a colonial character – Portuguese versus Brazilians.

The first elections in Óbidos after the ending of the Directorate in April 1799, for example, ended with rival families (the Printzes and the Picanços) locked in combat. Each ordered verbal injury claims (*Autos de justificação*) against the other, and each accused the other of nepotism and not following the rules for nominating candidates who were related by kinship.[64] Complaints followed against one part of the Printz family, whose head of household was an ex-military officer, José Ricardo.[65] He had offended a Portuguese settler and lieutenant in the local militia who had become so infuriated he sought to return to his native country. Given that José Ricardo's brother Joaquim Francisco, was a military officer in Santarém,

62 Prado, *Colonial Background*, 372.
63 In addition, the 1824 constitution was put to the councils of provincial capitals, who were expected to approve it (as they did) and who were assumed to speak for the entire province. See João de Palma Muniz, *Adesão do Grão-Pará a Independência*, Belém: Conselho Estadual de Cultura, 1973 for a list of councils and the letters of acclamation.
64 Pedro Estanistão Ferreira to the town council of Óbidos, Óbidos, April 6, 1799, APEP cod. 559, doc. 32, and accompanying letters.
65 Antônio José dos Santos to Prince Regent, Alenquer, before June 26, 1800, AHU Pará Avulsos, cx. 117, doc. 9045.

entrusted by Coutinho with ending the Directorate in the Lower Amazon, he was able to brush off the criticisms.

In Santarém and Óbidos, the two larger towns of the Lower Amazon, none of the previous headmen was elected to the councils. They became officers of the light militia only. In places like Monte Alegre, Alenquer, Vila Franca, and Alter do Chão, the Indian noble presence in one form or another remained until the Cabanagem (see Chapter 3). Coutinho wrote to one council that it did not matter whether the nominated candidate could read or write; what was most important, he said, was their moral character.[66] One alderman in Monte Alegre admitted he was not up to the job because he did not know many of the rules, but somebody had to do it and he felt he had the right kind of personality.[67] In Alter do Chão, the principal was elected as the "parish judge because none of the other residents could read," implying it was the non-Indians who were illiterate.[68] An anonymous memorial written at the end of the 1820s reflected that the council administration in most towns was incompetent because it was carried out by Indians, who did not read and write.[69] This comment cannot be taken at face value, since the author of the document more than likely was not a local and probably identified most people as Indian. Nevertheless, it was a claim also leveled by many people against judges and councillors from the afore-mentioned towns.[70]

One of the key responsibilities falling to the câmaras in this new period was the retrieval of escaped slaves and in this the élites were united. The câmara organized a detachment of local forces to seek out the often-remote hideaways of the slaves. If any slaves were recovered, they were imprisoned until their owners paid their share of the costs of the expedition.[71]

Town councils were not a distinct layer of colonial and postcolonial bureaucracy. They existed to represent local interests to a central command and vice versa. The competition for offices arose from the ability to grant contracts to one's friends and family, to control the taxes raised from shops (*tavernas*) and other smaller forms of revenue, and to curry favor from the

---

66 Manoel Antônio Souto Maior to governor, Santarém, March 27, 1799, APEP cod. 561, doc. 29, and the reply (dated April 10, 1799) by Governor Coutinho written in the margin on moral character, and preference should be given to those people who have married Indian women and had legitimate children.

67 Judge Adão José de Mirelles to governor, Monte Alegre, April 2, 1811, APEP cod. 623, doc. 175.

68 José Joaquim Pereira do Lago to governor, Alter do Chão, December 10, 1799, APEP cod. 575, doc. 48.

69 "Memória," Antônio Marcelino Marinho Gamboa to President of Pará, April 10, 1828, APEP cod. 857, doc. 145.

70 For example, against the judge in Vila Franca, Alfonso de Souza, by the judge in Santarém, José Thomas de Aquino, Santarém, April 1820, APEP cod. 707, doc. 77.

71 See, for example, page 167 and town council of Santarém to Governor, Santarém, April 24, 1811, APEP cod. 636, doc. 46.

governor. The post-Directorate legislation allowed for a consolidation of the varied interests at play and the council was a central element of the strategy to achieve stability and continuity of élite family ties. The effect of this consolidation was increased social division and conflict over labor and land.

International Dimensions of the Amazon, c. 1808

Another aspect of Coutinho's 1797 "plan" was his concern over an overland escape route to French Guyana used by Indians and slaves. People needed to be treated more justly in order to prevent them from pursuing these desperate measures, he thought, though slaves were nowhere else mentioned. The French Guyana border lay at the extreme northeast of Portuguese America, and the Cabo do Norte region had long been known as a refuge for Indians and the location of *mocambos* (also known as *quilombos*, runaway slave communities).[72] Coutinho had, in fact, been concerned by the possibility of an invasion from French Guyana and the spread of the French revolution, in addition to the need to put an end to the clandestine commerce taking place along the Atlantic coast between foreign vessels. However, he was never able to realize this particular proposal, which was left to a later governor.

The invasion of Guyana was precipitated by the departure of the Portuguese royal court to Brazil at the end of 1807. The fear that Napoleon's troops would land in Guyana and enter Brazil through its northern frontier forced the Overseas Council (*Conselho Ultramarino*) into action. As soon as Dom Joao VI arrived in Rio de Janeiro in March 1808, he declared war on France, paving the way to an invasion of Guyana.[73] The King's statement observed that "the total ruin of Cayenne [the capital of Guyana] would be greatly esteemed by Royal interests. Of this conquest your Royal Highness only asks your Excellency [the governor of Pará, José Narciso de Magalhães e Menezes] he conserves and plants for Pará the nutmeg tree, which exists in Guyana and his Royal Highness has never been able to procure."[74] Such were the spoils of war. By December 1808 a force of six hundred soldiers composed of Indians, mestiços, and freed slaves had been assembled in their uniforms of black vests and shorts, as required in

---

72 Arthur Reis, "A Ocupação de Caiena," 315–340, in Sergio Buarque de Hollanda, *História Geral da Civilização Brasileira*, Tomo 2, "O Brasil Monarquico," vol. 3, Bertrand Brasil, Rio de Janeiro, 2003; Gomes, "Safe Haven."

73 See Maria Beatriz Nizza da Silva, "Apêndice: *Política* Externa de D. João VI no Respeitante a Definição Territorial do Brasil," 389–393, in Maria Beatriz Nizza da Silva (ed.), *O Império Luso-Brasileiro 1750–1822*, (*Nova História da Expansão Portuguesa, Vol. 3*), Lisboa: Editora Estampa, 1986; and Patrick Wilcken, *Empire Adrift*, London: Bloomsbury, 2004.

74 Reis, "A Ocupacão de Caiena," 322–323.

Coutinho's plan.[75] The troops advanced up the coast by sea, accompanied by a British sloop of war, *Confiance*, under the command of James Lucas Yeo. Most soldiers landed at Oiyapock and went by land to Cayenne while the navy went on and organized a blockade of the capital. The local governor gave up after little defense in January 1809. The Portuguese occupied the capital for most of the next nine years until November 1817 following the Congress of Vienna (1815) when Portugal was able to negotiate reparations for losses during the Napoleonic offensive.

At the time of the invasion, Guyana was serving as a penal colony as well as one of France's sugar-producing slave colonies. Following the moderate backlash to the reign of terror in Paris, "undesirables" were shipped off to Guyana. Some of these men were priests who favored the "sans culottes" movement.[76] Slavery had been reinstated but the successful revolution of slaves in Haiti stood as an example to all who wanted to overthrow their tyrannical masters. The presence of a Portuguese expeditionary force brought Paraense soldiers into direct contact with this revolutionary world.

With the border secured militarily, the authorities paid little attention to other possible transgressions: in particular, the effect of the intermingling of Paraense soldiers with some of the radicals of the French revolution. One thousand three hundred soldiers were stationed at any one time in Cayenne and there was also a turnover of personnel. In other words, a significant number of Pará's colonial inhabitants came into contact with ideas that would have spoken to their experience of subjugation and abuse at the hands of a Portuguese and Brazilian élite.

Not only the occupying troops, but also the soldiers back home in Pará may have been radicalized by the encounters and transformed by their experience. During the nine years of Portuguese presence, French residents and "undesirables" came down into the region, particularly to Belém. One radical Franciscan was Luis Zagalo, who was likely a friend of João Gonçalves Batista Campos, also a priest and the dominant figure of Pará's years of rebellion from 1820 onwards. Zagalo was an exile, in the same tradition of political thought as François Babeuf, also deported to Guyana.[77] During his two years in Pará from 1815 to 1817, Zagalo is said to have stirred up slaves with his sermons in Belém and Cametá. Not only did he introduce revolutionary ideas to Pará but he also recounted what had happened in Haiti and France. In an otherwise oppressive intellectual environment with no printing presses (they arrived in Pará in 1821), few books, and hardly any schools, someone like Zagalo must have seemed like a beacon of hope and

---

75 Baena, *Compêndio das Eras do Pará*, 275.

76 Reis, "A Ocupacão de Caiena," 319.

77 Babeuf was a prominent revolutionary who demanded a radical redistribution of wealth, and fermented revolution in France.

courage. More than likely there were others from Guyana, and perhaps elsewhere, who came to the Amazon and introduced new ideas and sentiments. Zagalo was eventually expelled for "spreading subversive ideas," having upset the bishop for using the church against the state.[78]

The influence of the Haitian and French revolutions on Paraense society and its intellectual climate is in need of more research.[79] What can be said is that Pará was affected by transatlantic events directly (as outlined above) and indirectly (through modifications of policy). What is ironic about this Guyanan episode is the outcome was almost the opposite of the intention. What started as an attempt to secure a frontier from invasion led to the exposure of Paraenses to an insurrectionary world. These new ideas and pressures should also be juxtaposed with the ever-strong connection between Belém and Portugal; even though the latter was in French hands, there was still constant traffic of people and goods between the two places. On the ground, the innovative programs from outside and the old regime were in conflict, based in very different visions of society.

However, there were other important international dimensions to the Amazon. While Pará was invading Guyana, the ports of the Atlantic coast of Brazil were opened to friendly countries, principally Britain but also North America. This new policy arose as a result of British influence at the Portuguese court, especially strong since the British navy had helped the Court depart from Lisbon in a rush in November 1807. Previously, contraband commerce had been taking place, as mentioned above, along the coast to the north of the mouth of the Amazon. This traffic involved the French but could easily have involved ships of Britain, the United States, the Netherlands, and Spain coming down from the Caribbean, all of whom had a presence in Belém at the end of the second decade of the nineteenth century. The first British record of business in Belém dates from 1819 when there were seven agents for British trading enterprises in Liverpool and Glasgow.[80] At the time of independence, about ten British agents were based in Belém and a handful of correspondents placed upriver.[81]

---

78 Arthur Reis, *Dom Romualdo Coelho de Souza*, Belém, 1941, 26; Vicente Salles, *O Negro do Pará*, 1971.

79 See Rosa Acevedo Marin, "A Influência da Revolução Francesa no Grão-Pará," in José Carlos da Cunha (ed.), *Ecologia, Desenvolvimento e Cooperação na Amazônia*, Belém: UNAMAZ, UFPA, 1992, 34–59.

80 The first consular correspondence in Belém can be found in "Consûles Estrangeiros," APEP cod. 673. A new book on the Hesketh family, which came to my attention once this manuscript was complete, sheds light on the work of being a foreign consul and presents research on the dramatic lives of the three Hesketh brothers who lived in Brazil: William, Robert, and John. John witnessed the Cabanagem firsthand and died of illness shortly after the rebellion, leaving his Brazilian wife and family destitute. (Ian Sargen, *Our Men in Brazil: The Hesketh Brothers Abroad*, Lancaster: Scotforth Books, 2009.)

81 This calculation is made from correspondence between John Hesketh and the British Minister in Rio between 1824–1828 in the National Archives, London, Foreign Office, General Correspondence with Brazil before 1906, e.g. NAL FO 13, 13 (1825), when John Hesketh was vice-consul in Belém.

By the time of the Cabanagem, there were eighteen British men in Belém and also consulates from France, Russia, Britain, and the United States in addition to a number of foreign traders, sailors, mercenaries, and other itinerant individuals. In 1849 there were 1,666 foreigners in Pará (including 1,118 in Belém and 171 in the Lower Amazon, 96 around Manaus).[82]

The coincidence of the occupation of Cayenne and the opening of the ports put an end to the illegal commerce on the Atlantic Coast of the Cabo do Norte region – though it may have continued in some measure to avoid the taxes imposed on foreign goods. Late in the 1810s the presence of foreign traders meant an increase in such goods as wine, oils, tools, cloth, and luxury items, which few people could afford and most had little use for. From being an economy that supplied the mother country with a few natural products and brought in few goods, Pará became a net importer in the 1820s and 1830s.[83] The situation would not change until rubber exports increased in the late 1840s.

Economic Aspects of Amazonia in the Early Nineteenth Century

At the end of the eighteenth century, Amazonia's export products were of a relatively high standing. Exports provided significant revenue for the royal treasury, much of which was derived from Indian labor, and the region had the fifth largest port (in terms of export values) in Brazil. The main exports were cacao, coffee, and rice, produced privately and from Indian villages. Cacao was by far the greatest single source of revenue, accounting for nearly all of the Portuguese empire's production and a quarter of the world's. Its quality was rather second-rate, however, and its harvest liable to spoil if the flood of the Amazon River was high. The reforms of 1798 benefited the richer planters who were able to afford Indian labor and profit from the changes, such as buying up formerly state-owned lands when they were auctioned as part of the reforms. Indeed, the two key areas of the region most affected by these shifts at the end of the century were the main cacao-growing regions of the lower Tocantins River around Cametá and the Lower Amazon around Santarém.

Before considering the singular importance of cacao and the agrarian structure, the general economic picture should be described. As has been

82 James Henderson, *A History of Brazil, Comprising its Geography, Commerce, Colonization, Aboriginal Inhabitants*, London: Longman, Hurst, Rees, 1821, 464, 10–15 ships from Liverpool, 1–2 from London. In 1829, 21 ships arrived from Britain, John Hesketh to British Minister, Belém, July 1830, NAL, FO 13, 77 (1830), f. 99; "Mapa Estatistica da População do Pará em 1849," BNRJ I – 32, 10, 4.

83 For a list of goods, see Ignácio de Cerqueira e Silva Accioli, *Corografia Paraense, ou Descripção Fisica, Historica, e Política, da Provincia do Gram-Pará*, Bahia, 1833, 155. For imports and exports data see Santos, *História Econômica da Amazônia*, 30, 37, 290, British Consular Reports in the NAL, and presidential addresses from Pará.

mentioned, Amazonia never succeeded in developing a plantation economy; environmental and labor constraints prevented dependence on a single export. Instead, its economy was generally diverse, seasonal, and cyclical; this has consistently been one of the characteristics that separates Amazonia from the rest of Brazil. Furthermore, at least since colonial times, people have moved across environments (flood plain/uplands and rural/urban) to pursue opportunities and coordinate different seasonal activities. The general economic character of the early nineteenth century was based around the provision for local subsistence needs and the export market. The economy involved extraction, or collection of the drogas do sertão, agriculture, hunting, and pastoralism. Frequently, peasant hamlets combined these activities over the course of the year and pooled their labor.[84] Economic specialization was hardly an option for peasant households.

In the absence of archival documentation on the domestic economy to support this claim, the following argument can be offered. Little is known of the internal market for goods at the beginning of the nineteenth century. Indeed, it appears that there were few if any markets in the Amazon. Writing in 1784 the naturalist Alexandre Rodrigues Ferreira complained that Belém had no place to buy fruit, vegetables, or fish or any other thing he wanted to buy.[85] Indeed, it appears Coutinho instituted the first market (*feira*) for goods in Belém at the very end of the eighteenth century. Writing about the Amazonia of the missionary phase, that is, the early to mid eighteenth century, the missionary João Daniel says that what also set the region apart from the rest of Brazil at the time was the lack of markets in the villages; instead, settlers and Indians visited each other's dispersed homesteads to trade, sometimes on very disadvantageous terms. He also mentions the river traders who went from one riverbank house to the next, buying products for resale, often in exchange for rum (one of the main forms of "currency" at this time). Some of these products would have been cultivated and others collected.[86]

Daniel attributed the absence of markets to the low level of economic development in Amazonia. There were not enough of the right kinds of products to sustain a local economy. Most goods of monetary value went down river to Belém for export. He remarked on the near total dependence of human life on the river, which recalls Bates' observation at the opening of

---

84 See Ciro Flammarion Cardoso, *Economia e Sociedade em Áreas Coloniais Periféricas: Guiana Francesa e Pará*, Rio de Janeiro: Graal, 1984, 126, for a summary of Pará's economy in the late colonial period. Cardoso's study is well-researched and takes little for granted, focusing on slavery and its economic importance.

85 Cited in Cardoso, *Economia e Sociedade*, 129.

86 João Daniel, *O Tesouro Descoberto no Máximo Rio Amazonas*, Rio de Janeiro: Editora Contrapunto, 2003, vol. 2, 225–227.

Chapter 2.[87] All those who lived near rivers had canoes or boats and looked after their own sustenance; there was little left over. Because their work did not produce goods, missionaries and administrators thus had nowhere to buy their food. They also lacked canoes to travel. Without markets or transport, how could they obtain food to eat? Daniel recounts that this meant those like him had to hire canoes and paddlers to go from house to house begging for food. At the beginning of the nineteenth century, the situation was not much different. Family networks (and other informal mechanisms) were the means for the distribution of foodstuffs. In other words, the political significance of the family is matched by its economic importance. This meant that the work done producing goods to be sent down river had to be set against subsistence activities. One shaped the other.

What about women's economic role? We have already seen the constraints placed on some men's labor in the form of their compulsory labor service. Did this place an extra burden on women who remained at home? Women's work, as we saw partly in the previous chapter, involved agriculture, especially the making of manioc flour and related products. They also took part in collecting expeditions, especially of turtle eggs and Brazil nuts, and they produced artisanal goods such as hammocks, ceramics, and calabash dishes. It is likely they fished and hunted if men were absent. Women also worked on cacao plantations, opening the pods and drying the seeds, which needed turning every so often.[88] Their economic role, particularly in the providing, preparing, and serving food, was paramount to the functioning of peasant households. This characteristic may have given a matrifocal stress to the peasant economy, which contrasted with their near political invisibility on town councils.

In order to further highlight the economic singularity of Pará it is worth comparing it with neighboring Maranhão. There, the population profile was quite different, revealing the dissimilar basis of their economies. Forty-six percent of Maranhão's population owned slaves (compared to 25 percent in Pará), and consequently more freed blacks at seventeen percent (figure unknown for Pará), only five percent Indians in Directorate villages (30 percent in Pará), and the rest were classified as white.[89] As Colin Maclachlan points out, the greater slave body indicates the dependence

---

87 Daniel, *O Tesouro Descoberto*, vol. 2, 213.

88 This list is based on a variety of sources: unpublished documents that mention women's gardens, the images in the Alexandre Rodrigues Ferreira *Viagem Filosófica* collection, and contemporary accounts. See also Sommer, "Negotiated Settlements," 123–131, which discusses women's economic activities during the Directorate. She argues that women's agricultural focus was not because men were absent but part of traditional division of labor in Indian groups.

89 Colin MacLachlan, "Slave Trade in Amazonia," in Robert B. Toplin (ed.), *Slavery and Race in Latin America*, 1974, Westport: Greenwood, 136–137.

of Maranhão on servile labor picking cotton and planting rice, whereas Pará was predominantly an economy based on the extraction of wild products from the backlands. The fact that there was a class of white people in the census suggests a greater degree of hierarchy than Pará, as well as the ongoing attempt in that place to reduce the significance of racial divisions.[90]

Despite its significant slave population, Pará was unable to develop the plantation economy in the way Maranhão had. Its immense territory dwarfed all other continental areas, but its population was only four percent of Brazil's total and its economy provided for four percent of the value of Brazil's exports.[91] In numerical terms, Maranhão had almost double the slaves of Pará (but a lower total population and a much smaller area of land) and provided twelve percent of exports from Brazil. Imports reveal another aspect of the economic and social character of the Amazon at the dawn of the nineteenth century: Maranhão imported nine percent and Pará five percent of the total imports to Brazil in the period 1796–1807, before the opening of Brazilian ports to international trade. In other words, Pará was importing (5 percent of total value) slightly more than it was exporting (4 percent value). This imbalance would worsen in the first decades of the nineteenth century with the entry of English, U.S., and French traders keen to place their goods. It led to an outflow of coinage from the region, the introduction of counterfeit money, and the devaluation of existing currency, all of which climaxed in the early 1830s.

Cacao and the Agrarian Sector

Cacao had been the Amazon's dominant export since the 1730s, when its prices on the world market were high and produced profits for settlers and missionaries alike. It grew wild along the riverbanks throughout the Lower Amazon from Manaus downwards, including tributaries such as the Madeira, Tocantins, and Trombetas. The wild cacao from the Amazon was preferred to the cultivated sort grown in places such as Venezuela, which allowed for larger and more reliable harvests each year. Throughout the eighteenth century, Indians harvested cacao in their seasonal village

---

90 Figures for Pará derive from the "Mapa Geral da População de Capitania do Pará em 1797," BIHGB IM 5. 5. 1. Of the 19,560 Directorate Indians in 1797, only 2,971 (2,249 men and 722 women) were available for work in the Indian-administered villages. The rest were too young, old, or ill to work and yet had to be supported by the others. By 1849 (when the transatlantic commerce in slaves had been stopped for fifteen years), there was a more even spread of slaves with about forty percent of slaves working outside of Belém, mostly on cacao plantations and rice farms.

91 Dauril Alden, "Late Colonial Brazil 1750–1808," in Leslie Bethell (ed.), *Colonial Brazil*, Cambridge: Cambridge University Press, 1991, 287; Alfred Russell-Wood, "Ports of Colonial Brazil," in his *Society and Government in Colonial Brazil*, 211.

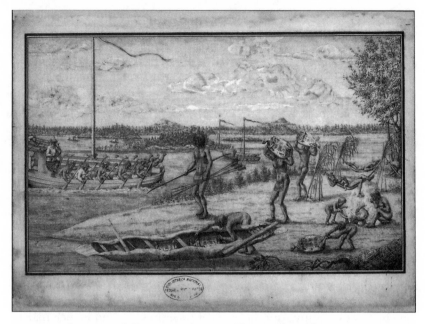

Image 4.1 Collecting expeditions and hunting for turtles, c. 1785

expeditions, but increasingly the crop came to be planted along the river banks by colonists and peasants.[92] The seeds had to be broken out of the pods and then dried before being dispatched in palm baskets and taken downriver to Belém to satisfy the European market in drinking chocolate.

During the first half of the Directorate, the production and export of cacao was a monopoly of the state. After 1777, however, the company's contract was not renewed and once again cacao was open to free trade and world prices. Production remained stagnant until the 1790s when Coutinho encouraged existing cacao growers to extend their properties, cheaper prices for slaves as an incentive and from this time it is possible to perceive more cacao being exported.[93] Wild cacao was being planted in what Dauril Alden calls "cacao corridor" – between Óbidos and Santarém.[94] In 1803 Coutinho

---

92 See Daniel, *O Tesouro Descoberto*, vol. 2, 84, for a description of these collecting expeditions. In the period 1761–1772 it is possible to differentiate between Indian and cacao planter levels of production. For an excellent recent analysis of their significance, see Heather Flynn Roller, "Colonial Collecting Expeditions and the Pursuit of Opportunities in the Amazonian Sertão, c. 1750–1800," *The Americas*, 66, 4, 2010, 435–467.

93 Baena, *Compêndio das Eras*, 237, 252.

94 Alden, "Cacao Production," 126, n. 173, citing the pastoral visits of Bishop Caetano Brandão who traveled the region a number of times in the late 1780s. See Luís A. de Oliveira Ramos (ed.), *Diários das Visitas Pastorais no Pará de D. Fr. Caetano Brandão*, Porto: Universidade do Porto, 1991.

wrote specifically to the town councils in that area instructing them in the use of new techniques for planting cacao seeds. In this way this area was set up to lead the development of cacao production.[95]

In 1797 the communal cacao plantation of the Indians in Óbidos had four thousand trees – a medium-sized orchard – and some individuals had five thousand trees (*pés de cacau*) and a few up to twenty thousand.[96] These plantations were stretched thinly following the riverbanks on the higher parts of the floodplains, and relied on a mixture of slave and Indian labor, though it is likely that after 1800 more slaves were used in attempt to expand production. One person could manage about two thousand trees through the year, work that would involve weeding, cutting dead branches, and so on. But during the harvest, many more people were needed to collect and open the pods, put the beans out to dry, and rotate them regularly.[97]

Cacao from Belém accounted for an average of sixty-one percent of the value of exports between 1756 and 1777 and fifty percent between 1776 and 1822; the drop is entirely due to the lower price of cacao, since production levels doubled or even tripled over the period.[98] In the disparity between the two figures lies one important economic origin of the Cabanagem rebellion, which as always in the Amazon has the special configuration of labor and land at the centre: little labor for large-scale production, lots of land but little in favored areas, and low levels of capital and technology.

In his study of the economic history of cacao production in the Brazilian Amazon from the time of the missions to the end of the colonial period, Dauril Alden concludes that:

95 Baena, *Compêndio das Eras*, 252.
96 For example, Mauricio José Valadão, Rio Surubi-Assú [Alenquer]. Conc. 20 de maio de 1803. Livro 19, para. 188, APEP "Catálogo das Sesmarias." The length of the land for the five thousand tress was deemed to be a half league of land, which was about two thousand five meters or just under two miles. The figure of twenty thousand trees has been calculated from the size of the land (about two leagues) and the stated use of the land in the land grant application.
97 According to Paul Le Cointe, each cacao tree can produce about between 200–300 grams of dried cacao; which means that a medium-sized orchard of five thousand trees could yield between 1,000 kg and 1,500 kg of cacao or between 68 and 102 arrobas. The price for cacao in 1800 was 2,400 réis per arroba in Belém, which means overall the owner will receive at least 163,200 réis from a harvest. In that year, a total of 127,181 arrobas were sent out from Belém, which means this hypothetical planter contributed roughly 0.08 percent of the total. Two years later, the price for an arroba of cacao was 1,150 réis, which would have meant more than a halving of gross income, Paul Le Cointe, *L'Amazonie Brésilienne*, Paris, vol. 2, 1922, 113–129.
98 According to a personal communication from Heather Flynn Roller, the level of cacao production from the Indian collecting expeditions in the first part of the Directorate (1761–1772) amounted to about twenty percent of this total. The rest was supplied by private parties who either collected or cultivated it. Her figures are based on the "Mapas Gerais do Rendimento" in AHU Pará Avulsos (for example, cx. 80, doc. 6627) for the period and the total cacao exports in Alden, "Cacao Production," 126–127.

It was cacao that encouraged the settlement of the Amazon during the eighteenth century and that produced a large share of the crown's income from that region. In the long run, however, cacao may have been disadvantageous to regional growth (because it was too dependent on a single crop). Certainly it did not bring about unlimited prosperity. As with staples in other production areas, prosperity for some, such as the merchants of Belém and Lisbon, meant misery for others, including the Indian paddlers, black slaves, and many marginal orchard owners. But who the people actually were and how much they benefited from the cacao industry are questions to which answers still need to be discovered.[99]

What is relevant here is the agrarian structure and the effect of this cacao boom for local society. What was the nature of the misery, which Alden reckons was the consequence of the boom? Let us recall that under the Directorate, Indians – especially the officer or noble class – had gained some standing in Pará's colonial world and could negotiate the terms of their inclusion in it. Following the end of the Directorate, they came to be at odds over the labor supply with owners of large orchards (or plantations) in the Lower Amazon, the most significant site for cacao in the Amazon. These relatively large cacao producers were the men who had been ceded land grants (as shown in the previous chapter). (This chapter also includes a land-grant image of cacao trees.) Many other large-scale planters did not seek to register their lands.

The rise in production, which can be viewed in Figure 4.1, is a consequence of more cacao being planted, more people planting, and the increased use of slave rather than Indian labor. From having no more than a few hundred slaves in the 1790s, the Lower Amazon and Tocantins areas came to have many thousands in the 1820s, mostly working in and around cacao plantations. The lands taken over for planting cacao bordered the rivers around the larger towns in the interior, Santarém and Cametá. Travelers in the early to mid-nineteenth century describe the monotony of the river banks in these places – the stumpy, wide-branched cacao tree for miles on end.[100] The lands where Indians once had their gardens and homes were progressively being taken over by land-grabbing cacao planters, who also bought up the old communal land auctioned off at the end of the Directorate. Certainly this happened in Óbidos, Alenquer, and Santarém, where Indians complained they had been thrown off the land they were

99 Alden, "Cacao Production," 132. For a discussion of control of cacao production in an earlier period see Dauril Alden, "Economic Aspects of the Expulsion of the Jesuits from Brazil: A Preliminary Report," in Henry Keith and S. F. Edwards (eds.), *Conflict and Continuity in Brazilian Society*, Columbia: University of South Carolina Press, 1969.

100 For example, see Henry Lister Maw, *Journal of a Passage from the Pacific to the Atlantic*, London, John Murray, 1829, 341–342. Also William Edwards, *A Voyage up the River Amazon including a Residence at Pará*, London: John Murray, 1847, 105–107.

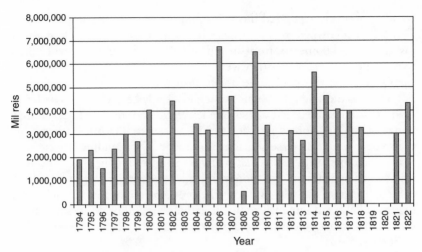

Figure 4.1 Cacao production in the Amazon, 1794–1822[101]

working. Planters responded by saying the Indians were not using it profitably. Land near towns on the main trunk of the Amazon River was at a premium in the first decades of the nineteenth century.

There is evidence to support the claim that Indians and other small-holders were at best marginalized and at worst thrown off their plots of land. *Grilhagem* (land-grabbing) is nothing new in the Amazon and took place with each successive economic phase. Priest André Fernandes de Souza worked with Indians as a missionary in the Upper Amazon region. Writing a report to Pedro 1 on the condition of the region, he stated that six kilometers above Manaus is a small river called Taroma: "At its mouth is the cacao plantation of the ex-governor [of the Rio Negro captaincy] José Joachim Victorio, in forming which he removed all the population, and obliged them to work on it with no other payment than a very slender subsistence, which was the principal cause of the desertion of the Indians."[102] This is unlikely to have been an isolated incident, but indicative of a general pattern taking place.

Generally, land could be possessed easily by constructing a hut and having someone live there for a year and a day.[103] As mentioned, the holding

---

101 Data from Alden, "Cacao Production," 133–134.
102 André Fernandes de Souza, "Notícias Geográphicas da Capitania do Rio Negro no Grande Rio Amazonas," RIHGB, 1848, 10, 410–504; part of which has been translated by William Smyth, "Account of the Rivers Amazon and Negro, from Recent Observations," *Journal of the Royal Geographical Society*, 1835, 15.
103 On land policy in Brazil at this time, see Emilia Viotti da Costa, *The Brazilian Empire: Myths and Histories*, Chapel Hill: University of North Carolina Press, 2000, 80–82. For Pará, see Itala Bezerra da Silveira, *Cabanagem: Uma Luta Perdida* . . . , Secretaria de Estado da Cultura, Belém: 1994, 123–134.

could be formally registered but this option frequently was not exercised. Formally, land owned by non-Indians had to be more than two leagues, or just under ten kilometers, from an Indian village. The rule allowed Indians to cultivate land near where they were supposed to settle. With the ending of the Directorate, this land came under great pressure from cacao planters: not only was the land near towns but it had already been cleared. The Jesuit João Daniel remarked that whites often preferred not to clear forest so they bought land and houses off the Indians at a very low price. Over time the settlers would increase the size of the land by expanding it with new gardens and orchards. Moreover, many non-Indian families had parcels of land spread out over an area, one with cattle, one with cacao, and so on.[104] Although Daniel was writing about the pre-Directorate period, such practices could only have intensified by the end of the century. More support for the gradual displacement of Indians from their village lands is presented in Chapter 5.

By 1828 a memorial from the Lower Amazon asserted that in the municipal districts of Santarém, Óbidos, and Alenquer, almost all land was covered by cacao trees.[105] The only land that remained unplanted was where the risk of flooding was too high. Other towns in the region had cacao but were more inclined to fishing and the making of manioc flour. As more and more land was swallowed up by men wanting to plant, some smallholders were pushed out to peripheral areas further away from towns and between plantations. So their efforts to create viable peasant households were disrupted by the cacao planters. This sheds a slightly different light on the comment by the judge from Vila Franca that Indians were dispersed in the districts. Rather, they were squeezed out. Whether they had moved voluntarily or forcibly in the space of thirty years, the agrarian structure had become more divided: more larger orchards worked by slaves, more small-scale peasant farms.

Annual exports of cacao fluctuated because the harvest depended on many factors, such as the care of the trees and the ground around them, their spacing, the age of the tree, and the strength of wind.[106] Although there was an increase in the volume of cacao exports, as shown by Alden's data, their value varied considerably on world markets.

An important factor in this period is the price of cacao on the world market. In the 1790s prices advanced as Venezuelan production was lost.[107] Prices then fell for all products in the following decade and fluctuated until

104 Daniel, *O Tesouro Descoberto*, vol. 2, 10–17.
105 Anonymous, "Memória" [of the Lower Amazon], December 1, 1828, APEP cod. 851, doc. 74.
106 Le Cointe, *L'Amazonie Brésilienne*, vol. 2, 113–129.
107 Alden, "Cacao Production," 129.

independence, so much so that a planter could receive two to three times the amount of money for the same quantity of crop from one year to the next. After independence, all Pará's main exports declined rapidly, possibly because Lisbon's merchants were prevented from trading.[108] From 1821 to 1830 the price of Pará's cacao dropped tenfold. During this decade the value of imports overtook the value of exports for the region and led to an outflow of cash. These factors put planters, slaves, workers, smallholders, and merchants under intense pressure in the 1820s and early 1830s. This economic crisis was combined with political instability and violence over independence.

The rise in price in the mid- to late 1790s may explain Coutinho's championing of cacao. But export levels did not rise, which Alden suggests was due to the lack of shipping. However, there is a complementary explanation: the ending of the Directorate was motivated (aside from the factors outlined above) by the need to supply extra labor and land for private cacao plantations. The rise in production did not really begin until the very early years of the 1800s, which fits the timescale rather well, for it takes about five years for a cacao tree to start producing fruit. Yet overall, the

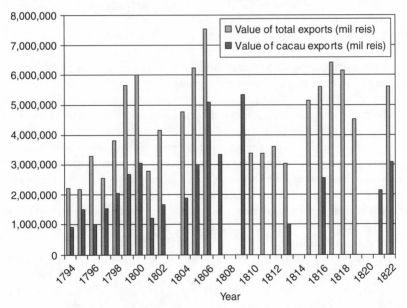

Figure 4.2 Relative value of exports from Pará, 1794–1822[109]

108 Santos, *História Econômica da Amazônia*, 31.
109 Data from Alden, "Cacao Production," 127.

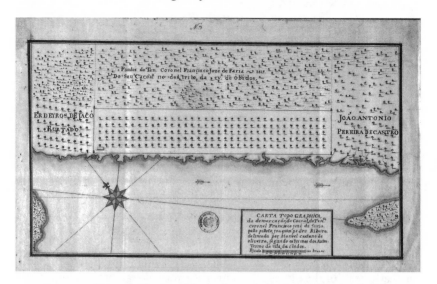

Image 4.2 Topographic map of the land grant belonging to Francisco José de
Faria, 1814 (*Carta topográphico do cacaol do tenente Francisco José de Faria pello
piloto Joaquim Pedro Ribeiro, delimitado por Manoel Caetano de Oliveira,
segundo os termos dos autos. Termo de Vila de Óbidos, 1814*)

returns varied from year to year as prices were affected by world events and
the demand in Europe.

Thus a single crop dominated the environmental, economic, and political situation of Pará, not just in the eighteenth century but also in the early
nineteenth century. Planters and their extended families dominated the
municipal councils in the more important economic districts outside
Belém. Given that the economy depended on cacao whose price and harvest
fluctuated, capital investment was highly restricted. All that could be done
was to try to harvest more, which meant occupying more land. In turn, the
workers who worked the trees and the pods, whether slave or peasant,
bore the brunt of this instability with increased pressure on their labor
and lands. The rise in cacao orchards was the nearest the Amazon had come
to a plantation style economy. Yet, general prosperity, as Alden says, never
resulted from cacao.

Planters may have controlled Pará during the first decades of the nineteenth century, but there was much other activity as well. Outside the
orchards were smallholding peasants who provided food for themselves
and supplied an export market. Some men were tied to a system of conscription to the militia for labor service; others were exempted. In some small
towns the smallholders had control of the councils. These people had diverse
origins: economically, they were peasants knowledgeable of seasonal resources who sold their labor and had extensive kinship networks. Connected by

trade and family to these people were some Indian nations, particularly the Mundurucu, Maués, and Mura. As we will see in the following chapter, there was a permeable boundary between Indians who lived in the forest and in riverine settlements near towns and plantations.

The balance between these various assemblies was delicate, not least because of the internal differences within them. Pará was a relatively mobile and seasonally organized society where continuity of residence and use of resources required great skill and management of labor. It was the heady mix of economic and agrarian crises and political conflict in postindependent Pará, both of which aggravated existing colonial divisions, that would feed into the explosive days of the Cabanagem.

This chapter has taken stock of the reforms introduced at the end of the eighteenth century and their impact in the nineteenth century. These changes were essentially economic in character. They were intended to take the state out of the control of labor and the ownership of land and to hand over responsibility of managing local resources to town councils and army barracks. The absence of physical markets for the sale of food was one sign of the uneven nature of Amazonian development. Nevertheless, there was an active economy albeit focused on exports and their sale in Belém. The Paraense experience of economic liberalism of the 1790s would give way to political changes in the 1820s and 1830s, the subject of future chapters. The overriding effect of the reforms examined here was to remove Indians from the center of attention in Pará and to shift the focus to the local élites who had managed to secure powerful positions in the countryside and the towns. But the Indians did not go away or disappear, as some commentators have implied. They remained intimately connected to colonial Pará and sought to defend their interests. Yet officially they were no longer treated as a collective body. Thus some of their interests converged with those of other peasants, mestiços, freed blacks, and poor whites.

5

Forms of Resistance in the Late
Colonial Period

Just minutes before he was declared the new president of Pará province, Eduardo Angelim made a speech that was of special importance. The date was August 26, 1835 and he stood in front of the neoclassical building of the Governor's palace in Belém. The city had just suffered great violence and destruction in the previous eight months and particularly in the last nine days. Rebels had managed to overtake the Rio-appointed president, Manuel Jorge Rodrigues, sent from the south and in post for only nine days, who escaped with British help. There followed great jubilation, but also massacres. Sixteen imperial soldiers, who were not advised by Rodrigues of his departure, took refuge in the beautiful baroque church of the Carmelite order at the end of the street leading along the river from the fort. They were eventually found by the rebels and taken out into the streets where they were cut up with swords and machetes. The partying continued, for once again the city was back in rebel hands.[1] The music could be heard even from the British naval ships anchored out of cannon shot from the shore. But the city could not go on in such disorder. Rebel leaders realized that discipline had to be imposed or the impostor forces would return. With most of the other leaders dead or imprisoned, Angelim, twenty-one years old, emerged as a young hopeful. He understood the significance of this moment.

Angelim started off by addressing the crowd as "Courageous people of Pará, valiant defenders of the homeland, and of liberty! After nine days and nights of murderous fire, we are the lords of the fair city of Belém, capital of this province." Instead of saying he was a revolutionary – which is how historians have portrayed him – Angelim calls Rodrigues the rebel because he had no mandate from the people. "Each one of you now should be like a father, protecting the innocent and handing down the future the homeland (*patria*) deserves."[2] The people, he pleaded, must moderate their warlike ardor. He ended his speech on a note of good leadership. Soon, he went on,

---

1 Domingos A. Raiol, *Motins Políticos, ou História dos Principais Acontecimentos Políticos da Província do Pará, desde o ano de 1821 até 1835*, Belém: Universidade Federal do Pará, 1970 [1865–1890], vol. 3, 922.
2 Raiol, *Motins Políticos*, 926.

"We will proclaim a new leader who deserves our esteem, trust and respect. Worthy leaders of all units, all of you deserve the greatest praise and glory for your valor, strength and loyalty." His last sentences invoked two figures from the past: "Long live descendents of the Ajuricabas and Anagaibas! Long live the free people of Pará! Long live Pará!"[3]

This appeal to two Indian leaders from a hundred years earlier is extraordinary. Mindful that a new president was needed, he placed himself in an oral tradition of resistance against the Portuguese oppressor that would play well with the crowd. What interests us here is not Angelim's ambition; rather, the invocation of Indian anticolonial rebels from at least a century before the Cabanagem. A direct continuity was being established between the insurgents of the past and the actions of the present. Both groups were fighting against the same kind of enemy – tyrannical, abusive, and despotic. Angelim seemed to be saying: We – the rightful and deserving owners of Pará – are the descendants of these fine leaders of yesteryear. There were no other mentions of these insurgent indigenes in his other printed proclamations. The purpose, though, was clear: it legitimized the current conflict by placing it within the lineage of freedom fighting, which had a vibrant life in the oral traditions of the people of Pará.

Ajuricaba was the legendary chief of the Manao Indians from the middle and lower reaches of Rio Negro in the 1720s. In textual history, he was a strong warrior who sold members of other Indian tribes into slavery to the Dutch. It is alleged that he used to sail with a Dutch flag in a deliberate attempt to provoke the Portuguese. A war was launched against him and his followers and eventually he was captured and put on a boat to Belém in 1725. Ajuricaba and his group were considered official enemies of the Portuguese, which meant a "just war" could be waged against them; if caught, they could be enslaved (friendly Indians were put into missions). On the ship taking him downriver, Ajuricaba tried to organize a mutiny, which failed and, still in irons, he managed to jump overboard to his death rather than face punishment by the Portuguese.[4]

"Anagaiba" is more difficult to locate. He may have been the chief of the Nheengaibas, an Arawakan group that once lived on Marajó Island. These Indians waged war against the Portuguese in the early to mid-seventeenth

3 The whole speech is reproduced in Raiol, *Motins Políticos*, 925–926; also printed in *Brasil: 500 Anos em Documentos*, 195–198, Ivan Alves Filho (ed.), Rio de Janeiro: Mauad Editora, 1999.

4 David Sweet, "A Rich Realm of Nature Destroyed: The Middle Amazon Valley, 1640–1750," Ph.D. dissertation, University of Wisconsin, 1974, 534–546; Antônio Baena, *Compêndio das Eras do Pará*. Belém: Universidade Federal do Pará, 1969, 147; Francisco Bernardino de Souza, *Lembranças e Curiosidades do Valle do Amazonas*, Belém: Typographia do Futuro, 1873, 214. Sweet is, however, not convinced of Ajuricaba's greatness as a leader. There is also a play by Márcio Souza of his life, characterized as a Christ-like figure, which was first performed in 1974, *A Paixão de Ajuricaba*, Manaus: Editora Valer 2005.

century and earned a particularly fierce reputation. In the 1660s Antônio Vieira, the famous Jesuit missionary, persuaded them to desist. After that time, little is known about what happened to them; they are mentioned in some eighteenth-century chronicles as continuing in the same area.[5] If it is correct that Anagaiba was a particularly famous headman of the Nheengaibas and there exist no textual references to him, this would have significant implications for understanding the Cabanagem. (It is also conceivable that Angelim was referring not to a person but a collective entity.) The existence of a powerful verbal tradition of anticolonial resistance in the 1830s must have been extremely threatening to the provincial administration.

It is possible that Angelim had read the accounts of Ajuricaba (or had them read to him) since there were at least two accounts extant at the time, one of which dated from 1777 and tried to recover Ajuricaba's good name as an anticolonial hero.[6] Obviously, Angelim never would have evoked the names of culture heroes if the reference had not resonated with his audience. It seems likely, then, that such struggles from the past, heroic or otherwise, gory or not, were a lively part of popular culture. This tradition should be interpreted as Amazonian in character rather than part of a national discourse associated with anti-Portuguese sentiment (lusophobia or nativism). Although I do not trace in full the development of two centuries of anticolonial sentiment and activity, the need to appreciate its depth and potency is inescapable.[7] Work by John Hemming has already demonstrated the significance of the long view for understanding how Brazilian Indians fought against the colonial presence. In short, an accumulation of memory and experience fed into the Cabanagem.

---

5 The story of their pacification by the Jesuits is told in detail in Serafim Leite, *História da Companhia de Jesus no Brasil*, vol. 3, 235–246. Antônio Vieira, in a letter cited by Leite, reports the Portuguese belief that, with the conquest of the Marajó region, the Amazon became impenetrable from the outside. The Portuguese justified the massacres of the Nheengaibas because of their alliance with the English and Dutch in the early part of the seventeenth century (Leite, *História*, 246). See also João Daniel, *O Tesouro Descoberto no Máximo Rio Amazonas*, Rio de Janeiro: Editora Contrapunto, 2003, vol. 1, chap. 18, 368–369; and Antônio Porro, *Dicionário Etnohistórico da Amazônia Colonial*, São Paulo: Cadernos do Instituto dos Estudos Brasileiros, 2007, 73–74, who cites Bishop Queiroz (1763), José Monteiro de Noronha (1768), and João Vasco Manuel de Braum (1789) as his sources. John Monteiro writes that *Nheegaiba* was a generic term used for non-Tupi speaking groups in the Marajó area; John Monteiro, "Escravidão Indigena e Despovoamento na América Portuguesa," in Francisco Faria Paulino (ed.), *Brasil: Nas Vesperas do Mundo Moderno*, Lisboa: Commisão Nacional, 1992, 156.

6 Sweet, "A Rich Realm of Nature Destroyed," 536.

7 This effort fits with calls in Andean studies to extend the short timeframes of some historical analysis in order to recognize the depth of local oral histories; for example, Steve Stern (ed.), *Resistance, Rebellion and Consciousness in the Andean Peasant World, 18th to 20th centuries*, Madison: University of Wisconsin Press, 1987.

Nevertheless, Angelim was fully versed in liberal politics, having participated in previous attacks on and petitions against the government in the 1830s. Somehow he was able to provide a bridge between radical liberalism and a colonized Amazonian culture. The opening references to the "future the homeland deserves" and liberty in the speech derive from liberal thinking. The characteristics of the leaders – courageous, strong, and loyal – appear locally meaningful and aimed to connect with those who identify with Indian chiefs who led their people against the Portuguese. His singular success may explain why he was able to command the fifth most important city in Brazil from August 1835 to May 1836.

These oral traditions suggest the study of the Cabanagem be placed in the colonial period. Of course, conflicts surrounding independence, fears of recolonization, and the liberal policies of the regency are also centrally important. Understanding the current of anticolonial activity prior to independence will help students appreciate the full force of the rebellion and why the élite radical liberals abandoned their one-time allies in 1835. Élites in Pará mobilized popular discontent to achieve their political goals but in Pará with independence a new motivation came into being. Élites' call to arms was responded to because they conformed to existing grievances and frustrations. In order to prepare the ground for the violent episodes during independence and after, this chapter surveys the different kinds of resistance in the late colonial period.

Forms of rebellion ranged from individual and collective desertion to opposing incorporation into the colonial world. Included here are slaves escaping their masters and setting up a community in a remote district; and attacks on property, kidnapping. and murder. Yet these defiant acts did not contemplate the end of colonial rule in the same way, if at all.[8] The motivation and effect of each one was different. For example, an attack by Mundurucu warriors on a colonial settlement was not the same as the escape of African slaves. The aim of this chapter is to review the various challenges to élites and colonial authorities and to consider the differences between them.

Colonial expansion into the interior of the Amazon was dependent on establishing trade circuits and settlements, farms and ranches. As inroads were made, Hal Langfur has argued more generally for Brazil that property, and its cultural perceptions, came to define identities in the frontier zones of colonial incorporation. Thus colonists depended on land and tools to make a living, while collective Indian groups were not tied to one parcel of land and could move around as necessary. Violence was the main form of communication in the frontier and was an expression not of the

8 David Sweet and Gary Nash (eds.), *Struggle and Survival in Colonial America*, Berkeley: University of California Press, 1981.

breakdown of order but the intensification of contact. The Botocudo, for example, sought to halt colonial advancement in the interior of Minas Gerais by attacking frontier farms and destroying tools, gardens, and animals.[9] This argument can be applied to Pará and the Upper Amazon in the late eighteenth and early nineteenth century, where there were few secure colonial zones. Tribal Indians assaulted villages regularly along the main river and the lower stretches of its tributaries (the settled zone) until the Cabanagem. These were attempts to push back colonial frontiers and challenge Portuguese sovereignty over their territory. Similarly, within the insecure colonial world, peasants acted to defend their autonomy when it was threatened (as it was by those seeking their labor power and wanting their land). This does not necessarily mean these people shared cultural perceptions, and placed the same value on property, especially land subject to flooding in river areas. It is difficult, then, to separate the frontier from the settled zone in the Amazon for the distinction was not present in the manner of the rest of Brazil.

With the ending of the Directorate, it is easier to learn about the wars with indigenous peoples for it was dealt with by the overseas council in Lisbon and there exists a long paper trail. Everyday acts of resistance concerning labor and the stealing of provisions were no longer the direct concern of the governor and those above him. However, desertion, escape, and loss of supplies were among the biggest quotidian problems for village authorities in this late colonial period.[10] Collectively and indirectly, these challenged the colonial system as much as open warfare. Even though this daily defiance of the élite may not have been directly concerned with the end of Portuguese sovereignty, the authorities interpreted it as such because it signified lack of revenue and ideological subordination. It is important to see all these forms of rebellion not as knee-jerk survival strategies but as part of a people's moral and cultural understandings.

Large-Scale Anticolonial War and Its Partial "Pacification"

The original interest of the Portuguese in Amazonia was geopolitical. The French, British, and Irish had established themselves at the mouth of the Amazon at the end of the sixteenth century. They had formed alliances with Amerindian nations, exported goods to Europe, and were expanding upriver at the beginning of the seventeenth century. By 1616 the Portuguese had expelled most of the unwanted European presence

---

9 Hal Langfur, *The Forbidden Lands: Colonial Identity, Frontier Violence, and the Persistence of Brazil's Eastern Indians,* Stanford: Stanford University Press, 2006, 231.

10 Flávio dos Santos Gomes, "A 'Safe Haven': Runaway Slaves, Mocambos, and Borders in Colonial Amazonia, Brazil," *Hispanic American Historical Review,* 2002, 82, 3, 493.

but were left with an abundance of hostile Indian nations. According to the Treaty of Tordesillas, Amazonia was the property of Spain. With the Portuguese in *de facto* possession of the mouth of the Amazon and with no European competitors, they sought to establish their presence over a much wider area and protect it with forts and a military presence. Soon, however, the Portuguese saw new opportunities, in particular for those who could not find a hold in the sugar dominant areas to the south. The reported large numbers of indigenous people along the Amazon River made prospects for economic development all the more attractive. As a result, the Portuguese, seeking slaves, waged war on the Indian nations along the riverbanks. And the natives resisted incorporation and submission.[11]

For much of the eighteenth century, the Mura (and, to a lesser extent, the Mundurucu) had attacked colonial settlements. They also resisted the *descimentos* (the forced or voluntary relocations of people) that would have incorporated them in Mendonça Furtado's Directorate.[12] Then, in 1784, a peace treaty was signed by a band of Mura on the Solimões River, a long way from their base on the Madeira River. Eleven years later, the Mundurucu performed the same act with the Portuguese in Santarém. The Mundurucu also formed an alliance with a neighboring nation, the Maués, who were smaller in number. The main area covered by these peoples stretched along the south side of the Amazon River and its various tributaries from between the Tapajós and the Madeira rivers further westward into the Autazes and on to the Solimões River.

Despite the coincidence of the peace treaties, the Mura and the Mundurucu had little else in common. They had fought each other for

---

11 The destruction of these Amazonian Indian nations in the seventeenth century by disease, slavery, and war is recounted by John Hemming in *Red Gold: The Conquest of the Brazilian Indians*, London: Macmillan, 1978, among various other articles and books, as listed below. João Daniel has a chapter devoted to the manner in which Indians of the seventeenth and eighteenth century declare war (using drums), the technology of war (large and small arrows, and wooden clubs), and motivations for waging it. See "A Guerra dos índios do Rio Amazonas," *O Tesouro Descoberto*, vol. 1, 316–320. Daniel says an Indian can fire ten to twelve arrows in the time it takes a Portuguese soldier to load his shotgun. Despite this skill few soldiers, he continues, were required to overcome an army of Indian warriors, who apparently were given to beating a retreat out of cowardice.

12 The overall picture is well supplied by the section on "Amazonia Meridional" in Manuela Carneiro da Cunha (ed.), *História dos Índios do Brasil*, Companhia das Letras, São Paulo: 1992; Hemming, *Amazon Frontier: The Defeat of Brazilian Indians*, London: Macmillan, 1987; Carlos de Araújo Moreira Neto, *Índios da Amazônia, de Maioria a Minoria, 1750–1850*, Petropolis: Vozes, 1988; Sweet, "A Rich Realm of Nature Destroyed"; Francisco Jorge dos Santos, *Além da Conquista: Guerras e Rebeliões Indígenas na Amazônia Pombalina*, Manaus: Editora da Universidade do Amazonas, 2002. Amerindian societies have their own history, which cannot be understood only through the lens of their contacts with colonial society. The objective here is to see how the presence of the three indigenous societies contributes to the general state of anticolonial resistance in the late colonial period. All these peoples participated in different ways in the Cabanagem.

many years and had different modes of social and economic organization.[13] The Mura were nonsedentary and had little agriculture; the Mundurucu lived in large villages with malocas and fields.[14] It is likely, then, that each nation's reason for giving up the war against the colonists was different. The ethnohistorian David Sweet speculates that despite the success of the Mura offensives, they were exhausted by the enterprise; Mura society was threatened by the continuation of hostilities, mainly due to the absence of men from communities.[15] Thus the pressure on women became too great and they in turn persuaded the men to find a compromise. The Mundurucu, I would speculate, also had their own dynamics. They were the dominant group along the main Amazon River around Santarém and the Tapajós River. Perhaps they sought to consolidate this position by favorable relations with the Portuguese; certainly some of them helped suppress various rebellions in the proceeding period and were rewarded for their services.

The Mura

The Mura were known in the earlier colonial period as pirates of the waterways.[16] They raided colonial villages and kidnapped Indians and African slaves, sometimes with the intention of recruiting them into their midst (discussed in the following paragraphs). The Jesuit João Daniel offers an anecdote in order to explain why the Mura had a "deadly hate of all whites."[17] A missionary had succeeded in persuading them to "leave their forests" and settle in his mission. He said there would be food, clothes, and tools for all, and if they did not want to they would not have to have gardens – normally the sure sign of settled and pacified wild Indians.

---

13 On the interethnic war, see David Sweet, "Native Resistance in Eighteenth-century Amazonia: The 'Abominable Muras' in War and Peace," *Radical History Review*, 1992, 53, 77; Moreira Neto, *Índios da Amazônia*, 261; and Jorge dos Santos, *Além da Conquista*.

14 Santos, *Além da Conquista*, 118–120.

15 Sweet, "Native Resistance," 77.

16 Sources on the Mura include Santos, *Além da Conquista*; Johann Spix and Karl Martius, *Viagem pelo Brasil 1817–1820*, Belo Horizonte, Editora Itatiaia, 1981, vol. 3; Sweet, "Native resistance"; Henrique João Wilckens, "Muhuraida ou o Triunfo da Fé – 1785," ABNRJ, 1989, v. 109, 79–165; Alexandre Rodrigues Ferreira, *Viagem Filosófica: Memorias, Antropologia*, Rio de Janeiro: Conselho Federal da Cultura, 1974; "Illustração," in Moreira Neto, *Índios da Amazônia*; Marta Amoroso, "Corsários no Caminho Fluvial: Os Mura do Rio Madeira," in Cunha (ed.), *História dos Índios do Brasil*; Universidade Federal do Amazonas, *Autos de Devassa Contra os Índios Mura do Rio Madeira e Nações do Rio Tocantins (1738–1739)*, Facsimiles e Transcrições Paleográficas, Manaus: Universidade do Amazonas, 1986; and Curt Nimuendaju, "The Mura and the Piraha." In Julian Steward (ed.), *Handbook of South American Indians*, 255–266. Bulletin 143: Bureau of American Ethnology, 1948.

17 Daniel, *O Tesouro Descoberto*, vol. 1, 360.

Image 5.1 A Mura Indian snorting tobacco (paricá), c. 1785

A Portuguese man found out about this move and with a large boat went to the Mura, saying that the missionary had asked him to fetch them. "How could he have?" some replied, "He has not had time to prepare the place yet." But the white man, with "intentions worse than a black man," according to Daniel, tricked them in to believing that the missionary really was ready; and put as many as he could on his boat. He promptly sold his boatload into slavery, separating children, women, and men by selling them to different settler families. When those who had stayed behind found out the dreadful fate of their kinsfolk, they vowed revenge on all whites.[18]

Travelers and missionaries who had contact with the Mura wrote disparagingly of the appearance of their villages and people.[19] Some of the Mura had come to occupy a marginal and dependent role in colonial society; this may explain why their poverty and misery was so apparent. An anonymous report in 1826, probably written by a missionary, said

18 Daniel, 360–361.
19 Spix and Martius, *Viagem pelo Brasil*, vol. 3; Bates, *A Naturalist*, vol. 1, 324. See also John Hemming, *Amazon Frontier*, 208–209.

"they never make nice houses for themselves" to protect against the annual floods. This meant they did not build their houses on stilts, perhaps preferring to leave the flood plain during the time of the high water.[20] The priest in Óbidos had a similar opinion of Mura architecture, saying they were building their "ridiculous houses" in the vicinity.[21] Whether these were communal houses, which was unlikely given later reports, or built less durably is unclear.[22]

Apart from their own language (which was not part of the Tupi group), the Mura were said to have another altogether different way of communicating, which was "very guttural and hardly perceptible." They used this form of communication when they wanted to talk in secret, especially on boats with whites, or planning an insurrection, robbery, or assassination.[23]

Although the Mura occupied the Madeira River at the beginning of the eighteenth century, by the end of the century they were spread out along the lakes and lower tributaries of the main trunk of the Amazon. Around 1786 the Mundurucu succeeded in eliminating the Mura from the Madeira areas.[24] They resisted settlement by missionaries and colonists and, in adaptation and resistance, became virtually nomadic, moving around in relatively small numbers.[25] The Mura around the time of the peace accord were settled in various communities of a couple of a hundred people in the Upper and Lower Amazon.[26] These communities reformed themselves over the course of the early nineteenth century; some moving around and others becoming more settled. Certainly those in the Lower Amazon appeared in one place and then reappeared elsewhere.

For example, the Mura were present in the north bank areas of the Lower Amazon in the Directorate period. They raided the farms and gardens of the residents of Silves, Serpa, Moura, Faro, and Óbidos on a regular basis.[27]

---

20 "Illustração," 249, in Moreira Neto, *Índios da Amazônia*.
21 Vicar Pedro José Ribeiro Pinto to Governor of Pará Francisco de Souza Coutinho, March 21, 1791, Óbidos, APEP cod. 478, doc. 7.
22 Spix and Martius's description in *Viagem pelo Brasil*, 152.
23 "Illustração Necessária e Interessante, Relativa ao Gentio da Nação Mura, [1826]," in Moreira Neto, *Índios da Amazônia*, 264.
24 "Illustração," in Moreira Neto, *Índios da Amazônia*, 261; Santos, *Além da Conquista*, 140.
25 Hemming, *Amazon Frontier*, 217; Marta Amoroso, "The Portrayal of Indians in the Colonial Epic," in Bernard MacQuirk and Solange Ribeiro de Oliveira (eds.), *Brazil and the Discovery of America: Narrative, History, Fiction, 1492–1992*, Lewiston: Edward Mellon Press, 1996, 122.
26 Sweet, "Native Resistance," 67; for names, places, and "Illustração," in Moreira Neto, *Índios da Amazônia*, 256.
27 "Illustração," in Moreira Neto, *Índios da Amazônia*, 250–251; Director Joaquim Francisco Principe [Printz] to Governor of Pará João Pereira Caldas, September 12, 1779, Óbidos, APEP cod. 346, doc. 11; and Director Joaquim Francisco Principe [Printz] to Governor of Pará João Pereira Caldas, October 1, 1779, Óbidos, APEP cod. 346, doc. 24; Governor of Pará João Napoles de Menezes to Director of Faro, April 25, 1780, Pará, APEP cod. 356, doc. 33.

Before the peace treaty some village Indians and whites were so afraid of the Mura that they did not go to the interior. Soldiers were sent regularly to "pacify" the Mura. On one occasion, troops surrounded a *maloca* and took it by surprise. The men tried to keep the troops at bay while the women and children swam to an island in the river. More than three hundred Mura drowned en masse because it was dark and they could not see the way.[28] The director of Óbidos wrote in 1778 that the Mura were present in three villages on the Trombetas River, and on the Amazonas about three days' journey away.[29] Following the peace accord, Mura settlements on the Trombetas acquired quieter, more formal relations with the colonial towns.[30] Óbidos' priest, though, heard that all was not so peaceful. Since January 1791 the Mura on the Trombetas had been trying to familiarize themselves with the townspeople, but were in fact causing great problems. They stole food from gardens as well as tools and canoes, "all that which they can take." "We cannot tolerate them near us," he said. The possible source of the problem was the fact that the Mura settlements attracted village Indians (ones doing compulsory labor service), since they saw it was easier to be a "wild Indian (*gentio*)."[31]

Around this time the Mura of the Trombetas region had extensive contact with a man called Manoel de Souza Piedade. He was a Portuguese trader and the owner of a cacao plantation, one of the best in the region apparently. However, he had no sons, only daughters, only one slave, and no workers to help him on the farm. In June 1791 he wrote to the governor informing him of his friendship with one Mura group in which he had invested much, offering tools and cloth. What's more, the group wanted to make a little village and gardens and never return to their old huts. In sum, Piedade believed that they did not want "eternal enmity" with the Portuguese. The principal of Maraca-assu Mura (Southwest of Óbidos) had 153 Indians in his care, and he had a brother on the nearby Iruri River who said that in the summer of that year more people would come, and there were two other *principais* at the mouth of Faro River (now known as the Nhamundá) who had a large number of people. This was just the beginning, according to Piedade. However, Piedade was really "buttering up" the governor for his main proposition, which was permission to do business

---

28 "Illustração," in Moreira Neto, *Índios da Amazônia*, 250–251.

29 Vicar Mauricio José e Souza to Governor of Pará João Pereira Caldas, July 9, 1778, Óbidos, APEP cod. 331, doc. 35; Director Manoel Antônio da Costa Souto Maior to Governor of Pará, Óbidos, January 1, 1774, APEP cod. 73, doc. 66; Vicar Mauricio José e Souza to Governor of Pará, September 4, 1778, Óbidos, APEP cod. 324, doc. 29.

30 Director Carlos Daniel de Seixas to Governor of Pará, Óbidos, August 10, 1789, APEP cod. 458, doc. 114.

31 Vicar Pedro José Ribeiro Pinto to Governor of Pará Francisco de Souza Coutinho, March 21, 1791, Óbidos, APEP cod. 478, doc. 7.

with the Mura. Piedade's suggestion was to make a settlement of about 250 Mura at the mouth of the Trombetas River and encourage them to collect forest products. For Piedade, the Mura could be persuaded only when it was in their interest; they could not be forced. The presence of a large village in the area would make available some good commercial opportunities.[32] The governor refused to countenance such a move, for it would have undermined the state's control of Indians and potentially lead to a minifiefdom. He recommended, however, that Piedade employ some Mura on his farm and pay them a daily wage.[33]

Given the conflicting reports of Mura intentions in the Lower Amazon, an inquiry was set up in May 1792 to determine the true situation.[34] Eleven witness statements attested to the continued hostility of the Mura to colonial society. They were accused of stealing from gardens and attacking the residents – Indians, slaves, and whites. Most seriously, the Mura had killed the daughter of an Indian official from Óbidos and five slaves when they tried to stop them from raiding a garden. There was little ambiguity in this report.

Nevertheless, it is possible to perceive the willingness of the Mura to seek peace with others, as in their agreement with the Portuguese some years earlier. Given the history and the numbers involved, it was likely that there would be ongoing tension in the relations. Although the voluntary peace accord of the Mura at the end of the eighteenth century was a form of self-pacification, the confrontation with colonial society continued in the nineteenth century.[35] With more support and integration, the Mura may have become more friendly. The author of the 1826 report says they were never helped once they settled in communities and that without tools and cloth they continued to plunder nearby villages and farms, whereas the Mundurucu and the Maués were offered all sorts of incentives and goods to keep faithful.[36] We can speculate that the Mura–Portuguese agreement was never meant to be taken seriously. Once the Mundurucu had attained dominance over other Amerindians in the Lower Amazon and had signed up to peace, the Portuguese had their

---

32 "*Que pello interesse dellas comprar suas vontades ... e ficando asim huma grandioza povoacao se poderao descobrir por elles alguns bons negocios,*" Vicar Pedro José Ribeiro Pinto to Governor of Pará Francisco de Souza Coutinho, March 21, 1791, Óbidos, APEP cod. 478, doc. 7.

33 Governor of Pará Francisco de Souza Coutinho to Manoel de Jesus da Piedade, October 16, 1791, Pará, APEP cod. 466, doc. 350.

34 "Auto de inqueirição de testemunha a respeito dos índios mura," Commander of Óbidos Fort Luis da Rocha Lima Barros, May 13, 1792, Óbidos, APEP cod. 470, doc. 38 [anexe].

35 Marta Amoroso and Nadia Farage (eds.), *Relatos da Fronteira Amazônica no Século XVIII: Alexandre Rodrigues Ferreira e Henrique João Wilckens*, Série Documentos, NHII/USP, 1994.

36 "Observação Addicionaes a Illustração sobre o Gentio Mura, [1826]," in Moreira Neto, *Índios da Amazonia*, 261.

allies. The Mundurucu were a more attractive proposition than other Indian groups, particularly the Mura, for they were sedentary, even if expansionist, more organized, and larger in number. The Mura may have returned to outright hostility partly in response to their neglect.

Another valuable source of information on the Mura is the poem on the Mura mentioned previously (see page 82). Marta Amoroso has argued that it can be usefully read as an alternative to the "official version of the group's pacification and settlement into missions" in the mid-1780s. The Portuguese perceived the Mura to be omnipresent in the second half of the eighteenth century; they were said to enslave other Indians, to violate the bodies of victims of their raids on colonial settlements, and specialists in guerrilla-type warfare, which contrasts with the larger-scale forms of warfare of the Mundurucu.[37]

The poem also mentions the practice of incorporating – or "murifying" – Indians who either deserted or were captured as a result of intertribal warfare. These people were apparently even more Mura-like than the original Mura – more fierce and anticolonial. It seemed to the colonial authorities the Mura were everywhere and settlements were constantly under threat. Amoroso argues that their mobility gave the impression of being more than they actually were. Nevertheless, prior to the peace treaty, colonial officials did fear a revolt on an Amazonian scale. In these details, the Mura can be seen as active participants in the colonial world and attempting to situate themselves favorably within it.

As mentioned, recent commentators on the colonial Mura have noted their ethnic diversity. They were composed not just of Indians but also of blacks and mamelucos. The best example is Ambrosio, the headman of the Mura, who negotiated the peace treaty and was described as black and tall. Some scholars have suggested the local use of the term *Mura* probably came to stand for anybody who opposed the Portuguese in the main Amazon River. In addition, the Mura were known to kidnap women and children from villages and farms. This forced and voluntary incorporation of outsiders undoubtedly strengthened their numbers and made them into the feared force they were. The processes can be seen as a "murification" of those on the fringes of the Portuguese world and was a powerful act of rebellion.[38]

Such was the case of the Mura at the end of the eighteenth century. In the very early part of the following century, there are few direct references to the Mura except in the published travel or scientific literature (none of

---

37 Amoroso, "On the Portrayal of Indians in the Colonial Epic," 115. This leads the poet to perceive the Mura as "*sem ley, sem pouzo, e sem autoridade/ So os acidentes tem da humanidade* (no law, no home, no authority/ Only in accident do they represent humanity)."
38 Amoroso and Farage, *Relatos*, 11; Sweet, "Native resistance."

which describes indiscriminate violence on behalf of the Mura). Nevertheless, many letters from officials in the Lower Amazon in the early part of the nineteenth century recount violent and sporadic attacks by "Indians." Invariably, no ethnic identity is given. These events were fairly serious offensives on people and property. The insults appeared to the writers as random events and took everyone by surprise. But it is likely that these attacks were planned and undertaken by the Mura with the aim of obtaining supplies and munitions and undermining colonial relations. In this light they should be seen as examples of bandit-style behavior.[39]

The Mura are an example of an Amerindian group who opposed assimilation and disintegration. Like many others, they resisted and fought to maintain their separate identity. Still, they were transformed by the wider Amazonian situation and became dependent on it. Their ethnicity was reconstituted as they received refugees and recruits, perhaps developing a stronger anticolonial position. Nevertheless, some did enter into peaceful relations and moved closer to colonial settlements. Officials in the interior may not have mentioned them by name because their identity was too sensitive a topic. Indians were supposed either to have lost their tribal affiliation or to be living in recognized *aldeias* run by missionaries (ideally in remote locations), as we will see was the case with the Mundurucu. The Mura were in the system but not playing the role the state wanted. Their proximity was a reminder of the policy failure to transform Amerindians into Portuguese-style vassals.

The Mundurucu

Throughout the eighteenth century, the Mundurucu were in expansion; they attacked all groups, not just the Portuguese, in the Lower and Middle Amazon area.[40] Their method was to announce their bellicose intentions with the blowing of a trumpet.[41] In the eighteenth century they regularly attacked canoes and boats on the Tapajós bringing produce from the interior. From the 1780s onward they began to harass and wreak violence on residents in the Lower Tapajós areas near Santarém, "stealing and killing without reserve or piety," according to the governor writing to the Overseas Council in Lisbon in 1781. "Of all the Indian nations which are near to us," he continued, "the Mundurucus are presently the most

---

39 See, for example, "Auto de sumário de testemunha," October 2, 1810, clerk Lourenço Justiano Figueira, judge José Claudio Pagones, APEP "Documentação Judiciaria," Óbidos, 1810. Also, Baena in 1833 briefly mentions the Mura's persistent attacks on all kinds of people, *Ensaio Corográfico*, 28–29.
40 Santos, *Além da Conquista*, 65 and 129.
41 Spix and Martius, *Viagem Pelo Brasil*, 276; also see Bates on the chilling memories of Santarenos of this noise, *A Naturalist*, vol. 2, 10.

Image 5.2 The use of a trumpet by an Amazonian Indian [Mundurucu?], c. 1785

terrible, as much for their large numbers, as for their unlimited capacity for barbarity." In fact, "they take no notice of age or sex of their victims, just to the great number of them in order to increase their inhuman practice of collecting heads."[42]

In one of these raids, a Mundurucu warrior was captured with his arms of war and sent to Belém to the governor. In turn, the governor was so impressed with the appearance of this fine specimen that he put him on the next ship to Lisbon. "He is a most recommendable example of their nation ... with a black painted face and design on his chest in the manner of a necklace." Despite the exotic interest in this Mundurucu warrior, regular soldiers were sent to the Tapajós to protect residents and their

42 Governor of Pará Martinho de Souza e Albuquerque to the Minister of Overseas Affairs, August 17, 1788, letter transcribed in Santos, *Além da Conquista*, 189.

property, and ensure that commercial trade could move freely.[43] At the same time, a strategy of pacification was adopted that did benefit the Portuguese. The then-governor of the Upper Amazon, Manuel da Gama Lobo de Almada, had been pursuing a policy of seducing the Mundurucus with commodities. Captured warriors were taken to Portuguese settlements, treated very well, and given every luxury. They were then returned to their communities with a number of goods. This policy was employed from the early 1790s; by March 1795 a peace treaty had been signed that, at its heart, established Mundurucu in new villages on the lower and middle parts of the Tapajós River. In return, the Mundurucu were to be showered with tools, clothes, and manufactured items for their convenience. The prisoners of the Mundurucu had to be returned and a few children of the chiefs were handpicked for education in Belém at the request of the governor of Pará.[44] The Maués were also at war with the Mundurucu during their expansionist phase, but they made a truce alongside the Portuguese and also became their allies.[45]

The main area for Mundurucu resettlement was Santa Cruz, on the left bank of the Tapajós, about five days' journey in canoe from Santarém. From 1800 there were irregular influxes of about two hundred people each time, monitored by the military authorities at first and then by a missionary.[46] Despite the care given to the process, tensions ran high over a number of incidents. Three men from Óbidos were found to be trading in arms with the Mundurucu, which was illegal for obvious reasons.[47] José Florindo, an Indian military officer registered in Santarém, impregnated the daughter of a Mundurucu headman, then refused to marry her and deserted his company.[48] The soldiers who manned the boats carrying

---

43 See paintings by Hercule Florence in Mario Carelli (ed.), *Les Carnets du Naturaliste Hercule Florence*, Paris, Gallimard, 1992.

44 Santos, *Além da Conquista*, 148–163.

45 Spix and Martius, *Viagem Pelo Brasil*, 279; Seth Leacock, "The Economic Life of the Maués Indians," *Boletim do Museu Emílio Goeldi* (Série Antropologia), 19, 1964; Francisco Jorge dos Santos, "Dossiê Mundurucu: Uma Contribução para História Indígena da Amazônia Colonial," *Boletim Informativo do Museu Amazônico*, vol. 5, no. 8, 1995. More generally on the Maués' social organization and religious practice, see Nunes Pereira, *Os Índios Maués*, Editora Valer, Manaus, 2003 [1954].

46 Military commander of Lower Amazon Manoel Antônio da Costa Souto Maior to Governor of Pará Francisco de Souza Coutinho, Santarém, April 25, 1800, APEP cod. 575, doc. 35; Governor of Pará to Secretary of the Navy and Overseas Affairs, October 27, 1803, Pará, AHU Pará Avulsos, cx. 127, doc. 9773.

47 Judge Romão José de [?] to Commander of Amazonas, [May 1805?], Pinhel, APEP cod. 610, doc. 151.

48 See letters by José Florindo to Governor of Pará Francisco de Souza Coutinho, December 2, 1799, Aveiros, APEP cod. 575, doc. 10; and military commander of Lower Amazon Manoel Antônio da Costa Souto Maior to Governor of Pará Francisco de Souza Coutinho, July 1, 1800, Santarém, APEP cod. 575, doc. 20. Florindo had been a head man (*principal*) in Aveiros on the Tapajós River at the end of the eighteenth century. "Relação dos novos alistados," Captain Joaquim Francisco Printes to Governor of Pará Francisco de Souza Coutinho, Santarém, April 24, 1799, APEP cod. 561, doc. 34.

Image 5.3 A Mundurucu Indian on the Tapajós River by Hercule Florence, 1828

people to Santa Cruz were regularly accused of stealing goods from the Mundurucu. Despite these infelicities, the efforts of the colonial military commanders and Mundurucu headmen were to maintain the convenient relationship.

One commander, José Marinho Lisboa (the head of the army in Santarém), met with one headman on Christmas Day 1801. They spoke lingua geral through an interpreter. The headman and his retinue were given clothes to wear, shown around Santarém, taken to church, and offered a special banquet in honor of their visit. The headman was so impressed he said he wanted to build a maloca in Santarém and make friendship with the commander.[49] Lisboa made further advances in cementing relations with this group over the coming months, convincing them to settle in Santa Cruz and to clear land for gardens. The headman asked for a priest to teach them the Christian doctrine, which Lisboa provided, and he promoted the Mundurucu interpreter to the post of military officer, giving him a uniform and a wage. Most importantly, though, the Mundurucu needed to be protected from the traders "who come more to steal than do business."[50] There was much rivalry between competing traders, and accusations that each was exploiting Indians and supplying arms.[51]

Another significant individual in creating good relations with the Mundurucu was José Rodrigues Preto, a Paulista and one-time village director of Silves on the Amazon River, and an excellent speaker of lingua geral.[52] Rodrigues brought a couple of a hundred Mundurucu and Maués Indians to a new establishment near the mouth of the Madeira River. A priest baptized sixty children, two headmen, and their wives. Mostly, they built malocas but there were some new smaller houses and a wooden enclosure for protection around the village; near the village were fields of maize and manioc.[53] A year later, this habitation had grown to four hundred. After José Rodrigues requested permission to set up an élite army of Mundurucu and Maués warriors to serve the Portuguese, he was named captain of the force.[54] Their main obligation was to defend commercial enterprises operating along the Madeira River, which reached all the way down to Matto Grosso.

These incidents and developments suggest that there was no coherent or general strategy on behalf of the Mundurucu to resettle *en masse*. Rather, it was up to individual headmen to move their people when and how they wanted and set up the kinds of relations they desired. On the other hand, the signing of the peace accord required some level of coordination between headmen, and some may have opposed it. From the Portuguese view, it was a case of not just incorporating the Mundurucu and Maués Indians through

---

49 Captain José Marinho Lisboa to Governor of Pará Francisco de Souza Coutinho, February 11, 1801, Santarém, APEP cod. 575, doc. 61.

50 Captain José Marinho Lisboa to Governor of Pará Francisco de Souza Coutinho, July 12, 1801, Santarém, APEP cod. 575, doc. 110.

51 For example, Angelo Gatto to Governor of Pará Francisco de Souza Coutinho, August 4, 1800, Óbidos, APEP cod. 572. docs 1 and 2; judge Romão José de [?] to Commander of Amazonas, [May 1805?], Pinhel, APEP cod. 610, doc. 151.

52 Spix and Martius, *Viagem pelo Brasil*, 278.

53 Vicar Francisco Antônio de Sancta Catharina (Carmelite missionary) to Bishop of Pará Dom Manoel de Almeida, June 5, 1803, Silves, APEP cod. 601, doc. 47.

54 "Requerimento de José Rodrigues Preto," before June 15, 1804, Silves, AHU Pará Avulsos, cx. 129, doc. 9951.

trade and bribery: they wanted to turn them into vassals of the Crown. The Mundurucu and Maués' new role as mercenaries accorded them a privileged status in the coming conflicts, though this is far from generalized for all. It was reserved for those who received uniforms and wages, and acted as scouts to locate insurgents and those slaves who took flight.

Before their peace agreements, the Mura and the Mundurucu appeared not to distinguish between Indians in the colonial system and those outside it. They attacked all those who were not on their side – whites, mamelucos, and other Indians. This suggests that there was no shared identity between what outsiders called Indians. On the ground, some groups or villages had closer relations with the colonial sphere than others even when they belonged to the same nation. There was both an individual and a collective movement across the colonial/noncolonial boundary, and a refiguring of the friendly and hostile relations depended not just on force and bribery but also internal and interethnic factors. We know little about these latter aspects and can only speculate, given the circumstantial evidence.[55]

The ending of hostilities between "nations" marks a shift in the general opposition to colonial rule. Almost two centuries of interethnic war had come to an end. The colonial élite finally felt they had "pacified" the areas that meant the most to them and could provide revenue. If they were optimistic, the coming decades would give little comfort and reassurance that their investments would reap rewards. On the contrary, a new phase opened with the peace treaties where the energy for revolt spread. The Mura and the Mundurucu may have been tired of their wars, but they may also have been confident that their grievances were shared by others and would be taken up sooner or later. These two peoples offer contrasting examples of the ways in which natives rejected colonial integration. One was spread-out, mobile, and inclusive, while the other was concentrated and boundary-conscious. Consequently, the way they opposed the colonial world differed, even when they entered into formal peaceful relations. Neither suddenly approved of colonial rule but sought a mode of accommodation that suited them. Autonomy was no longer possible due to the expanding colonial frontier.

In the period immediate prior to Independence, we can conclude there were no settled zones free from Indian attack. At best, the edge between the

---

55 On population numbers: Maués were said to number up to 40,000 people, Spix and Martius, *Viagem pelo Brasil*, 276; the letter from Governor of Pará to Secretary of the Navy and Overseas Affairs (October 27, 1803, Pará, AHU Pará Avulsos, cx. 127, doc. 9773) says there were 100,000 more Mundurucu in the forest; the author of the "Illustração," in Moreira Neto, says there were 60,000 Mura in 1826; according to Spix and Martius, there were about 40,000 in 1819. See Santos, *Além da Conquista*, 81, for difficulties in estimating the numbers of these "nations."

frontier and the colonized shifted backwards and forwards depending on the overall situation. For example, during conflicts in 1824 and in the early to mid-1830s, all kinds of people clashed and there were no safe areas. There was therefore no secure or single authority over the region until the ending of the Cabanagem. The Amazon was yet to be conquered in the early nineteenth century.

Other Kinds of Assault (*Rebeldia*)

The large-scale ethnic conflicts that had taken place throughout the colonial period were matched by small-scale group or individual acts against the Portuguese and local Brazilian élites. These appear as isolated, if ongoing, events. The question is whether they added up to more than annoyances to the colonial order. Three aspects are relevant here. The first concerned the importance of geographical mobility, which should include escape from abusive masters and bosses (and search for better patron rather than total separation from colonial world). The second was the need for supplies, so that attacks on towns, boats, and farms were related to stealing and gaining food and munitions. Destroying property was an extremely good way to undermine the colonial system. The third was the attempt to avenge an injustice and redress some harm done to oneself or one's family. Much of the rebellious behavior surrounded labor obligations but this does not exhaust all possibilities; that would imply individuals did not seek a form of political expression for their grievances and just did not want to work. It was more than recalcitrance, as will be seen presently. The case study of the Royal Cacao plantation and Royal Fishery reveals some of the tensions at the heart of local and daily life, wrapped up in conflicting persuasions and intentions.

Disorder in Vila Franca and the Royal Companies

Located between Óbidos and Santarém on the south side of the Amazon River was the Royal (later Imperial) Cacao plantation. The trees were planted on an area of high flood plain land. A full-time administrator, appointed by the governor, managed the company and scores of Indian workers were employed to work the trees. The manager was formally linked to officials in Óbidos, and the workers came from Vila Franca. This division and its administrative autonomy was the source of many conflicts since its formation in the late 1750s when the Crown confiscated the plantation from the Jesuits. About thirty people were employed from one year to the next, and most of these were women.[56] Levels of

---

56 Judge Ignácio Ferreira to the provincial president, Vila Franca, April 1, 1825, APEP cod. 862, doc. 29.

production were never very high compared to private production. In 1814, for example, 1,348 arrobas were exported to Belém from the Royal Cacao plantation; in same year 177,643 arrobas were shipped to Portugal.[57]

On the large lake to the northwest of Vila Franca was one of the royal fisheries (there were others on Marajó Island and in Bragança), engaging periodically 120–150 Indian men. These laborers were registered with the part-time militia, which meant they were obliged to work as directed by their officers. Canoes were made when required. Fish were prepared for export by gutting and salting them. Founded in 1783 by royal decree, the company came under the control of the provincial treasury in 1801.[58] A house by the church in Vila Franca acted as a salt deposit and store. Various fishing techniques were used, including net fishing and harpoons. Fish was much less significant than cacao as an export, however, since it was mostly produced for internal consumption and the provisioning of military, commercial, and scientific expeditions.[59]

These two royal services in the Lower Amazon were the site of a series of conflicts over the period of the study, concerning the tyrannical conduct of the men running each of these operations and the resistance of Indians to forced labor drafting. Among the Indians' interests was the desire to remain in control of their labor power. The administrator's aim was to increase collective production and generate profits. This push-and-pull led to a series of confrontations between Indians and their bosses.

A dominant employer and occupier of lands, such as the royal companies, had an important place in local life. In 1802 the Indians working on the Royal Fishery were much agitated and the manager, José Miguel de Sá Barreto, thought they were on the verge of a rebellion against him and his family. "These Indians are rebels and criminals and not frightened to murder," he wrote. He requested at least fourteen soldiers to protect royal interests and prevent the Indians from taking their disquiet any further. In a letter to the military commander of the Lower Amazon, João Bernardo Barralho, the manager of the royal fishery, opined that with this "class of people" (that is, the Indians), they behaved peacefully only if they remembered the punishment they would receive for bad

---

57 Manoel Barata, *Formação Histórica do Pará: Obras Reunidas*, Belém, 1973, 306. In 1814, the royal service employed nineteen women for about half the year to prepare beans for export and seventeen men in various forms of support, such as carpenters and woodcutters, Administrator of the Cacoal Real Herculano Cezar Miranda to Governor of Pará, January 9, 1815, Vila Franca, APEP cod. 674, docs 78; and Administrator of the Cacoal Real Herculano Cezar Miranda, "Relaçám das praças que são empregados em defrentes servicios neste cacoal real de vila Franca," January 9, 1815, Vila Franca, APEP cod. 674, doc. 79.

58 Antônio Baena, *Ensaio Corographico Sobre a Província do Pará*, Brasilia: Senado Federal, 2003, 231.

59 The top four exports were cacao, rice, café, and cotton; see Santos, *História Econômica da Amazônia*, 37.

conduct.[60] He thus made the presence of soldiers an open invitation for them to repress and abuse, rather than maintain discipline and order. He did have some basis for complaint, however. He had overheard some Indians, as they were carrying a bag of manioc flour to the Royal Fishery boat (*canoa*), exclaim that they should all rise up against him and end everything in one go: kill him and then do whatever they wanted with his family. Furthermore, he said that the Indians were being protected by the municipal judge of Vila Franca, Alfonso de Souza, who was an Indian himself and would not enforce the orders of the governor (something the governor knew not to be the case, though the manager could get away with this deception because he was writing to the regional military commander). Barralho's request for military backup to avoid an uprising was not fulfilled. He got nothing and was told that the militia from Vila Franca should be used.

Tensions were heightened when the manager tried to increase production following the rise in the price of cacao during the 1810s. Herculano Cesar de Miranda ordered a Vila Franca judge to conduct an investigation into the resident (*morador*) Paulo José Francisco, who was suspected of trying to spur the Indians into destroying the cacao plantation. While the judge was trying to gather evidence, Francisco was imprisoned. Unable to find any evidence to support the accusation and because the judge had no food for the prisoner, he was released. In the same breath, the judge informed the governor that he was unable to fulfill his orders because of the "great rebelliousness in which the Indians of the town can be found. They disobey openly and if you force them to do anything they escape to nearby towns, where they stay with families and friends." Since the judge had no authority, the Royal Cacao plantation had few workers.[61]

It is significant that Vila Franca was a source of social conflict. In the censuses of the period, the town had one of the largest number of Indians and smallest numbers of slaves and whites of any of the Lower Amazon towns. This strong Indian presence in official municipal positions must have given them a confidence unlikely to have been shared by Indians in other towns in the district. Alfonso de Souza, then a captain of a light infantry division of Vila Franca and said to be a *tapuio* (Indian), wrote in 1818 that Vila Franca was one of the most populous towns in Pará, with a militia some 300–400 strong.[62] Despite this, he went on to say that it was almost impossible to get the militia to work because of their

---

60 Administrator of the Royal Fishery in Vila Franca João Miguel de Sá Barreto to military commander in Santarém João Bernardo Borralho, September 17, 1802, Vila Franca, APEP cod. 595, doc. 96.

61 Judge of Vila Franca Flauzino José Guilberto to Governor of Pará, August 7, 1815, Vila Franca, APEP cod. 623, doc. 198.

62 Captain Alfonso de Souza to Governor of Pará, August 23, 1818, Vila Franca, APEP cod. 684, doc. 77.

rebelliousness (*"por sua rebeldia"*). They lived in mocambos and spread themselves out in distant parts, reluctant to be ruled. Subtly, he reminded the governor of the emancipation of Indians in 1799, but they were still obliged to perform unreasonable duties, such as private royal service. De Souza recommended that the militia be exempt from working for others, or they would never be willing and productive vassals. His argument was that the Indians were more productive when left to work on their own accord.

Another important element here was a conflict of interest between civil and military authorities, such as the judges, councilors, and ranked officers. All these parties competed for labor in a private or official capacity. The demands on a recalcitrant labor force came to be more than oppressive. As mentioned in the previous chapter, all Indian men between ages 12 and 60 were registered as soldiers and were under the command of locally elected officers. This made it quite easy to call the men up for duty, which often included serving the private interests of their officers, such as working on their farms. But because women were not registered in the census, they lay outside direct colonial control of labor but this marginality also made them vulnerable to abduction by colonists and domestic slavery. The situation was made even more complicated and conflictual because the same officials moved between elected or appointed positions with different responsibilities and yet used their public officers for the pursuit of private interest, considering themselves above the law.[63]

On April 16, 1818, the militia captain from Óbidos, José Cavalcante, wrote to fellow officers in Santarém and Vila Franca asking them to arrest the heads of a revolt against the administrator of the Royal Cacao plantation at the beginning of that year. After various vain attempts to apprehend them, Cavalcante wrote back that he "cannot capture the authors of those responsible for the disorders."[64] He had also relied on a good friend, Joaquim Perreira, to track them down. Perreira wrote to Cavalcante that the Indians involved had either retreated to distant parts or had escaped from prison. All the other Indians were working obediently in their gardens. This state of affairs apparently was cause for optimism and he recommended that nothing else could be done. The man who had released the captives from prison was arrested, but Perreira reckoned that the judge and militia captain, Alfonso de Souza, had organized the release, not least because one of the leaders was his relative. Indeed, Perreira said that de Souza could not be trusted, since he was an Indian and completely

---

63 See judge Antônio de Silva Barreto to Governor of Pará, April 27, 1819, Santarém, APEP cod. 684, doc. 136, on the abuse of child labor by soldiers and the judge's protest to the governor.
64 Captain of militia José Cavalcante de Albuquerque to Governor of Pará, August 28, 1819, Óbidos, APEP cod. 684, doc. 148.

incompetent, not even able to write or read.[65] De Souza's relative, militia lieutenant Francisco Caetano da Silva, was eventually arrested in December 1819. De Souza then gave sworn testimony that his lieutenant acted alone in the revolt against the administrator and that he should be punished for indiscipline.[66]

Perreira, who had a royal land concession in the district Vila Franca, in the vicinity of the plantation reflected, pleaded that something be done about the "inveterate intrigue" between the municipal officials and the administrators of the Royal Cacao plantation.[67] He did not come up with any recommendations or support either side. The officials in Vila Franca were largely Indians and protected their own, while the royal services took labor away from local enterprises, or at least reduced the pool of available hands. Even though the Royal Cacao plantation depended on relatively few workers, there was a continual precariousness of the administration of production.

This brief outline of the chronic disturbances surrounding the employment of Indians in royal services reveals some of the critical tensions in the area before independence. From the Indian point of view, their labor was embedded in a system of social relations and given value not just through its products but also by its place in their moral universe. One phrase stands out as expressing this view: One Indian told a military commander that "I am not your servant and not a servant of anybody else either."[68] The tensions were certainly about the control of labor and were the central preoccupation of the colonial authorities, as has been convincingly demonstrated by other scholars.[69] However, the flashpoint was what labor meant to a person – personal autonomy and social rather than economic value, as anthropologists have argued.[70] It would be wrong to assume that this notion of self-determination automatically meant a blanket rejection of the colonial world. On the contrary, the kinds of arguments outlined above can be seen as a collapse of the relations between various parties. Working Indians were not so much resisting authority or desirous of full autonomy as searching for better and fairer treatment that respected their

---

65 José Joaquim Perreira do Lago to captain of militia José Cavalcante de Albuquerque, August 15, 1819, Vila Franca, APEP cod. 684, doc. 149.

66 Judge José Thomas de Aquino, December 31, 1819, Santarém, APEP cod. 707, doc. 59.

67 José Joaquim Perreira do Lago to captain of militia José Cavalcante de Albuquerque, August 15, 1819, APEP cod. 684, doc. 149.

68 "*Não sou seu criado nem de ninguem,*" Pedro Alvarez Borges to Governor of Pará, June 26, 1752, Óbidos, APEP cod. 73, doc. 1. Borges said this was the worst insult anyone had issued toward him in his service in India as well as Brazil.

69 For example, see Colin Maclachlan, "The Indian Directorate: Forced Acculturation in Portuguese America, 1757–1799," *The Americas*, 1972, 28, 4, 257–387.

70 See Stephen Gudeman with Alberto Rivera, *Conversations in Colombia: The Domestic Economy in Life and Text*, Cambridge, 1991; for contemporary Amazon floodplain; and Mark Harris, *Life on the Amazon: The Anthropology of a Brazilian Peasant Village*, Oxford, Oxford University Press, 2000.

values. In this way, the disputes were about doing away with a bad master rather than completely doing away with the system itself.

Care should be taken, then, in presenting the colonial worlds as dualistic: slaves and laborers on one side and bosses on the other, neatly separate and opposed. A spectrum ran from remote pocket communities of Indians (and slaves, see below) to those who had isolated farmsteads and others who had relatively larger farms nearer to a market, and to those élites who had royal land concessions on prime land on the riverbanks. Individuals could move between these poles, as seen in the Alfonso de Souzas – Indians, competent in carrying out official tasks and seeking position and influence. There were divided and mixed-up loyalties rather than a chasm in between the colonizers and the colonized.

Mocambos in the Sertão and Slaves in Towns

According to regional authorities, the flight of slaves from their masters was one of the most serious problems of the late colonial period.[71] Escaped slaves typically established their own communities or camps (*quilombos*) in remote places up tributaries and would attack farms, burn houses, kill cattle, and kidnap women and other slaves. Often they were armed and defended their homes with devices such as trenches and traps. In these ways the quilombos of the Amazon were no different from those elsewhere in Brazil and the Caribbean.[72] There were some regional variations, such as the importance of Indians in helping slaves escape, the complicity of traders in supplying quilombos, and the network of rivers and dense forests that aided escape and obscurity. Some in the northeast of the Amazon had connections with the French in Guyana.[73] The main runaway slave communities were situated around Belém and the Tocantins River (the areas with the largest numbers of slaves and sugar plantations), Marajó Island and on the Pará–Maranhão provincial border, and in the Lower Amazon around Alenquer and Óbidos.[74]

---

71 Flávio dos Santos Gomes, "A 'Safe Haven': Runaway Slaves, Mocambos, and Borders in Colonial Amazonia, Brazil," *Hispanic American Historical Review*, 2002, 82, 3, 493.

72 There is a multitude of literature on mocambos; see, for example, Clovis Moura, *Quilombos: Resistência ao Escravismo*, São Paulo, Ática, 1989; Flávio dos Santos Gomes, *Histórias de Quilombolas: Mocambos e Comunidades de Senzalas no Rio de Janeiro, Século XIX*, Rio de Janeiro: Arquivo Nacional, 1995; João José Reis and Flávio dos Santos Gomes, *Liberdade por um Fio*, São Paulo: Companhia das Letras, 1999; and Stuart Schwartz, *Slaves, Peasants and Rebels: Reconsidering Brazilian Slavery*, Champaign: University of Illinois Press, 1996.

73 Gomes, "A Safe Haven."

74 Ronaldo Vainfas (ed.), *Dicionário do Brasil Colonial* (1500–1808), Rio de Janeiro: Editora Objectiva, 2000, 494–495; Vicente Salles, *Vocabulário Crioulo*, Belém: Instituto de Artes do Pará, 2003, 198–199 and 222; Salles, *O Negro no Pará sob o Regime da Escravidão*, Rio de Janeiro: Fundação Getulio Vargas, 1971, 205; Beatriz Maria Nizza da Silva (ed.), *Dicionário da História da Colonização Portuguesa do*

The term *quilombo* is derived from the African Bantu language. The documents from Pará mostly used *mocambo*, which strictly refers to a hut with a palm roof and no walls, but came to be used interchangeably with quilombo. The Portuguese made a noun and a verb of the terms, so a *mocambeiro* or *quilombola* describe the people in camp and *amocambado* refers to the act of having set one up. No distinction was made between Indians and African slaves who had taken flight. Any camp with more than five people was considered a quilombo. In the Lower Amazon during the time of the Directorate, desertion, absenteeism, and flight were constant aspects of social life, impossible to prevent. A village director of Óbidos in 1780s, Joaquim Francisco Printz, wrote to the governor that nine Indian men and eleven Indian women with their children had left the village for a mocambo on the Trombetas river, apparently without any reason other than "their laziness with which they are much in love"; it would seem that in this case they did not join any slaves. Two of the Indian men had already been in a mocambo and had conducted various hostilities against settlers from there.[75] Repeated escapes were a characteristic of slave as well as Indian life. Furthermore, as we shall see, Indians helped to find suitable routes and locations for their African counterparts. By the end of the Directorate, Indian mocambos were less common because Indians were no longer under the colonial thumb in the same way.

Rural flight was a widespread strategy of resistance used by those who were enslaved or felt abused; it could be temporary or permanent, small or large scale. Sometimes, it involved removing to areas difficult to access; though more daringly camps were placed strategically on commercial routes where inhabitants could conduct banditry. Some lasted days or weeks; others survived much longer with increasing numbers and more equipment.

In late 1799 came news of "a formidable mocambo" of slaves. No one knew where it was but it had started "insulting" residents of the north bank of the Lower Amazon with continuous attacks. They had run off with the canoes and arms of their masters. The governor ordered a military expedition to rid the district of the "menace" and put the people at peace. Within a year, locally organized scouts had located a group of runaways on the Curuá River. Troops from Alenquer and Óbidos went to recover them and encountered fierce resistance, resulting in many deaths on both sides though no numbers were given.[76] The soldiers found a well-organized

Brasil. São Paulo: Verbo, 1994; Angela Vianna Botelho and Liana Maria Reis, *Dicionário Histórico Brasil: Colônia e Império*, Belo Horizonte: Autêntica Editora, 2003, 146–147.

75 Director Joaquim Francisco Principe to Governor of Pará, January 27, 1780, Óbidos, APEP cod. 354, doc. 14.

76 Captain of militia Lourenço Justiano Siqueira to Lower Amazon military commander João Bernardes Borralho, December 24, 1801, APEP cod. 575, doc. 207; captain of militia José Antônio de Oliveira to Governor of Pará, October 8, 1805, Alenquer, APEP cod. 610, doc. 171.

and -supplied community with clothes, rolls of cotton, and plenty of goods, including sacks of manioc flour (*farinha*).[77] The soldiers who destroyed the camp shared those goods, counting them toward the payment for expenses. The captors only released the slaves from prison when their masters paid for the rest of the costs of the campaign. Two slaves whose previous owners no longer wanted them were sold to another party. The recovered goods suggest a relatively settled community. The presence of manioc flour indicated agricultural production and an established community; though it could also have been gained by stealing.

A year or so later, at the end of December 1801, a group of slaves prepared to escape from their masters in Óbidos. Knowing their owners were in town taking part in the festivities, the slaves planned their departure. They enlisted the help of two people, an Indian and a mulatto, Prudente José and José Antônio de Lira, respectively. Somehow, the authorities found out about the "conspiracy of slaves of the residents of this town to get themselves ready to escape during mass." They arrested the two guides and questioned them as to the slaves' intentions. The whites of the town were extremely worried about this news, since the slaves had only just been recovered from a previous flight and further loss would upset the fine equilibrium of social and economic life. Some thought the slaves just wanted to run away, whereas others suspected that they were waiting for their masters to arrive in town, then there would be a general attack on the place. In consequence, the masters wanted to return to their farmsteads but were told by the judge to remain in Óbidos so as to protect their families.[78]

Since the breakup of the Curuá mocambo, there had been no more large-scale escapes in the Lower Amazon. Then in 1805 the flights resumed and the attacks by the runaways had become "excessive with not just stealing from farms but also burning houses and kidnapping free women from their homesteads in order to satisfy their brutish appetites." The whites considered slaves to have no fears: punishment made no difference to how they behaved (in contrast apparently to Indians). No form of control could prevent the enslaved from moving as they pleased because "the farmhouses were so spread out." The Africans were the worst enemies of the masters, especially those from Santarém. A resident of Alenquer heard that an escaped slave couple belonging to him was living in the garden of an Indian woman in Vila Franca. He invited some companions to rescue them, certain there would be little resistance because the male slave was seventy years old. The couple was spotted on a lake in a small canoe. As soon as the slave saw his master, he shot him without a word and

77 Judge Fernando Ribeiro Pinto to Governor of Pará, September 20, 1800, APEP cod. 572, doc. 39.
78 Captain of militia Lourenço Justiano Siqueira to military commander of Lower Amazon João Bernardes Borralho, December 24, 1801, Óbidos, APEP cod. 575, doc. 207.

the slave catcher fell dead at the bottom of the canoe. "There is nothing in God's world we can do to avoid this rebelliousness," one man wrote describing the event.[79]

Yet, some measures were discussed to remedy the situation. A judge from Alenquer recommended that the governor nominate "mestiços and *descalços*" (literally, those without shoes, meaning the destitute) as *capitães do mato* (official slave catchers). These "quality of men" live from fishing and collecting the *drogas de sertão* and will not demand anything, reckoned Antônio de Oliveira, the judge. Whites, he continued, were just not interested, since they were well-established in these parts, had their own lands, and did not seek to take on extra work. So they will absent themselves from military campaigns, not taking their responsibilities seriously. He also argued that the governor should issue tickets (*bilhetes*) to all slaves and require them to be carried at all times. This way it will be known who should be where and who belonged to whom. Moreover, the punishment of the enslaved should be carried out by those who have earned their freedom, the exslaves, who know what a good whipping means. "These procedures could perhaps counteract all or part of the relentless escapes and attacks of these enemies, the most horrible, powerful and fearsome there are in this province."[80]

Clearly from the first decade of the nineteenth century, enslaved Africans were troublesome to their masters. What is more, talk of freedom following the ending of the Directorate was ever present, as was the disaffection with the unchanging circumstances of the majority of people. Desertion from the army, duties, work parties, and slavery were classified in the same way as rebellion, and treated accordingly, using military type offensives. Property owners were outraged, not just because their slaves were absent but because they also were being attacked and stolen from. How systematic this was and whether the level of violence was being exaggerated we cannot know for sure (in order to justify harsh repressive measures that might otherwise be condemned). Yet in this first decade of the new century, there appeared to be little that could be done to prevent the formation of "formidable mocambos" and their incursions into neighboring farms and towns. These challenges grew even stronger in the next decade.

One of the flashpoints between slaves and masters was public punishment. Taking place in the town square, the most common castigation was a whipping, sometimes a hundred lashes being administered while victims were tied to the *pelourinho*, the whipping post in the town square. For

---

79 Captain of militia José Antônio de Oliveira to Governor of Pará, October 8, 1805, Alenquer, APEP cod. 610, doc. 171.
80 Ibid.

example, Francisco, the slave of Manuel José de Faria, was punished for looting and desertion. He had been living in a mocambo near Lake Cucuí (situated between Alenquer and Monte Alegre) with other fugitives. From their hideout, they would raid farms for farinha and cattle meat, and invite other slaves to return with them.[81] A hero to his fellow slaves, Francisco's ordeal led to looting in the town and the flight of more slaves. On the other hand, some authorities were unable to carry out a penalty. The town council of Alenquer complained to the governor that "the residents continually live under the threat of the invasion of escaped slaves ... the slaves do not stop from attacking and stealing from the houses of their masters, which results in 'total rebeldia.'" The masters could not even punish these "criminals": even the lightest form of punishment encourages them to leave with their families. Their mocambos were apparently a "secure refuge" from which they would come and go as they pleased.[82]

Mocambos were safe for reasons other than their hidden location. Soldiers would not set out unless there was a sufficiently large group, which meant considerable time and effort were needed to prepare for an expedition. The authorities did discover the location of some hideouts, following the questioning of recovered or arrested slaves. To find these remote and inaccessible places, scouts were employed from the increasingly reliable Mundurucu Indians who, only a decade or two earlier, had been one of the most hostile groups the Portuguese faced in the Amazon.[83] The Mundurucu knew only too well the kind of places people could go to avoid being found easily. Their enlistment proved to be a success, for they found a series of mocambos in the Lower Amazon.

As slave owners grew more desperate, the slaves' increasing confidence was manifested in their forms of collective organization. Slaves taking flight had been going to the Curuá River since at least the end of the eighteenth century. By 1812 and early 1813, three mocambos located by Mundurucu scouts were destroyed in that area using regular troops. From the information collected after the destruction, it is possible to sense something of the new forms of relations that had emerged. Seventy-four slaves, including fifteen children, were captured from communities known as Cipotema, Inferno, and Caxange.[84] The very fact that the mocambos

---

81 Certificate of Lourenço Justiano Siqueira, November 24, 1810, Óbidos, APEP cod 636, doc. 05.

82 Town council of Alenquer (headed by judge Alvaro José Ribeiro) to Governor of Pará, January 2, 1811, Alenquer, APEP cod 636, doc. 3.

83 Judge Domingos Corrêa Picanço to Captain Antônio Joaquim Coutinho, April 28, 1811, APEP cod. 623, docs 176–179; see Salles, *O Negro no Pará*, 232, and Euripides Funes, "Nasci nas Matas, Nunca tive Senhor: História e Memória dos Mocambos do Baixo Amazonas," 623–641, in João José Reis and Flávio dos Santos Gomes (eds.), *Liberdade Por um Fio: História dos Quilombos no Brasil.* São Paulo: Companhia das Letras, 1999, 474.

84 See Funes, "Nasci nas Matas," 477.

had names suggests how settled they were. This is confirmed by the job descriptions of some of those captured. Heading the mocambo was a man named João Caxange, a slave of José Ricardo Picanço. The mocambo included a priest, a slave of Francisco José Perreira, and a sacristan, Caetano, suggesting the existence of religious practices and ritual objects. One inhabitant, Ana Joaquina, was described as a queen (*rainha*) and was the slave of Simplício Antônio Corrêa.[85] There was also a justice of the peace, Silvestre. An Indian woman, Valentina, listed last, was also found among the slaves.

Three hundred and seventy-five soldiers and twenty Mundurucu guides were involved in the operation headed by Captain Bernardo Marinho de Vasconcelos.[86] Eight slaves were killed in the attack, though no soldiers died. The seventy-four recovered deserters were the property of twenty-three masters including two apparently belonging to one-time Governor Francisco de Souza Coutinho. The significant military force indicated the seriousness with which the repression was considered. However, mocambos continued to form and slaves to steal and insult their masters; indeed, the practice would continue until slavery was abolished in 1888, way past the Cabanagem. There is evidence, though, that a less aggressive stance was taken toward runaway slaves from the 1840s on.[87]

After the raid on Cipotema, "The quilombo was raised to the ground, everything was reduced to dust and all that was planted was thrown into the river."[88] Despite such physical annihilation, the spirit of freedom could not be extinguished. Mocambos continued to form in the Curuá area; and at the beginning of the 1820s groups were reported to the west on the Trombetas River, which runs north to south and parallel with the Curuá.[89] During another large military expedition in 1816, eleven slaves were recovered, three died in the fighting, and others escaped into the forest.[90] The head of that quilombo ruled like a king and sought recruits from all over the region. The official of that expedition believed the slave king deserved a harsh punishment, so he was sent to Belém where his fate was decided by the governor.[91]

85 Funes, "Nasci Nas Matas," 477, 479, 485; Salles, *O Negro no Pará*, 232.

86 Ibid.

87 Salles, *O Negro no Pará*, 208.

88 Funes, "Nasci nas Matas," 486, quoting Captain Vasconcelos. I was unable to find this quotation in the original documents.

89 See Anaiza Vergolino-Henry and Napoleão Figueiredo (eds.), *A Presença Africana na Amazonia Colonial: Uma Notícia Histórica*, Belém: Falangola Editora, 1990; and Salles, *O Negro no Pará*, 233.

90 Juis ordinario Narciso Ignácio Ferriera to Governor of Pará, December 13, 1816, Santarém, APEP cod. 676, doc. 31.

91 "*O capitao do quilombo que se dono minava rei,*" Judge Narciso Ignácio Ferriera to Governor of Pará, September 9, 1816, Santarém, APEP cod. 676, doc. 32.

The monarchical form of social organization was mentioned by a later visitor to the Trombetas area. Tavares Bastos, a national deputy who traveled the Amazon widely, said in 1866 that the mocambos along the Trombetas River contained criminals and deserters, for a total of about two thousand people. "The blacks, perhaps trained by other companions in exile, live under a despotic regime (*governo despotico electivo*)."[92] These elements are suggestive of the attempt to create an alternative type of social organization, distinct from slavery. The mocambos, though, were interdependent with colonial society, relying on it for food, tools, arms, and recruits. Increasingly over the nineteenth century, traders came to interact with them, seeking alternative sources of goods and new clients.[93]

However, not all mocambos were distant from towns. According to the town's judge in 1813, Santarém suffered from persistent attacks by the fugitives in a new mocambo in the forest on the outskirts. That year there was regular thieving from the houses in the town.[94] The fact that slaves were openly disturbing the town was a serious concern. These attacks could not just have been about securing supplies; they may also have included an element of revenge and redressing past injustices. Whether they were systematically conducted or opportunistic, however, should be left open due to lack of evidence. In the next section we shall encounter a case of a slave resistance at the heart of town life.

It is not known exactly how many quilombos existed at that time or how many people they secured. Still a pattern can be detected to the development of mocambos in the region. Alenquer, Monte Alegre, Óbidos, and Santarém were the only towns in the Lower Amazon with a slave population of more than 50 in the period from 1800–1821.[95] The Curuá River is a long and substantial river on the north bank between Monte Alegre and Óbidos. It is not surprising that the first mocambos in the Lower Amazon formed some way up that river at the end of the eighteenth century and continued to attract people as they managed to build up supplies and perhaps hide them before an attack. The mocambos on the Trombetas form later on in the 1820s, as the slave population grew and sought alternative areas.[96] Another piece of evidence corroborates this view. As indicated earlier, during the late 1780s the Mura had settled along the Trombetas River, near some lakes. Residents of the mocambo Moura told João Barbosa Rodrigues, a chronicler from the 1860s, that before they

---

92 A. C. Tavares Bastos, *O Valle do Amazonas*, São Paulo: Companhia Editorial National 1937, 201.

93 Captain of militia João Gama de Lobo to Governor of Pará, April 20, 1827, Monte Alegre, APEP cod. 835, doc. 100.

94 Judge José Fernandes dos Reis to Governor of Pará, August 22, 1813, Santarém, APEP cod. 623, doc. 183.

95 José Maia Bezerra Neto, *Escravidão Negra no Grão Pará*, Belém: Editora Paka-Tatu, 2000, 118.

96 Salles, *O Negro no Pará*, 233.

lived there, there was a maloca of "wild Indians."[97] Knowing the Mura were settled in the area may have put off runaway slaves from going there until favorable relations had been established or the Mura had moved on. By the mid-1820s there were said to be no *gentio* living in or near the town of Óbidos.[98] At this time, independence from Portugal causes further disruption, since the slaves also "expect liberty" and they knew of the slave rebellion in Haiti (see the next chapter).[99]

"O Preto Antônio"

The scattered and incomplete information on "Antônio, the black man," as he was referred to, elaborates the themes of geographical mobility and family networks. Antônio was a slave belonging to the captain of the second company of the militia troops based in Vila Franca, José Joaquim Perreira Lago, the aforementioned friend of José Cavalcante.

In 1805 Antônio was accused of being the "head of an uprising" of fellow slaves that took place in Santarém. The group threatened to kill nine leading whites in the town for their abuse of slaves in their care. In turn, the whites were deeply "shocked" by this terrorization. Due to the absence of other information, it is likely that little or no damage was done to person or property and the threat was the part of a display of drunken bravado exaggerated by the authorities. The slaves managed to leave the town unhindered. Nevertheless, the town's judge ordered the perpetrators be caught. Antônio was not arrested because he was helped by his master. In fact, Antônio had been sent to a friend of his master in Gurupá with a suspected forged letter from the governor asking his friend to look after Antônio for a while.

Ten years later, Antônio went to the farm of an unnamed resident in the region of Ituqui (about five kilometers downstream of Santarém on the south side of the Amazon River). There he smashed open the head of a man and broke his arm, but did not kill him. Antônio moved on to a neighboring house and there wounded a woman with a knife as well as

---

97 "*Gentios,*" cited in Euripides Funes, "Mocambos do Trombetas: História, Memória e Identidade," *Estudos Afroamericanas Virtual,* Universidade Federal do Ceará, 2004, 13, www.ub.es/afroamerica/EAV2/gomes_d.pdf.

98 Antônio Marcelino Marinho Gamboa, "Memória [do Baixo Amazonas]," April 11, 1828, APEP cod. 857, doc. 145.

99 João Bento to Governor of Pará, July 1, 1825, Alenquer, APEP cod. 815, doc. 61; Arthur Reis, *História de Óbidos,* Rio de Janeiro: Editora Civilização Brasileira, 1979, 40, citing a document I was unable to locate; Salles, *O Negro no Pará,* 208. According to the administrator of the Royal Cacao plantation, the cause of the problem was not the way the whites treat the slaves but a massive ethnic divide. See Administrator of Royal Cacao plantation to Governor of Pará, [?] May 1825, Alenquer, APEP cod. 815, doc. 51.

"treating her very badly," which could mean that he raped or beat her. On December 25, 1816 he again was in Santarém and was said to have "insulted some women at the church door," saying that they should "raise the whip" (a bull's pizzle) and he showed them what he meant by demonstrating on some Indian men and women bystanders. All this was aided and abetted by his master, who was heard to say to another captain, as he observed the scene, that when military uniform became cheaper he would buy a suit for "his preto Antônio."[100]

Antônio's antics become even more extraordinary the following Christmas 1817. A group of Antônio's friends were sitting together drinking on the outskirts of the Santarém under the warm night sky and toasted Antônio's health saying, "Long live our governor Antônio and death to the whites." To this he was heard to reply, "And my master will be the first." Later that night, he was said to have caused another disturbance, this time at the church door where he was prevented from entering. The second mass of the day was being celebrated and all the whites of Santarém were there in their best clothes. As the host was being raised and the priest invited people to receive communion, Antônio shouted out, "Raise the devil and the beast (cativeiro) and the whore who gave birth to them." At this point he was arrested and put in the town prison. But there he was treated like "the best kind of white man" by his master.

The manner in which Joaquim Perreira indulged treated him was not specified. Perreira may have provided food and clothes or he may have paid a fine and had him released. In any case, by January 12 of the following year, Antônio was heard to have spoken with much arrogance and threatened many people with "offensive words," and not just whites. He went into the house of Antônio José Auzier (a commissioned officer in the town) with a razor in his hand. He demanded to know the whereabouts of the mameluca who once lived there. He wanted to behead her for having said something against him in the past.[101]

Some seven weeks later, on April 2, 1818, he again came back to Santarém. This time he attacked the town's judge, Antônio Luis Coelho, the top civil official in the town. He appeared at the judge's door at eleven o'clock at night and banged so hard that he left marks on the wood. Antônio threatened him and told him to expect the "sad consequences" of his revenge. Luis Coelho reported that he had never been so badly spoken to in all his eighteen years in Santarém. Even the slave's master Joaquim Perreira spoke rudely to the judge when Perreira was told to bring Antônio into line. According to the

---

100 "*Levar o vergalho e o mesmo practicou com varios índios e indias sendo tudo apoiado pello senhor,*" sworn statement of alferes Antônio José Fernandes do Reis, June 20, 1818, Santarém, APEP cod. 700, doc 125A.
101 Sworn statement of judge Antônio José Auzier, June 20, 1818, Santarém, APEP cod. 700, doc. 125.

judge, Perreira was "an enemy of good order." Still, Antônio, while a slave and therefore someone's property, was moving relatively freely and all the time seemingly "supported" by his master.

Things came to a head on the night of Maundy Thursday, April 1818. Having made his way into the town armed, Antônio broke into the army's stores as mass was being celebrated and stole a flask of gunpowder. Apparently, he wanted to create disorder and sought revenge for those who had put him in prison.[102] Antônio headed for the church, where a black guard stood at the entrance. Antônio slashed at him with a knife and ran away. The next day, Antônio José Fernandes dos Reis tried to arrest him for stealing the gunpowder, but again his master protected him, though eventually he was brought into custody.

Luis Coelho decided Antônio should be sent to Belém with a list of his crimes. He believed the governor should deal with Antônio because the whites of Santarém could not live with him any more, even in prison. "He continues to threaten and promises revenge on all those who helped to arrest him."[103] On the day of his embarkation for Belém, Antônio was accompanied by a group of his friends and Perreira, his master. Perreira told him that there was no need to worry because "a letter from his [Perreira's] father [to the governor] was worth more than all the judicial investigations." Meanwhile, Luis Coelho made sure the provincial authorities were in no doubt as to Antônio's ability for licentious subordination: "he governs the slaves in Santarém more than their masters ... he must be dealt with as your Excellency sees fit."[104] Antônio's actions were portrayed as "large crimes" and to have caused "a great deal of disorder." He was arrested many times but each time escaped and was given asylum by his master, who "supported him throughout the exploits, perhaps because he feared him." Indeed, the judge wrote that Antônio always triumphed with the help of his master. Whether his master's special protection continued to secure his fate is unknown.

This account is a curious, but exceptional, story. A slave was actively sheltered by his master and treated like a white man. This elevation was not lost on his fellows who also made him into governor, the top provincial job of the time. Antônio disrupted the segregation of women by addressing them directly and in an overtly sexual way. He also had no respect for the church and overturned the most sacrosanct of Catholic rites with blasphemy. What is more, he appeared to move around freely in the

102 Military commander Antônio Luis Coelho to Governor of Pará, April 13, 1818, Santarém, APEP cod. 700, doc. 124.
103 Judge Manuel Joaquim Bentes to Governor of Pará, June 23, 1818, Santarém, APEP cod. 700, doc. 123.
104 Military commander Antônio Luis Coelho to Governor of Pará, January 12, 1818, Santarém, APEP cod. 684, doc. 23.

region from farm to farm, from town to country and back again, almost as if he could choose his comings and goings. This was a parody of race, gender, and religion. If Antônio was challenging these hierarchies, we may assume he was one of many renegades, even though his case stands out from other examples of the "weapons of the weak."[105]

This chapter has examined the ways in which various actors fought Portuguese rule and challenged the tyranny of their masters and, in the case of Antônio, opened up new spaces for self-expression. These were different kinds of resistance with various outcomes for the colonial world. That world was neither firmly in place nor was its foundation threatened (as it would be in the early 1820s). Rather, groups and individuals sought to gain advantage within it. This was achieved by seeking new bosses, moving to a new town, and maintaining diverse sources of livelihood. Versatility was a key characteristic of Indian and mestiço strategies for survival, such that they would participate selectively in colonial markets and labor relations, and change bosses, if they saw fit. For the runaway slaves and indigenous nations, their choice was to remain outside the colonial system, yet they wanted to benefit from some of its spoils. Perhaps it was their dependence on these rewards that made them a menace, for they had to raid and fight for tools, kidnap victims, and so on. The extent to which these items were required for the continuity of livelihoods indicates these groups' lack of will to end colonial rule. Instead, their motivation was to control the manner in which they engaged with it. In this way, they shared the same interests as other individuals and groups mentioned in this chapter. These histories of violent interaction and their responses not only provide the background to the years of intense conflict between all parties from 1820–1840, they also acted to structure the range of viable options open to those unable to participate directly in the political process.

Many of the anticolonial grievances found resonance in oral histories of injustice, exclusion, loss of land, and unending demands for labor service, taxes, and conscription. The wealthier Brazilian cacao planters, administrators, and cattle ranchers would too have experienced discrimination at the hands of the Portuguese who assumed they had the right to rule. It was only in the very early 1820s that these variously oppressed groups in Pará found common ground in their opposition to Portuguese domination. This is not to say that they shared the same interests or means of pursuing them. Rather, there was a sudden congregation of diverse actors with liberal persuasions, Amazonian peasant values, and enslaved experiences.

---

105 This is a reference to James Scott, *Weapons of the Weak: Everyday Forms of Peasant Resistance*, New Haven: Yale University Press, 1985.

6

Independence, Liberalism, and Changing Social and Racial Relations, 1820–1835

By way of introduction to the events surrounding independence and ongoing conflict up to the Cabanagem, some reflections are required on the difference between peasant and enslaved political worldviews and liberalism. The basis of Amazonian opposition to colonial authority has been presented as a series of loosely associated characteristics, including geographical mobility, the use of diverse economic skills, the speaking of lingua geral, long-distance family networks, and flight from oppressive masters. These features did not form a coherent body of ideas or practices; on the contrary, they were the haphazard outcome of the actions of those forced into the colonial world as they contended with Portuguese policy. By the very nature of this kind of opposition, they would have been composed of regional histories and cultural parameters. So far, this book has argued that Amazonian popular cultures of resistance involved an attachment to places and people through the innovative and locally meaningful adjustments of existing material and cultural resources. This process was inclusive rather than exclusive: natives could be anybody who showed a willingness to join in, as it were. In this way, interethnic alliances were integral to the establishment of peasant and enslaved political worldviews.

This should be contrasted with the history of "nativism" in Brazil, which some have argued goes back to the wars against the Dutch in the mid-seventeenth century.[1] The Dutch expulsion was said to have united all those in Brazil, regardless of background, with a sense of belonging and togetherness.[2] Most frequently, nativism is associated with vehement anti-Portuguese activity and exaggerated defense of the privileges of the native-born. It did not begin as a political movement seeking to purge elements considered alien until independence, when it became associated with radical liberalism and an anti-Pedro I faction. Nativism and other forms of liberalism in the period are only part of the story in this book. Rebels or liberals did not

---

1 Luciano Figueiredo, *Rebeliões no Brasil Colônia*, Rio de Janeiro: Jorge Zahar, 2005, 11–14.
2 Bradford E. Burns, *Nationalism in Brazil: A Historical Survey*, New York: Praeger, 1968; Ronaldo Vainfas (ed.), *Dicionário do Brasil Colonial, 1500–1808*, Rio de Janeiro: Objetiva, 2000.

use the label *nativism* at the time. Brazilian historians first used it at the end of the nineteenth century to refer to the origins of nationalism.[3]

For most commentators on the first half of the nineteenth century in Brazil, nativism is a radical type of liberalism. Roderick Barman, for example, understands nativism to be a strong form of patriotism and contrasts it with nationalism, since local loyalty overrode wider belonging. Certain liberals who favored federalism and republicanism were, following Barman, "Nativists."[4] Similarly John Chasteen, writing about Pará in the same period, uses the term *nativist* as a political label. Yet he also understands the term to be protonationalist in the sense that it shares with nationalism a sense of a territorially defined people.[5] The problem with this formulation is that it implies that nativism comes into being fully formed. Recently, Gladys Sabina Ribeiro has argued that Brazilian national identity was progressively constructed in the 1820s as it developed in opposition to the Portuguese presence in Brazil. She also demonstrates that popular identification with the nation and the patria was not a mere imitation of élite sentiment, but developed its own characteristics and interpretations.[6] As should be clear, peasant opposition in the Amazon before independence is eminently practical – the sense of togetherness arises from living together and communicating common experiences. The patria was the environment of rivers and forests of the Amazon, not Brazil in general. This popular concept of the homeland had to be worked at and developed according to present conditions. It did not define *a priori*, the collective experience of those who opposed Portuguese rule. Perhaps for these reasons the notion was not powerful enough to unite élite and popular perceptions of patria. Yet the Cabanagem was not a mere defense of the homeland; it was about participation in nation building and the political process. All sorts of expectations and commitments had been set off by the multiethnic alliances achieved in independence. A new political consciousness had begun to emerge in 1820.

Nativists, peasants, and slaves were often allies in seeking to realize their aspirations in Pará. The main demands of liberals all over Brazil in the early

---

3 See Gladys Sabina Ribeiro, *A Liberdade em Construção: Identidade Nacional e Conflitos Antilusitanos no Primeiro Reinado*, Rio de Janeiro: Relume-Dumará, 2002; and Ron Seckinger, "The Politics of Nativism: Ethnic Prejudice and Political Power in Mato Grosso, 1831–1834," *The Americas* 1975, 32, 4.

4 Roderick Barman, *Brazil: The Forging of a Nation, 1798–1852*, Stanford: Stanford University Press, 1988, 111.

5 John Chasteen, "Cautionary Tale: A Radical Priest, Nativist Agitation, and the Origin of Brazilian Civil Wars," in Rebecca Earle (ed.), *Rumours of Wars: Civil Conflict in Nineteenth Century Latin America*, ILAS, London, 2000, 105, n. 6.

6 Ribeiro, *A Liberdade em Construção*; also on lusophobia, see Jeffrey Mosher, "Political Mobilization, Party Ideology, and Lusophobia in Nineteenth-Century Brazil: Pernambuco, 1822–1850," *Hispanic American Historical Review*, 80, 4, 2000, 881–912.

nineteenth century were for a constitutional monarchy that safeguarded individual rights, limited royal power, and promoted a free market.[7] Liberals in Pará wavered in their support of liberals in Portugal, rather than Brazil, and had to rely on the support of the region's local inhabitants to bolster their own political designs and careers.[8] For this reason, liberals at times sounded more radical than they were prepared to be (inflammatory language was the order of the day: anti-Rio, anti-Portuguese and, less often, anti-white). Thus liberalism in Brazil, whose history really starts in the very early 1800s with economic liberalization, coincided with Amazonian anti-colonial resistance. Liberalism lent local forms of opposition a language and ideology, but not necessarily one that articulated everything people felt and knew. The coexistence ended in the first months of the rebellion. As a consequence, nativists turned to repression, allying themselves with the regency government in Rio (which was by then performing its own u-turn), something which may have cost them much personal anguish. Such a retreat permits the conclusion that Paraense élite liberals were never interested in promoting political equality and regional cultural identity, such as using lingua geral or deepening the connections with the oral histories of oppression. They were much more concerned with their own careers and defending certain liberal ideals at the expense of their rivals. As Emilia Viotti da Costa says, liberal ideas were like "ideological weapons" that could be used to achieve very specific goals.[9]

Potential common ground between Paraense liberalism and anticolonial resistance also lay in the revolutionary idea of universal emancipation, which attracted slaves, Indians, and mestiços. The connections were based in the claim that all Brazilians had something native in common and they used the same language of regional regeneration by harnessing the riches of the province and valuing local identity, not necessarily in conflict with the national.[10] The aims of a limited monarchy, popular sovereignty, and possibly federalism could be achieved only by ending the rule of tyrannical leaders and all they stood for. A graphic illustration of their conjuncture comes from the early copies of the liberal newspaper *O Paraense* from early 1822, which apparently (none have survived from that time) showed on the

7 See Jeffrey Needell, *The Party of Order: The Conservatives, the State, and Slavery in the Brazilian Monarchy, 1831–1871*, Stanford: Stanford University Press, 2006; Ronaldo Vainfas, (ed.), *Dicionário do Brasil Imperial (1822–1889)*, Rio de Janeiro: Objetiva, 2002; Lucia Maria Bastos Paschoal Guimarães and Maria Emilia Prado (eds.), *O Liberalismo no Brasil Imperial: Origens, Conceitos e Prática*, Rio de Janeiro: Editora Raven, 2001.

8 See Geraldo Mártires Coelho, *Anarquistas, Demagogos e Dissidentes: A Imprensa Liberal no Pará de 1822*, Belém: CEJUP, 1993.

9 Emilia Viotti da Costa, *The Brazilian Empire: Myths and Histories*, Chapel Hill: University of North Carolina Press, 2000, 56.

10 John Chasteen, "Cautionary tale," 111.

front cover two interlocked hands, one black and the other white.[11] Yet liberalism could not sustain such revolutionary rhetoric. Its ideas had to be applied and in this process liberalism lost its radical force: "Rights defined as universal became the privilege of the minority, the minority of those with property and power" is how Viotti da Costa has put the change.[12] The realities of the social and economic conditions restricted the adaptation of ideas from Europe. Nevertheless, the brief encounter between radical liberalism and local traditions of undermining colonial authority during the years of 1821 through 1834 in Pará had provided enough time for revolutionary ideas to take root, as this chapter will recount.

Local factors also shaped liberalism in Pará. The apparent lack of interest in the region aggravated radical liberals, who never attained the influential positions in government. Although there may have been little to separate democratic liberals in Pará from those in Rio, there was a profound mistrust of regional élites on behalf of those in Brazil's capital. Furthermore, some wealthy Paraenses had a strong sense of attachment to Portugal, maintained by the import and export of goods, family connections and, in a few cases, university education. These people, known as *luso-paraenses*, were in favor of equality between Brazil and Portugal and a free market. When Brazil became independent, these people hoped Pará would remain part of the Portuguese empire. From the 1820s many factions developed among the élite; it is impossible to distinguish clear ideological divisions. For the most part, this was due to the fact that liberal politics was full of contradictions as well as particularities. The best-known contradiction in Brazil was the liberal justification of slavery.[13] For the same reasons, the roots of Amazonian resistance were not lusophobic, rather anticolonial. It is not difficult to understand why the two may have been mixed up.

In order to highlight the various élite positions of the time as they were perceived by a commentator and a group from the National Assembly based in Rio, the following two quotations will be offered.

The first difficulty which the new monarch [Dom Pedro 1 in 1822] began to experience, in the administration of his kingdom, was an appearance of republican, or democratic principles in some of the northern provinces, which necessarily occasioned him considerable uneasiness. In order to prevent the growth of delusive theories which, in so mixed a population, could not fail to be attended with fatal consequences, he, on the 9th of August, 1823, addressed a proclamation to the

11 See Baena, *Compêndio das Eras do Pará*, Belém: Universidade Federal do Pará, 1969, 328; and Arthur Reis, "O Grão Para e Maranhão," in Fernando Henrique Cardoso (ed.), *O Brasil Monarquico, Part 4, Dispersão e Unidade, História da Civilisação Brasileira*. Rio de Janeiro: Bertrand Brasil, 2004, 92.

12 Emilia Viotti da Costa, *The Brazilian Empire*, 57.

13 See Roberto Schwarz, "Misplaced Ideas: Essays on Literature and Society in Late Nineteenth-century Brazil," in his collection, *Misplaced Ideas: Essays on Brazilian Culture*, London: Verso, 1992, 19–32.

Brazilians, in which he says, 'some of the chambers in the Northern Provinces, have given to their deputies instructions, breathing a democratic spirit. Democracy in Brazil! In this great and vast Empire, it would be an absurdity. **** Brazilians! [sic] trust to your Emperor and Perpetual Defender. He wishes no power that does not belong to him; but he will never allow that to be usurped, to which he is entitled, and at the same time so indispensably necessary to secure your happiness. Let us wait for the constitution of the Empire, and let us hope that it will be worthy of you. May the supreme arbiter of the universe grant to us union and tranquillity – strength and perseverance; and the great work of our liberty and independence will be accomplished!¹⁴

[...] Brazilians! Your conduct has been above all praise ... Let the adopted Brazilians who have been seduced by perfidious suggestions, acknowledge that it was the love of liberty and not the thirst after vengeance which armed us ... The Brazilians abominate tyranny, they regard the foreign yoke with horror ... Fellow Citizens! We now have a country, we now have a monarch the symbol of your union and of the integrity of the Empire, one who educated among us, can receive almost in the cradle the first lessons of American liberty, and learn to love Brazil, where he first drew breath; the cradle of anarchy and of the dissolution of the provinces has disappeared and has been substituted by a more cheerful scene ... Viva a nação Brasileira! Viva a constitução! Viva o Imperador Constitucional o Senhor Dom Pedro II!¹⁵

In the first quotation, taken from a book originally published in English in 1828, the proclamation by Pedro I indicates some of the contradictions in his own position. He wanted a constitution, yet he wanted to be the absolute monarch and not lose any of his powers. Democracy was, for him, a move too far, even though by it he meant a few good men (*homens bons*, as citizens who had the right to vote were known) electing a limited number of local officials. Constitutional reform (based on the French 1791 constitution) was a basic liberal demand because it ensured Brazilian sovereignty. It would end tyranny, despotism, and the arbitrary use of the law. According to Eric Hobsbawm, these kinds of liberal constitutionalists were not interested in universal suffrage or equality or abolition, but in having a proper, well-thought-through legal document.¹⁶ These demands became intrinsically

---

14 Paulo Midosi, *Portugal, or Who is the Lawful Successor to the Throne?* London: John Richardson, 1828, 15–16.

15 Quoted in John Armitage, *The History of Brazil*, London, 1836, 294–297.

16 Eric Hobsbawm, *The Age of Revolution, 1789–1840*, London: Abacus, 1977, 80–81. For a discussion of the class-based aspect of the 1824 Brazilian constitution, see Clarence Haring, *Empire in Brazil*, Cambridge: Harvard University Press, 1958; and more generally for Latin America, see R. A. Humphreys and John Lynch (eds.), *The Origins of Latin American Revolutions 1808–1826*, New York: Alfred Knopf, 1965.

linked to the press and the first printing of newspapers in Brazil. Presses had been banned until 1808 and their introduction was primarily to advance political argument, especially on the liberal side. They proliferated in all the provinces, with the copying of large sections of news and polemic from one region to another. As a result, Brazilians became conscious of themselves as citizens through divisive political arguments. In Pará much of the conflict concerned the nomination of provincial presidents by the Court in Rio, but also the freedom to publish newspapers and have influence in government.

The second proclamation was made on the day after the abdication of Pedro I, April 8, 1831. It was issued by the deputies who happened to be present in Rio and gathered informally. Brazil had just entered a period when the son of Pedro I was too young to rule, so a regency administration was put in place which lasted until July 1840. If April 7, 1831 was the date when the proper "political existence" of Brazil began because the Portuguese-born emperor sailed back to his home country, it would also inaugurate a new cycle of violence between Brazilians themselves. And there remained unfinished business between the Portuguese and Brazilians. For the next three years, bloody urban and rural battles, especially in the northern provinces (Bahia, Pernambuco, Maranhão, and Pará) took place between the "restorationists" (*restauradores* or *caramurus*) and the radical liberals. Not until late 1834, when news arrived of Pedro I's death, did the Portuguese factions retreat from the center stage and Brazilians no longer feared a recolonization effort from Portugal. Yet the violent conflicts continued in various forms, with regional challenges to central domination a major element. From the abdication to the conservative backlash (*regresso*, literally "return movement") starting in September 1837, radical liberals were in control of the regency government and ceded some autonomy to provincial administrations. The regional rebellions allowed a conservative élite into power in 1837, though by the mid-1830s many liberals were backing away from their ideals. The liberal experiment was over; and conservative-minded politicians established, in the words of one recent commentator, "the sort of centralized, authoritarian regime that Pedro I had wanted, one in which power and legitimacy flowed from the emperor."[17] Still, the conservative ascendancy produced its own regional rebellions, ending only in 1848 and serving to remind national élites that their political worldview was not yet hegemonic.

---

17 Jeffrey Mosher, "The Struggle for the State: Partisan Conflict and the Origins of the Praiera Revolt in Imperial Brazil," *Luso-Brazilian Review*, 2005, 42, 2, 41. For the regresso, see Thomas Flory, *Judge and Jury in Imperial Brazil: 1808–1871: Social Control and Political Stability in the New State*, Austin: University of Texas Press, 1981, 131; and Needell, *The Party of Order*.

Belém, 1820–1824

The following narrative is concerned with the appearance of liberalism as an ideological force and its alliance with anticolonial movements.[18] Essentially, this means concentrating on the relations between different kinds of Brazilian-born people (though not exclusively so), including the use to which the élite Brazilians put their allies in their arguments. Unfortunately, the repression of liberal journalism was so complete that very few printed materials remain. Batista Campos, as the (second) editor of the first newspaper to be printed in Belém, must have written a great deal, but only a handful of his letters survive to this day.[19] This means relying on commentaries made later on and contemporary accusations against the liberals, neither of which can be totally trusted given the context. A brief example will suffice: Palma Muniz, one Pará historian, gives full biographical details in his 1930 study of the main protagonists in the events surrounding independence in Pará.[20] Yet he fails to include an entry on Batista Campos. This can only be explained by an ideological blindness still in place a hundred years later.

Aside from the general transatlantic movement of ideas and the invasion of Guyana, the rising liberal tide can be given a precise date in the case of Pará. This is the arrival in December 1820 of a young man on a boat from Lisbon.[21] He had recently graduated from Coimbra University and had witnessed the O Porto constitutional revolution in August of that year. Clever and shrewd (though apparently given to mental instability), Felipe Patroni disembarked in Belém full of energy for reform, clutching the news from Portugal.[22] The Lisbon-based Portuguese courts (*côrtes*) were to be recalled (after two hundred years); each region of the empire would be represented, so no longer would Pará be dependent on absolutist and centralized rule from Rio. Provincial governments (*juntas provisórias* and *conselhos gerais*) would be elected and gain legitimacy through their new representatives. The buzzword was regeneration (*regeneração*), so decadent

---

18 Useful general sources for this section include Raiol, *Motins Políticos*; Guilherme Mota, *1822: Dimensões*, São Paulo: Perspectiva, 1972; Arthur Reis, *O Grão Pará e o Maranhão*; Barman, *Brazil*; John Armitage, *The History of Brazil*, London, 1836; Manoel Barata, *Poder e Independência no Grão-Pará*, Belém: Conselho Estadual da Cultura, 1975; Antônio Côrrea, *A Fragata Leopoldina e a Missão Grenfell no Pará*, Belém: UNAMAZ, 2003; Felippe José Pereira Leal, "Memória Sobre os Acontecimentos Políticos que Tiveram Lugar no Pará 1822–1823," *RIHGB*, 1859, 22, 161–200; Chasteen, "Cautionary Tale"; and Coelho, *Anarquistas*.

19 Issues 32 and 44 and a supplement to issue 40 from September and October 1822 are transcribed from the AHU in Coelho, *Anarquistas*, 311–330.

20 João de Palma Muniz, *Adesão do Grão-Pará a Independência*, Belém: Conselho Estadual da Cultura, 1973.

21 Pereira Leal, "Memória Sobre os Acontecimentos," 163.

22 See Baena, *Compêndio das Eras*, 319.

and impoverished had life become.[23] Support for constitutional renewal was unanimous among the white oligarchs. For the Portuguese loyalists it meant direct contact with Lisbon; for the Brazilians the elections answered their call to have a political voice. In the absence of a governor in the second half of 1820 (who had apparently run off with a love interest), a provisional junta was installed as the government of Pará. It consisted of nine administrative, religious, and military leaders. This junta on January 1, 1821 declared Pará to be in favor of a constitutional revolution.[24] By April 1821 the other provinces had followed suit, and King João VI had been finally persuaded to return to Lisbon, only to try to throw out the constitution and reinstall an absolutist state.

The Côrtes remained in place, however, and deputies were elected, three from Pará and the Rio Negro, though they would not take their seats until the end of 1821 – by which time the days of the Côrtes were numbered, as far as Brazil was concerned. Patroni managed to gain an audience with King João VI in late 1821 in Lisbon, where he raised the possibility of the abolition of slavery, only to receive an extremely strong rebuttal.[25] In a speech to the Côrtes by Patroni on April 5, 1823, something of the way with which he approached the battle of ideas of the time can be seen, though he appeared to have dropped the calls for the end of slavery. He laid out his belief that since the arrival of the Portuguese, despotic rule had put deep roots in Pará. There had been a plundering of all its riches, and there was nothing to show for this: Paraenses had lost it all. Only Paraenses had a real love of their homeland (*patria*) and because they were just as capable as the Portuguese, they should be allowed to rule.[26] Patroni also apparently favored the forging of alliances with Indians in the movement toward independence. It was not difficult to imagine the wider significance of someone like Patroni questioning slavery and appealing for support to Indians. Even if he were being mischievous, he would have divided opinion and raised the stakes.

However, the provisional governments of Pará remained faithful to constitutional renewal and the Portuguese Côrtes up to August 1823, refusing to adhere to the newly independent Brazilian nation, announced some eleven months earlier (September 7, 1822). It was only the threat of force by a British mercenary, John Pascoe Grenfell, that brought Pará reluctantly

---

23 On *regeneração* in Pará, see Coelho, *Anarquistas*, 149.
24 Baena, *Compêndio das Eras*, 321; James Henderson, *A History of the Brazil*, Longman, Hurst, Rees, London, 1821, 464; Patrick Wilcken, *Empire Adrift: The Portuguese Court in Rio*, London: Bloomsbury, 2004, 230–235.
25 Pereira Leal, "Memória Sobre os Acontecimentos," 162. The British were trying to end to the Atlantic slave trade at the time; see Leslie Bethell, *The Abolition of the Brazilian Slave Trade: Britain, Brazil and the Slave Question 1807–1869*, Cambridge: Cambridge University Press, 1970.
26 "Discurso Pronuciado na Sala das Côrtes, Sessão 5 de abril [1823?] por um das mais Illustres Deputados do Pará," 8 pages, BIHGB, lata 403, doc. 3.

into the Empire of Brazil with Pedro I at its head (his coronation was December 1, 1822).[27] Before continuing with the episodes surrounding this imposition of "freedom from Portugal," it is necessary to return to the initial triumphs of Paraense liberalism.

Between January 1821 to January 1823, the Amazon was ruled by a largely liberal élite; Batista Campos and Felix Malcher were elected to government but there were also significant Portuguese loyalists. In itself, the impact of this rule was not great. But the effervescence of ideas and the general sense of regeneration had far-reaching consequences. One concrete example is the introduction of the first printed newspaper in the Amazon, called *O Paraense*, probably first printed in April 1822 on presses brought over by Patroni (we do not know exactly when it started, since only a few later editions have survived).[28] The significance of this newspaper should not be underestimated: it was the focal point for debate and dissemination of news from the rest of Brazil. It was a sign that, for the first time, the region could be proud of itself: something colonial rule had denied Paraenses.

Educated Brazilian liberals saw themselves as giving leadership to the new alliances between Indians and slaves; a kind of benevolent paternalism. They were unlikely to have been interested in the lives of the people they claimed to be representing, other than trying to bring fair implementation of the law for all. The leaders were not calling for a new kind of society, as the leaders of the slaves of Haiti had. The support of the lower classes was necessary for the local élites to have legitimacy, but it is unlikely to have gone farther than that. Batista Campos himself owned a sugar cane mill that used slave labor, and he had a personal slave for his daily chores. Nevertheless, at the time, slaves saw both men as their redeemers.[29]

The call for the abolition of slavery in this period originated in particular from Patroni and was linked to the need for popular support. As mentioned above, the Paraense circular was printed in an early edition with an image of two hands shaking, one black and the other white. This was supported by text saying that it was hoped the order of things would soon change. Concretely, Patroni argued that slaves should be included in the calculation of electoral districts. The constitution stated that for each thirty thousand people there should be a deputy. In the official view, slaves were not full

---

27 For a biographical sketch of Grenfell and other British mercenaries, see José Honório Rodrigues, *Independência: Revolução e Contra Revolução, As Forças Armadas*, vol. 3, Rio de Janeiro: Livraria Francisco Alves, 1975, 113–133; and Brian Vale, *Independence or Death!: British Sailors and Brazilian Independence, 1822–25*, London: Tauris Academic, 1996.

28 Pereira Leal, "Memória Sobre os Acontecimentos," 163.

29 Pereira Leal, "Memória Sobre os Acontecimentos," 162. This word perhaps derives from a denunciation of Patroni by slave owners around Belém, Raiol, *Motins Políticos*, 19, n. 8. "Libertador" is also used.

persons and therefore could not be counted. But Patroni, through another widely circulated newspaper, said that slaves must be included because that way they could work toward restoring their "rights" (*direitos*). Patroni apparently saw himself as the William Penn of Pará. One contemporary relays a joke circulating at the time. On a visit to a house, Patroni became thirsty and asked for water; once the cup was finished, he stood up and told his host, who was a black slave: "Thank you, you are a being as free as I am, but the law of tyranny has made you a slave, I hope that ... " [sic, presumably the punch line is he hopes slaves will become free soon]. Yet this commentator notes that Patroni's main ambition was to become a deputy to the Côrtes.[30] The people who would elect him were the rich and powerful, not the slaves, and neither Indians nor the poor, for that matter. Their inclusion in the consideration of electoral districts was symbolically significant but not much else. Still, abolition was a key radical liberal idea being discussed in the early 1820s. Patroni, however, seems to be the main individual pushing this cause; others like Batista Campos seem less concerned with it. By the time Patroni leaves the political stage in the mid-1820s, abolitionist calls had been mostly abandoned.

While liberals were in the ascendant, the Portuguese sympathizers were gathering their forces. The creation of a new position, governor of arms (basically the vice president), appointed from Rio (in addition to the president) saw the arrival of a strongly loyalist Portuguese officer, José Maria de Moura, in April 1822. In May of that year he arrested Patroni for spreading "incendiary ideas" through *O Paraense*, and deported him back to Lisbon. Batista Campos took over as editor, employed the same rhetoric, most of it culled from other newspapers circulating at the time. News arrived that along with Pará, only Maranhão, Ceará, and Piauí remained loyal to Portugal in early 1823. A municipal council election in Belém saw only Brazilians elected, but still they could not persuade the governing junta to recognize Pedro I and independence. The new councilors wrote: "now is the time of the Brazilians ... our constitutionally composed chamber will show those Europeans that the country is ours and that they are foreigners."[31] Then, on March 1, the pro-Portuguese group deposed the whole municipal chamber and governing junta, putting their members under house arrest. New representatives were elected and fidelity to the Portuguese king expressed.[32] In response to

---

30 Baena, *Compêndio das Eras*, 328. See also Raiol, *Motins Políticos*, 18–19, n. 8, who transcribed the denunciation of Patroni. His pamphlets were said to have spread ideas about freedom for all individuals and the need to thrown off the shackles of bondage. Some slaves even thought slavery had been abolished.

31 Pereira Leal, "Memória Sobre os Acontecimentos," 166.

32 Pereira Leal, "Memória Sobre os Acontecimentos," 168; Raiol, *Motins Políticos*, 27.

this outrage, a group of a hundred men, some soldiers, others administrators and politicians, planned an uprising for mid-April, but they were caught and arrested before they were able to act. There followed a debate as to whether to execute them all. Arguing against the proposal, the bishop of the Province said that they could not be executed because it would weaken the perception of white people among slaves. If the slaves witnessed the capital punishment of those fighting for freedom, what "ideas of liberty will ferment in their heads, it could lead to the fatal catastrophe of San Domingos?"[33] Under colonial law, élites could be judged for capital crimes only in Lisbon, and the types of crimes depended on one's status. The logic in the quotation is then that if the enslaved Africans saw the whites executed, that is treated as though they were commoners, the aura of their status would be eroded, and the slaves might rebel as they did in Haiti.

O Paraense was forced to close as a result of the new regime. In its place and somewhat predictably, a new periodical opened called *O Luso-Paraense* (literally "The Portuguese Paraense"). The forces sent by Pedro I to ensure that each province adhered to independence were moving northward, capturing a Portuguese warship on the way. Lord Cochrane made it as far as Maranhão, taking command of it in July 1823 with a trick. He used the Portuguese warship to approach the provincial capital port of São Luis. The loyalist governing junta in turn sent out its own ship thinking it was heading for an ally and was duly secured. Cochrane told the captain that behind him was the whole Brazilian navy ready to bombard the place if they did not recognize the political reality of independence. It worked; and Cochrane's deputy, Grenfell, was sent on to Pará to fit the last piece in the jigsaw of the new Empire. Grenfell used the same trick with the frigate *Leopoldina* in Belém. August 14 saw the governing junta, full of loyal Portuguese, grudgingly sign away their colonial past.[34]

Rather than sail immediately, Grenfell remained in Belém, probably because he sensed the new situation could undo itself amid conflict between armed factions. Despite the proclamation of independence, the Portuguese remained in government, much to the discontent of the liberals. About a thousand armed soldiers marched on the Governor's palace on October 15 and demanded the deportation of the enemy Portuguese and the nomination of Batista Campos as president.[35] They were dispersed peacefully and with promises of a favorable acceptance of their demands. These soldiers

33 Raiol, *Motins Políticos*, 35.
34 See Thomas Cochrane, *The Autobiography of a Seaman*, vol. 2, London: Constable, 1996; Barman, *Brazil*, 102–106; Antônio Eutalio Corrèa, *A Fragata Leopoldina e a Missão Grenfell no Pará*, Belém: UNAMAZ, 2003; Brian Vale, *Independence or Death!: British Sailors and Brazilian Independence, 1822–25*, London: Tauris Academic, 1996.
35 Raiol, *Motins Políticos*, 46, says 3,000, but this seems an exaggeration.

were mostly part-time reservists, made up of Indians and mestiços. The next day the junta did step down, but disturbances continued. On the night of October 17, a group of soldiers attacked Portuguese property in the city. Grenfell ordered the men to be locked up. The next day he picked five randomly from the barracks and immediately executed them in the square in front of the governor's palace. Batista Campos himself was tied around the mouth of a cannon with the fuse lit in order to force a confession concerning the leadership of the attack. He denied any involvement and none could be proven, indicating a rupture between the élite liberals and soldiers with liberal sympathies. A further 256 soldiers were arrested and squashed into the hold of the prison ship, *São José Diligente*, afterwards known as *Brigue Palhaço*, the Brig *Clown*.

Crowded and almost unable to breathe, and suffering alike from heat and thirst, the poor wretches attempted to force their way on deck, but were repulsed by the guard, who, after firing upon them, fastening down the hatchway, threw a piece of ordnance across it, and effectually debarred all egress. The stifling sensation caused by this exclusion of air drove the suffering crowd to utter madness; and many are said to have lacerated and mangled each other in the most horrible manner. Suffocation with all its agonies succeeded. The aged and the young, the assailant and his antagonist, all sank down exhausted, and in the agonies of death. In the hope of alleviating their suffering a stream of water was at length directed into the hold, and towards morning [of 21st October] the tumult had abated, but from a cause which had not been anticipated. Of all two hundred and fifty three [sic] four only were found alive, who had escaped destruction from having concealed themselves behind a water-butt.[36]

It is not known who was directly responsible for the deaths.[37] To the soldiers and most others from the popular classes, this episode revealed the true colors of the new regime in Rio. Pedro I was held personally responsible for the loss of the soldiers' lives, since it was he who sent Grenfell. The tragedy traumatized Belém and as news of it spread upriver and around the Atlantic towns of the Amazon delta, it entrenched an already tense situation. It continued to be cited as a motive for hatred of Pedro I until he abdicated and more generally of the Rio regime for years to come. It was recounted to many of the travelers and scientists who traveled to Belém in the mid-nineteenth century.[38] What made the situation worse was the fact that a

---

36 Armitage, *The History of Brazil*, 108.

37 Raiol, *Motins Políticos*, 46–52. Paraense historians of the first half of the twentieth century were convinced Grenfell was directly responsible for the order to block up the exit. A recent study by naval historian Brian Vale of British involvement in Brazil has argued that in fact no shots were fired nor was the exit secured: Vale, *Independence or Death!*, 86–87.

38 For example, James C. Fletcher and Daniel P. Kidder, *Brazil and the Brazilians. Portrayed in Historical and Descriptive Sketches*. Boston: Little, Brown, 1879, 544.

handful of the Portuguese loyalists, including some who had tried to assassinate Grenfell, were imprisoned on the same ship on which the British mercenary was commander, and apparently treated well. The Brazilian navy had come to force independence on a few hundred ardent luso-paraenses, and had ended up killing those who supported independence. The irony (hence the change of the ship's name) and the sense of treachery were not lost on those who witnessed events. The catastrophic loss of life deepened the belief that if the region really was going to have its regeneration, it was going to involve new multiethnic alliances. If leaders were to promote their worldview and give shape to the new consciousness, they would have to prepare themselves better for the tasks ahead.

Increasing bitterness grew during the final months of 1823 between Pedro I and political representatives in the Constituent Assembly in Rio. Pedro reacted by dissolving the assembly and exiling key liberal leaders of the time. From this point, various Brazilians no longer saw him as serving the cause of independence but his Portuguese friends. He and his advisers drew up a constitution, which was seen by radical liberals as not recognizing the liberty of Brazil. More anti-Portuguese attacks took place in many cities.

The most sustained was a rebellion starting in Recife in late 1823. It was led by Manuel Carvalho de Pais Andrade, who was elected provincial president by the governing junta. (His revolutionary credentials had been established in his involvement in the 1817 uprising in the city.) His appointment was overturned by Pedro I and a naval squadron sent to bring order. The movement that resisted Rio's influence was openly republican (that is, against the Portuguese king), and federalist rather than secessionist. It called itself the Confederation of the Equator and was proclaimed on July 2, 1824; it hoped to be joined by the other northern provinces. Some did adhere but not Maranhão and Pará. Imperial troops under Thomas Cochrane staged a naval blockade and gained control of Recife from the land. The rebels were tracked down and sixteen leaders were executed, including the ideologue Father Caneca. This time, there were no qualms about how others might perceive such a penalty.[39]

---

39 See Dênis de Antônio Mendonça Bernardes, "Pernambuco e sua Área de Influência: Um Território em Transformação (1780–1824)," in Istvan Janscó (ed.), *Independência: História e Historiografia*, São Paulo: Editora Hucitec, 2005, 379–410; and Jeffrey Mosher, *Political Struggle, Ideology, and State Building: Pernambuco and the Construction of Brazil, 1817–1850*, Lincoln: University of Nebraska Press, 2008. In a passage from *Motins Políticos* (79–80), Raiol says that some key individuals from the rebel movement in Recife came to Pará in April 1824 and joined forces with Paraense liberals. Their plan was to proclaim the Confederation of the Equator in Belém but they were arrested beforehand. Recently, Machado has called into question the veracity of Raiol's claim who gives no sources. Machado could not find supporting evidence in the state's archive, APEP, André Machado, "A Quebra Mola Real das Sociedades: A Crise Política do Antigo Regime Português na Provincia do Grão-Pará (1821–1825)," Ph.D dissertation, University of São Paulo.

Alliances and Rebellion in the Interior

As news of the *Brigue Palhaço* tragedy left the capital, tensions worsened. The fight over independence quickly moved from the urban center to actively involving large portions of the people, often self-organized, in the whole region. In this context, new alliances were forged in a campaign against a common enemy identified as the colonial order and those who upheld it. Even though whites were fewer in the interior, there were still enough people to advocate colonial rule and to be in a position to enforce their beliefs.[40] There were rumors about the freedom of slaves and the end to abusive and violent treatment of Indians by whites, as well as a vague expectation that life would get better; these were given concrete form in what follows, especially in a proclamation of independence from a small town in the interior.

With Grenfell more or less in control of the capital, a mixed group soldiers and artisans outraged by the deaths in October congregated in the town of Cametá at the end of 1823. They razed the town in an anti-Portuguese attack and declared themselves to be standing against the "enemies of independence." Grenfell was supposed to have sent an expeditionary force to regain Cametá in February 1824. However, he refused, claiming to have discharged his orders. With £8,000 (40,000 milreis) in prize money, he headed for Rio de Janeiro. The rebels in Cametá remained and their cause spread upriver to the Lower Amazon.[41] By March 1824 there was serious concern that the whole Amazonas area was on the brink of large-scale rebellion and counter-rebellion.

The government in Belém responded by trying to secure a deal with the Cametá liberals and creating a provisional military junta consisting of four imperial military officials, based in Santarém, to suppress what was seen as a "counter-revolution."[42] Granted full powers, the junta declared a state of emergency that suspended all rights. The junta could conduct the suppression of the revolt with impunity. Quite simply, the junta saw its task as stopping the spread of the rebellion, which involved on the one hand Indians, slaves, and mestiços (ambiguously Brazilian from their point of view) and on the other Portuguese, who were against independence.[43]

---

40 See Reis, *História de Óbidos*, 40, for the condescending Portuguese perception of Brazilians in the interior.

41 Raiol, *Motins Políticos*, 53–82; Vale, *Independence or Death!*, 87–88; and Machado, "A Quebra Mola Real," 250–252.

42 Members of the Provisional Military Junta for the Defense of Santarém (led Antônio Luis Coelho) to Governo Geral do Pará, April 2, 1824, Santarém, APEP cod. 790, doc. 56.

43 The following narrative is a synthesis of ABAPP, Vol. 12, 1981 (which is a transcription of codex 776 from the APEP), and APEP cod. 783; cod. 789; cod. 790; cod. 798. Reis in his histories of Santarém and Óbidos also narrates the episode. After writing this section, I read Machado, "A Quebra Mola

The conflict came to a head in mid-March 1824, when a group of Indian rebels, possibly including some whites, attacked some of the north bank towns in the Lower Amazon. On March 13 insurgents came to Monte Alegre, picked on three white traders, stripped them of their clothes, and tied each person by their legs to a horse. The victims were then dragged through the streets and left for dead. Next, the rebels kidnapped Antônio Malcher, a prominent landowner, and his family and deposited them in a rural dwelling. Their next target was Alenquer, where they robbed and killed two prominent citizens. Before leaving town they took the icons from the church and broke them open to see if they contained gold, for it was commonly suspected that the Portuguese kept their riches under cover of a holy watch. Soon after the attacks, a letter was sent by a military officer in Monte Alegre saying that some "Europeans," who were against independence, had been involved in the incidents.

Then eyewitness reports told of slaves operating on the north bank of the river who had been armed by a few "Europeans" for the purpose of attacking the imperial army and rising up against their Brazilian masters.[44] The roving armed groups numbered an estimated four hundred people, "committing horrible atrocities without reserve against Brazilians and Europeans, attacking property and honor and cruelly taking life."[45] The imperial troops consisted of three hundred and sixty soldiers at this time, but by the end of April they had forcibly conscripted many more to stand on the front line. An order was sent to all men to leave their rural homesteads and report for duty in the nearest town.[46] This command was likely to have been not so much to recruit soldiers as to prevent them going over to the other side. As it was, there were many desertions; people left their posts when on watch, either to go to the other side or to escape into the forest.

It is clear that the slaves were organized and prepared for action. The Santarém junta observed, rather poetically despite themselves (though it is probably taken from a reactionary newspaper), that there was an "effervescence" among the slaves, and some had even declared themselves free

Real," who accords the events in the interior great significance in his characterization of political crisis of the old regime. In particular, he sees the uprising in the Lower Amazon as one sign of the uncertain future facing Pará at the time (272–288). The course of events could have gone in various directions. But with the defeat of the interior rebels one possible avenue was closed off definitively, namely a strong interior, possibly separate from Belém, controlled by its majority of poor and ethnically diverse inhabitants.

44 Council of Santarém (president Antônio Luis Coelho) to Governo Geral do Pará, April 2, 1824, Santarém, APEP cod. 790, doc. 54; [?captain in Monte Alegre] to Provisional Military Junta of Santarém, March 22, 1824, Monte Alegre, APEP cod. 798, doc. 2.

45 Provisional Junta of the Rio Negro to the Provisional Junta of Pará, March 26, 1824, Rio Negro, APAPP vol. 12, 8–80.

46 Provisional Military Junta of Santarém to the Council de Óbidos, April 23, 1824, Santarém, APAPP vol. 12, 53.

and held papers to attest to their new status.[47] Death was apparently declared to "all who are white without exception of sex."[48] There was also an alliance between Indians (*tapuias* as it was written) and blacks, even if they did not fight together in every area: "the enemy is composed of all the ordinary and stupid race of people."[49] Both Indians and blacks said they were "lords of themselves,"[50] having been encouraged to think in this way, some said, by the priest from Juruti, Antônio Manuel Sanches de Brito. A captain in Santarém told the junta there that these opinions so were offensive to the emperor and the country's independence that they had to be eliminated.[51] This was Amazonian political consciousness at its sharp edge, offering evidence that the rebellious activity was a continuity of the antagonisms in the preindependence period, yet also invigorated with liberal ideas.

The Santarém junta's first reprisal came at the end of March, when eighty soldiers marched on Alenquer. After an hour's battle, the rebels fled into the forest surrounding the town, having lost about half their numbers in the town; twenty men were killed and the same number taken as prisoners.[52] The rest were tracked down using twenty Mundurucu scouts supported by thirty soldiers. The jails were full by mid-April and some prisoners were probably summarily executed (though this punishment was never mentioned in the correspondence) or forced to serve in the army. Blockades were put in place outside each town and at entrances to streams and lakes. Mundurucu Indians continued to search for more rebel encampments outside the towns and the runaway slave communities.[53]

Throughout April more attacks took place and the insurgents gained a fragile control of Monte Alegre and Alenquer. They heard that many other towns had also been taken over by rebels and whites were afraid to go there: Gurupá, Melgaço, Portel, Óbidos, and Manaus as well as Cametá.[54]

47 The phrase is actually the "*efervescência da escravatura,*" Provisional Military Junta of Santarém to the General Government of Pará, Santarém, March 31, 1824, APAPP vol. 12, 59.

48 Provisional Military Junta of Santarém to Government of the Rio Negro, April 12, 1824, Santarém, APAPP vol. 12, 85–86.

49 Provisional Military Junta of Santarém to Council of Óbidos, April 22, 1824, Santarém, APAPP vol. 12, 54.

50 "*Senhores de si,*" Provisional Military Junta of Santarém to Captain Bibiano do Carmo, April 29, 1824, Santarém, APAPP vol. 12, 97.

51 Manoel dos Santos Falcão to Provisional Military Junta of Santarém, April 10, 1824, Santarém, ABAPP vol. 12, 88–89.

52 Provisional Military Junta of Santarém to Government of the Rio Negro, April 12, 1824, Santarém, ABAPP vol. 12, 85–86.

53 Provisional Military Junta of Santarém to Manoel dos Santos Falcão, April 15, 1824, Santarém, ABAPP vol. 12, 83.

54 Council of Santarém (president Antônio Luis Coelho) to Junta Provisorio do Pará, April 2, 1824, Santarém, APEP cod. 790, doc. 54.

However, Monte Alegre was the largest insurgent center in the Lower Amazon, attracting "all kinds of people." Rebels were also seeking new recruits by visiting communities along the Negro, Tapajós, and Xingu rivers despite the blockades. Farmsteads of whites were burned down and cattle, horses, and agricultural implements were stolen. But the sheer military might at the service of the Junta was threatening. They had a schooner with six revolving cannon, two igarités, about two hundred armed soldiers, and a hundred harquebuses at their disposal. There was evidence that some Brazilian liberals notably João Pedro de Andrade, a magistrate in Santarém, were supplying arms to the rebels throughout the conflict.

The rebellion could have spread during the previous months because each town's uprising of Indians, mestiços, and blacks spurred the next place on. A dynamic and empowering alliance had been set in motion. Quite what these people wanted to achieve is not obvious. Even when the military officer wrote "freedom from slavery" and "death to all whites" were the rebels' calls, it cannot be assumed that these were more than the necessary justifications for military suppression. How did he know when he did not talk to them or exchange letters? We know little about what forms of association the rebels wanted and whether they targeted specific whites, or all those in positions of authority.

What was to be the final assault to retake on Monte Alegre was repelled by the rebels at the beginning of May. For a few weeks a standoff was maintained, with potshots taken across the water. As a gesture of defiance, a black flag with a skull and crossbones was raised above the town. The imperial fighters' only response was to tighten their blockade on the town, yet they recognized people were still breaking the cordon and escaping. However, by mid-May, with the news that other towns were back in the hands of the government and amnesty granted to all, the rebels gave up and agreed to the conditions of a peace accord by the beginning of June. The agreement was to lay down arms, for slaves to return to their masters and to respect the authority of the imperial government. Whether these demands were honored by either side is not clear. The junta was dissolved at the end of June, having avoided a general outbreak of rebellion. However, small clusters of discord continued. Faro and Alter do Chão experienced rebel attacks on whites and their property in June, perhaps as a result of the squeeze out of Monte Alegre and a regrouping elsewhere.

This period is less interesting for the Portuguese reaction than (1) the way independence spurred other uprisings and gave confidence to all to challenge the dominant authority and political structures, there was no single independence movement, (2) the multiethnic alliances between slaves, peasants, and Indians, (3) the discourses of revolution and liberty and how they were interpreted by different groups, (4) the attack on property by rebels (destroying what was most valued by their enemy) and strategies used by the Portuguese and their supporters and the Brazilians, for example, killing cattle, guerrilla attacks, burning houses, and blockades, all of which recur during the Cabanagem. What is also striking about these events are the relatively small Portuguese losses compared with those among the rebel groups. Did the new Brazilian oligarchs fear much more the revolutionary potential of the masses than of those with property? Evidence for a positive answer can be found in a document from Alter do Chão on the Tapajós River, where the predominantly Indian administration expressed support for independence and their expectation that it would lead to liberty and equality. This is the point that previous discussions of the transition to independence have missed. The anti-independence reaction masked other fundamental and more threatening challenges to the colonial and post-colonial order.

The petition was fronted by a letter of complaint from the council of Alter do Chão, a village on the white sandy banks of the Tapajós River. The complaint concerned the spread of the rebellion near Monte Alegre in June. Some rebels came into the city threatening to kill "Europeans." As a result, the town was visited by an armed boat from Santarém, which pounded the place with artillery from the river. But the rebels had already left, so the attack was pointless. Residents fled into the forest for safety, only to return a few days later to find the town ransacked by the army. The letter was strongly and formally worded so as to demand reparation for the damage. Accompanying it was another demand, but this time the tone was very different.

It was written in the same hand as the council letter, but is much more colloquial, as if the clerk was told to write down exactly what was being said.

We the undersigned would like to make it known to your excellencies in the central government (*Governo Geral*) that this village has been very poor in recent years. We know that the much loved Emperor Dom Pedro I has urged us to engage in commerce and farming. For this reason, we want from today onward for the assessor of tithes to be a native son (*filho da terra*), rather than the contractor, who does nothing but promiscuously rob our widowers and widows. We spend all year giving tithes, and we always end up owing [more]. Another thing is that this câmara [of Alter do Chão] is always receiving orders from the village of Santarém to provide Indians to serve them, which is a great loss to this village. Freedom came for all those who are sons of Brazil, not the Europeans, [who] say they defend the fatherland (*pátria*) only to deceive the native sons .... They do nothing but harass us, taking away our wealth and property (*teres e haveres*), and that is the way that it has always been in this village. We took this action because they do nothing but threaten us, saying that we are monkeys and macaws (*macacos e araras*). To those who say that Independence is only for them, and not for the Indians: we, who have [been granted] freedom by our august Emperor, would say that even though we are

Indians, we are baptized as well as they are. From today onward we will seek to obtain from your excellencies an order to keep them from interfering with this village.[55]

The petition was signed by thirty names, by means of crosses in the middle of first and last names of each person. The surnames were the same as those of the five councilors from the first letter. We can assume that the municipal chamber was composed of the same families as those who were writing the second letter. There are a few important points to be drawn out here.

This short extract offers a window into what Indians living in the interior were thinking around the time of independence and for this reason it is highly significant, given the absence of documentation from elsewhere. It appears that they also held dear the declaration of independence from Portugal, having been cheated by outsiders for many years. Finally, they had the opportunity to influence people who would understand better their interests. Hence the call to have a native-born assessor of tithes. In the same vein, there was the complaint, replicated in many other places, that Indians were regarded as a source of ever-available, cheap labor. They should be free now of the colonial bondage (including conscription and labor service) and be able to work on their farms providing tax for the Emperor.

The other significant element is the distinction the writers of the petition drew between Europeans and those "who think independence is only for them." This indicates that there were some non-Indian Brazilians who did not consider themselves in the same category as Indians. Indians were simply not regarded as Brazilians, but a class apart who provided services for others and nothing more. From the Indian point of view, they were certain they were Indians and citizens of Brazil, and had just causes and claims on the state because they provided taxes, identified with the emperor, and so on. Moreover, even though the Directorate had abolished the separation of Indians from others, these villages were self-identifying as Indians. It is likely the attitudes expressed here were reasonably widespread at the time. In the absence of further evidence, it would not be unreasonable to link the violent conflict in the north bank towns of the Lower Amazon with the dissatisfaction felt about the constant pressure on labor and the lack of fulfillment over freedom and independence. If the government would not act, the Indians would.

There might seem something opportunistic about sending the petition at the same time as the letter of complaint, although arguably letters from Alter do Chão to the Pará government were not regular and it made practical

---

55 Council of Alter do Chão to Governo Geral of Pará, July 5, 1824, Alter do Chão, APEP cod. 789, doc. 2. This translation is by Heather Flynn Roller. I am very grateful to her for sharing with me her translation of this important document.

sense to send them together. Of course, nothing was done to address the issues in the request. Nevertheless, a pattern had been established: complaints or events in one domain occasioned others. In this sense, the accusation of opportunism can be rebutted. Having been submitted to colonial authority and violence for about one hundred and fifty years (in the Lower Amazon), rebellion had stopped being endemic and was about to become epidemic. Events in one place affected those in another in a similar way. The only strategy the government had was military. But pushing down in one place only caused the phenomenon to rise elsewhere. This was the immediate legacy of the 1820 to 1824 period in the Amazon, which effectively liberated the forces of antagonism of the past. But it would need some more provoking before they would unfurl and reach their full maturity.

In Alter do Chão the Indians were dominant, as they were in some other towns in the interior, such as Vila Franca. In some of the towns on the Amazon River itself, there were relatively more whites, some with slaves and others who could not afford them. As always, Indian labor was in high demand, particularly where slaves were absent, either because they had run away or were too expensive. Many whites, Brazilians or Portuguese or other Europeans, must have thought they still had a right to cheap Indian hands. Rather than enter into reciprocal labor exchanges with other whites (the peasant strategy to labor shortage), they sought to "employ" Indians. Most of the work was agricultural, such as preparing land, planting, harvesting, and preparing the product for sale. Those employed through obligatory service were working almost in a state of slavery, since they had little option not to work and were probably not paid, or only very little. They were probably threatened with violence if they refused. If this was not bad enough, the work regimes prevented the Indians (or mestiços) from working their own plots of land or attending to their domestic needs. Essentially, the conflict over labor had these two basic dimensions: forcible service to whites, which was illegal, and the detraction of time and effort from working for oneself. The second aspect then implied a third dimension, the right to land: if someone or a family was not working a plot of land, it could be claimed by someone else.

The response to these conflicts had often been desertion. But as we get nearer to the Cabanagem, there was growing reluctance to work for whites. In effect, this was part of the repeated call for more agriculture in the region, which dated from the end of the eighteenth century. In a long letter to the governor of Pará, the councilors of Itacoatiara town (then called Serpa) complained about the difficulty of recruiting Indian labor in the 1820s. They said they could not raise any money or taxes because there was no produce, which in turn was due to the lack of labor. "The Indians refuse to do service for the whites because they have their own *sitios*." The great problem, the municipal chamber said, was the lack of agriculture, but what they meant in fact was their own lack of farming rather than a general situation.[56] At the same time, other Indians near Manaus, a few days by sailing canoe from Parintins, were not so lucky. They had no time to work on their land and complained constantly to the priest of the abuse by colonists.[57]

The period between independence and the Cabanagem was a time when peasant and liberal ideas were disseminated throughout the whole province. The priests were generally responsible for reading out newspapers and pamphlets and, in the absence of schools and teachers, general education. One priest from the Lower Amazon, Antônio Manoel Sanches de Brito, a missionary with the Mundurucus and Maués at the time of independence, was said to have distinguished himself with his message to the Indians. A good friend of Batista Campos, as we will see below, he encouraged Indians to work for themselves, to be their own masters.[58] This message, his enemies said, was also extended to slaves, together with calls for their liberty. Sanches was an important figure in this period, since he worked with Indians and helped them settle in missions. The paucity of information on him and the fact it was mostly written by his adversaries makes it difficult to come to a proper understanding. What is certain is that during the Cabanagem rebellion itself, he played a decisive role, one that could not have been predicted by the preceding information.

It is likely that priests like Sanches campaigned for better treatment of Indians. Despite the growing confidence of some Indians, it was apparent that others were in a much worse situation, unable to control their own labor. In a memorial on the Lower Amazon written in 1828, an anonymous writer wrote "it is incredible the barbarity with which those miserable Indians are treated by those whites who order them around and are insensitive to their civilization. They are beaten with sticks of wood for even the smallest infraction."[59] Although such mistreatment abounded, it was not the exclusive experience of Indians at the time. There were contradictory messages of both liberation and independence and continued tyranny and violence, which sharpened the relations between the various actors.

No single group felt the contradiction more deeply than the enslaved Africans. Talk of the Haitian revolution spreading to Brazil was plentiful at the time. Slave traffic had diminished significantly, and new slaves appeared either through internal movement in Brazil or biological reproduction.[60] It

---

56 Council of Serpa [Itacoatiara] to President of Pará, October 24, 1829, Serpa, APEP cod. 884, doc. 93.
57 André Fernandes de Souza, "Notícias Geográphicas da Capitania do Rio Negro no Grande Rio Amazonas." *RIHGB* 10, 1848, 496.
58 Manoel Pereira de Souza to President of Pará, July 14, 1825, Óbidos, APEP cod. 815, doc. 65.
59 Anonymous, "Memória" [of the Lower Amazon], December 1, 1828, APEP cod. 851, doc. 74.
60 According to Machado, there is an almost complete silence in the Pará archives on questions of slave traffic and slave labor during the independence period, "A Quebra da Mola Real," 76–77. This silence is important to his argument since it shows that, despite all the tensions and conflicts between

would be logical to assume that this state of affairs led some masters to take better care of their slaves, to ensure their longevity and the healthy production of children. The evidence here is weak but there were some disputes after independence between slave owners about the treatment of slaves. In Alenquer, some masters apparently allowed their slaves weekends off (which allowed them more time to work on their gardens) and gave them drink in the evenings. This freedom was deplored by the members of the town council. Though it is not clear whether they were owned by "liberal" masters, some slaves held certificates of emancipation, apparently signed by Batista Campos.[61] They had been effectively freed with forged papers, and were wafting them teasingly in front of their masters. Nothing could have been more calculated to enrage a bureaucratically-minded councilor. When the Cabanagem came, slaves resorted to the same position: they had papers granting their freedom and so should join the rebels.[62]

There was much discussion in official correspondence of the level of agitation among slaves around independence.[63] The talk of Portuguese tyranny was easily applied to the slaves; they could say they were living a kind of double enslavement to their masters and the Portuguese Crown. Slave owners feared their charges would become masters of themselves, but it was far from conclusive that liberals were serious about ending slavery. The participation of slaves in the Cabanagem was not widespread: they fought on both sides (perhaps pressurized), and in the Lower Amazon they fought in their own groups and had their own positions.[64] Certainly the cabano presidents made no effort toward emancipation.

Between Independence and the Regency Administration, 1825–1830

Despite Portuguese recognition of Brazilian independence at the end of 1824, a strong Portuguese presence remained in the form of King Pedro I and the people who advised him (not to mention the Portuguese naval ships anchored in the Bay of Guajará in front of Belém). Increasing polarization in Pará was not a simple one between Portuguese and Brazilians, or merchants and planters. Liberals fought among themselves; though pro-Portuguese factions appeared more united. On a national and local level, similar

élites over independence, territorial integrity was not achieved through their eventual unity on the continuation of slavery.

61 João Bentes to President of Pará, July 1, 1825, Alenquer, APEP cod. 815, doc. 55.
62 Justice of the Peace Antônio M. Sanches Brito to Commander of the Alenquer Expedition Manoel Aragão Bentos, Pauxis, November 28, 1836, APEP cod. 1013, doc. 169 [copy].
63 See, for example, Reis, *História de Óbidos*, 40.
64 See, for example, Captain of the Naval Forces Antônio Firme Coelho to President of Pará Francisco José d'Andréa, on board Pataxo Januaria near Santarém, June 6, 1837, APEP cod. 1052, doc. 238; and Military Commander for the Lower Amazon João Henrique de Mattos to Captain Tenant of the Naval Forces of the Amazonas Antônio Firme Coelho, May 27, 1837, APEP cod. 808. doc. 141.

conflicts were reproduced, mostly violently and with little interest in a political resolution. Recent historiography has show how these levels were interwoven in an almost seamless fashion.[65] This connected nature of regional and national struggles should not be taken to imply the motives and outcomes of uprisings in the period can be characterized using the same brush.

All provinces had in common, however, ideological and physical clashes between property holders, religious and military leaders, high-level administrators, and merchants – "active citizens," as laid out in the 1824 constitution.[66] Active citizens were defined by their annual income, for the constitution determined who could vote and stand for election. The higher up the political scale (or nearer the center of power in the Rio), the more earnings were required to either vote or stand for office. The rest of the population was "passive citizens," equal to their richer counterparts in civil society but lacking political rights. I will discuss in the following paragraphs the implications of this division; for now I shall remain with the unstable élite factions.[67] Their squabbling intensified their inability to achieve dominance and impose a political solution.

From 1821 the fighting between those who intended to hold political office and determine the future of Brazil expressed itself in the form of depositions, imprisonments, deportations, and removal of public servants (in common with other provinces in the north). Violence frequently accompanied these maneuvers in Pará (as elsewhere). Recently, historian André Machado has argued that the inability of one élite group to achieve provincial hegemony in Pará was a result of their economic and political weakness. Dominant groups failed to find a common ground on which they could oppose more radical and popular forces from taking hold. This position allows Machado to address the established historiographical argument that the need to maintain slavery eventually united élites. It is assumed in turn that this guaranteed the continuity of production from the colonial to the imperial period and of an absolutist state with monarchical rule. Yet for Machado, the diversity of Brazilian regional systems prevented a unity of élite interests on a national and a local level in the early independence

65 For example, Jeffrey Mosher, "The Struggle for the State: Partisan Conflict and the Origins of the Praieira Revolt in Imperial Brazil," *Luso-Brazilian Review*, 42, 2, 2005, 40–65; and Machado, "A Quebra da Mola Real."

66 Ivan Alves Filho (ed.), *Brasil: 500 Anos em Documentos*. Rio de Janeiro: Mauad Editora, 1999.

67 The disparity between the types of citizens can be seen in the following. The town of Vila Franca had a population of 2,736 in 1833. In December of that year 69 men voted for the justice of the peace in parish elections. This indicates that roughly ten percent of men then had an income of 100 mil-réis (assuming that half the total were women, and of the male half, another half were under 25 years old), Council of Vila Franca to President of Pará, September 3, 1833, APEP cod. 947, doc. 86.

period.[68] The divisions became more polarized as the 1820s drew to a close. Lusophobic attacks and nativist attitudes became more widespread; and Portuguese factions more violent and provocative. On a cultural level, for example, the Portuguese sympathizers in Óbidos sang a variation on the hymn of independence, which deliberately insulted Brazilians, calling them goats and descendents of slaves from Guinea.[69] This kind of positioning racialized the conflict over independence, lumping together all Brazilians, rich and poor. The irony is that the Brazilian liberals would also racialize the uprisings of the 1830s in much the same way.[70]

Machado stresses that until 1824 there was a provisionality about the future of Brazil. In fact, the options became very limited from 1825 onward if territorial integration was to be maintained. No longer could one risk, as Patroni had done, criticizing established conventions. Liberal activity became focused on a series of legal reforms that were significant but lacked the imaginative force of the earlier era. They were essentially technical changes concerning the distribution of power to the regions and creating a more federalist type of nation. The key national reforms that impacted on Pará were the creation of local magistrate to oversee village legal matters, the *juiz de paz*, in 1827, and the National Guard (*Guarda Nacional*) in 1831. They were not aimed at forging a national identity, which would be taken up by centralizing conservatives in the regresso of the late 1830s. Nor were the constitutional adjustments aimed at greater political inclusion of those termed passive citizens. The lack of interest in ideological positions is put well by Thomas Flory in his study of political life at this time: "Brazilian liberalism was in fact less dependent upon foreign models than it was a reflexive, practical response to the transitional political and socioeconomics conditions of the early national period."[71] One of the translations of this attitude to the village level was the emphasis on order (*ordem*) and peace (*socego*). Without order and peace, social life was not feasible. It is no exaggeration to say that these terms were used in most official letters from councils, priests, and judges to the provincial governor in this period. They had become the prism by which to view every argument and development.

As the options became more restricted, so too was the space for inclusion in the political sphere. The lack of élite interest in addressing the grievances

---

68 Machado, "A Quebra da Mola Real," 13.

69 See Machado, "A Quebra da Mola Real," 257; and Reis, *História de Óbidos*, 49.

70 Leandro Mahalem de Lima, "Rios Vermelhos, Perspectivas e Posições de Sujeito em Torno da Noção de Cabano na Amazônia em Meados de 1835," Master's thesis, University of São Paulo, 2008, 142–145.

71 Flory, *Judge and Jury*, 6.

outlined in the petition from Alter do Chão, for example, and the military reaction to each uprising must have indicated to the majority of Paraenses that they were not going to become involved in the invention of the Brazilian nation. Still they felt they had helped to give birth to it by fighting against Portuguese interests in each town and had paid a high price in terms of lives lost (such as the Brig Palhaço disaster). In this sense, the idea of a new nation became one that Amazonian peasants found harder to relate to. The distance, at a very early point in the life of the new nation, was well expressed by the people from Alter do Chão: independence was apparently not for them. Undoubtedly this sentiment was shared across other Brazilian provinces.[72] It is no coincidence that the collective name chosen by rebels in the Lower Amazon was the "Forces of the United Brazilians" (*Forças dos Brazileiros Reunidos*, see Chapter 7). They aspired to be included but were locally marginalized and dispossessed. The identity displayed a national consciousness and implied a sophisticated understanding of liberal ideas.

The paradox is that they – the poor, with the exception of slaves – were considered citizens but literally submissive ones. Nonetheless, outside the political life granted them by the constitution, they were actively involved in pursuing their own interests and in forming alliances with élite factions in this new context. Inevitably these passive citizens were drawn into a wider set of conflicts and became aware of what was at stake. The same applied to the enslaved as they fought their own battles and were used by their owners against wealthy counterparts – as seen in the example from Antônio in the previous chapter. Excluded from holding office – both electoral, administrative, and legal – and having influence in a political process, these people were expected to submit to political authority. The problem in the second part of the 1820s was that the dominant classes did not recognize the new status of all citizens, let alone grant them more influence. The élites continued to demand free people's participation on work projects and military exercises, and punished them cruelly for minor infractions: nothing had changed. Even in front of the law they did not feel on an equal footing.

One way of developing this argument would be to consider what being a citizen meant to poor and enslaved Paraenses in the imperial period. But explicit information is not present in the documents. We could also ask how being a citizen differed from being a vassal (*vassalo*) in the colonial times and notions of the social contract had changed. The vassal was required to love, honor, and obey the monarch. In turn, the royal person would protect their vassals and bless them with their power.[73] In the case of newly independent

---

72 Machado, "A Quebra da Mola Real," 289.
73 For a general discussion of the social contract before and after the Rousseau, see Michael Lessnoff, *The Social Contract*, London: Macmillan, 1986, especially Chapter 2.

Brazil, this intimate bond had been broken and a new social contract (*pacto social*) had not yet come into existence.[74]

Machado entitles his study with a comment by the Bishop of Pará. As early as October 1823, the bishop saw talk of a liberal constitution as creating social confusion, for it gave way to "too much anxiety and freedom to the passions." This was clearly the old regime discourse but it captured the perception that freedom was an emotion, not a political cause, because people needed to know their place in society. The break from the past and notions of vassalage, smashed the basis of all authority, including religious. The bishop sums his view up of the rupture caused by the modern view with a rather attractive phrase, the end of the "Royal spring of well-constituted societies." The future stored up only more violence and social conflict.[75]

Nevertheless, the liberal call for popular sovereignty gave confidence to poor and marginal citizens to resist continued demands on their labor. As we saw in the previous chapters, during the colonial period élites were locked in a constant battle with Indians and mestiços concerning the deployment of the labor. This did not end with independence. If anything, attempts to recruit forcibly for seasonal or temporary work and short military campaigns intensified in the later 1820s due to the decreasing numbers of slaves and economic development in the countryside. Amazonian peasants sought to determine their labor, and interpreted the Constitution as granting them this freedom. So potentially damaging for social order was the Constitution that one town council decided not to publish it, claiming the Indians were too ignorant to understand it. Toward the end of the 1820s, the church in Óbidos was in the process of reconstruction. The priest requested "tapuios" to complete the task, and consequently had great difficulty in persuading them away from their daily economic activities. He exclaimed that the question of labor (*força de trabalho*) was a "stumbling stone" (*pedra de escândalo*), a reference to St Paul's letter to the Romans (9:33). The significance of this statement cannot be overemphasized. By drawing an analogy between the origins of Christianity the priest implied that for him this was the most important question of the period and how it would be resolved would influence the future direction of the province, if not the nation.[76]

Military recruitment had always been a source of conflict. In common with other provinces; Pará officers scoured the countryside for "volunteers." They sought out men whose origins were not officially known and accused them of desertion, being a vagabond, or any number of small crimes for

---

74 The conception of the new Brazilian nation, according to Machado, was as a political contract between men; "A Quebra da Mola Real," 93.

75 Machado, "A Quebra da Mola Real," 93. Machado generally emphasizes the variety of élite positions that arose out of the crisis in the old regime.

76 Machado, "A Quebra da Mola Real," 191.

which they could be arrested. Traveling without papers would lead to arrest. Prisoners were taken to Belém and trained for regular army work or sent to nationally owned factories, such as the cattle farm on the island of Marajó. On this farm, production was organized along military lines with commanders and colonels enforcing the orders of the president of the province. As frequently as they were arrested they would escape or lead mutinies.[77] Some were lucky to evade capture. A military commander from Chaves informed the president in January 1829 that it was impossible to arrest the Indians, excowboys who were attacking the imperial farms there. For the commander, this hopelessness prevented the implementation of the constitution (*pacto constitucional Brazilico*).[78] The national cacao plantation in Vila Franca was unable to gather the harvest in 1825 because its Indian employees ran away into the surrounding countryside. The manager did not know why they had left, but suspected they had been stirred up by talk of freedom.[79]

During the early 1830s in Pará, radical priests took up the cause of abolishing Indian servitude. This faction advocated the extinction of the nationally owned factories in the interior, including the cacao plantation and fisheries, claiming the enterprises were set up by speculators in order to cheat Indians. The pay was very low and workers were permanently tied by debt bondage to their bosses. Moreover, they were not permitted to leave the establishment and were threatened with violence if they tried, so they could not enjoy their freedom.[80] These efforts even had the president's support, but before they could be implemented, the president was deposed and exiled and one of the priests, Batista Campos, was arrested in the middle of 1832. It is not entirely clear, on the other hand, how genuinely interested the radical leaders were in Indians themselves. The proposal was obviously provocative and aimed to stir up social tensions. Certainly some revolutionary liberals no longer supported Indians in the mid-1830s, once the Cabanagem had begun. In their favor it should be said that deliberate aggravation of the other side came at significant personal cost – arrest, imprisonment, and temporary exile.

The liberal ascendancy, which Thomas Flory dates from 1827, has most often been considered an élite phenomenon. In line with more recent historiography such as Jeffrey Mosher's study of the early nineteenth

77 Manoel Lourenço de Mota to President Chermont, Chaves, February 18, 1828, APEP cod. 852, doc. 44. I am grateful to Leandro Mahalem de Lima for giving me the transcription of this document.

78 Carlos Francisco Saraiva to the President of Pará, Barão de Bage, Chaves, January 31, 1829, APEP cod. 852, doc. 91. Thanks to Leandro again for the transcription of this document.

79 Council of Vila Franca to Judge Paulo José Francisco [in Santarém ?], Vila Franca, APEP, cod 808, doc. 104.

80 Raiol, *Motins Políticos*, 202 and 228; Lima, "Rios Vermelhos," 102; Itala Bezerra da Silveira, *Cabanagem, A Luta Perdida* . . . , Belém: Secretaria de Estado da Cultura, 1994, 141.

century in Pernambuco, which also witnessed many uprisings, there is clear evidence in Pará of liberal ideas taking root among all Paraenses. The declaration from Alter do Chão, for example, and the willingness of Amazonian peasants to take sides indicate the extent to which the liberal tide took hold of people's imaginations, mixing with other currents of resistance to slavery, colonial and anti-élite rule. Among the élite of the provinces and the capital, liberal arguments may have resulted in practical responses, that is, laws and desire for order, but for the vast majority they embedded themselves as unfulfilled promises. Furthermore, they offered a kind of measure to judge the implementation of justice on a local level. If all citizens were equal in front of the law, why should family connection, class, or ethnic status affect the conduct of legal process?

In October 1827, the first reform marking the rise of national liberal political action in Brazil was the introduction of the *juiz de paz*, or justice of the peace. The reform was not intended to end corruption, however; rather, it was aimed to decentralize basic legal decision making by putting it in the hands of a parish-elected magistrate. It was aimed at strengthening local powers of arbitration in cases in which higher-level involvement was not necessary. This included adjudication on petty civil cases, reconciliation of prospective litigants, enforcing boundaries, and parish policing. The candidate did not need training, received no salary, and held the post for one year. The introduction of this position in the period covered in this book caused divisions to grow among élites and allowed judges to act with impunity in their treatment of the popular classes.

Pará's first justices of the peace were in place in 1829. Given the identification of the post with liberalism, Brazilian-born citizens sought election. According to Flory, many justices of the peace in Brazil were relatively poor but capable individuals whose families could not have afforded to send them to Portugal for a university education. In the Lower Amazon, many were cacao planters rather than merchants, and a few were priests. The immediate effect of the election in Óbidos, for example, was to set up rival camps between the municipal chamber and the judge over a series of matters. In an effort in early 1829 to limit violent fights in the countryside, the magistrate limited alcohol sales to the town and during daylight hours.[81] The councilors thought this was unenforceable and pleaded to the governor that payment for work was often made in rum and a ban would cause problems for employers. Yet there is probably more to the case than the councilors were willing to admit. In an anonymous memorial on the Lower Amazon dated 1828, the writer reported that slaves regularly stole from their masters and sold the goods to neighbors. The slaves mostly bought *aguardente* (rum) from river traders or their employers (for vastly inflated prices, the writer

81 Reis, *História de Óbidos*, 106–108.

added) with the money they received, which resulted in general disorder and their escape.[82] The sale of alcohol was under the jurisdiction of the magistrate but precisely why the councilors opposed the measures is not clear, unless their commercial interests were threatened.

In any case, conflicts between the various parties continued in the years preceding the Cabanagem. For example, crimes went unpunished, especially those committed by kinsfolk and friends of the magistrate.[83] One of the most significant arguments concerned the distribution of arms among the National Guard. The justices of the peace in Santarém and Óbidos did not want rifles to be given out to soldiers. If they were not armed, replied the officers, how would they be able to respond quickly to a call-up, which was their very purpose?[84] The juiz argued that, given the instability of local social relations, the presence of arms would increase tension and fear, and be used to further partisan interest. If order and peaceful social relations were the objective of the nation, then arms should be locked up in the local barracks. But it was the arbitrary and excessive punishment of some soldiers in Santarém by a judge toward the end of 1835 that sparked the takeover of the town and a massacre of the élite (events that are recounted in the following chapter). In other words, while position in these towns may have been occupied by liberals, they were perceived not to implement the law equally and fairly.

Though not a comprehensive review of the institution of the justice of the peace at the time, it can be argued that the new role added to the existing rivalries and deepened the tensions between different groups. It also gave locally powerful individuals another stick with which to beat those they considered below them.

The irony is that, as the 1820s drew to a close and the 1830s began, radical liberal reforms resulted in increased polarization, regardless of the matter in hand. A chronically fractured society had come into being, for no group could achieve hegemony. In Pará, there was no acceptance of alternative political identities. This would appear to support the historiographic view that the reforms gave too much power to the provinces since they lacked the ability to institutionalize regional power effectively. Against this argument, it can be said that it was not the fault of the reforms *per se* but the character of social relations in which they were situated. Not only were élite groups too weak, cross-class and ethnic alliances proved fragile. The range of viable choices for the future of Brazil that faced social actors in the early 1830s may

82 Anonymous, "Memória" [of the Lower Amazon], December 1, 1828, APEP cod. 851, doc. 74.

83 Maneol Pedro Marinho to President of Pará, Pauxis [Óbidos], March 6, 1834, APEP cod. 888, doc. 103.

84 Maneol Pedro Marinho to President of Pará, Pauxis [Óbidos], August 14, 1833, APEP cod. 888, doc. 103.

have become very limited, as Machado argues. Yet from the protagonists' perspective, this could not have been true, otherwise they would not have continued to defend their interests, to influence the course of events, and to consider alternatives open to them. In this context of persistent violence and challenges to authority, nothing could have seemed settled and lost. There was everything to fight for.

Pará, April 1831 to August 1835

The conflict between the different oligarchical groups reached a new level when news arrived of the abdication of Pedro I and his departure for Lisbon. For a number of years Pedro had been seen as nominating Portuguese officials to important positions and being responsible for a series of atrocities against liberals and nativists in Rio and in the provinces.[85] Known as the "April revolution" by Brazilians, the abdication was certainly a critical moment for them and popular mobilization.[86] Pedro left in his place his five-year-old Brazilian-born son, Pedro II. Almost immediately the Portuguese factions called for the return of the Duke of Bragança, as Pedro I came to be called, and they set up a new party, the Restorationists (*restauradores* or *caramurus*) to fight the cause. Violent confrontations broke out in most cities of the north, which in turn were followed by revenge action taken by whichever side felt aggrieved by the losses.

A volatile political sphere characterized Belém as much as, if not more than, anywhere else. Each piece of news was often colored by gossip or propaganda or lies (or "spin," as we would say nowadays). Thus Batista Campos was constantly accused of sedition and trying to get the slaves to revolt and destroy the civilized system of government, or of wanting to separate the province of Brazil and install a republic. There is little or no evidence to support any of these claims.[87]

In the early 1830s the class nature of the conflict took second place to the ethnic divisions, namely Portuguese and Brazilian. Though this should be qualified with the fact that outside Belém the Portuguese side was small and weak. The more moderate Brazilians perhaps were pushed into taking on their role. Portuguese sympathizers were composed of deserters from the Portuguese army, poor exiles, and wealthy traders, and resided almost exclusively in Belém. The liberal Brazilians were by now a much broader

85 Barman, *Brazil*, 160.
86 Chasteen, "Cautionary Tale," 110.
87 Salles, *O Negro no Pará sob o Regime da Escravidão*, Rio de Janeiro: Fundação Getulio Vargas, 1971, 239–270, for a good discussion.

group filled with new recruits, but one that was not unified. There were huge differences between radicals and moderates, each vying for political advantage. Moderate liberals often sided with the Portuguese in an effort to marginalize the others. A few radical leaders were classed as white, though most were artisans and farmers emboldened by priests and some held salaried army positions.[88]

When news arrived of the abdication of Pedro I, the Portuguese in Belém reacted by deposing the liberal president, the Viscount of Goiana, and arresting Batista Campos (this was linked to the cause of Indian freedom).[89] The immediate origin of the dispute was the election of Batista Campos as vice president. The Portuguese faction argued that the vote was a setup; in any case, the last thing they wanted was Batista Campos in the second most powerful position. As his friend and sympathizer, the Viscount of Goiana also had to go and was sent to Rio de Janeiro, while Batista Campos was forced into internal exile in order to get him away from the capital and prevent him from bolstering support in the south. It is interesting to note the way in which the deposition occurred. A group of armed soldiers turned up in front of the governor's palace and demanded a change of leader. Despite the threat of violence, this kind of assertive action indicates how politics was conducted at the time. Essentially, it was personalized and small-scale, and the collective group had to be mobilized quickly to be effective. Violence was legitimate if the opponent was perceived as acting outside the law. This was the context in which the entry of cabanos in Belém in January 1835 must be seen. Access to those in the highest office was relatively easy and persuasion was often achieved with the threat of aggression. This type of conduct of politics was probably not particularly unique to Pará.

An eyewitness account by the commander of arms, José Maria de Silva Bettancourt, said that he advised the new president not to send Batista Campos into internal exile. The commander considered Campos a criminal and implicated in seditious activities, including murder.[90] If Campos went into the interior he would only escape and seek support among the towns of the Amazon River. Indeed, this is just what Campos did: he persuaded his guard to take him not to Crato, the village prison for exiles on the Madeira River, but to Manaus. He sought refuge there but found little sympathy, perhaps because of ongoing tensions with Belém; a few months later, the region would declare itself a separate province from Pará (see the following discussion). Far from dispirited, Batista Campos settled with an old friend,

---

88 Salles, *O Negro no Pará*, 243.
89 See José Maria da Silva Bettancourt, "Documentos Relativos aos Acontecimentos do Pará de 1831–
    1836," 1864, *BNRJ*, II-32, 04, 015 (also copied in BIHGB Coleção Manuel Barata); Raiol, *Motins
    Políticos*, 227.
90 Bettancourt, "Documentos relativos."

Manoel Sanches, in Juruti. He immediately set about recounting the news from the capital, writing out proclamations and letters to those in nearby towns. No doubt his appeal worked them into line behind his own narrative of events, but it was mostly a case of self-interest. By February 1832 he was proclaimed the constitutional vice president of Pará in most of the towns of the Amazonas region on the basis of a popular mandate granted by some councils.[91] The municipal chamber of Óbidos sent its proclamation to the president in April 1832 declaring:

Viva a Nação Brazileira! Viva a Assembleia Geral! Viva o Dom Pedro II, Imperador Constitucional! Viva a Regencia! Viva a liberdade! Vivam os Obidenses! Viva o Excellentíssimo Senhor vice presidente da Província do Pará!

If there were campaign trails in the early nineteenth century, Batista Campos was working one. There was no mention of the end of slavery or the equality of all Brazilians in this proclamation, nor in anything else Batista Campos wrote in the little that has survived. Yet provincial president Machado de Oliveira (who replaced the Viscount of Goiana) spat out numerous letters to all local authorities not to let the "hellish hydra of anarchy" spread in their region.[92] He ordered them to arrest any follower of Batista Campos and to avoid at all costs "rivalries between existing authorities."[93] In other words, he knew Batista Campos would divide people between good patriots of Brazil and enemy Europeans. From Machado de Oliveira's point of view, there were good patriots – such as himself – and bad patriots – all those who supported Batista Campos.[94] Not surprisingly, the presence of Batista Campos and his "anti-European" talk caused a series of reactions from the Portuguese.[95]

From what has survived of Batista Campos's writing and accusations made by others, it seems he carried a simple message at this particular time. Independence had not brought full liberation from the colonial yoke, and the Portuguese remained in key positions in the province. There was an

91 Raiol, *Motins Políticos*, 240–246; Lucas Boiteaux, *A Marinha Imperial versus a Cabanagem*, Rio de Janeiro: Imprensa Naval, 1943, 56.

92 President of Pará Marcellino José Cardoso to Justice of the Peace in Santarém Agostinho Jozé Auzier, Pará, October 20, 1831, APEP cod. 918, doc. 224. The reference to hydra is very apposite: the monster in Greek mythology that had nine heads and was killed by Hercules; when one head was cut off, another grew instantly in its place.

93 President of Pará Marcellino José Cardoso to the Military Commander in Santarém, Pará, October 20, 1831, APEP cod. 918, doc. 222, and December 1, 1831, doc. 308.

94 See also the letter from Minister for Imperial affairs to Machado, reprinted in Ignácio Accioli de Cerqueira e Silva, *Corographia Paraense, ou Descripção Física, Histórica, e Política, da Província do Gram-Pará*, Bahia, 1833 230–232, which accuses Brazilians given to turbulent activities of waving "a flag of false patriotism."

95 Manoel Antônio Coelho, Captain Commander of the First Regiment of Pará to Commander of Arms [of Pará] José Maria da Silva Bettancort, Pará, February 8, 1832, APEP cod. 919, doc. 197.

"awaited liberty." The language of the Paraense regeneration from the 1820s constitutional revolution was replete with words such as "tyranny" and "despotism" and the need for justice, order, and the rule of law. This became an anti-Portuguese anthem, which in turn created the specter of a return to the old days of colonial absolutism and their lack of care for one's native soil. The Portuguese were seen as by nature anti-Brazilian and unwilling to compromise. The fight for true independence had to go on and would probably do so until all Portuguese were expelled from positions of political office, at least from Batista Campos's point of view. Although there is no clear evidence of this, the fact that he was so dominant in this period indicates his ambition to be the leader of such a movement; as Moses led the Israelites out of Egyptian slavery.[96]

If Pará's population was mostly illiterate, how did this message get across? First, Batista Campos had a network of like-minded clergymen, such as Manuel Sanches, who spread the word. Besides their spoken teachings, these people probably read out the pamphlets and newspapers that circulated widely at the time. They could relate the message easily to their own situation, memories, and experience. Even though the despots referred to in the newspapers were specifically Portuguese, the Indians and slaves who heard the term had no difficulty applying it to all masters and administrators, regardless of nationality or ethnic background. What was a matter of patriotism for Batista Campos was in fact a class struggle for most of his supporters. This difference can be clearly seen in the way many of the élite Brazilians, who sympathized with Batista Campos, fought against the rebels once the Cabanagem started. Moreover, only Indians and slaves were executed for sedition, never Batista Campos. It was not just that whites were not condemned to death but that he did not advocate general class or race war.

The rise of the Brazilian faction in the Lower Amazon in the first part of 1832 predictably led to a Portuguese reaction, with the formation of Portuguese armed mobs ready to kill anybody who posed a threat.[97] Santarém, with the largest Portuguese group, was the focus of these efforts, where soldiers and civilians stationed themselves outside the town and shot at anybody who approached them. Such conflict would continue on and off for the following few years, though not always involving armed combat. Having heard of the support he was receiving in the interior, Machado de

---

96 See discussion of Batista Campos in Salles, *O Negro no Pará*, 249–259, which is the best one I have read; and Chasteen, "Cautionary Tale."

97 Raiol, *Motins Políticos*, 244–257; Bettancourt, "Documentos Relativos"; Felipe José Pereira Leal, *Correções e Ampliações ao que sobre a Revolução que Arrebantou na Cidade do Pará em Janeiro de 1835 publicou o Conselheiro João Manoel Pereira da Silva*, Bahia, 1879.

Oliveira invited Batista Campos back to Belém to sit on the governing body of the province. By June 1832 Campos was sitting next to the president.

Apart from the fearful Portuguese, others were also fired up. The municipal council of Óbidos, which in the same month had made the proclamation supporting Batista Campos, passed some draconian and conservative measures to control its Indian and slave body. The new laws were:

(1) Anybody insulting those born in Brazil or those born outside of the empire will be fined 10,000 reis and receive ten days in prison.
(2) No gathering of more than five persons is allowed [same punishment as above].
(3) Slaves who cause disturbances will be whipped with fifty lashes and receive a fine and jail sentence.
(4) No sale of alcohol after 6 o'clock.
(5) No slaves allowed into taverns.
(6) No slave allowed out after 7 o'clock.
(7) Indians who are employed by a master are not allowed out at night.[98]

The council informed the president that these rules were a response to some recent problems, but omitted any reference to Batista Campos. In view of the forthcoming Holy Week and the congregation of people for the festivities, the councilors wrote that they needed to keep a heavy hand on any disorder. These rules were clearly about suppression; the first item was self-interested and concerned the élites of the town. Again, it is possible to see the separation of the élite's interests from the call for emancipation of all people. The radical liberal bent of two town councils was also in evidence when they changed the names of their towns from the Portuguese names to the pre-Pombal native ones: Santarém became Tapajós and Óbidos Pauxis in May 1833. This was a deliberate act of provocation on behalf of the Brazilians.

Like the multiheaded hydra, local rebellions could not be stopped. For Indians, the army had been a form of mobilization and organization for some years. It was also hated, as it detracted from the domestic labor pool, but it provided a way of obtaining munitions and discussing the political situation with like-minded others. A revolt in Manaus is a good illustration. A group of anti-Portuguese soldiers, led by Joaquim Pedro da Silva, rose up in Manaus in April 1832. They wanted to separate the Rio Negro region from Pará. At the time, the Rio Negro was a legal district of the Pará province, having been downgraded from a separate region with its own governor in the first decade of the nineteenth century. Pará was seen as pro-Portuguese, or at least stuck in an impasse between the parties. The troops

---

98 "Posturas da Camara Municipal da Vila d'Óbidos," sent to President of Pará, Óbidos April 22, 1832, APEP cod. 927, doc. 97; see also Reis, *História de Óbidos*, 111–112, for an update of the restrictions a year later.

bayoneted their commander, an outspoken absolutist and Portuguese loyalist, and burned some houses. One of these houses held the local archive: there can be little doubt this was a deliberate attempt to wipe out records that might be held against them in the future. The one hundred or so soldiers left Manaus in order to garner support from neighboring towns. The soldiers managed to persuade a group of Mura Indians living near Maués (Luzeia) of their cause, apparently telling them that if the Portuguese were to come back, they would enslave them all. As a result, the Mura killed thirty soldiers and some whites suspected of being Portuguese in Maués.[99] The insurgents, now numbering about thirty, continued downstream to Óbidos but were repelled by the town's forces and pushed to a farmstead northwest of Santarém, called Ecuipiranga.[100] Five years later, this place would become the redoubtable stronghold of the cabanos.[101]

For two months Manaus was in a state of limbo, for many of the wealthy families had left town fearing for their lives. The nativist soldiers returned there at some point and by June 22 held a popular meeting in the imperial factory warehouse. The group decided to secede from Pará and declare itself independent.[102] On receiving notification of the secession, the government in Pará sent a squadron upriver. The rebels offered little resistance and by the end of August the formal declaration had been ripped up. Twenty-five years later, though, the region became a province in its own right.

This episode was more than a mutiny.[103] It was not a localized uprising of soldiers who suddenly got excited. Rather, it reveals the proportion of the problems facing the region. The event sparked other reactions in nearby towns. Belém had to react quickly, diverting troops from its own needs in the capital. The Mura's involvement indicates the volatility of the situation: little encouragement was needed to spur people into action. Moreover, their participation shows the alliance sought by the nativist soldiers and the Mura, a relationship that would become crucial in the Cabanagem itself. About a year later, the Mura and some Indian and mestiço soldiers (including Joaquim Pedro) mounted an attack on the town of Borba on the Madeira River. About seventy men came armed with bows and arrows, spears, and some small arms, and killed two men and stole goods from their

---

99 Raiol, *Motins Políticos*, 270; Arthur Reis, "A Explosão Cívica em 1832," *Revista do Instituto Geográphico e Histórico do Amazonas*, 1932, vol. 2, 60; Lourenço da Silva Araujo e Amazonas, *Diccionário Topográphico, Histórico Descriptivo da Comarca do Alto Amazonas*, Recife, 1852, 274–275.

100 President of Pará José Machado d'Oliveira to Minister and Secretary of State for Business and Justice, December 29, 1832, Pará, APEP cod. 901, doc. 75.

101 John Hemming, *Amazon Frontier*, 227; Reis, "A Explosão Civica em 1832."

102 Raiol, *Motins Políticos*, 268; and Reis, "A Explosão Cívica em 1832."

103 Hemming, *Amazon Frontier*, 227.

houses.[104] The specific nature of this attack suggests some sort of revenge for an act committed in the past. As a result, the council requested that the Mundurucu come to guard the town and use their bows and arrows, for there were no shotguns in Borba.

The fear and suspicion that the Portuguese party was maintaining the upper hand is confirmed by a massacre of mostly Paraenses in April 1833 in Belém. Some ninety-five people were left for dead after Portuguese soldiers, led by a merchant called Jales, attacked the military barracks of the light infantry.[105] The main Portuguese leaders, Jales included, were killed, but none of the other participants was punished for their involvement.[106] Paraenses felt victimized, as if they were second-class citizens and nothing had changed since independence. A petition after the massacre called for equal rights for all people who lived in Pará, and tolerance of all views. It was signed by 367 people, all of whom had either already played a significant part in events in Belém or who would do so in the future, such as the two Angelim brothers and the three Vinagre brothers. The signatories also gave their occupations; these included artisans, property owners, soldiers, farmhands, and street peddlers. The fact that these people had a common cause and knew each other suggests their potential for collective organization. They may not have been planning the kind of rebellion they would enact some eighteen months later, but they had identified each other.[107] The French, British, Portuguese, and US consuls were so worried about the situation that they sought reassurance from president Machado that he would offer full protection to the lives and property of all foreigners in Belém.[108] In fact, the British consul had been worrying aloud since 1826 that the attacks on Portuguese would spread to all Europeans; a fear that was never realized, though one British merchant did lose his life in May 1835.[109]

By 1834 the conduct of daily life had become difficult throughout the province. Bandits attacked traders along the course of rivers and rustled cattle as a matter of course.[110] A stalemate had been reached between violent reactions of one side against the other, with the government vacillating in

---

104 Council of Borba to President of Pará, August 13–14, 1833, Borba, APEP cod. 947, doc. 51 and 52.

105 See "*O Cabanada do Pará*," Coleção Alencar Araripe, BIHGB, lata 316, doc. 15; and Chasteen, "Cautionary Tale," 112.

106 Raiol, *Motins Políticos*, 339.

107 Signatories to Manifesto [April 1833], Coleção Cabanagem: Revolta de Vinagre, BNRJ, II-32, 4, 16.

108 British vice consul John Hesketh and U.S. Consul Russell Smith to President of Pará, April 7, 1833, NAL FO 128, 16, part 1, 1833, folios 282–283.

109 British vice consul John Hesketh to General British consul Lord George Canning, May 8, 1826, Pará [Belém], NAL FO 13, 31, folio 9; David Cleary (ed.), *Cabanagem: Documentos Ingleses*, Belém, SECULT, 2003, 16.

110 The famous bandit of the time was called Jacob Patacho, also written as Jaco Pataxo, who was a mestiço soldier and deserter from the army. See Jorge Hurley, *Traços Cabanos*, 177 and 333; Raiol, *Motins Políticos*, 285; and the short story by Inglês de Souza on Patacho in his *Contos Amazônicos*, Rio

between. Arms were in short supply and regular soldiers had not been paid since the end of 1833. The commander of the National Guard in Óbidos wrote to the president in March 1834 that "it only leaves me to tell you that in this town the people have still not experienced the advantages of a constitutional system, and the citizens do not consider themselves secure in their homes, because at each moment there is a violation of the imperial constitution." He assured that it was not the natives of his town who make trouble but those who come from other parts, though he did not say where.[111] Ten years after independence, and political expectations still were not fulfilled.

However, a few months later, Pedro I died in Portugal from ill health, and the Caramuru party was left adrift without a cause in Brazil. Its supporters in Pará had been weakened by the massacre in April 1833, not least through assassinations, some of which Francisco Vinagre and Eduardo Angelim, both future presidents of Pará, were implicated.[112] Vinagre was accused of cutting off the head of a Portuguese man and blowing it up with gunpowder, and cutting off the ears of adversaries and using them as button hooks on his jacket.[113] These were common slanders for the time and it is not possible to verify them.

The difficulties arising from the circulation of false coinage also damaged relations between traders (mostly the Portuguese) and the producers and consumers (mostly poor Brazilians). For a few years, counterfeit copper tender had been in use, introduced from the south, apparently with the support of the government in Rio.[114] Gold and silver had become highly limited, probably as a result of the balance of payments favoring imports, and paying off the debts arising from independence. The arrival of false copper money caused high inflation and hardship; in 1833 noncounterfeit copper was circulating at two-thirds its intrinsic value. Since the Portuguese controlled much of the flow of goods and money, they were thought to be conspiring against the Brazilians and accumulating profit from the latter's misery. Despite this popular supposition, it was likely untrue. British traders complained to their consul that money was so scarce they had to operate an extensive credit system, which they did not like because clients did not

de Janeiro: Presença Edições, 1988. See also APEP cod. 888 for his movements in the Lower Amazon in 1832. British naval officers William Smyth and Frederick Lowe were warned of Patacho's ferocity but end up having a cup of coffee with him and thinking him quite decent, *Narrative of a Journey from Lima to Pará*, London, 1836, 300–301.

111 Commander of National Guards Manoel Pedro Marinho to President of Pará, Pauxis, March 6, 1834, APEP cod. 888, doc. 103; also in Reis, *Historia de Óbidos*, 118–120.

112 Bettancourt, "Documentos relativos," 1864; BIHGB, Coleção Alencar Araripe, *O Cabanada do Pará*, Lata 316, doc. 15, without named author and date.

113 BNRJ II-32, 4, 13.

114 Chapter 2, *O Cabanada do Pará*, BIHGB, lata 316, doc. 15.

always pay back their debt.[115] In February 1834, in an attempt to halt the crisis, the Pará government offered to exchange all copper for paper currency. They ordered each council to publish a notice informing people they had ten days to register their copper currency and receive the new currency. This relatively short timeframe was insufficient for all residents to act; thus, many people would have lost money, serving only to increase anger against a government considered to be siding with the Portuguese. Certainly one merchant in the Lower Amazon, the Scot John Hislop, failed to register because he was away trading up the Tapajós River. He lost 4,520$000 reis, about 500 pounds, most of which he owed to his correspondents in Belém, other British merchants.[116]

Democratically minded liberals were the dominant political force in Rio in the early part of the regency. They had been demanding more provincial autonomy since the abdication. Although the reforms were not as strong as some may have liked, they did manage to see through policies that allowed some decentralization. Another key reform was a change to the constitution with the Additional Act of August 1834. This was debated in the middle of 1834. The Act's central aim was to create a regional legislative assembly with local tax-raising powers. If the local president disapproved and the measures were provincial, a two-thirds majority in the Assembly could overrule his veto. Members would be elected for a two-year period. The act was sent to the provinces for implementation. Just as plans were being drawn up and the president, Lobo de Souza, was dragging his feet about doing anything, the rebels moved in.

Although it is difficult to identify a beginning to the Cabanagem rebellion proper, matters come to a head in this gap at the end of 1834. A journalist from Maranhão and friend of Batista Campos, nicknamed Papagaio, had been writing fiery attacks on the government, which in turn tried to stop him. He retreated to the farm of Felix Malcher on the Acará River (Malcher had also escaped the capital) and there, with Batista Campos, discussed some ideas for the takeover of the presidency. Batista Campos and Malcher had long had a personal feud but now realized they could support each other. A group of soldiers went to arrest Papagaio but were forced back when the commander was killed by shots coming from the farmhouse. A much larger force was then assembled with the aim of arresting all the dissidents and putting an end to their plans. President Lobo de

---

115 In 1836 10$000 mil-reis was worth about 10 pounds, Consul John Hesketh to British General Consul in Rio, May 9, 1838, Pará, NAL FO 13, 148, f. 151.

116 British vice consul John Hesketh to Henry Fox, Envoy extraordinary and minister plenipotentiary, September 10, 1834, Pará, NAL FO 128, 19, folios 367–387 (including supporting documents); Hislop appears in various Victorian chronicles, most notably Richard Spruce.

Souza accused Malcher of republicanism, of supporting the abolition of slaves, the expulsion of all Portuguese, and the appropriation of their goods. Pedro Vinagre was killed along with some others and Malcher arrested, but the ever-plucky Batista Campos managed to escape.[117] However, he died from septicemia at the end of year. Apparently, a shaving cut had become infected and, in the absence of medical help, he passed away quickly.

His death did nothing to diminish the appetite for change. From their hideout in the forests a few days' canoe trip from the capital, those who remained planned their assault for the festival of São Tome on evening of January 6. They wrote a manifesto listing recent atrocities committed by the government and the Portuguese faction, including mistreatment of slaves, tying soldiers to posts as punishment and leaving them to die, the burning of their periodicals and preventing publication of pamphlets, and introducing paper money that had no value. The manifesto also accused the president of being a mason and against the Catholic Church.[118] Gangs of men were to be placed on the islands around Belém, which would then cross the river and meet up with soldiers and armed civilians gathered together for the festivities. By daybreak, various forces had assembled and occupied different positions. Middle-ranking officers in the barracks were shot first, then the president, and then the top military commander and British mercenary James Inglis, who had led the attack on the Acará river farm. The prisons were opened; Malcher was declared president and Francisco Vinagre, the military commander. Looting and murder of some twenty Portuguese traders ensued. The rebels were in control of the city.

That day Malcher issued "the act of the extraordinary council of assembled citizens." It announced that Lobo de Souza was dead because of his despotic acts carried out during his reign as governor, and that Pará wanted nothing more to do with the Regency government until Pedro II came of age.[119] This was signed by over six hundred men, though the British consul said they were threatened with immediate death if they refused to sign. The next few days saw new measures instituted to bring some calm and normality to the region: the abolition of the National Guard who had been seen as pro-Portuguese, the call to carry on with production of goods and trade, and a return to the exclusive use of copper currency, apparently now almost valueless, and the reassurance of the consuls that foreign property

---

117 "Correio Official Paraense," Coleção Cabanagem: Revolta de Vinagre, BNRJ II- 32, 4, 03; Cleary, *Cabanagem: Documentos Ingleses*, 29; João Manoel Pereira da Silva, *História do Brazil na Menoridade do Pedro II*, Rio de Janeiro: Havre, 1888, 172–178.

118 "Manifesto," Pedro Joaquim de Santa Isabel, Coleção Cabanagem: Revolta de Vinagre, November 1834, BNRJ II, 32, 4, 04.

119 "Acta do Conselho Extraordinariá de Cidadaos Reunidos na Salla do Conselho do Governo," January 7, 1835, Coleção Cabanagem: Revolução de Vinagre, BNRJ II, 32, 4, 17.

would be respected. Each copper coin was declared to be worth only a quarter of its face value.[120] New coinage was introduced by restamping old coins with a new face value.[121]

An eyewitness to the first few months of the cabano rule, British consul John Hesketh opined that "if the regency will not be able to resist this act of insubordination this province is lost to the Brazilian Empire, and by successive cause of misrule will ultimately fall under the power of the Negro population to the extinction of the white, or what is more probable the insults offered to the subjects of other nations when redress cannot by obtained from the capital, may induce some foreign powers to take possession of it."[122] He pleaded that the British secretary for foreign affairs consider the military takeover of this province, for its citizens would welcome the end of anarchy. This call was not taken too seriously, though it is apparent the possibility was suggested to president Angelim by various consuls and a British naval officer.

Within a month, fatal arguments had broken out between Malcher and Vinagre and their respective supporters. The former occupied the castle and the latter the arsenal, and recriminations were shouted at each other. Still, the Brazilian navy waited patiently in the bay, out of cannon shot of the city. In an attempt to impose order, Malcher sent the journalist Papagaio into exile, where he continued to write pieces attacking presidents, and arrested Angelim. Fighting broke out between opposing factions, leaving many dead and Malcher under arrest. Vinagre sent him to one of the Brazilian navy boats but then asked for him back. Before Malcher could be imprisoned in the city's jail, he was murdered and picked apart with bayonets, and Vinagre was proclaimed president and military commander. Malcher was then portrayed as another despot in the line of all the other presidents, the new savior being Vinagre himself. Moreover, Malcher had not backed the regency administration but Vinagre did – an attempt to portray himself a more legitimate leader. He also never raised the possibility of separation from Brazil or an end to slavery, and explicitly asserted the importance of law and order, the union between all Brazilians, the empire of Pedro II, and the constitutional authorities.[123]

Whatever Vinagre's personal hopes and ambitions, he was not able to assert his authority and achieve recognition from Rio. A spy in Belém wrote

120 "Paquete do governo no. 1: Acta extraordinario de cidadaós reunidos na salla do conselho do governo," January 31, Pará, NAL FO 13, 122, folio 124–125.

121 Some of these coins can be viewed in the Museu do Forte, Belém.

122 British vice consul John Hesketh to John Bidwell, Superintendent of His Majesty's Consular Services, Foreign Office London, February 6, 1835, NAL FO 13, 122, folio 118.

123 "Exposição do Presidente da Provincia do Pará ao seus Concidadaós," February 27, 1835, Coleção Cabanagem: Revolução de Vinagre BNRJ II, 32, 4, 01; see also his proclamation to the people of the Lower and Upper Amazon, Raiol, *Motins Políticos*, 625.

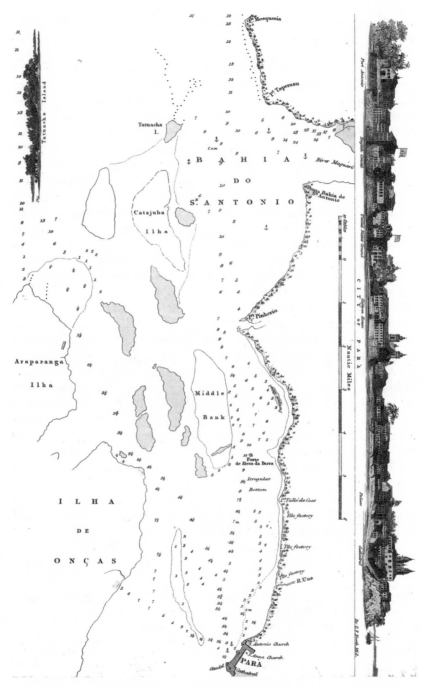

Image 6.1 Profile of Belém, by E. F. North [inset to River Pará, Image 8.1], 1835

to the imperial officers watching events in their ships that Vinagre said, echoing Batista Campos, he wanted to be like Moses: leading people to the promised land. In addition, the spy wrote, Vinagre's closest confidantes were a black man and an Indian (as though this was a condemnation).[124] The regency insisted the vice president at the time of Lobo de Souza's death was the current lawful president, and at the end of April sent another president with another British mercenary, John Taylor, to Belém to enforce the situation, arriving in late May. Nevertheless, at this time Vinagre was in contact with imperial naval commander Pedro da Cunha, stationed on the river.[125] After the vice president's disastrous attempt in May to retake the city, Vinagre was persuaded to stand down, much against his will, since he feared for his life, but given his support of legal process he found himself forced to give up his post. The new president, Manuel Rodrigues, was installed in late June but to little effect. Once again, relations descended into violent confrontation between factions. Francisco Vinagre and other leaders were arrested, but Angelim escaped the city with some other rebels and immediately recruited from the surrounding district for another assault. On August 14 two thousand Indians, mestiços, and blacks wearing red shirts staged an exceptionally well-planned assault on the city. They attacked both from the river side and from inland, dividing the imperial troops (which were small in number, since all the volunteers and part-time soldiers had deserted). After nine days of fighting, the rebels regained the city they had lost over a month earlier.[126]

By this time, most of the whites, about five thousand, had fled to the boats and ships at anchor in Guajará bay.[127] The holders of the city, for a few days without a leader, proclaimed an end to slavery and "declared war on people not of their race," according to John Taylor, who led the imperial army. However, when Eduardo Angelim was proclaimed the sixth president of the year, he imposed a new discipline and order on the city. He disarmed the slaves (though whether he sent them back to their masters is not clear); he shot the ringleaders of an attack on a farm which freed some slaves; and

---

124 Commander of Naval Forces stationed in Pará John Taylor to Minister of State Affairs and the Navy, June 13, 1835, Belém, "Arquivo Particular do Barão do Rio Branco," AHI Lata 875, Maço 01, pasta 02. See also correspondence by Marechal Manoel Rodrigues, June 1835, Coleção Cabanagem: Revolução de Vinagre, BNRJ II-32, 4, 13.

125 Correspondence between Francisco Pedro Vinagre and Pedro da Cunha, June 1835, Coleção Cabanagem: Revolução de Vinagre, BNRJ II-32, 4, 11.

126 Cleary, "'Lost Altogether to the Civilized World': Race and the Cabanagem in Northern Brazil, 1750 to 1850," *Comparative Studies in Society and History*, 1998, 40, 1, 121–123; Cleary, *Documentos Ingleses*, 58–65; Raiol, *Motins Políticos*; see F. P. Vinagre to [?] no date, Coleção Cabanagem: Revolução de Vinagre, BNRJ II-32, 4, 10 for a handwritten and undated letter by Vinagre calling for *patricios* and *amigos* to lay down their arms and accept the new imperial president, written sometime in June 1835.

127 Tenente General Manoel Jorge Rodrigues to the Minister for War, August 25, 1835, "Arquivo Particular do Barão do Rio Branco," AHI Lata 875, Maço 01, pasta 01. I am grateful again to Leandro Mahalem de Lima for giving me copies of this and the following document from the AHI.

imprisoned someone who slashed a picture of Pedro II and said he did not want him as emperor. A new mood was ushered in with the young Angelim. If the rebellion were to succeed in keeping its locally nominated president, control and authority was needed to impress on the regency government the significance of the rebels' demands.

Just before he was forced to leave the city, John Taylor captured something of this change, again raising the specter of the Haitian revolution.

It is necessary to reflect a little on the population of this province which is composed of the most part of freed slaves, cafuzes, mulattos, mamelucos and Indians or Tapuios. Amongst all these castes the Indian is the best, because he is more likely to follow a leader than take independent action. The others are not demoralized and do not have the lack of interest the Indians have in plan of the Haitians ... If the Vinagre brothers were not of the same opinion they would be dead now. The goal of the revolution of 7th January has now entirely changed. Then the fight was about personal interest, it was jealousy and greed that did away with Law and Order. Today it is the war of these diverse castes of people in conjunction with the lives and property of the whites in order to make the country more prosperous. But it is worth noting that the tapuios are less enthusiastic about this objective. This is my opinion formed from talking to the sensible people of Pará.[128]

Angelim's leadership qualities appeared to come from nowhere. He was only twenty-two years old and although he had accompanied Batista Campos, he had spent most of his life as a farmer in the interior. His family had migrated from Ceará when he was seven years old and for most of the last eight months he had not figured as a leader alongside the Vinagre brothers and Malcher. In the situation, personal skills and appeal went a long way in bringing unity, but he clearly achieved this at a cost to the broader participation of the movement. Angelim was a serious and thoughtful man with a presence and judgment that inspired confidence. In these qualities he was different from the previous leaders, who led more by energy and rhetoric. An undated portrait of Angelim in the old governor's residence in Belém reveals a determined man, with a touch of anger. Even Angelim's nemesis General Andréa, who led the repression, could not fail to be impressed by Angelim when he interviewed him after his arrest in November 1836. Asked by Andréa if the soldiers who had arrested him had treated him properly, Angelim answered that they had and added:

I know that I am a rebel and a criminal, but it was not me who was the author of all the atrocities. Others made these crimes happen, and many who now ask for my head were my masters and teachers. Now they call me a "malvado" [a wicked

128 Commander of Naval Forces stationed in Pará John Taylor to Minister of State Affairs and the Navy, August 9, 1835, Belém, "Arquivo Particular do Barão do Rio Branco," AHI Lata 875, Maço 01, pasta 02.

person] because I did not want to link myself to them or their ends. I could have saved myself but I could not leave this city without a leader. You have no idea of the crimes which would have been committed had I gone. I was very tough on punishing crimes committed when I was president.[129]

Andréa wrote that Angelim did not show pride, humility, or regret. He was sure of himself and honest. Signing the order for his deportation, Andréa said he was moved to cross out the part that said "in chains," for which Angelim thanked him most civilly.

Whatever Taylor's reading of the situation and Angelim's attempt to bring order, the province was in a state of general revolt. It is quite apparent there were many different aims and motivations among those in the uprising. Slaves were a part of some rebel groups but not others. Some rebels sought revenge on specific individuals and were uninterested in assuming power in the towns or supporting Angelim. Others attacked whites *en masse* but these latter forms were the exception and occurred in very few documented instances. The most well-known was a massacre in Vigia of about seventy whites at the end of July 1835, before Angelim took power. There had been disagreements for some months between whites and Indians about elections to the municipal chamber, which descended into tragedy.[130] The young Scot seaman Alexander Paton, who survived the slaughter of the rest of crew of the brig *Clio*, spent a number of weeks in Vigia, a town on the Atlantic coast, in October and November 1835. One of the widows from the Vigia massacre showed Paton the houses in which the whites had been killed. Blood stained the mud floors, and the wooden windows and doors "were all full of shot holes."[131] Paton also recounts the punishment of a slave for running away from his master in Vigia. A group of Indians had tied his hands to the bars of a window, his feet about two feet above the ground. For a quarter of an hour they flogged him "with great pleasure."

In summary, the end of 1834, the various factions fighting for power in Belém had reached deadlock. The 1820s had begun with the opening up of various possible futures, even if the people had not articulated them as such. The politically powerful agents pushing these possibilities were either dead by January 1835 (for example, Batista Campos and the Portuguese restorationists) or did not understand the potential unleashed in taking over the governmental apparatus after storming the capital. Malcher and Francisco Vinagre's only clear and substantial demand was to nominate the provincial president without interference from Rio. And yet they were in a position few

129 *O Cabanada no Pará*, BIHGB, lata 316, doc. 15.

130 See Raiol, *Motins Políticos*, 748–759, for the account in which his father was counted among the white victims.

131 Alexander Paton, *Narrative of the Loss of the Schooner Clio of Montrose*, 1879 (originally 1837), Montrose, 29–30.

rebels can ever hope to be in – holding the reins of government with mass popular support. The opportunity was wasted by their own subsequent infighting and rivalry, lack of leadership, or connection with their supporters, and their protection of class privilege, fearing the backlash by the regency administration.

The kind of prospect that faced the rebels in 1835 is revealed in an anecdote from Alexander Paton's account of his escape from the massacre of the *Clio* crew in October. President Lobo de Souza had ordered a shipment of arms from Britain at the end of 1834. The Clio left Liverpool in August with a crew of seven and a cargo of guns and dry goods, without knowing of the rebellion or the death of the president. It stopped at a prearranged Atlantic seaport to await a pilot to direct the boat to Belém. In order to locate the pilot, two crew members went ashore and one of them let slip to a local the contents of the schooner. After a day or so, the villagers gathered together and killed all but two of the crew, who managed to run away into the forest. For the next ten days these two men survived, swimming across streams, running in the forest, eating the buttons on their shirts, and sleeping in trees. Then William Lloyds drowned and Paton was left to roam. He stumbled on some houses and was offered food, and the women took care of his sore and scratched feet. In the house, he noticed some soap from the schooner. He was too weak to move by now so he was carried to another house where he was looked after by someone specially sent from Belém. As he moved between houses, he kept noticing goods, and especially the muskets which had once been on the Clio. They had been distributed equally among the people, rather than hoarded, and each family in the neighborhood was given a gun. This small fact reveals the degree of cooperation and organization developed in the time of the rebellion.

National and regional developments in the buildup to the rebellion are central to understanding the changing perception of race in this period. The alliance between peasants, soldiers, priests, and other liberals brought whites, mestiços, blacks, and Indians together for the first time. Similarly, Portuguese sympathizers lumped all natives of Pará together. By the time of the rebellion, the tense alliance had been shattered and the rebels consisted of a less diverse range of people. From the Brazilian oligarchical point of view (that is, the representatives of the conservative backlash from 1837), the rebellion was an anarchic monster and all Brazilians should defend themselves against the rabble. The rebels had no political rights and should have no say in the future of the country (remember the opening quotation from Pedro I). From the cabanos' point of view, the rebellion was against some of the élite who had no right to impose an unconstitutional tyrannous political system and favor their friends. The rebellion then reconfigured the complex and fluid ethnic relations and simplified racial perceptions that deepened the exclusion of nonpropertied Brazilians from any political responsibility.

7

The United Brazilian Encampment
at Ecuipiranga, 1833–1837

In his 1845 geographical and historical dictionary of the new empire of
Brazil, the French diplomat Sainte-Adolphe has a short and tantalizing entry
for "Cuipiranga."[1] He had never visited the Amazon region and must have
received some of the information for his dictionary from combing newspaper reports and listening to military officers whose bloody instinct had
been sharpened in the north. The entry is hardly a line long and reads
"Cuipiranga: a Brazilian fort, on the margins of the Amazon River."[2] The
specification of Brazilian is odd: of course it is Brazilian, since it is in Brazil.
So why mention it? Furthermore, it is well known that there were forts only
in strategic towns – Barcellos, Óbidos, Santarém, Gurupá, Macapá, and
Belém. So what was the status of this particular fort? How had the reputation of this small, remote military outpost found a place in a work giving
expression to the birth of an independent nation with its own heightened
sense of territory and history? Cuipiranga, or Ecuipiranga or Icuipiranga as it
was also known, is not mentioned in later dictionaries either of Brazil or the
Amazon region, for example, Carlos Rocque's *Encyclopaedia of Amazonia*.
Yet its significance in the rebel movement is indisputable: first as a strong
ally of the cabanos in Belém under Angelim, and secondly as the center for
the rebel movement when Belém fell.

The name *Ecuipiranga* is derived from the lingua geral and means "red
dust" (*cui* is dust, sand, or bits and *piranga* red). Although I have not found
references to the place prior to the 1830s, the term must have been in use
before. The land is indeed covered in red dust, which has spread to
the beaches, where it mixes with the white sand. But to the people of the
region, the term has another meaning aside from the geological. In the
contemporary oral history of the Tapajós region, the color comes from
the blood of the people killed there during the Cabanagem. On various
occasions, people told me so much blood was spilled, it will never be

---

1 Millet de Saint-Adolphe, J. C. R. *Diccionário Geográphico, Histórico e Descriptivo do Imperio do Brazil.*
  Paris, 1845.
2 Saint-Adolphe, *Diccionario Geográphico*, 314.

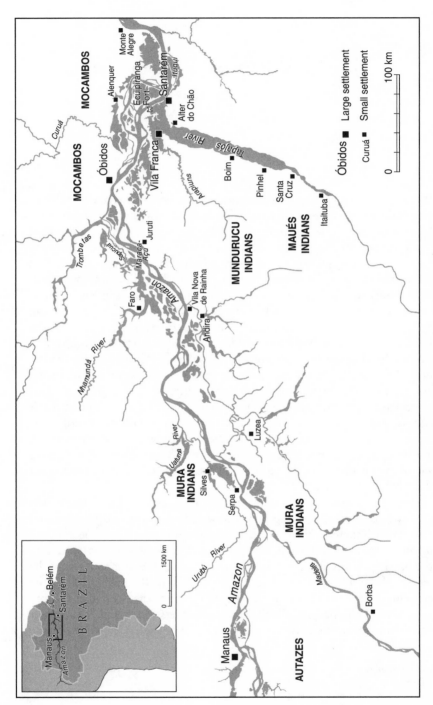

Map 7.1 The Lower and Upper Amazon during the Cabanagem

washed out.[3] This raises the intriguing possibility that the site was chosen by rebels because of its prior connection with insurgency.

The critical significance of Ecuipiranga has come to be lost to a view of the rebellion dominated by Belém with marginal support in the interior. Yet it was actually the largest and most successful of the rebel strongholds in the interior during the Cabanagem. Observers portrayed it as a "famous" and "terrible" place since it was the base for planning and launching rebel military operations from late 1835.[4] Some of the imperial commanders (also known in the documents as *legalistas*, or the legal ones on the side of the empire) saw it as the "cradle of all anarchy" in the Amazon. One of these military officers in the Lower Amazon, João Henrique de Mattos, wrote in 1842 that Ecuipiranga was where the "agitators of public peace established the largest and best fortified point in their campaign. They had all the resources they needed; soldiers were commanded by the main leaders, and it was where they had their last hopes of salvation."[5] At its apotheosis toward the end of 1836, it housed more than a thousand men and their families, and possibly many more. These people were of various kinds: whites, mestiços, Indians, and freed blacks. However, it seems that escaped slaves were not part of the community.[6]

At this point it is worth outlining the principle phases of the revolt. The period 1835 to 1840 can be divided into three parts: (a) the uprising in Belém and its spread, 1835–1836; (b) the arrival of Andréa, the retake of the capital, and the concomitant strengthening of rebel positions outside of the capital,

3 The symbolic association of rivers and blood during times of social conflict is well known. These particular comments were made to me on two visits to Ecuipiranga and Vila Franca in July 2004 and December 2006, respectively.

4 Domingos Antônio Raiol writes "um lugar celebre," and "um lugar terrivel," *Motins Políticos, ou História dos Principais Acontecimentos Políticos da Província do Pará, desde o ano de 1821 até 1835*, Belém: Universidade Federal do Pará, 1970, vol. 3, 905. In fact, Raiol's phrases are lifted from João Henrique de Mattos' manuscript cited below in the BNRJ. Other sources that mention Ecuipiranga are Lourenço de Araujó e Amazonas, *Dicionário Topográfico, Histórico, Descritivo da Comarca do Alto-Amazonas*, Recife: Typografia Comercial de Meira Henriques 1852, 281–282; Felipe José Pereira Leal, *Correções e Ampliações ao que Sobre a Revolução que Arrebantou na Cidade do Pará em Janeiro de 1835 publicou o Conselheiro João Manoel Pereira da Silva*, Bahia, 1879; Francisco de Bernardino de Souza, *Commissão do Madeira, Pará e Amazonas*, Rio de Janeiro: Typographia Nacional 1874–1875, part 3, 23. More recently the historian João Santos published a pamphlet recovering the history of the period using published sources, *Cabanagem em Santarém*, Livraria Atica, Santarém, 1986. Special mention should be made of Pereira Leal's account. He was a participant in the repression of the Cabanagem and, like Mattos, spent months in the Lower Amazon attacking Ecuipiranga. His contribution is, as the title says, a correction and elaboration of the text on Brazil in the 1830s by Pereira da Silva, though Leal's only deals with aspects of the Cabanagem in Pará. Leal also wrote a short account on independence in Pará.

5 João Henrique de Mattos, "Roteiro das Viagens da Cidade do Pará até as Limites do Rio Negro," 1842, BNRJ 05, 4, 009.

6 Military Commander for Lower Amazon João Henrique de Mattos to President of Pará Francisco José Soares de Andréa, July 18, 1837, Garrison in Santarém, APEP cod. 888, No. 6, doc. 202.

1836–1837; and (c) the attempted repression, including mutinies and kidnappings, and the development of guerrilla-type attacks and the involvement of tribal groups on both sides, 1837–1840. Essentially, the first two phases are continuous with each other and are motivated by similar political visions. During the final phase the conflict is turned into a race war by imperial propaganda, and rebels are pushed into enclaves. In addition, a new policy is introduced to force the rural poor into public service projects or private work for bosses. This frees up more land in the countryside and counteracts the labor shortage as a result of the repression.

The Camp

Geographically, Ecuipiranga was a site of supreme strategic importance. By choosing it as a base for their work in the Lower Amazon, the rebels pursued the Portuguese tradition of combining military and residential considerations in occupying the region. The main location was about twenty miles on the south side of the Amazon River from Santarém and fifteen miles north across land, streams, and lakes from Vila Franca. This site was linked to another point, also known as Ecuipiranga, on the south side by an *estrada* (literally, road) through the jungle from a beach at the mouth of the Arapiuns River as it flowed into the Tapajós. The path was about three miles long and runs through interfluve forest from the south end to the north. At the north end, overlooking the Amazon, was a plot of land that belonged to sympathizers of the movement, cacao planters, and fishermen. The land here was about a hundred feet above the river with a sharp rocky front. Ecuipiranga on the north side was the only place for a couple of miles either side with access to the Amazon River, a small path following a break in the hard red rocks down to the beach. The view from this point was clear and ships and canoes going up and down the river were easily spotted by lookouts. The southern end also offered a panoramic view of the vast bay of the Tapajós River before it was forced eastward into the Amazon River at Santarém. From the bluff above the bay, where the chapel was situated, guards looked out to the black river (*rio preto*), as the Tapajós River was also known. The north-south road was crossed by another that ran east-west from the most easterly point at the mouth of the Tapajós to Juruti, a small mission for Mundurucu and Maués Indians. It may even have gone further to Luzea and the Autazes, where there were other rebel positions.[7]

---

7 This description is based on visiting the area in July 2004, and from the documents in APEP and published sources. I am grateful to Francisco for introducing me to the area and answering my questions. It is likely that some of these roads are very old, going back to preconquest times though their precise location may have moved, see also Raffles, *In Amazonia: A Natural History*, Princeton: Princeton University Press, 23–33, for an excellent description of the Arapiuns basin.

Life in the encampment was much the same as elsewhere. There were shelters made from palm thatch, hammocks slung between trees, clay hearths for cooking, with dogs, chickens, and ducks wandering freely. Manioc grew outside the camp and there were ovens for making manioc flour (*farinha*). The communal life contrasted with isolated family houses of the interior. There was also a military fortress with wooden bulwarks. A chapel was situated some way from the main camp near the beach on the south side. They referred to themselves as the *Forças dos Brazileiros Reunidos,* or United Brazilian Forces. This self-description indicated their loyalty to an independent Brazil, and antipathy to those who would undermine the well-being of the country by exploiting it and ruling without legitimacy. Moreover, the term "united" indicated plainly the congregation of interests behind the movement.

Sometime in early 1836 a number of cannon were placed at the north and south ends of Ecuipiranga, apparently stolen from an armored naval boat that had been seized by the rebels and dragged ashore. The imperialist forces could see these cannon from the river. In addition, the south side beaches were protected by large trenches and stakes. Some trenches were covered over to make a trap and others were gaping holes in the soft sand and soil at the river margins. Munitions came from the plundering of riverside towns and attacking ships on the waterways. Some arms even arrived from Cuiabá, about two thousand kilometers up the Tapajós. Food was taken from neighboring farms and gardens, since many of their white owners had fled in fear, leaving behind many possessions. Horses and cattle were most prized, the latter squashed on to ships or herded across land for slaughter in the camp. The ones left over were killed on the spot and the farmhouses were burned down. A system of communication using horses and sailing canoes linked the various rebel groups and towns. Care was taken never to send letters in case the courier was intercepted. Messages were relayed by word of mouth; even so, if one were captured by the enemy or found out as a spy, the punishment was one that few could survive – a whipping of two hundred lashes. In such an apparently unassailable strategic position, with numbers growing in early 1836, hopes for achieving a more just and less despotic system of governance were high. President Eduardo Angelim had managed to gain a measure of stability, and many towns had declared their support for his presidency and administration.

Prior to its settling as a camp and the building of fortifications in 1835, Ecuipiranga was simply another rural "estate" sandwiched to the east and west by other landholders. About seven miles upstream toward Óbidos is the national cacao plantation. However, Ecuipiranga's geographical significance must have been appreciated for some time. As mentioned in the previous chapter, in mid 1832 a band of mutinous soldiers who had taken over Manaus in April and then had to escape to avoid persecution, took refuge there.[8] Their choice of the area for refuge suggests that it had a reputation as a meeting point for those involved in the cabano movement.

The connection between soldiers, rebellion, and Ecuipiranga was strengthened in the years to follow. The leaders of the military camp were mostly from the National Guard, and from their point of view were fulfilling their duty in protecting the Amazon from impostors and those who would take it over for the benefit of foreigners. But in the opinion of the legalistas, they had defected and were traitors. Worse still, they were assassins, robbers, evildoers, sectarians – in short, "scum" (*faciosos*). Moreover, when any of these soldiers joined the Ecuipiranga camp, they were likely to have taken arms and munitions.[9]

Miguel Apolinário, nicknamed Maparajuba, was a well-known leader in the early part of the rebel campaign. Maparajuba was a man "gifted with much vivacity and courage."[10] He was a part-time soldier who had served in the light infantry division of Santarém and had taken an oath of allegiance to the new Brazilian nation; he probably had a smallholding with cacao trees and manioc. His nickname was derived from one of the hardest woods of the rainforest, which had a deep red color and was used in construction (in the same family of trees as *massaranduba*, Sapotaceae). Like president Angelim, who also had a species of tree as a nickname, Apolinário was firm and strong. The tree names also indicated a sense of standing upright and holding still in righteous certitude. As with Angelim, Maparajuba was thrown to prominence by the revolutionary conditions of the time.[11] Maparajuba was well placed within the military and was in this sense inside the world that had to be overthrown. He imposed strict discipline on the soldiers in the camp and demanded unity of spirit. In an open letter to his fellow men, he wrote "Blessed are the meek. And what does meek mean if not obedience?" And ended it with vivas to the young Pedro II, the Catholic religion, Brazilian defenders of the peace.[12]

The men at Ecuipiranga were made up mostly of locals who had fled their homes in search of safety and to lend their support to the movement. Some had brought their families and household belongings in their canoes. These

---

8 President of Paré José Joaquim Machado de Oliveira to Honório Carneiro Leão, Minister and Secretary for Homes Affairs and Justice, June 22, 1832, Belém, APEP cod. 901, doc. 75.
9 Paulo Rodrigues dos Santos, *Tupaiulândia*, Santarém, ICBS/ACN, 2000, 200.
10 Bernardino de Souza, *Commissão do Madeira*, parte 3, 23; and Santos, *Cabanagem*, 19–20.
11 See C. L. R. James, *The Black Jacobins*, Harmondsworth: Penguin, 2005, on the making of leaders in revolutionary times.
12 Bernardino de Souza, *Commissão do Madeira*, parte 3, 23–24. He says he found the letter in his travels and copies it out in full. There are many biblical references and one to Bonaparte's armies.

men had come from a variety of backgrounds: many were farmers and fishermen, others cowboys and artisans; some were deserters who may have been on the run for a while; a few were escaped prisoners or internal exiles. In other parts of the Amazon, an American and an Argentinian had joined the rebels, and there were rumors that the French were attacking imperial positions in Amapá.[13] As a result, the countryside of the Lower Amazon – the farmsteads and the huts – was almost empty; people were grouped in towns or camps for security, or else had fled to remote parts, perhaps joining or moving near runaway slave communities. After the fall of Belém in May 1836, the contingent of Ecuipiranga was increased by rebels moving upriver seeking other battles. The collective form of organization contrasted with the more atomistic type lifestyle of the interior. The camps lent themselves to a party-like atmosphere, with music, singing, and dancing as well as discussion and debate.

The rebel army was described by one imperial commander as "numerous and well armed."[14] But another observer claimed that in fact the enemy comprised only a "few score of inexperienced *tapuios*, infested with vermin, fishermen, cowboys, all extracted from their work under threat, who have little idea how to use a gun. They know only how to use a machete, drink rum, and when drunk how to commit crimes and exercise violence."[15]

At least, the rebel army had a new and independent organization and structure of command. It was headed by many leaders rather than one, though obviously there was some level of coordination of movements between bands. Rebel soldiers operated in units, each with their own chief rather than under a central command. There was equality rather than hierarchy among commanders, for positions were numbered. A captain was "Captain One" or "Captain Two," and so on. Presumably, military titles were awarded on the basis of campaigns launched, successes, and collective responsibility.

Rebels identified themselves in various ways. They dyed their clothes red with *muruci* palm fruit and put a cross on their straw hats. Until September 1836 it was commonplace to see people with a crossed hat, and so long as the wearer was not bearing or using arms he or she was tolerated. In the repression it became a crime to wear a hat with a cross, potentially punishable by

---

13 American John Priest gave a statement to British naval officers concerning his role in the murder of the crew of the Clio; see David Cleary, *Cabanagem: Documentos Ingleses*, Belém: Secult, 2003, 98–100; Paton, *Narrative of the Loss of the Schooner Clio*, Montrose, 1879; Lucas Alexandre Boiteaux, *Marinha Imperial versus Cabanagem*, Rio de Janeiro: Imprensa Naval, 1943, 343; and Hurley, *Traços Cabanos*, 157–161 and 232–233.
14 Santos, *Tupaiulândia*, 209.
15 Quoted in Santos, *Tupaiulândia*, 209.

summary execution.[16] More generally, clothes were in scarce supply in this period. The local imperial soldiers had no uniform, in fact hardly any had clothes; they "look like Africans" because all they had *tangas* – strips of cotton barely covering their genitals.[17] It had also been reported that rebels, having recently attacked one town, killed only to steal clothes from their victims.[18]

Documented instances of rebel brutality were surprisingly few. Manoel Sanches, the most voluminous and insightful correspondent from the Lower Amazon of the time, described an attack by Diniz Marcelino de Souza. "Diniz, without order or law or authority, attacks, kills and robs ... in Maracá-assu near Óbidos he smashed up the chapel into small pieces, took escaping residents as prisoners, killed cattle, stole manioc flour and then asked for peace. When I refused to offer a peace treaty he encircled Óbidos, drummed on his boxes and shouted in the custom of wild Indians, only they are more honorable."[19] Eventually they agreed a peace deal sometime in September 1836 and Diniz, a military official from Santarém, went over to the imperial side and became a trusted ally of Sanches. Diniz then helped conduct a series of operations against Ecuipiranga and in the final one he was killed by rebels.

While Ecuipiranga was the largest in the 1835–1837 period, there were many other rebel strongholds dotted along the rivers and lakes of the whole region. They came and went depending on their success in defending themselves and their own strategies and movements, and tended to be smaller affairs with a few to a hundred men in position. Many were well fortified, with trenches, traps and armored canoes guarding the port. Known as a "meeting" (*reunião*), they were likely to have been camps dedicated to guerrilla attacks on local towns and farms to maintain stores and supplies. Each had a leader and an extensive system of communication with other positions. These networks were a prime concern of the legalista forces: if they could stop movements and communication between groups, they might prevent a build up of force. Thus blockades were one of their main methods in this regard – sitting outside a meeting with armed ships. Of course, many town councils were sympathetic to president Angelim, though this did not mean they necessarily sympathized with the rebels.

16 Justice of the Peace Antônio M. Sanches de Brito to Justice of the Peace and other officials in Vila Franca, Pauxis [Óbidos], September 18, 1836, in Arthur Reis, *História de Óbidos*, Rio de Janeiro: Editora Civilização Brasileira, 1979, 124.

17 Justice of the Peace Antônio M. Sanches de Brito to Commander for the Tapajós River, Lourenço Justiniano da Serra Freire, Pauxis, May 26, 1837, APEP cod. 888, doc. 141 (copy).

18 Justice of the Peace Antônio M. Sanches de Brito to Justice of the Peace and other officials in Vila Franca, Pauxis, September 18, 1836, in Reis, *História de Óbidos*, 121.

19 Justice of the Peace Antônio M. Sanches de Brito to Justice of the Peace and other officials in Vila Franca, Pauxis, in Reis, *História de Óbidos*, 123.

In the first part of the Cabanagem rebellion in the Lower Amazon – effectively all of 1835 and up to September 1836 – small bandit like groups called *magotes* patrolled the countryside, terrorizing people and plundering what they could. There appeared to be little overall organization to these movements and their motives were a combination of revenge and justice. These groups were chiefly self-organized and worked in parallel to the military rebels in Ecuipiranga, especially in the absence of a sustained opposition or an army to repress them until September 1836. After that time the navy moved upriver and as the imperial forces became organized, *magotes* began to consolidate and unify, "all the time getting bigger."[20] The "interior is inhabited only by rebels," one imperial captain exclaimed.[21] He nevertheless feared these diverse entities would "make one large body" led from Ecuipiranga.[22] From his point of view, the smaller meetings the better, for the groups could then be destroyed more easily. There was danger, the commanders recognized, in proceeding too quickly on the rebel positions without a coordinated strategy. They might re-form into one large muster, which could prove to be indomitable. On the other hand, the guerrilla-style tactics of small dispersed bands were also valuable to the rebels.

Aside from the disparate nature of their movement, the rebels faced other difficulties in consolidating their support. Until September 1836 in the Lower Amazon, and perhaps elsewhere, rebels could not be easily distinguished from imperial soldiers. Even though some rebels wore crossed hats and red clothes, it was not always obvious who was on what side. The problem was twofold: both factions had generated only wavering support and no one really knew what either side stood for. There were no clear divisions. Furthermore, as mentioned previously, people changed sides for no apparent ideological reason. Presumably Diniz Marcelino de Souza changed sides because he had enough of the nomadic life and the aggression. He was a commander general of the United Brazilian Forces until September 1836 and, before that, a captain in Santarém's national guard. He may have foreseen the rebels' failure, having experienced what he felt to be their disorganization and lack of leadership and ideals. He may also have known that the return of the ruthless General Andréa to Pará in early 1836 would mean no effort would be spared in repressing the rebel movement. I will return to Diniz and the circumstances of his defection later in this chapter.

<hr>

20 Commander of Imperial Forces in Vila Franca Diniz Marcelino de Souza to Justice of the Peace Antônio M. Sanches de Brito, Ponto de Santa Anna, November 11, 1836, APEP cod. 1013, doc. 163.
21 Without author or date, sent around December 1836 to President of Pará José Soares de Andréa, APEP cod. 1013, doc. 186.
22 Justice of the Peace Manoel Aragão Bastos to Antônio M. Sanches de Brito, on Schooner *São João III*, December 3, 1836, APEP cod. 1013, doc. 178.

Most of the Portuguese in the Lower Amazon had either left or been murdered by March 1836. Remaining were the moderate liberal Brazilians (a small group of whites) who ran the town councils and local businesses; the more radicalized military officers and soldiers; the artisans and farmers and fishermen; and the slaves and Indians who worked for daily wages and had their own plot of land. The splits between these people were far from obvious and certainly not insuperable. Furthermore, a good many people were holding out since it was not clear what was going on in Belém and what repercussions there would be. After three centuries of dreading what came from downriver, it was understandable that some were reluctant to express firm support for any side. "Let's wait and see" was one sensible option. Furthermore, the so-called rebel side made themselves "respectable, covering their actions with legality" in order to obtain declarations of support.[23] From September 1836 and the start of the period of zero tolerance of rebels along the main course of the Amazon, the factions became better demarcated and people were pushed willingly or unwillingly into one of them. What had been a general movement among Paraenses against despotism and for more inclusion became a war between "patriots" who supported a new independent Brazil and everyone else, who were seen as "evildoers" who did not deserve to be a part of the nation. This shift was one of the most amazing developments in the history of the region.

The Cabanagem in the Lower Amazon

At the end of 1835 serious accusations arose against the chief judge and head of the police force in the Lower Amazon, Joaquim Rodrigues de Souza, and, to a lesser extent, the mercenary Ambrosio Pedro Ayres. (Souza had been appointed early in 1835 by Felix Malcher, the first president of the Cabanagem period.) The pair was accused of punishing supporters of Angelim with arbitrary imprisonment and violent punishments, especially the participants in a Christmas uprising. A rebel attack launched from Ecuipiranga, which had the support of some Santarém residents, had brought turmoil to the town on Christmas Day 1835. The assault was violently put down by Pedro Ayres and sixty of his men.[24] Both men sought to punish all those they could lay their hands on and, in so doing, they wildly exaggerated their powers. According to Maparajuba, Souza had embarked on a march to destroy all political activity,[25]

---

23 Without author or date, sent around December 1836 to President of Pará José Soares de Andréa, APEP cod. 1013, doc. 186.

24 Judge of the Lower Amazon Joaquim Rodrigues de Souza to President of Pará Marechal Manoel Jorge Rodrigues, Macapá, March 23, 1836, APEP cod. 1000, doc. 69.

25 "*Uma marcha antipolítica,*" writing in May 1836 from Manaus, which he had just stormed, to the municipal council of Santarém.

Reducing the homeland to a prison, making free citizens into slaves, misrepresenting our struggle as robbery and murder, imprisoning people who are not guilty, putting others in irons without a trial, and tying some to a large wooden wheel with the greatest cruelty, and, lastly, accusing us of burning houses and pillaging their contents. Whereas all know the executor of these last crimes is the captain Ambrosio Pedro Ayres, who in February of this year smashed up a Meeting near Alenquer. We demand that the same law be used to try the captain as all others ... we will bring down the colossus of despotism which has been built against the well-being of our sacred rights ... and we will enjoy the fruits of our sacred constitution in the shadow of a free government, whose only desire is to see the reign of liberty, the law, and the peace, to oversee the prospering of laws, industry, and commerce. These last two should be drawn to your attention. We should deploy to provide for our subsistence, but even this is entirely paralyzed by political activity, which equally causes prejudice to our national income.[26]

By the time this complaint was written, the judge had, in fact, fled Santarém. Fearing he could no longer stay in the town, Souza took to the imperial naval ship *Guajará* at the end of February with some local families. After a tumultuous voyage downstream, which saw the ship taken over and redirected to Gurupá with its captain shot dead, the *Guajará* found safety in Macapá, where military operations in the Lower and Upper Amazon were orchestrated. From there Souza received reports of events in Santarém, returning a year later when the town was retaken by imperial forces. On the other hand, Ayres, who was nicknamed Bararoa (after the town on the Negro River where he had settled), had a very different experience. He conducted his repression with much brutality. It is not clear on whose authority he acted or when and how he came to be there, but for the next two years he acted as a mercenary with a band of imperial soldiers, searching for rebels in remote parts.[27]

In October 1835 Angelim wrote to the United Brazilian camp at Ecuipiranga to request loyalty to his presidency and to ask whether the other towns in the area were sympathetic to him.[28] Angelim knew he had the support of Belém and a few other neighboring towns, but he also was aware that key towns such as Cametá and Macapá were held by those who disputed his authority. Six months later he received notification that most towns in the Lower Amazon recognized his presidency, the most important being Santarém, not only in size but for its links to the south up the

---

26 Raiol, *Motins Políticos*, 1038.
27 Few documents have survived from the 1835 period of the Lower Amazon so we cannot be clear about what was going on. Much more is known about events in and around Belém since it was clearly at the center.
28 Angelim sought a request for support of his government and presidency in October 1835, Raiol, *Motins Políticos*, 953.

Tapajós.[29] Less a soldier than politician, Angelim hoped that general recognition would legitimize his presidency with evidence of widespread support (see Chapter 8).

As a leader, Maparajuba was also concerned with the general well-being and the maintenance of order amid the rebellion. As shown in his letter above, Maparajuba insisted on the proper functioning of the economy and the fair implementation of justice and discipline. It was precisely the apparent despotic use of law and the arbitrary and exaggerated acts of punishment of the past three hundred years of Portuguese occupation that had been at the forefront of rebel protests in this period. Now, with Brazilians in control of their own country, Maparajuba seemed to say, "We don't need to put up with this anymore, either from the Portuguese or our own élite." Along with Angelim's request for loyalty, the tyrannical violence of Souza and Pedro Ayres sparked a series of events that launched the rebel, or United Brazilian, campaign proper in the Lower and Upper Amazon. The irony was that at about this time the man who would defeat the rebels arrived from the South of Brazil and positioned himself near an island in front of the city of Belém, and prepared for suppression.

The Santarém council's acceptance of Angelim as president seemed to be a result of a deal done with the military commanders at Ecuipiranga. Whether the council members were threatened or not is unclear, but peaceful relations were negotiated early in March 1836. The allegations against Souza were resolved by his flight from the place; yet the council refused to sack him at the end of February because they thought he basically had patriotic sentiments and was capable of maintaining law and order.[30] The council members revealed that he was threatening to abandon the town of his own accord, as were many others. Their stated reason was the descent of the region into total anarchy and ruin of the province.[31] The council decided it was time to negotiate and nominated a commission to organize peaceful relations with the United Brazilians in Ecuipiranga.[32] Council members and military officials Manuel Raimundo Ferreira, João de Deus Ferreira Canumam, and Antônio Manuel Brancher were named as intermediaries. They carried with them the council's request that the United Brazilian forces put down their arms and keep the peace. In fact, these people were chosen not just by the council but by local authorities and other citizens. The recognition of the importance of popular interest was given further weight in future sessions of the council. From April for the next few months, ecclesiastical, civil, and military officials and various citizens were

---

29 Raiol, *Motins Políticos*, 1033.
30 Ibid.
31 Raiol, 1031.
32 "*A fim de tratar a paz*," Raiol, *Motins Políticos*, 1032

invited to take part and vote on decisions. This small detail was suggestive of wider public participation in council sessions and perhaps a revolutionary move to more inclusive democracy.[33]

The agreement reached between the commission and the United Brazilians is unknown. For sure, no arms were laid down. Nevertheless, some assurances may have been extracted from the rebels not to attack the town while it was sympathetic to Angelim. The result was an imbrication of civil and rebel positions and personnel. The following letter by the United Brazilians and the proclamation by the Council, written a few days after peaceful relations were established, expressed in their own words some of the tensions and interests at stake.

To the President and members of the Council of Tapajós.

In order to maintain the public peace and the tranquility of this district and to combat the spirit of the deluded, we have resolved in this meeting to nominate as commanders to this District the citizens Bonifacio Nunes de Arruda and Hermengildo Fernando Valente, who are peaceful Brazilians and friends of the law, not that some would say they are. However the urgency of the times demands your Lordships' help, the administration of the law so that the peaceful citizens can live in tranquility, respecting the law in all the Brazilian properties, as well as those of allied nations, which must not suffer the minimum insult or attack. In order to fortify this unhappy district the aforementioned commanders will patrol with fifty armed soldiers, which this District needs because it has become known to us that the slaves have run away and are grouping and threatening the town wanting to take possession of it. We must take every precaution and be on our guard all the time in this respect. This Meeting has the honor to inform your Lordships of the Proclamation included which we are sending to make public to the Council. Your Lordships are now in the intelligence that today we live only under the supreme law, and any act to the contrary will be treated with the severest penalty. Your Senhores should take these considerations into account with all the maturity that such an important undertaking requires; so delicately poised is our well being and so strong the ignorance which endures amongst us, the measures needed are ones with much subtlety. Only in this way will we be able to impose the law. We praise your Lordships and request all efforts be extended to our troops when they take quarters in Santarém. God keep you well.
Encampment of Ecuipiranga, 16th March 1836.

[signed] Bras Antonio Correia, first general commander of the forces;
Francisco Antonio Batista, *alferes* second commander;
Antonio Correia Picanço,
Pedro Antonio Correia Vianna,
Manoel d'Oliveira da Paz,

33 Raiol, 1036–1040; see the list of people present at beginning of each report.

Raimundo Elias de Carvalho,
Bernardo Antonio de Aragão,
João Pais Pedroso,
Domingos de Conceiçao Ferreira, first commanders of the trenches;
Julião Correia Jatai, second commander of the trenches;
Lourenco Raimundo Martinho, third commander;
Martinho Bras, fourth commander;
João Ferriera Leal, justice of the peace of the Meeting.

With this official letter is being sent a Proclamation which was published in Santarém, and is being sent to all the councils of the district in order for them to be filled with the patriotism of the United Brazilians in Ecuipiringa.[34]

Proclamation

Honorable Tapajoense citizens. Calm your spirits! The Meeting of Ecuipiranga does not offend you. On the contrary, it exists to guarantee your rights, which were almost taken away by the Judge of this district, Joaquim Rodrigues de Souza. Already through an intermediary of this Council a deal has been made with the Meeting. We recognize the person of Eduardo Angelim as president of this province and will defend the individual rights of all people in this district. Long live the Holy Catholic faith and the apostles of Rome! Long live the Brazilian Dom Pedro the Second and the Regency government in his name! Long live our brothers in Ecuipiranga in the defense and maintenance of the individual rights of the citizens of this district. Long live the virtuous Tapajoenses![35]

This handwritten proclamation was pinned to the door of the church in Santarém. Although few could read, people crowded around and listened to the news and participated in the discussions.

To be clear: the first of these documents was written by soldiers at Ecuipiranga and the second comes from the hand of the council of Santarém. There were both significant differences and strong overlaps. Both stressed the importance of law and order. The rebel letter mentioned the supreme law, which was the Catholic faith and its moral authority. This would imply that the revolutionary aspects of Christianity were an important motivating factor for rebels.[36] Maintaining order in the region was to be

---

34 Raiol, 1035, but the proclamation is not transcribed there.
35 Passed in the "town of Santarém March 9, 1836 in the 15th of Independence and the Empire," Hurley, *Traços Cabanos*, 69.
36 On the religious aspects of the rebellion, see Hurley, *Traços Cabanos*, 72–73, for a letter about the importance of the Catholic faith and Maparajuba's biblical references in his letter. Sanches de Brito's also sought to outlaw any mention of Sebastianism, in Reis, *História de Óbidos*, 124. (N.B. I was unable to find the original of this document.)

achieved through the patrolling of fifty soldiers, who would respect all property, not just that of Brazilians but also of allied nations, principally referring to the Portuguese but there were two British citizens – John Hislop and Edward Jeffreys – and a French citizen in Santarém at the time.[37] The insistence on protecting property, combined with the Council's endorsement of Pedro II and the regency government in the proclamation, indicate the nonrevolutionary interests of the United Brazilians.

Of course, these were official pronouncements. So we must be alert to the possibility that the rebels were positioning themselves in order not to arouse too much suspicion or fear. It should not be forgotten that the writers of these letters were probably peasants, artisans, military, and civil officers. However, it would seem that these claims were not a smokescreen for more revolutionary intentions. For example, there were no calls to end slavery on behalf of the main cabano leaders. Had there been a move to abolish slavery, likely all the other institutions surrounding property and class would have tumbled down.

To make this claim more concrete, we can return to the letter written by the United Brazilians, where they revealed something of their true colors. They seem to imply the collapse into anarchy was not their fault or due to Angelim's presidency, but rather to the slaves in their encampments – the property of Brazilians. This pronouncement was designed to justify their patrols of the area in maintaining law and order and preventing pillage. It shows the United Brazilians had no interest in ending slavery or forming alliances with runaway slave communities. If there was one way for rebel leaders to gain respectability in the eyes of the regency government, maintain the racial hierarchy, and incorporate liberal political reforms, this was it.

One qualifier should be added here: The rebel movement was heterogeneous. Some rebels shot white slave owners, skinned at least one trader, and freed slaves. But some of the soldiers who had committed these acts were themselves executed very publicly by Angelim.

The conciliation process in Santarém worked, but suffered at least one major hiccup in Santarém at the end of March 1836, only a few weeks after it began. On March 23 a band of soldiers – Indians and whites – came into the town led by Thomas Antônio de Faria, a "cabano without equal." As Faria entered the town, he was asked what he wanted and was said to reply "Nothing really, only death to the Portuguese, Caramurus [conservative Portuguese], and masons, and then everything will be peaceful." On their arrival the group killed some civilians and soldiers, at least three being

37 For accounts, see Bates, *The Naturalist*, vol. 2, 1–70 on Santarém in the early 1850s; and William Smyth and Frederick Lowe, *Narrative of a Journey from Lima to Para*, London, 1836, 299–300, among other references.

"Brazilians of the highest quality."[38] Not satisfied, the next day they mistook a religious brotherhood meeting in the town for a conservative plot and massacred all the participants. After three days about thirty people were left dead, including José Policárpio and a prominent naturalized Brazilian (that is, Portuguese-born) Miguel Antônio Pinto Guimarães. These men were slave owners with extensive lands in the region. Faria was accused of being a hypocrite because he was the son of a prominent Portuguese military officer – "Enemies, indeed, who was your father then?" one woman reportedly asked. The rule of law was clearly not imposed on this occasion since this question demanding Faria's arrest was written down in February 1837, once Santarém was back in imperial hands. Faria, the writer went on, was one of the worst "authors of widowhood and parentless children" in the region, and his band of men were "monsters for human blood."[39]

A few weeks earlier in March 1836, a similar attack had occurred in Monte Alegre, this time led by Francisco Rodrigues Lobo Bentes, known as the *Sertanejo* and from another relatively well-placed family. A group arrived in the town and linked up with some friends there. They assassinated ten people, including the leading mason and captain, Nicoláo da Gama Lobo. According to an eyewitness, the ears of the unfortunate dead men were chopped off, put on a rope, and hung up in the main square.[40] Monte Alegre fell into United Brazilian hands; a week later, Rodrigues de Souza tried to take refuge there as he escaped from Santarém, but left once he realized who was in charge. Cutting off ears was common practice in the early colonial period: soldiers used them as proof of their valor.[41]

As Santarém, Almerim, Gurupá, Alenquer, and Parintins declared their adherence to Angelim's presidency, Manaus was stormed by Francisco Bernardo de Sena and a contingent of 1,800 soldiers in early March. Sena writes on March 7 to the Council in Santarém that he had no authority, he was "only a soldier," but he wanted to see a constitutional Brazilian government in place. This meant one that was in accord with article 165 of the constitution, that there be a "Brazilian born provincial president who administers justice in a fair and fraternal way to the people of Pará."

38 Judge of the Lower Amazon Joaquim Rodrigues de Souza to President of Pará Marechal Manoel Jorge Rodrigues, Macapá, April 18, 1836, APEP cod. 1000, doc. 96.

39 Maria Margarida Pereira and 20 other signatures to Commander of Land Forces in Lower Amazon, February 5, 1837, Santarém, APEP cod. 1052, doc. 65; and Francisco Ignácio Pereira to Military Commander, February 5, 1837, Santarém, APEP cod. 1052, doc. 67.

40 Judge of the Lower Amazon Joaquim Rodrigues de Souza to President of Pará, March 23, 1836, Macapá, APEP 1000, docs 67 and 69.

41 The bandeirantes in the sixteenth and seventeenth centuries collected Amerindian ears. The Jesuit missionary João Daniel mentions slavers made necklaces from teeth as well as ears; *O Tesouro Descoberto no Máximo Rio Amazonas*: Rio de Janeiro: Contrapunto, 2003, vol. 1, 278.

These remarks were hardly threatening and the demands quite unrevolutionary and resonated with Angelim's in Belém. In fact, Article 165 of the 1824 constitution does not quite say what Sena claims it does: "There will be in each Province a President, appointed by the Emperor, who can remove him, if it is in the best interests of the State." This reading reveals a significant dimension of the popular interpretation of the constitution. Clearly, there was comprehensive knowledge and critical engagement with centralized authority among large parts of the population. Sena may not have deliberately misread the article, but chose to understand it in his own way.

Sena had been in Santarém late in 1835, and supposedly participated in the uprising of Christmas Day that year. He claimed to have been a victim of the barbarity of Rodrigues de Souza, who had arrested him and sent him under armed guard to Belém. Released by rebels, Sena left Belém and made his way up to Ecuipiranga, where he found a "force ready to defend the Imperial Constitution, his Imperial Majesty and Brazilian nationhood."[42] Then he went to secure Manaus for the movement.

Although the democratic version of liberalism was dominant among the rebel leaders, the United Brazilian side held a variety of opinions. Moreover, the defenders of the constitution (as they interpreted it) and property among the rebels were not able to control their "allies" or maintain discipline over their forces. The question, then, must be whether those like Faria or Lobo Bentes were really part of the United Brazilian front or something different, and perhaps allied. If they were part of the United Brazilians, were they acting alone or with the knowledge of their commanders, revealing their professed respect for the constitution and property to be a sham or a ruse? After all, judge Souza did call them the "false friends of order."[43]

The most likely answer is that there was a general movement and agreement over basic principles – only Brazilians to be in power, respect for the law, no arbitrary implementation of justice, and so on. Given the diversity of groups in the region, it is not surprising that small bands formed with their own ideas, even if they were linked to a wider network. At the center were those with military experience who formed the largest and most coherent force and deliberately set out to persuade councils to adhere to Angelim. Others, like Faria and Lobo Bentes, thought this was not enough – the Portuguese and their sympathizers would never go away quietly; a cleansing was needed, blood for blood. At this time the United Brazilians may have

---

42 All quotes from Raiol, *Motins Políticos*, 1036–1037. Sena, a freed slave, was exiled from Pernambuco for murder. He went to manage cattle ranches on the Branco River but was accused of corruption. Mattos, "Relatorio do Estado da Decadência em que se Acha o Alto Amazonas," RIHGB 1979 [1845], 325, 160.

43 Judge of the Lower Amazon Joaquim Rodrigues de Souza to President of Pará Marechal Manoel Jorge Rodrigues Macapá, March 23, 1836, APEP cod. 1000, doc. 69.

refused to support and offer protection to these men. So it is likely Faria and others and their followers lived as bandits, looting farms and exacting revenge. This may have radicalized their understanding of the situation. Nevertheless, the dividing lines were unclear, and would remain so until the repression moved upriver. Moreover, the support for the rebels from town councils was lukewarm; violent attacks served only to reinforce reactionary fears.

A shift toward an anti-cabano position is clearly seen in a council meeting that took place in Santarém on May 27, 1836. Belém had fallen into imperial hands on May 13. Angelim was trying to negotiate safe passage to Ecuipiranga but Andréa refused to agree, forcing Angelim to escape, and allowing Andréa's repression to begin with the imposition of martial law, arbitrary imprisonments and executions.[44] But it is unclear whether the council chamber knew what was happening downstream or what significance they attached to the events. They did know there was much fighting downriver. In particular, rumors from Belém suggested "a declaration of war against whites and mamelucos, with no exceptions made for the small and innocent." The council was debating a letter from Manoel Pedro dos Anjos, a United Brazilian officer stationed near Manaus, proposing the separation of the Lower and Upper Amazon districts from Belém and her neighboring region. The point of the separation was to distance themselves from the events downriver and to exempt themselves from responsibility for the crimes.[45] A blockade could be maintained to control movement up and down the river. The council threw out the proposal because it decided unilateral separation would be an illegal act in itself. The declaration of war against whites and mamelucos was possibly genuine, but if so must have been made by either Indians or blacks, that is, those not identified as the victims. It could also have been an inverted comment derived from Andréa or one of his commanders, who came with every intent of declaring war not on whites but on all who supported the rebel movement.

Attending this council meeting was Joaquim Fructuoso, a Mundurucu headman.[46] He asked to address the meeting after the debate on the

---

44 Raiol, *Motins Políticos*, 977–978, says Angelim requested to go up to "Amazonas." My supposition is that he would have aimed to go to where his support was strongest.

45 See also Joaquim Rodrigues de Souza to President of Pará José de Soares Andréa, Macapá, June 21, 1836, APEP cod. 1000, doc. 152, on the dismemberment of the two regions.

46 See also Hemming, *Amazon Frontier*, 548, on the Mundurucu tuxaua Joaquim Manoel Fructuoso. Revealingly, in 1852 tuxaua Joaquim met the American naval explorer William Lewis Herndon in his village on the Tapajós River. The headman told the visitor "in bad Portuguese," "I am the Tuchão, Joaquim. I love whites, and have never betrayed them. I left my friends, my cacoaes and my house on the borders of the Madeira to defend them. How many cabanos have I not killed when I showed my war canoe that never fled? Now I am old and infirm; but if I remain in the midst of these women, and do not soon leave for the fields to chase away these brigands of Muras, who lay waste my cacoaes, I will be bewitched and die like a dog." William Herndon, *Exploration of the Valley of the Amazon,*

separation. Once permission was granted, he got to his feet, gave a great and elegant bow, and spoke: "Your illustrious lordships and honorable citizens: from what I have seen since I came to this town and from what I have heard in the letter from Manoel Pedro dos Anjos, I see clearly that the lowest class is working mercilessly against the lives of the most noble and learned citizens, as are the whites and mamelucos, with the most refined atrocities. It is impossible for us of sound reason to ignore the abyss in which this vast and rich province is falling as a result of such barbarous and iniquitous projects. For this reason I have already offered to your Lordships the whole body of the Mundurucu nation, for the defense of your lives, families and goods."[47]

This short speech reveals how the general movement was splitting over reforms and the imperial constitution (not to mention the shrewdness of Joaquim Fructuoso in sounding like an élite property owner). There may have been an alliance between the civil and military officials for the past few months, but now some of – if not all – the United Brazilians, the military rebels, were being pushed out by another alliance: one between the civil authorities and the Mundurucu Indians. The United Brazilians had failed to convince others of the legitimacy of their purpose. Perhaps they were also unable to contain the various groups with whom they were linked, even if this was only in the popular imagination. If we bracket off the appeal to ethnic groups in this process, the United Brazilians had lost their respectability.[48]

The question remains, though: What was the link between the United Brazilians and the "lowest class," those who were not seen as white and mamelucos by the Mundurucu headman? Fructuoso may have had his own hidden motivation here, which was to label all non-Mundurucu Indians as inferior and treacherous. More generally, it is inconceivable that some of the rebel leaders mentioned previously were not white or mameluco. For example, Faria was the son of a white Portuguese lieutenant-colonel (though his mother was an Indian). More likely, an interpretation is that the

Washington, Taylor and Maury, 1854, 315–316. Hemming says he was rewarded for his service but Herndon says he was not because he disobeyed a Brazilian officer, who subsequently discredited the headman's record of loyalty. Given the poverty and diseased state with which Herndon found Fructuoso, it is more likely he was not paid. He was also accused of assassinating a Mundurucu woman in 1840; Antônio Rodrigues to Commander of Expeditionary Forces in the Lower Amazon Colonel Manoel Tavares, August 16, 1840, Ponto Brazileira Legal, APEP cod. 1141, doc. 151.

47 Raiol, *Motins Políticos*, 1040. The Mundurucu served as scouts for the imperial army, see for examples references in military letters from the Santarém sent in June 1837, APEP cod. 888, doc. 185; May 1838, cod. 906, doc. 35; June 1837, cod. 1052, doc. 238), with scarce public funds used to buy their support, see Agnello Petra Bittencourt to President Francisco José Soares d'Andréa, October 29, 1836, APEP cod. 1013, doc. 64.

48 The sacking of the arms-carrying British ship *Clio* and the murder of all but two of its crew in Salinas in October 1835 is an example of the distance between Angelim and his supporters.

identification of the violence and excess with a class and an ethnic group was part of a deliberate process to undermine the rebel movement. The appeal to racial prejudice and colonially derived hierarchy was clearly aimed to discredit the movement. It was a way of dismissing the participants – if they acted like bad Indians, they were and should be treated as such.

In summary, the civil and ecclesiastical authorities in Santarém were divided and wavered in their support in the first part of 1836. The priest for Santarém, João Antônio Ferreira, witnessed a rebel attack in June 1836 involving two hundred soldiers, or "anarchists," consisting of eleven days of fighting and looting though apparently no deaths or injuries. Forces from Óbidos had to help the imperial drive; the result was the arrest of the rebel leader and some of his men. Ferreira said with obvious relief that the town was "back in the hands of the legal side," though this turned out not to be the case.[49] The backing for the rebels was finely balanced, showing the tremendous effort put in by both sides to bolster their position. In the repression spreading upriver, the imperial troops – stronger and better armed – came to be synonymous with the whites and Brazilian patriots, even if their supporters had been sympathetic to other ideas. The question of political legitimacy was never considered again and would get buried beneath the "war of race hate" (as will be discussed in the next chapter).

The Gathering Imperial Forces

By September 1836 the Upper and Lower Amazon presented a confused picture of successes and failures on each side. Maparajuba had been killed in Manaus some months before, and new leaders had replaced him. New rebel musters had formed in Maués (then Luzea) and Curuá, as well as some towns, and others were held by imperial troops. Manaus had returned to the legalistas with the help of Bararoa and his men. Sena had been shot dead by one of his own soldiers. A commander general of the United Brazilian forces in the Lower Amazon was Diniz Marcelino de Souza. Diniz, like most of the other leaders, was in the military and had become radicalized by liberal ideas. Óbidos was the most important town between Manaus and Gurupá to remain in the hands of the legalistas, and Diniz and his troops had been trying for the past few months to take it and extend the United Brazilian position in the region. His counterpart at the time was a missionary from Juruti, Manuel Sanches, who was recently elected as a judge in Óbidos.[50]

---

49 Military commander Antônio José da Gama Malcher to the Commander of Forces for the Lower Amazon Jõao Henrique de Mattos, Monte Alegre, July 2, 1837, APEP cod. 888, doc. 127; and Justice of the Peace Antônio M. Sanches de Brito to Commander of Forces for the Lower Amazon Jõao Henrique de Mattos, Ponto de Santa Anna, APEP cod. 888, doc. 128, July 8, 1837.

50 Extraordinary session of the town council of Óbidos, December 17, 1836, APEP cod 1050, doc. 93.

While he had also been radicalized (see Chapter 5) and opposed abuse and mistreatment of Indians, Sanches was firmly against the rebel movement.

Diniz and Sanches became personally embroiled sometime in August 1836. They exchanged letters and probably came face to face, with the outcome being a declaration of peace by Diniz and his soldiers. The adversaries met in Vila Franca, though there was little negotiation. Sanches was suspicious and cautious, but Diniz was willing to give up the fight. The proclamation by Diniz was as follows:

It is the duty of all citizens to work for the growth, greatness and happiness of their country, and to maintain rights of the Sovereign, and those of each person; and to this end I have fought against the violence of absolutism ... in order to prove incontestably my true Christian and peaceful sentiments, I have agreed a ceasefire with the town of Óbidos ... once and for all we [the troops under my command] can give to Brazil, a proof that good Brazilians do not want the disgrace of their country, nor the pains of its patriots, everyone together can build a peace which can be trusted by all the responsible authorities ... I also order that no one can take revenge resulting from past events and those who do will be considered a disturber of the peace, and any threats will be considered a crime against the nation and in all rebel strongholds, rivers, lakes and streams all will be required to maintain good order.[51]

Diniz's men were not to be broken up and disarmed (demobbed) but stationed in the barracks in Óbidos. Sanches de Brito wrote to the imperial Lower Amazon commander to confirm the arrangement six days later, though he added "the greatest prudence" was needed in dealing with such a declaration. He continued with eloquence and insight:

I must first make sure that I have secured him, that I have not tricked myself, when I gave consent to what Diniz has said, but for sure his word is firm, and sincere demonstrations have been given that peace is desired, and he is forcing himself to bury once and for all the spirit of the party [presumably the rebel side or "anarchist," a word Sanches uses frequently elsewhere]. But one should not doubt that the direction of a heterogeneous people, with diverse inclinations and without discipline and perfect subordination, cannot possibly be impressed with a single orientation and reduced to one path of obligation. It would be such a change, either the fruit of a miracle, or of some well-reflected and prudent ideas which have matured over time. For this reason it is indispensable that those whose role it is to pursue peace should keep a watch on the whole situation and work towards a felicitous ending.[52]

51 "Bando" [copy], Commander of the United Brazilian Forces Diniz Marcelino de Souza to all towns in the Lower Amazon, September 4, 1836, Vila Franca, APEP cod 1013, doc. 86.
52 Justice of the Peace Antônio M. Sanches de Brito to Commander of the United Brazilian Forces Diniz Marcelino de Souza, September 10, 1836, Vila Franca, APEP cod 1013, doc. 86.

Why did Diniz agree to peace with Óbidos? It is not clear, but he went on to fight for the empire most valiantly, according to one observer.[53] Toward the end of September Diniz requested the priest of Óbidos, Raimundo Sanches de Brito (who was also the elder brother of Sanches) to come to Vila Franca "to take mass or at least baptize some children, and you will bring with you some of the salvation of Óbidos, and for this reason you must come."[54] Though he had other interests, Raimundo came. Like his brother, Raimundo was committed to the imperial forces. He encountered a demoralized troop at Ecuipiranga and informed his brother that there was "a general disposition for peace. It is only a small exalted part that works for our disgrace. For this reason I will work hard to remedy such evil ... it is necessary to conduct yourself with moderation [i.e. do not attack rebel positions for the moment] ... I am also working to win over Diniz to the party of law, who is well disposed to this end."[55] As the result of his visit, the priest Sanches wrote to the military commander, Bittancourt, arguing that they should try to squeeze the rebels into one place; and that Manaus must remain in imperial hands, so a schooner of war must go there and keep the peace.[56] The fight should be in the Lower Amazon.

The moderation Raimundo asked of his brother had a purpose. Diniz's troops had gone to Óbidos and stationed themselves in the barracks following the peace accord. Presumably unknown to Diniz, some of his troops staged an attack on residents during the early morning of September 16, killing a handful of men, terrorizing the women, and ransacking some houses. The legalistas, as feared, had been tricked into trusting the soldiers. In a long letter to Bittancourt reflecting on the times, Manoel Sanches reveals much of his own antipathy for the rebels. They supported Angelim, he says, though he was not even "a son of this province" (he was born in neighboring Ceará and had come to Pará with his parents at age five). The rebels had tricked Indians into supporting them by offering false promises for their freedom. As in Spanish America, the Indians would soon realize that supporting the rebels would not lead to freedom. All the rebels wanted to do was kill and steal. A revolutionary movement, according to Sanches,

---

53 Captain of the Naval Forces of the Lower Amazon Agnello Petra de Bettancourt to President Francisco José Soares d'Andréa, November 12, 1836, Escuna rio da Prata, near Santarém, APEP 1013, doc. 107.

54 Commander of the United Brazilian Forces Diniz Marcelino de Souza to Priest of Óbidos Raimundo Sanches de Brito, Tapajós, September 23, 1836, APEP cod 1013, doc. 83.

55 [Priest] Raimundo [Sanches de Brito] to brother [mano] Antônio [Sanches de Brito], September 25, 1836, Vila Franca, APEP cod 1013, doc. 85.

56 "Todos fazem huma só reuniao," Justice of the Peace Antônio M. Sanches de Brito to Captain of the Naval Forces of the Lower Amazon Agnello Petra de Bettancourt, September 29, 1836, APEP cod. 1013, doc. 84.

should not be about disobedience to the law.[57] On the basis of this evidence it would appear that Manual Sanches was opposed to the cabano rebellion partly because of the lack of Indian leadership. Thus, from Sanches' perspective, the rebel leaders sought to impose only another form of slavery on the masses. Of course, this assumes that the Indians had been tricked into supporting the rebels, rather than knowingly joining them to pursue their own interests or there being a convergence of motivations.

The important point here is that four years earlier, Raimundo and Manoel Sanches were housing Batista Campos – the intellectual force behind the nativist movement in the Brazilian Amazon (see Chapter 6). Indeed, Óbidos set itself up as capital of a new region in order to distance itself from the despotic and foreign presidents in Belém. Batista Campos was the new leader. Was the rebel movement so far removed from what these people wanted? Had they changed their ideas over this period to come to support the tyrannical presidency of Andréa, who himself was a foreigner, born in Portugal to a Brazilian father and Portuguese mother? Or were they fighting for what they had always believed and it so happened that meant being on Andréa's side? I suspect that this last gets nearest to the political machinations of the time.

In any case, another agreement with far-reaching consequences was signed a month later. Manoel Sanches and Bararoa made a pact to work together in the "destruction of the evil-doers" of the Lower and Upper Amazon in October 1836.[58] Aboard Bararoa's boat, the *Bararuense*, at the port of Óbidos with the members of the council and a number of citizens, Sanches was formally acknowledged as the civil chief of the Upper Amazon, though it effectively made him civil leader over the Lower Amazon also. Under the terms of the declaration, Bararoa was subordinate to Sanches.

Bararoa was as complicated a character as Sanches, though for different reasons. His origins were obscure; some said he was a foreigner of either German or Peruvian descent. He was already infamous for violence. We have already seen how he fomented some difficulties in early 1836. He was known to have shot a town official when he disagreed with him, and to have killed wounded prisoners and even whole families who supported

57 Reis, *História de Óbidos*, 124–125.
58 Commander of the "Forças Bararuaense" Ambrozio Pedro Aires to Justice of the Peace Antônio M. Sanches de Brito, on board the *Bararuerense*, October 19, 1836, APEP cod. 1050, doc. 91. Other information on Bararoa can be found in Hurley, *Traços Cabanos*, 167, who says he was a republican who had been exiled from Pernambuco to the Amazon in punishment for crimes not entirely clear. Boiteaux, 381, on his murder; Reis, *História do Amazonas*, 172; Hemming, *Amazon Frontier*, 234–235; Mattos, "Relatório," 159; de Souza, *Lembranças e Curiosidades*, 21–22; Raiol, *Motins Políticos*, 906; and Riviere, *Absent Minded Imperialism*, 33.

rebels.[59] He demanded hefty sums from town councils for ridding the nearby region of rebels. Furthermore, he pursued rebels up the narrowest and remotest rivers, unlike the imperial battalion, who were less knowledgeable and more fearful. Bararoa's force consisted of his boat, the *Bararuense*, and 254 soldiers, though only 127 worked on the boat.[60] Sanches' pact with such a mercenary could only further legitimate his operations. He had now a formal military position, a recognition of the existing situation. Sanches and Bararoa were, in effect, both mercenaries, working with their own soldiers and somewhat marginal to the imperial army under Andréa's command.

Their deal was nevertheless official in the sense that it was recognized by the military commanders of the region. And it certainly accorded with the full militarization of all positions of authority. This was because Andréa would only recognize military personnel – "he wants a purely military administration in order to achieve pacification and tranquillity."[61] Andréa installed new chief military commanders in Manaus and Santarém, with subsidiary ones in Marajó and Cametá. What Andréa thought of Sanches' assumption of local authority in this growing military complex is unclear. It is likely that Andréa wanted his men only in key positions and did not want complicated local arrangements since they could lead to weak leadership. Still, Sanches had much popular support. One captain remarked that he was amazed what Sanches was able to achieve. His secret was his dependence on a group of devoted friends and supporters to realize his ideas and plans.[62] The captain added that he knew Sanches did not like Andréa, though he recognized his authority. What is more, Sanches was heard to say at the height of the repression that "the man to save Pará has not arrived yet," an obvious reference to and criticism of Andréa.[63]

Meanwhile, about five hundred troops advanced upriver in three schooners of war (the *Rio do Prato, Leal Cametense,* and *Riograndense*).[64] They attacked rebel strongholds on the way in a sweep of firepower. Santarém was their main objective since this was the most important town outside of Belém. Accompanying the ships of war was a convoy of two hundred–odd ships, mostly sailing canoes and montarias. The first vessels arrived October 3, 1836, and for most of the next day, there was much resistance until the town

59 Reis, *História do Amazonas,* 179.

60 Commander of the "Forças Bararuaense" Ambrozio Pedro Aires to Justice of the Peace Antônio M. Sanches de Brito, on board the *Bararuerense,* October 19, 1836, APEP cod. 1013, doc. 94.

61 Boiteaux, *Marinha Imperial versus Cabanagem,* 342.

62 Manoel Thome Fialho d'Albuquerque, Minutes of an extraordinary meeting of the council of Pauxis, Pauxis, January 4, 1836, APEP cod. 1050, doc. 3.

63 Captain Antônio Firme Coelho to President of Pará Francisco José Soares d'Andréa, June 6, 1837, Santarém, APEP cod. 1052, doc. 238.

64 See Boiteaux, *Marinha Imperial versus Cabanagem,* 360, for information on these schooners, such as numbers of cannon.

was regained by mighty force at around 4:30 P.M., by which time the rebels had fled into the forest. José Pereira Leal, who led the imperial troops, estimated six hundred rebels had fought, of whom sixteen were left dead. They were judged to be well-armed with pistols, rifles, blunderbusses, swords, daggers, and bows and arrows, and were captained by Saraiva, Albuquerque, Barboza, and Carlos Pereira, the brother of Maparajuba. To protect the trenches, the rebels had placed barricades at the edges of the town, consisting of thick skins of leather, cotton, and vegetable fibers.[65] The other side lost only two men and suffered eight injuries.[66] Many houses were ruined by bullet holes, probably from the many town skirmishes. The invaders enjoyed the food the rebels left behind. Rebels also lost the armed yacht *4ᵗʰ October*, the schooner *5ᵗʰ October*, and various canoes and igarités. These prizes were sold and the money divided up between soldiers and commanders.[67] Like other towns, Santarém had suffered greatly. There was little food or money and much violence, suspicion, anger, and fear.

The military force of the empire continued to establish itself. The chief commander wrote to all rebel towns to lay down their arms; if they did not, they would suffer the consequences. Sensibly, the people of Alter do Chão, for example, fled their town upon receiving this demand. When the force of one hundred and fifty strong landed, the town was deserted, though still well fortified. All the saints' icons, ornaments, and religious symbols had been removed from the church. The troops searched nearby farms but found nothing.[68] Presumably, residents of Alter do Chão had escaped to one of the safe places, such as Ecuipiranga or further up the Tapajós. Slowly other towns came under the control of the imperial units – Alenquer in October, Faro in November, and Monte Alegre in December – though these towns also suffered further attacks and more deaths as rebels attempted to take them back or seek revenge.[69] Pushed out of the towns, the rebels fled to the rural strongholds and sought new forms of fighting the enemy. Increasingly, the differences between the sides became more exaggerated as the fighting continued, with people forced to join sides.

65 This description of the barricades comes from Hurley, *Traços Cabanos*, 40; and there are many others in the unpublished documents.

66 Officer Felipe José Perreira Leal to Captain of the Naval Forces of the Lower Amazon Agnello Petra de Bettancourt, October 5, 1836, Tapajós [Santarém], APEP cod. 1013, doc 31, no. 1. Boiteaux's source says 114 rebels died, as did 15 imperial soldiers, and 67 soldiers wounded in the attack, 363; see also Santos, *Cabanagem em Santarém*, 23.

67 "Conta das presas feitas em Santarém no dia 4 d'outubro de 1836," Captain of the Naval Forces of the Lower Amazon Agnello Petra de Bettancourt, May 25, 1837, Santarém, APEP cod. 1052 doc. 223.

68 Diniz Marcelino de Souza to Justice of the peace Antônio M. Sanches de Brito, October 31, 1836, Ponto de Santa Anna, APEP cod. 1013, doc. 101 [copy].

69 Commander Antônio Marques Farias to Captain of the Naval Forces of the Lower Amazon Agnello Petra de Bettancourt, December 12, 1836, Tapajós [Santarém], APEP cod. 1013, doc. 213, no. 8.

The Defeat of Ecuipiranga

The soldiers used their ships to blockade rural rebel strongholds, preventing food from coming in as well as communication and personnel movement. These blockades proved to be almost useless, however, since the cabanos knew the area so well they could move freely through forests and along rivers without detection. Nevertheless, the blockades served a purpose: making the presence of a threatening force visible. Patrols of heavily armed ships along the main waterways supported this visibility.[70] The main imperial strategy at this time was to take back the towns and push the rebels into their camps, then attack the smaller ones, gradually pushing them into a more confined space.[71] One set of commanders attacked from Santarém and another from Manaus, to contain the rebels on the south side of the river between the Madeira and the Tapajós rivers (later known as Mundurucania). However, this vast area was a labyrinth of streams, lakes, and rivers, and afforded easy communication with the south via the Tapajós River.[72]

Between October 1836 and May 1837, the confrontations occurred almost weekly, and sometimes even daily.[73] Patrols of imperial soldiers sought rebels, and rebels sought to regain the towns they had lost. Though Belém was in the hands of an imperially recognized regime, many other areas of the region were embroiled in continuing violence. In particular, Marajó Island, the Acará River, south of Belém, and the Lower Amazon experienced significant continuing conflicts between rebel and imperial armies. Indeed, these areas not only contained the cabanos' main encampments but also provided significant recruiting grounds for the movement – old and numerous colonial settlements and peasant economies tied to small-scale export production.

The ongoing unrest enraged Andréa and his commanders and increased their fervor in repressing the rebellion. More arms and soldiers were

70 Special commissions were set up to go up and down the rivers with armed ships, massacring rebels. This marks the beginning of the downfall of the rebels and imperial forces' concerted attempts to regain control.

71 Justice of the Peace Antônio M. Sanches de Brito to Captain of the Naval Forces of the Lower Amazon Agnello Petra de Bettancourt, November 4, 1836, Pauxis, APEP cod. 1013, doc. 100.

72 There were various military positions around Óbidos in October 1836, involving 597 men in the area: Trombetas River patrol (20), Curuá River patrol (15), Sapucuá River patrol (100), Muratuba (10), Juruti (100), Curumucuri (16), on Guajará boat (90), Santo Antônio boat (60) and 186 men in the town, "Mappa em que se mostra a força militar desta vila de Pauxis e os differentes pontos em que achão occupados," Captain of the National Guards, João da Gama Lobo Bentes, October 22, 1836, Pauxis, APEP cod. 1013, doc. [96?]. This was a significant investment of men. In Santarém about 800 men were stationed in town and in the points of Santa Anna on the Amazon River, Caxião on the Arapiuns River, and others were stationed at the blockade of the south side of Ecuipiranga on the Tapajós River.

73 Angelim was arrested in October 1836.

dispatched to new positions. More commanders were posted and those who failed were relieved of their duty. One hundred and nine naval officers headed military operations; seven of those were killed in action.[74] In terms of regular or part-time armies, all men over twelve years old were conscripted into fighting against the rebels or face imprisonment.

It is impossible to know with certainty the numbers fighting on either side or the scale of losses suffered (see pages 279–281). There were an estimated three thousand cabano soldiers in the Lower Amazon, about a thousand at Ecuipiranga, and the rest stationed in smaller strongholds of Luzea (Maués), Andira, the Curuá River, and Barreiras (near Monte Alegre).[75] Their weapons were the same as those of the legalista force since they had either looted military sources or received supplies from elsewhere. The weapons included shotguns of various kinds (front-loaded and top-loaded), some with bayonets, pistols, swords, and bows and arrows as well as the ubiquitous machete. A continuous supply of lead, gunpowder, and bullets was necessary to use the guns. The need to ration ammunition must have affected strategy and plans. Horses were also in use, though they would have been of limited use in the riverine landscape.

Rebel tactics were not the same as imperial ones, however. One strategy was to take a town by surprise by disembarking in the middle of the night in large numbers. The rebels would pick their victims carefully – those who had abused their positions of authority. Rarely would they indiscriminately kill, since they knew the town and its people. Their objective was to replace their enemies with more sympathetic agents. Another tactic was to attack patrols and passing river traffic for supplies and to disrupt communication. This was consistent with the more guerrilla-style approach to warfare that developed with the strengthening of the imperial side in urban centers.

The center of all operations was Ecuipiranga. With the fall of Belém and the takeover of towns, the city's importance grew for the cabanos. For the legalistas, it was the "place from where all evil comes."[76] The importance of destroying the encampment became paramount. Without sustenance and encouragement, the networks that spread out from it would wither.[77] Its destruction became Sanches' obsession: he rarely missed an opportunity to

74 Boiteaux, *Marinha Imperial versus Cabanagem*, 403–405.

75 Justice of the Peace Antônio M. Sanches de Brito to Captain of the Naval Forces of the Lower Amazon Agnello Petra de Bettancourt, December 5, 1836, Pauxis, APEP cod. 1013, docs 176 and 178; and Justice of the Peace Antônio M. Sanches de Brito to Bras Antônio Corrêa, January 18, 1837, Pauxis, APEP cod. 1052, doc. 42, no. 6.

76 Antônio M. Sanches de Brito to Captain of the Naval Forces of the Lower Amazon Agnello Petra de Bettancourt, October 24, 1836, Pauxis, APEP cod. 1013, doc. 95.

77 Antônio M. Sanches de Brito to Captain of the Naval Forces of the Lower Amazon Agnello Petra de Bettancourt, November 9, 1836, Pauxis, APEP cod. 1013, doc. 159, no. 1.

mention it. Sanches devised a plan and distributed it widely.[78] It would take time to achieve since it first required a long-term blockade. The *legalista* strategy was containment to weaken, followed by annihilation.

However, having lost many towns by the end of 1836, the rebels tried to unite the various strongholds in rural areas and organize themselves collectively in "one large body."[79] One *legalista* commander said "the interior is infested with rebels, and only in some honorable situations is it not inhabited by them."[80] In particular, they sought to build a coalition of the villages on the middle and lower reaches of the Tapajós and the smaller strongholds between Gurupá and Manaus, which were both in imperial hands. Despite the Mundurucu chief's alliance with the imperial army, some of their bands did join the rebels.[81] Under the leadership of chief Clemente, Mundurucu warriors were expected to play a significant role in a concerted effort to retake Santarém. About a thousand men headed by Thomas de Albuquerque, excluding the Mundurucu, were mustered to attack the town at the end of March 1837. They arrived just before dawn, managing to evade the lookouts. They established themselves at the east and west ends of the town. With the first shots, the alarm bell (*arrabate*) was rung. As the church bells rang wildly, houses were shut up and some people hid in their gardens or up trees, or even fled to the nearby forest. The imperial soldiers in the barracks came out to confront their attackers, immediately establishing themselves outside important people's houses and forming their lines along the roads. Other soldiers and officials were stationed on ships in the port and came ashore and to hold the riverfront. The Mundurucu Indians were supposed to arrive shortly after the cabanos, but they failed to materialize, either paid off or being uninterested. An intense exchange of fire followed for the rest of the day along the three streets of the town. The sun's power was too strong for open field warfare, so the houses and shacks provided shade as well as protection. As darkness fell, the rebels fled, leaving 86 dead.[82] Only eight imperial soldiers were killed. A leading officer was almost killed and provided the following account of how a fellow soldier dealt with the officer's assailants.

---

78 Justice of the Peace Antônio M. Sanches de Brito to Captain of the Naval Forces of the Lower Amazon Agnello Petra de Bettancourt, December 5, 1836, Pauxis, APEP cod. 1013, docs 176 and 178.

79 Justice of the Peace Antônio M. Sanches de Brito Pauxis to Captain of the Expeditionary Forces of the Lower Amazon Agnello Petra de Bettancourt, [?] January 1837, APEP cod. 1052, doc. 39, no. 5.

80 [?] to President of Pará Francisco José Soares d'Andréa, [? December 1836], [?], APEP 1013, doc. 186.

81 Military commander of Santarém Lourenço da Serra Freire to President of Pará Francisco José Soares d'Andréa, March 29, 1837, Santarém, APEP cod. 888, doc. 129.

82 Commander of Land Forces for the Lower Amazon Felipe Pereira Leal to Captain of the Naval Forces of the Lower Amazon Agnello Petra de Bettancourt, March 6, 1837, Tapajós, APEP cod. 1052, doc. 102; Boiteaux, *Marinha Imperial versus Cabanagem*, 368, says 248 rebels were killed.

Seeing that his commander had been attacked by three rebels, Rezende [the soldier] who in the place of a shot gun took one of the blunderbusses of the schooner *Riograndense* and discharged a shot at one of his enemies who shortly fell down dead. Rezende then chased another and landed a massive blow to his head with the gun, the enemy quickly collapsed, the gun having been broken by the hit. Finally the third, who was also trying to flee, was caught up with and dispatched with a dagger's stab to the liver. He expired after a while of suffering.[83]

The high number of rebels killed in this failed attack suggests how much the Mundurucu let them down. The rebels had counted on their support. It is doubtful that the rebels wanted to do anything other than take over the town and establish their authority. They sought a show of force by intimidating their enemy rather than killing them off to achieve control. The fatalities suggest also their lack of munitions; they were cornered and defenseless. They had wanted to reactivate their one-time supporters in the municipal administration and have a gradual and relatively peaceful return to rebel rule; they used machetes, daggers, and knives rather than rifles and pistols to achieve their aims. Having failed, they retreated, though they continued to build smaller positions in the vicinity.

By the end of May the circle was being squeezed ever more tightly on Ecuipiringa. The legalista forces' blockade, stopping communication and supplies, seemed to be working. Their ships were positioned on the north side of Ecuipiranga and on the south side by the chapel. They also claimed to have cleared the island areas in the stretch of the Amazon between Óbidos and Santarém, which had contained a handful of small rebel musters, using abandoned farm houses as their camps. Manoel Sanches and Diniz led their groups of men in the destruction of these rebel bases.[84] One of their twenty-four prisoners, however, reminded Sanches and Diniz of the futility of their maneuvers. Questioned about rebel plans and positions the prisoner, an Indian woman, confessed that they were re-forming on the Curuá River, near Alenquer and Barreiras, near Monte Alegre.[85] In other words, the squashing of one location merely caused another to appear. Once attacked, people ran off into the forest, hid, and waited to regroup.

News had also arrived of a large assembly of slaves on the Lago Grande just west of Vila Franca.[86] It was reputed to be growing by the day, well

83 Boiteaux, *Marinha Imperial versus Cabanagem*, 368–369.

84 Justice of the Peace Antônio M. Sanches de Brito to Military Commander of Tapajós João Henrique de Mattos, May 26, 1837, Pauxis, APEP cod. 888, doc. 142.

85 Military Commander of Tapajós João Henrique de Mattos to Commander of Naval Forces Antônio Firmo Coelho, May 29, 1837, Tapajós, APEP cod. 888, doc. 159.

86 "*Reunião dos escravos*," Justice of the Peace Antônio M. Sanches de Brito to Military Commander of Tapajós Lourenço Justinianno da Serra Freire, May 26, 1837, APEP cod. 888, doc. 141. See also APEP cod. 1013, docs 159, 169, 194 on the movement of slaves at this time.

armed and very well fortified with trenches. Compare now the confidence enjoyed by the rebel movement with the physical state of the soldiers from Pauxis under Manoel Sanches's command. The imperial troops had no uniforms, he exclaimed; in fact, they were virtually naked and had few arms and munitions. If support of a cause was helped by wearing a smart uniform and holding a gun, then this was no army in a fit state.

Sanches' plans for a major assault on Ecuipiranga were well under way by April 1837. The blockade was in place, even though it was impossible to know how successfully. More imperial soldiers from the northeast of Brazil had arrived and there were a number of warships in the area. But Sanches, the archstrategist, knew there had to be a psychological element to the suppression. In mid-June 1837 he wrote to João Henrique de Mattos, a military commander for the Lower Amazon, that not only should they encircle Ecuipiranga, but "we have to foment discontent [in Ecuipiranga], which I have heard already exists. There has to be a counter-revolution from inside," he arrogantly demanded. It seems reasonably clear that he had at least one informant among the rebels, who supplied information on the kinds of defenses at Ecuipiranga, the number of soldiers and their positions, the kinds of arms they had, the supply routes, and so on. With this information it was decided to launch an attack involving five ships and about one thousand men coming from the south. A further three ships should wait on the north side to block off the escape route from there.

This plan was nine months in the making, dating from when Sanches was elected as a judge in Óbidos and had signed the agreement with Bararoa. Why he devoted his considerable energies to this task in particular we do not know, though there is a punitive or revengeful feel to his zeal. But the fact that such a considerable force, relatively speaking, was being amassed is testament to the importance of Ecuipiranga to all parties and to Sanches as an aspiring candidate for high political office. Most of the repression of other rebel positions was conducted by single ships with a well-armed crew. They pursued rebels where they could and did as much damage as possible where they found them; hardly a military strategy, rather repression by opportunity and chance. In response, the rebels had to take evasive tactics and establish themselves in small mobile bands with a few well-situated assemblies. The situation of Ecuipiranga was very different since it was more organized and an attack on it thus required better strategic planning.

What did rebels know of these plans? They too would have had their informants among the imperial soldiers and townspeople. Likely they knew little or nothing of the precise details; commanders would have been aware of the possibility of information leaking out. Moreover, there may have been little new to add to what was already known. The blockade was visible after all. Not since the terrible events of March that had so devastated the rebel army had they attempted any more attacks on imperial positions or towns.

They must have expected a large-scale attack sooner or later. Certainly one of their strategies at this time was a regrouping (as can be inferred from the prisoner's confession) in order to settle somewhere else and to avoid heavy losses in the expected assault.

The major assault on Ecuipiranga was organized for June 20, 1837. Three schooners of war and two other ships would synchronize their arrival on the south side. The soldiers would fire from their vessels and first secure the beach. Behind the beach lay the forest on rising land, so the next aim was to remove the rebels from the areas nearest the beach. From there, a regrouping could take place before entering the dense interfluve forest and walking the few kilometers to the fortress on the north side. About five hundred soldiers were to take part in the operation, under the command of eight officers and three mercenaries.[87]

What actually happened was an embarrassment for all concerned and occasioned a series of subsequent letters to identify a culprit. Only the three warships arrived (*Rio do Prato, Brasileiro,* and *19th October*) and with about a hundred "professional" soldiers from Maranhão. Commanders who failed to turn up at the appointed hour – including Sanches, who got stuck in Alter do Chão – gave lack of wind as an excuse. Nevertheless, the attack resulted in the capture of the beach and the chapel. The legalistas also destroyed all the fortifications near the shore, some houses, and the manioc flour-producing equipment.[88] But they refused to continue with so few men and little knowledge of the area, so they returned to Santarém, angry at not having completed the operation. Sanches turned up after their departure and, with Joaquim Fructuoso and a band of Mundurucu soldiers, they landed to survey the scene. The group went some way into the forest after the cabanos but found nothing and did not want to pursue them, fearing guerrilla tactics. We do not know how many people died in this botched episode. The imperial side suffered a few injuries, one of which was to prove fatal: Diniz had been shot in the chest by the rebels and died on June 23.

Sanches' reason for his lateness may well have been genuine, but there may also have been another factor involved. He must have contacted

---

87 The names of the officers were Antônio Manuel Brancher, captain, on the schooner *Santo Antônio*, patrolling the Tapajós River; Francisco Vieira Leitão, colonel, on the schooner *Rio do Prato*; José Luis Coelho, captain, on the yacht *5th October*; João Henrique de Mattos, captain, on the brig *Brasileiro*; Antônio Firme Coelho on the schooner *19th October* (with 2 cannon), with 30 men; and Agnello Petra Bettancourt, Lourenço Siqueira Freire, and Felipe Ferreira Leal, who commanded from Santarém and occasionally from a naval vessel. The mercenaries were Diniz Marcelino, on his own boat (name not known) with about 50 soldiers known as the "Força Tapajoense"; Ambrosio Pedro Ayres, with the *Bararuense* and about 150 men at the time; and Manoel Sanches, with 120 men known as the *Forças de Pauxis* on his own boat (no name).

88 Commander of Naval Forces in the Lower Amazon Antônio Luis Coelho to Military Commander of Tapajós João Henrique de Mattos, June 21, 1837, APEP cod. 888, doc. 175.

Bararoa, who arrived in the area only at the beginning of July, presumably to take part in the assault. Perhaps Sanches did not want the assault to commence until his ally was present. Many rebels had somehow dispersed to other locations, but about five hundred remained in the fortress at Ecuipiranga. With the help of the Mundurucu, the inland roads were blocked by felled trees and traps and guards by June 25 to prevent any more "leakage." The scene was set for a major battle.

But Antônio Manoel Brancher insisted that one last attempt be made to avoid the battle. He persuaded his commanders to hold off while he delivered a letter saying that if the rebels put down their arms, amnesty would be offered to them. João Henrique de Mattos wrote the letter. The boat arrived with white flags at the north side of Ecuipiranga just before dawn. At daybreak the sentinel, somewhat surprised by the apparition in front of him, walked forward and asked Brancher, "What kind of boat is this?" The reply: "This is a boat sent by his Illustrious Excellency, the military commander of Tapajós, and it has come to show you the path you should follow."[89] Brancher met with the commander of the Ecuipiranga forces, Bernardo Pereira de Mello Genipapo. A joint letter was signed in the fortress there, though the voice in the quotation below was that of Genipapo and he was making his point of view reasonably clear.

I have the honor to reply to your letter. With the serious news that a force is coming in protection of the law which has been so roundly destroyed by absolutist power ... I call for a meeting of the various people involved in this situation. And through their judgment we can respond to your demands. It is necessary to safeguard all the authorities in the whole region. To this end many months are needed before a solution with sound judgment can be worked out and one in which we can all trust. In the meantime we ask you not to fight against us and we will also keep the peace because it is most dreadful to spill the blood of one's brothers. The other action you should take to show good will is to order the retreat of your forces which exist in these districts ... God keep you well for many years.

Barracks of Ecuipiranga, 28th June 1837.

Antonio Manoel Brancher and Bernardo Pereira de Mello Jenipapo.[90]

Mattos said he could not have anything to do with this plan; Andréa would recognize only those on the legalista part. Therefore, Mattos ordered Brancher to tell the commander of the *partido cabanal* (his term) that the military commander for the Lower Amazon was giving the orders for a

89 Commander Antônio Maciel Brancher to Military Commander of Tapajós João Henrique de Mattos, June 27, 1837, Ecuipiranga port, APEP cod. 888, doc. 199 (copy).

90 This is a "loose" translation of the letter from Commander Bernardo Pereira de Mello Genipapo to Commander Antônio Maciel Brancher, June 28, 1837, Ecuipiranga fort, APEP cod. 888, doc. 200 (copy).

decisive blow (*golpe*) to the enemy positions. "This is the order of the government of his Majesty the Emperor. Unless he [Genipapo] puts down his arms we will attack him."[91]

And that is what happened on July 12. This time, the arrival of the ships was coordinated. The rebels were well-positioned in their trenches and ready for battle.

In reality [wrote Sanches], they did not need firearms to defend themselves and repel whatever force came their way. They are highly accustomed to carrying out attacks [*aguerrear*] that you have to see to believe how dangerous and hot-blooded was their onslaught. We lost eleven men and seventy-eight were wounded. They lost only five in the trenches. As the expedition moved on to abandoned areas we found many fresh graves by paths, fields and houses. More than three hundred people have turned themselves in, among them men, women and blacks. The Amazon River region can now count on being returned to the old order.[92]

In fact, more than five hundred people gave themselves up. Each prisoner received one hundred lashes as punishment in the following days. But they were not put on ships and sent downriver to be punished in Belém; only their leaders faced that fate.[93] Some of the captured were made to fight for the imperial forces, which explained why desertions were so frequent. Mattos was ecstatic, claiming the whole region had been pacified and all the other points of resistance now had lost their source of strength.[94] This was emphatically not the case, as will be seen in the following chapter.[95] Ecuipiranga, however, had been razed and no longer would its name cause fear on the imperial side. Ships would be able to travel upriver close to the south bank of the Amazon near Ecuipiranga without fear of looting or being shot by one of the formidable cannon overlooking the bluff. Indeed, when

91 Commander Antônio Maciel Brancher to Military Commander of Tapajós João Henrique de Mattos, June 29, 1837, Ecuipiranga port, APEP cod. 888, doc. 201 (copy). The jointly signed letter is significant for it indicates that the repression of Ecuipiranga took place observing certain formalities of warfare. There would have been little point in writing and sending a messenger to the encampment if commanders really believed in Andréa's secret pact between all nonwhites to kill whites (see next chapter). The soldiers at Ecuipiranga were the enemy, but they were human.

92 Justice of the Peace Antônio M. Sanches de Brito to Military Commander of Tapajós João Henrique de Mattos, July 15, 1837, "Ponto queimado de Ecuipiranga [lit. burnt out point of Ecuipiranga]," APEP cod. 888, doc. 203; also in Reis, *História de Obidos*, 140.

93 President Francisco Soares Andréa to Minister of War, December 30, 1837, Belém, in Hurley, *Traços Cabanos*, 40. The prisoners who gave themselves up after the collapse of Ecuipiranga went back to the other side, took over a boat, and went to a rebel muster on the Curuá River.

94 Military Commander of Tapajós João Henrique de Mattos to President of Pará Soares d'Andréa, July 18, 1837, Santarém, APEP cod. 888, doc. 202.

95 For example, in early July Faro had suffered an attack by so-called rebels who had apparently killed some of the town's council officials; Military Commander of Tapajós João Henrique de Mattos to Justice of the Peace Antônio M. Sanches de Brito, July 8, 1837, Acampamento em [Santa] Anna, APEP cod. 888, doc. 147.

Sanches arrived at the fort, he sought out these infamous cannon and found them not to be real. They were in fact palm trunks painted black with the genipapo dye and placed on wooden boxes. Holes the length of the trunk had been drilled out to drive smoke through to make the cannon appear even more fearsome. The imperial forces had been tricked into panic.[96]

These false cannon appear emblematic of the whole episode. Ecuipiranga rose as a military center using the language of radical liberalism and with the support of Amazonian peasants. The United Brazilians wanted to replace the unjust officials with ones who would administer fairly. They broadly supported Independent Brazil, the young emperor, and inclusive political participation. The revolutionary potential of the rebel movement, as it was expressed at Ecuipiranga, was exaggerated by legalistas. Like the cannon, the cabanos were feared unnecessarily on the basis of prejudice rather than informed knowledge. The rebels appeared fierce and may have committed some atrocities, but their interpretation of liberalism and popular consciousness was unthreatening to the territorial integrity or future organization of the empire. But political opinion had moved on in the center of power and, more to the point, the cabano rebels were the wrong kind of people clamoring for political participation and reframing state institutions.

The insurgents at Ecuipiranga were finally defeated by an alliance of certain individuals in the villages and towns along the rivers (and their small armies) and the imperial forces. For the first time, the Paraense elite was able to unite and challenge the core of the rebellion that had spread out over the vast hinterland. Had there not been this link between the interior and the provincial capital, Pará conceivably would have remained in rebel hands, for cabanos may have been strong enough to retake the capital and hold it. For this reason the dynamics in the sertão are critical to understanding the Cabanagem as a whole.

---

96 In fact the story about the false cannon exists only in oral history and I have imagined the episode of Sanches searching for them. I could find no mention of them in the documents of the period, except as defending the fort with formidable force. The story is, however, widespread in the Santarém area and fits with the theme of trickery and deception mentioned in the Introduction. Rodrigues dos Santos, in his history of Santarém, says that the false cannon "have not entered history but remain conserved in popular tradition" (Rodrigues dos Santos, *Tupaiulândia*, 240). He implies that its revelation at the time would have brought down scorn on local military commanders from Andréa. So it was suppressed. The other written mention of the cannon is in the booklet on the Cabanagem by another Santarém based historian João Santos, *Cabanagem em Santarém*, 26.

8

"Vengeance on Innocence"

The Repression and Continuing Rebellion, 1837–1840

The fall of Ecuipiranga signaled the end of the formal phase of Pará's great uprising. It had begun in Belém in January 1835 with the successful takeover of the provincial administration and the engine of its government. Angelim sought to spread the revolution by seeking the backing of the municipal councils. If they declared allegiance to him, Rio de Janeiro would have to listen to their demands. A front of solidarity – "United Brazilians," as they called themselves – was their strongest weapon. However, once Belém was returned to imperial rule, the uprising maintained its momentum by consolidating in the interior. At that point, though, the outcome could still not have been predicted. It is clear from the reports, and the correspondence between Andréa and his commanders, that the repression took place in an atmosphere of uncertainty and insecurity. Only with the support of the key characters in the interior was Andréa able to break up the fortified camps, especially Ecuipiranga in mid-1837. From that moment, the Cabanagem changed its character. It was dominated by survival against the repression and the strengthening hand of the imperial forces. Some rebels became guerrillas and others stayed put in their rural homesteads and were at the receiving end of the punishments metered out to those suspected of crimes.

This chapter will examine the repression and its effects on the people of Pará. In fact, the rebellion ended only because of amnesty. The period 1837 to 1840 coincided with the backlash against the radical liberals in the regency administration. That did not make much difference to the cabanos, for they had never received any support from that group. Rather, it created an environment for Andréa, his officers, and his successors as president to end, without fear of recrimination, what they perceived as a caste war.

In order to understand the full implications of their position, we need to go back to Angelim in August 1835. Knowing that the imperial authorities would not recognize his presidency, he sought to establish his legitimacy as president through popular endorsement – in contrast to all previous presidents of the province. "People of color" (*gente de côr*) would not be excluded from government on the basis of their ethnicity and ancestry.[1] After his nomination in August 1835, Angelim wrote a manifesto that sought to put recent events behind and look forward to a new era.[2] He ended with the following:

Know this, Regency government and the whole of Brazil, that Paraenses are not rebels. Paraenses want to be citizens, but they do not want to be slaves, particularly of the Portuguese. Paraenses want to be governed by their country-fellows, who treat compassionately those suffering from the calamities of life, and not by a Portuguese fortune seeker such as Marshal Manoel Rodrigues [the imperial nomination as president who was stationed on a ship near the island of Tatuoca, just across the river from Belém]. Paraenses want to be governed by the rule of law and not by arbitrary judgments. We are all waiting with open arms to receive a government nominated by the Regency administration, but only one with the confidence of the people of Pará. Otherwise they will prefer to die on the field of battle rather than deliver themselves once more up to the shackles and chains of despotism. If the Regency government dares to subjugate us by force, we will dare to prove ourselves with the bravery of a free people who can forget death when they want to defend their liberty.[3]

As we saw in the last chapter, Angelim's demands were much the same as those expressed by rebels in the Lower Amazon: an end to colonial-style domination by a distant power, the local determination of leaders, the love of the homeland of Pará, and the fair implementation of the law. There is no evidence here of a push for disintegration of the Brazilian empire or republicanism or any wish to depose Pedro II (many proclamations end with a recognition of his supreme authority).[4] All rebellions and revolutionary movements have a range of aims, arguments, and means. But Angelim, his supporters in Belém, and the Ecuipiranga leaders occupied the center ground of the Cabanagem. On the margins were other, perhaps more radical, voices, perhaps those who felt

---

1 Domingos Antônio Raiol, *Motins Políticos ou História dos Principais Acontecimentos Políticos da Província do Pará, desde o ano de 1821 até 1835,* Belém: Universidade Federal do Pará, 1970, vol. 3, 938.
2 The proclamation is reproduced in full in Raiol, *Motins Políticos* 936–939.
3 Raiol, *Motins Políticos,* 939. There are a number of other proclamations by the three cabano presidents (Malcher, Vinagre, and Angelim) and many transcribed by Raiol in the third book of his study. A handful of originals (pertaining to Malcher and Vinagre) can be found in the BNRJ in the "Fundo Cabanagem: Revolta de Vinagre" and the NAL Foreign Office Correspondence. Angelim's proclamation offered just before he fled Belém on May 8, 1836 can be found in "Documentos relativos a evacuação da cidade de Belém," Coleção Particular do Barão do Rio Branco, AHI Lata 875, Maço 01, Pasta 04. I am grateful to Leandro Mahalem de Lima for bringing this document to my notice.
4 See also the British consul report from October 1835 in which Angelim is said to have "declared himself and those under him subject to the Brazilian Empire but they will never submit to a president who is not a native of the province, and of their own choice. Their only want is gunpowder, and this they manufacture near the city, but there is little doubt that two American schooners are engaged to supply them." David Cleary, *Cabanagem: Documentos Ingleses,* Belém: Secult, 2003, 70. On the subject of separation from Brazil, according to Raiol, Angelim explicitly refused an offer of British help should he wish to detach Pará from the rest of Brazil; see Raiol, *Motins Políticos,* 944.

disenfranchised from the centre – slaves and "bandits" (in the Hobsbawmian sense of those seeking redress for social injustice) from previous decades. These last people had little to lose in the settling of scores and were quick to take advantage of the situation. What was new and threatening in this period was the organized takeover of state institutions and their commanding by popular leaders. Otherwise, the proposals espoused were liberal and widely shared across other rebellions during the regency period.

Angelim's other concern was discipline and order. In front of the governor's palace, he executed a number of his fighters who had been involved in the killing of the imperial soldiers near the church of Carmelite order, mentioned at the opening of Chapter 5. Officers who had freed slaves from estates near Belém were also shot by firing squad. The people's president then threatened to continue such punishments if his orders were not followed.[5] These episodes show that he tried hard to impose his authority and that there was some dissent, for not all shared his antipathy to full emancipation. This makes the Amazonian situation not dissimilar to that of San Domingo (Haiti) in the early stages of its revolution, where some of the free population, the mulattos and freed slaves, refused to ally themselves with plantation slaves.

The question then becomes, How did a movement with a mixture of liberal, peasant, and radical demands become transformed into one characterized as a war of race hate, threatening the territorial integrity of Brazil?[6] The answer is to be found in the way Andréa suppressed the rebellion and the tactics and propaganda his commanders used.

We might recall here Euclides da Cunha's account of the distortion of the Canudos revolt of 1896–1897 in northeast Brazil. The republic had just been proclaimed and he reports some instability in the capital caused by those wishing a return to monarchy and slavery, but nothing significant. In the backlands of the arid northeast, a small colony of religious fanatics had formed, attracted to a mystic named Antônio Conselheiro who had few political interests. They refused to pay taxes and they burned local registers. Yet the miserable residents of the isolated village were transformed into a vanguard of a vast monarchical conspiracy that somehow repelled three heavily armed campaigns against them. No wonder they believed in miracles, Cunha writes. The misrepresentations then not only justified the repression, they also obliterated competing interpretations. Cunha does not reveal whether he considered the distortions deliberate.[7] The same kind of machinations were present in the Cabanagem and with consequences just as

5 Raiol, *Motins Políticos*, 934.
6 "*Odio de raças*," Raiol, *Motins Políticos*, 925.
7 Euclides da Cunha, *Rebellion in the Backlands*, Chicago: University of Chicago Press, 1944, 277–279. On the misinterpretations of Canudos and a compelling reinterpretation, see Robert Levine, *Vale of Tears: Revisiting the Canudos Massacre in Northeastern Brazil, 1893–1897*, Berkeley: University of California Press, 1995.

debilitating, for despite all the talk of integration and unity, no one considered that the political inclusion of all people, and not just land, should be a part of that same understanding.

Andréa and the War of Race Hate

The notion of a war of race hate originates from outside the Amazon in a continent-wide discussion surrounding independence, which had become prominent in Spanish-speaking America. Elite Brazilians were reluctant to see their own divisions in such terms, but Pará was different and basically unknown to the southern Brazilian upper classes at the time. The Portuguese had a larger presence there and had cultivated its geopolitical significance from the point of view of their Atlantic empire and the Amazon's borders to the west and the north. This separateness permitted misconceptions to develop. On hearing about the uprising, the liberal journalist and constitutionalist Evaristo de Viega wrote in the periodical *Aurora Fluminense* about cabanos in highly dismissive terms, as scum, anarchists, and rabble (*gentalha*, *crápula*, and *massas brutas*). He also observed that Pará looked more like Spanish America than Brazil because it had more Indians.[8] Although no other published report readily confirms this opinion, it is likely to be representative of views in the Rio government towards the Cabanagem rebels. Portraying the leaders and their followers as part of the brutish masses foreclosed any negotiation with them.

Padre Feijó, Viega's friend and prince regent during the early part of the Cabanagem, was equally condemning of the situation in Pará. In his *Falas do Trono* of 1836 and 1837, he linked the Cabanagem with other disorders, in particular the Farroupilha revolt in Santa Catherina. On May 3, 1836, he addressed the opening of Parliament as regent and reasoned that the "lack of respect and obedience to the authorities ... excites universal clamor all over the Empire." In reference to Pará, he exclaimed, "For good or for ill, it [the city of Belém] will be wrenched from the wild beasts which dominate it." Prefacing that predication with "good or ill" suggests recognition of the brutality to come in the name of restoring imperial control. The same message was reiterated a year later: even though Belém was in the hands of the imperial government, full order had not returned and the costs of supplying the army were very great.[9]

The concern of the regency administration was the reestablishment of its version of peace and tranquility. The person Feijó selected to achieve that

---

8 Leslie Bethell and José Murilo de Carvalho, '1822–1850', in L. Bethell (ed.), *Brazil: Empire and Republic, 1822–1930*, Cambridge: Cambridge University Press, 1989, 70.

9 Diogo Antônio Feijó, "Fala do Trono (1836)," in Jorge Caldeira (ed.), *Diogo Antônio Feijó*, São Paulo:, Editora 34, 1999, 176 and 178.

goal in Pará was brigadier Francisco José Soares Andréa. He was brought out of early retirement, which had been necessary to quiet liberal critics who accused him of the abuse of civilians in the 1820 campaigns of independence in Pernambuco. At age sixty-three, Andréa's reputation was in tatters: he had been close to the Portuguese royal family during their exile and associated with calls for the return of Pedro 1.[10] His nomination letter to the top civilian and military posts of Pará nevertheless exonerated him of the crimes with which he was associated and required him "to ensure the full and proper observance of the laws of freedom, security and prosperity."[11] He positioned himself on the island of Ituaoca (or Tatuacha Island, see Image 8.1) in February 1836 with a formidable fleet of one frigate, two brigs, and eight schooners. He had about 2,500 soldiers with him, some 800 from Rio de Janeiro and the rest picked out of prisons in Pernambuco and Maranhão.[12] The prisoners were presumably offered their freedom once they completed the task of counter-insurgency in Pará. The use of convicted murderers and robbers to achieve the noble ends of the Rio government was necessary because there were few funds and soldiers. Andréa was probably desperate for men, since regular soldiers had been drafted to fight the rebellions elsewhere; perhaps rough-and-ready men would do anything to get out of prison without asking questions. Whether they remained faithful to Andréa and his officers remains unknown.

The first measure taken by Andréa on arrival in Belém in 1836 was to suspend all individuals' constitutional rights.[13] In fact, it was argued that for the previous six months (that is, more or less since Angelim became president), the constitution had not been in place in Pará and this measure was a mere continuation, justified by the need to end the rebellion. For Andréa, the suspension meant that guarantees of individual rights, such as trials, could not be invoked and people could be arrested on suspicion of support for rebels and kept in prison indefinitely.[14] These emergency powers were granted him by the Rio government, but were not explicitly stated in his nomination letter.

10 José Andréa, *O Marechal Andreia nos Relevos da História do Brasil,* Rio de Janeiro: Biblioteca do Exercito, 1977.

11 "Cartas Imperiais nomeando Francisco Andréa para o presidente do Pará e exonerando," Coleção Manoel Barata, BIHGB Lata 279, pasta 15.

12 Pasquale Di Paolo, *A Cabanagem: A Revolução Popular da Amazônia.* Belém: Conselho de Cultura, 1985, 331. See also Cleary, *Cabanagem: Documentos Ingleses,* 126; and the summary of forces in August 1836 by a British naval officer, which does not make mention of the fact that the Pernambucan soldiers were ex-prisoners.

13 See Leandro Mahalem de Lima, "Rios Vermelhos, Perspectivas e Posições de Sujeito em Torno da Noção de Cabano na Amazônia em Meados de 1835," Master's thesis, University of São Paulo, 2008, 146–161, on the suspension of legal rights. He argues that the Cabanagem had elements of a "just war," echoing the Portuguese employment of that ideology in its confrontation with indigenous people in the seventeenth and eighteenth centuries.

14 Raiol, *Motins Políticos,* 974–975.

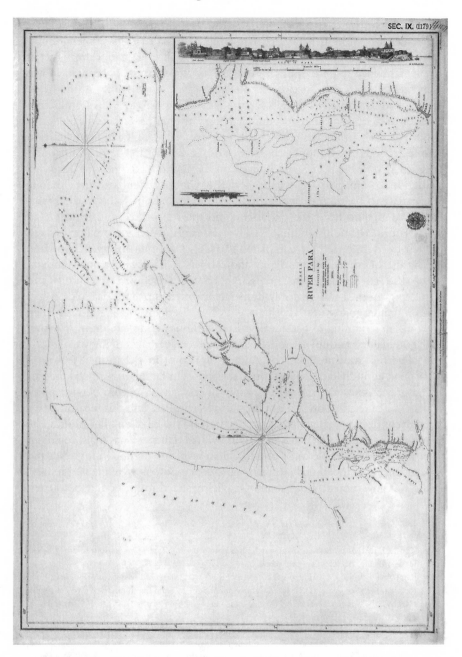

Image 8.1 River Pará surveyed by Captain Sir Everard Home, Baronet and Mr. Byron Drury, Mate of HMS *Racehorse*, 1835 (published 1836)

There was some debate among liberals in Belém, and also in Rio, about these matters and criticism of the extreme actions taken by Andréa.[15] In early 1838, almost two years later, Andréa justified the continuing absence of constitutional rights because

The state of war gives us the authority to attack the enemy on all fronts until we have annihilated its force. For this measure to have effect it was necessary to dispense with the formalities with which the law defends criminals. All men who are accused of a crime should be certain that they will be found and arrested without their being able to evade prosecution. All disorders will be corrected with imprisonment, which for the most part will happen in military offensives, because their authors [of the crimes] can mostly be considered soldiers. Visits to domiciles and house-to-house searches, which today are so odious to the sacred rights of the citizens, have taken place out of public necessity. These actions have scared all wrongdoers, preventing reason and justice being used as a form of protection for criminals. This city and the whole of this province has fallen into the hands of many rebels who now find themselves imprisoned or have already ended their days in prisons or hospitals. If they were to be freed we would be very worried, as some are still causing us anxiety in some parts.[16]

The characterization of the Cabanagem was no longer as a rebellion but a war; the political demands were expunged. Prisoners faced indefinite imprisonment merely on suspicion of a crime and many would die sooner or later from the terrible conditions in which they were kept. A few, such as Angelim and Francisco Vinagre, were sent into exile but these were the handful of leaders caught early on who were carefully detached from their bands and supporters. Others either died fighting or were bribed to move over to the legalistas, as we saw in the last chapter. In his three years as president of Pará (1836–1839), Andréa succeeded in the delegitimization of the genuine demands of the rebels and transforming the movement into one of race hate.

As for recruitment, it should be said that this province should not have soldiers who are sons of the region. The best groups to follow in the constant exchange of personnel are those from the provinces of the south. All men of color born here are linked in a secret pact to end to all that is white. This is not a made-up story and experience has proved it to be true. It is indispensable then to put arms in the hands of others and indispensable to protect by all possible means the growth of the white

15 Raiol, *Motins Políticos*, 980, but much of the Paraense documentation was lost when the box in which Raiol kept these documents was destroyed by sea water in Fortaleza in 1883, 974.

16 Opening speech by Andréa to the Provincial Assembly of Pará, March 2, 1838, "Discurso com que o presidente da Provincia do Pará fez a abertura do 1a sessão da Assembleia Provincial," Typographia Restaurada de Santos, e Santos menor, Pará, 1838, 16–17; also in Raiol, *Motins Políticos*, 980–981, and parts in John Hemming, *Amazon Frontier: The Defeat of the Brazilian Indians*, London: Macmillan, 1987, 233–234, though my translation is slightly different.

population. If the government agrees with these means I seek to exchange as many troops from this province as I can with other provinces.[17]

Whether this claim was part of a carefully orchestrated campaign on behalf of Andréa or an article of his class-based faith, the effect was the same. It "naturalized" the conflict, turning one's participation in it into a question of birth. This process of naturalization helped the repression by demarcating sides very clearly. Rebels could be identified not by their participation or by their political beliefs but simply by the color of their skin – and, as we shall see, their residence in rural areas in much the same way "white" or "Portuguese" or *bicudo* (long-snout) were also shorthand for slave owners, the rich, and so on, combining race with class. Given the complex and variable nature of perception of racial characteristics, the term *gente de côr* should not be taken to refer literally to skin color, but a complex of characteristics, including ancestry, appearance, popular perceptions, clothing, and place of residence. The new focus on observable characteristics heralded a shift to a form of racism that conflated physical attributes with class, dwelling, and occupation. These forms of discrimination fitted in well with unofficial pacification of the region. Areas, especially small hamlets, suspected of harboring rebels were attacked. If people of color lived there, they were "naturally" against the imperial government and therefore should be arrested or exterminated.

This shift is present in the very term used to refer to the rebel movement. The term *cabano* came to be used in the early nineteenth century around independence to indicate the person who lived in rural huts, and from the authorities' point of view were marginal, petulant, and sometimes rebellious.[18] The neologism *Cabanagem* came to describe the uprising sometime after the movement had been wiped out; Bates encountered the word in 1849 on Marajó to refer to the revolutionary days of 1835–1836.[19] Raiol used it in the 1880s in quotation marks, perhaps indicating its uncertain status. The shift is towards seeing the movement as composed exclusively of backward rural types and their "invented" political demands as symptomatic of their menace and "stupidity." Furthermore, the rebellion was not confined to rural areas, as should be abundantly clear. In sum, the term *Cabanagem* has its semantic roots in various negative connotations, which distort the rebels' central achievements and aims.

Prisoner records provide the most important evidence to undermine the racialization of the rebellion, offering a small but highly significant view of the

---

17　Francisco José Soares d'Andréa to the Imperial Minister of War, Belém, December 18, 1837, quoted in Jorge Hurley, *Traços Cabanos*, Belém, Oficina Gráfica do Instituto Lauro Sodré, 1936, 284. Mattos said the rebels wanted "the extinction of people of white colour" in 1845, by which time the propaganda had been fully digested, João Henrique de Mattos, "Relatório do Estado da Decadência em que se acha o Alto Amazonas," RIHGB, 1979 [1845], 325, 145.

18　Basilio de Magalhães, "A Cabanagem," RIHGB, 1936, vol. 171, 278–305.

19　Henry Walter Bates, *A Naturalist on the River Amazons*, London: John Murray, vol. 1, 1863, 196–197.

generalized participation. Five bound volumes of prisoners taken between 1836 and 1840 exist in the Public Archive of Pará in Belém. One of them has been badly damaged and cannot be read; the other four document the names, crimes, ethnic category, and locations of arrest, and occasionally birthplace and other information. Some of this data has been processed by John Chasteen in an article on people and politics in 1830s Pará; he argues the Cabanagem was not a "caste war."[20] Together, the four volumes list 1,405 prisoners, some of whom died while incarcerated. The largest single category listed is *índios* and *tapuios* (terms indicating indigenous parentage) who composed twenty-eight percent of the total; then *pardos* and *mulatos* (of European and African descent) with twenty-three percent; *brancos* (whites), seventeen percent; *mamelucos* and *mestiços* (white and Indian parentage) sixteen percent; *cafuzos* (Indian and African descent) ten percent; and *negros* and *pretos* (African ancestry) six percent. These figures represent about one fifteenth (1/15) of the number of people who may have died and a much smaller fraction of those who were taken prisoner but not sent to Belém for processing. Nevertheless, they reveal that whites were a significant part of the overall movement. Such a large number of whites is also surprising given the dominant perception that the rebels were mostly Indians. What is also significant here is the relatively small numbers of arrested slave rebels. This could be a reflection of the lack of interest in abolition among the other rebels, but it could also be the possibility that, once caught, slaves were returned to their masters, owing to their economic importance. Alternatively, they could have been killed and their bodies left to rot or tossed into the river.

All wars need their propaganda. The one that animated the imperial repression concerned the fear that whites would be exterminated. There were indeed some documented instances of rebels allegedly proclaiming "death to whites." Whites were targeted not because of the color of their skin but because of their ties to holders of political or military office, judges, and merchants. Given the importance of racial categories at the time, it is hard to believe the rebels carelessly mixed up race, class, and nationalism, as some have claimed.[21] The Cabanagem was not a war of race hate, but was presented as one by those who sought to impose imperial order.

20 John Chasteen, "Cautionary Tale: A Radical Priest, Nativist Agitation, and the Origin of Brazilian Civil Wars," in Rebecca Earle (ed.), *Rumours of Wars: Civil Conflict in Nineteenth-Century Latin America*, London: Institute of Latin American Studies, 2000. Bernardo de Souza Franco, Pará's president after Andréa, calculated that 2,085 people had been arrested and put into prison, and 504 died in their place of incarceration. He estimated that four thousand more were arrested and imprisoned without being officially recognized, and that at least a thousand of these nameless people died in prisons. A further thousand men were sent to the south of Brazil to fight in the repression of rebellions there, Raiol, *Motins Políticos*, 1000. It is likely Souza Franco's sources for this first figure were five codices at the APEP 1004, 1014, 1024, 1025, 1026.
21 Jeffrey Needell, *The Party of Order: The Conservatives, the State, and Slavery in the Brazilian Monarchy, 1831–1871*, Stanford: Stanford University Press, 2006, 27.

The Rebellion Moves On

In the immediate aftermath of the destruction of Ecuipiranga in July 1837, the military commander of the Lower Amazon, João Henrique de Mattos, produced a report for Andréa that claimed there had been "a complete and satisfactory destruction of all rebel points in the region." Camps had also been destroyed, supposedly "annihilating the rebel party in the Amazonas river area." In the process, however, this "rich part of the province," he says, "has been reduced to hunger and misery, which presently plagues its inhabitants." For example, six thousand head of cattle existed before the conflict; the figure was reduced to a fraction of this number in 1837. Mattos requested a further hundred regular soldiers with good officers in order to build small mobile artillery boats for negotiating the riverways – the "only kinds able to wage the war in this country."[22] Although this appears to be the first time Mattos used the term *war* to describe his military operations, nowhere does he use ethnic or racial categories to refer to the enemy. They were still called evildoers (*malvados*), rebels (*rebeldes*), and less frequently *cabanos*.

The economic decline of the region had a dramatic effect on the availability of food. As Mattos mentioned, there was hardly any meat due to the lack of cattle, but there was fish when it could be obtained from the fishermen. One of the most important events at the ending of rebel activities in the Santarém area was the reintroduction of the fruit and vegetable markets. But these too were very limited in the range of products and depended on the goodwill of nearby farmers who dared bring their goods to town. Commercial life in Santarém had been at a standstill for two years. Houses had not been repaired from the marks of gunfire, looting, or burning and great gaping trenches were spread out along the edges of the town. The richer townspeople refused to venture out of the city or, if they had a farmstead, to go back to it. They feared the continuing possibility of rebel attack. Indeed, terror must have been a very vivid sentiment in these times, no longer tempered by new world hope or economic prosperity. Even in the early 1850s some whites were too scared to go their old farms, according to Henry Bates. It was, as Mattos says, a wretched place in which to live. In contrast, there was calm at the time in Óbidos, whose council says in September 1837: "Once again the residents are starting to breathe freely emerging from the bloody battle of the past few years."[23]

It was the presence of the three hundred or so other soldiers from the northern province that was most intimidating in the Lower Amazon region.

---

22 Military Commander of Tapajós João Henrique Mattos to President of Pará Francisco José Soares d'Andréa, July 18, 1837, Santarém, APEP cod. 888, doc. 202.
23 Council of Óbidos to President of Pará Francisco José Soares d'Andréa, September 14, 1837, Óbidos APEP cod. 1050, doc. 131.

Their actions were unpredictable and they placed a heavy demand on food supply. To make matters worse, there was insubordination, defection, and disagreements between commanders about the course of actions. Some were cautious, like Mattos about the repression, and others, like chief naval commander Joaquim Luiz de Souza, were more than enthusiastic about the pursuit of rebels. Soon after the fall of Ecuipiranga, a series of arguments broke out among commanders concerning the requisition of food from locals and the movements of boats. Soldiers had been forcing fishermen at gunpoint to give up their catch without payment, and in their raids on farms and houses they had taken food from local stores.[24] These were common occurrences all over the Amazon during the repression. Worse was carried out – rape of women, attacks on children, summary executions – most of which has failed to find a way into the records. Raiol does not "contest that the agents of the government abused the arbitrary power that was given to them and with it they carried out criminal acts against innumerable unfortunate citizens ... we know there were many and serious abuses committed by the imperial forces."[25] Even Andréa had to remind military commanders not to attack women and children and burn down houses.[26]

Raiol and various visitors to the region during the mid-nineteenth century confirm the use of excessive violence by imperial forces. In addition, a lively oral tradition developed around the terrifying and horrendous punishments, one that continues to exist today.[27] The usually reliable Raiol writes that

Rebels, real or suspected, were sought out everywhere, and persecuted like wild animals! Tied to tree trunks, they suffered barbarous forms of torture, which frequently led them to their death! ... I knew of one celebrated commander of these expeditions, who proudly described his atrocious acts, such as putting venomous snakes on their [the rebels'] bodies informing them they would never be pardoned. He used to throw strong men into the middle of rivers, and others, already imprisoned, he would order to be shot on the pretext that they wanted to escape from their incarceration! On days when he was in a bad mood he would hang up from the roof inside his house those who inspired his greatest antipathy, and he used to take pleasure in hurling them against the walls. Since their hands and feet were tied up, they had no means to avoid the terrible shocks which broke their bones.[28]

24 Military Commander of Tapajós João Henrique Mattos to President of Pará Francisco José Soares d'Andréa, August 2, 1837, Santarém, APEP cod. 888, doc. 207, no. 10.
25 Raiol, *Motins Políticos*, 981; see also 999 for some stories.
26 See Articles 20 and 23 in Francisco José Soares d'Andréa, *Instrucçoens Geraes para os Commandantes Militares da Província do Pará*, Palácio do Governo do Pará, 04 de abril de 1837.
27 See Thiago Thorlby, *A Cabanagem na Fala do Povo*, São Paulo: Paulinas, 1987.
28 Raiol, *Motins Políticos*, 999.

Raiol did not excuse Andréa of authorizing – legitimizing – such abuse by his officers and soldiers. Instead, the large majority of it was the fault of their insubordination: they simply could not be held in check and disciplined. "Their training is in the starting and ending of rebellions and to this end they even assassinate their own officers".[29] A conspiracy of silence swathed the cruel retribution delivered by these individuals. Raiol considered that "we should not call the abusers to account and those who hid the truth of the facts ... [such episodes] are a sad consequence of civil war."[30] Nevertheless, Raiol did not offer any suggestions for remedying the bloody and open wounds of the war – he was, after all, writing about fifty years after the conflict. The only way forward was indeed Andréa's "expert" suppression of the "cancer eating away at the insides of Paraense society."[31] This argument apparently united all those who opposed the rebels. Travelers to the region in the late 1830s and 1840s believed the grief caused by the violence was ever present, as we shall see below.

In the Lower Amazon, Mattos tried to persuade his fellow officers that the people of Santarém were a peaceful people who should not be persecuted. In late July 1837 in the middle of the night shortly after the fall of Ecuipiranga, some shots were heard and church bells were rung as the alarm to defend the town. The town was under attack once again, or so it was supposed. There was much commotion but nothing happened. The next day a number of soldiers and townspeople were arrested on suspicion of helping the rebels in the neighboring districts and preparing an attack. Mattos thought the whole episode was a fake. Some individuals had staged the shots and alarm to justify more repression and revenge.[32] Yet the officer in charge did nothing to control his army. This was the same group that was taking food from locals at gunpoint. Mattos wanted boats to leave the port only if they had permission from their commanders for a specific expedition or task. As it was, soldiers came and went on their boats as they wished. Those under the command of Luiz de Souza, according to Mattos, considered the rosaries made from the dried ears of cabanos "an emblem of their glorious struggle."[33] It was worth noting that Luiz de Souza was the chief commander of the first forces to make their way into Belém on the afternoon of May 13, 1836. He would not have done so if he did not have a reputation for leading strong offensives, a feature he clearly brought to the pacification of the Lower Amazon. The significance of Mattos' intervention

---

29 Andréa, *Discurso*, 1838, 19.
30 Raiol, *Motins Políticos*, 981–982.
31 Raiol, 981.
32 Military Commander of Tapajós João Henrique Mattos to President of Pará Francisco José Soares d'Andréa, August 2, 1837, Santarém, APEP cod. 888, doc. 207, no. 10.
33 Raiol, *Motins Políticos*, 999.

was his efforts to get others to realize that peace would not be achieved if the pacification was subverted by a continuation of injustice.

About a year later, the overseeing priest for the Lower Amazon was in Alenquer to celebrate the town's festival of its patron saint. He was celebrating mass for two thousand people when he was abruptly arrested by soldiers, taken on their boat, and questioned; he also claimed to have been hit a few times. He was accused of "holding dangerous opinions."[34] Writing from prison in Santarém, the priest implored Andréa not to allow this "vengeance on innocence" (*vingança contra a inocência*). He mentioned two other leading members of the council of Santarém who were also in prison. It is not known what he did or his fate; though elsewhere the priest had been said to have provided medical assistance for injured rebels. He was present in Santarém throughout the previous years and therefore could be seen as guilty by association. If proximity to rebels was a crime, then this could cover many people. The phrase "vengeance on innocence" is carefully chosen here: a biblical reference to the slaughter of Jewish newborns by the Roman Herod.

This priest's voice was one to have broken through. The implications of these scattered pieces of evidence were that the repression of the rebel movement took place in a state of terror and panic. A rebel was identified on the basis of the color of his skin – since all dark-skinned people were supposed to have a secret pact against the whites. Appearance would, at least, have given an excuse to interrogate or arrest. Other indicators such as place of their residence may also have indicated a person's status. Rural areas were almost synonymous with rebel hideouts and safe houses. Andréa's instructions of early 1837 to military commanders made clear the need to search for military hardware in all establishments and to hunt down rebels wherever they might be.

Overall, these strategies appear to be more than a repression of the rebellion. They seem more like a deliberate continuation of war, spurred on by Andréa's orders to his commanders to rid the district of rebels. Certainly, the war was continuing because some rebel positions were resisting. Despite Mattos' conviction that he had ended rebel activities in the Lower Amazon region, it quickly became obvious that this was not the case. Not only had groups moved elsewhere, but the subsequent pacification of the movement was to create division, and possibly more recruits to fight against the people perceived as the illegitimate lords of power.

Daniel Kidder, an American protestant missionary, was in Belém in early 1838, having made his way along the Atlantic coast from Maranhão. He had many acute observations and had clearly discussed recent events with various people. Andréa, he said, pre-empting Raiol's words, stood

---

34 General vicar of the Lower Amazon Raymundo Antônio Fernandes to President of Pará Francisco José Soares d'Andréa, July 9, 1838, Santarém, APEP cod. 854, doc. 145.

Accused of tyranny and inhumanity in his course towards rebels and prisoners; but the exigencies of the case were great, and furnished apologies. One of the most disgraceful things charged upon him and his officers, was the abuse made of their authority in plundering innocent citizens, and also in voluntarily protracting the war so that their selfish ends might be advanced. Certain it is, that there was loss of life; the ruin of property, and the declension of morals were all combined and lamentably continued; and yet in this state of things we see nothing but the fruits of that violence and injury which, from the first colonization of Pará by the Portuguese, had been practiced against the despised Indians.[35]

In this view, the Cabanagem was an almost inevitable result of the manner of the region's colonization. In the present of 1838, however, the overwhelming need to bring peace justified the ends, even if some winced in horror.

As a consequence of the onslaught, the rebels sought less accessible, but equally strategic, strongholds. They were pushed up the Tapajós River and westwards towards the Autazes. An arc of rebel positions formed across the land, swamps, and rivers linking the middle Tapajós River to Madeira River. Here new alliances were formed with the Mura and some rogue Mundurucu bands. There were still rebel points on a north bank tributary, Curuá River, and in Mauná on Marajó Island. In the words of one commentator, the rebels were "like mushrooms after rain," they sprouted everywhere.[36] Andréa estimated two thousand rebels were located in the Curuá muster at the end of 1837.[37] A further eight hundred were believed to be occupying various islands near Gurupá. With these developments, the Cabanagem was decisively entering a new phase, whose character was different from the broadly liberal aims that started the rebellion.[38] This period was more about survival and escaping persecution, and occasionally resorting to guerrilla tactics and bandit-like raids. By setting up impregnable strongholds, they were continuing the colonial tradition of creating safe places, mocambo-like refuges. They could launch attacks for provisioning but essentially these mocambos were defensive and not offensive locations.

In a separate development, the imperial authorities feared the French would take advantage of the unrest by joining the rebels. Although an earlier dispute over the border to French Guyana had been settled in 1817 (see

---

35 Daniel Parish Kidder, *Sketches of Residence and Travels in Brazil*, Philadelphia: Sorin & Ball, 1845, vol. 2, 318–319; also quoted in Hemming, *Amazon Frontier*, 234.

36 Lucas Alexandre Boiteaux, *A Marinha Imperial versus A Cabanagem*, Rio de Janeiro: Imprensa Naval, 1943, 373 and 374; Araújo Lima, *A Amazônia: A Terra e o Homen*, São Paulo: Companhia Editora Nacional, 1975, 128–129; Arthur Reis, *História do Amazonas*, Belo Horizonte: Editora Itatiaia, 1989, for information on rebel positions in late 1837.

37 Boiteaux, 374.

38 Guns and rifles were seldom used due to the lack of gunpowder, so knives, bows and arrows, and spears were the weapons. In turn, tactics changed to maintain an element of surprise.

pages 127–128), the French were apparently making new incursions into Brazilian territory, and claimed that Cabo do Norte, present-day Amapá, was theirs.[39] Like the British and the Americans, the French were present during the 1835 revolt in Belém. Sometime in 1836 a group of French soldiers with horses on two steamers had moved down the Atlantic coast and settled on the north side of the mouth of the Amazon, near Macapá. This had caused much anxiety to Andréa – the invasion could also mean the breakup of the new empire and loss of control of significant commerce. French Guyana was also perilously near the provincial capital, Belém, so plans were drawn up for an invasion (though how they could be realized was not clear).

However, in terms of the Cabanagem the French threat could not be underestimated. Should the French have started to supply the rebels the whole movement would take on an altogether different dimension. With more arms and new leaders, there would be a reinvigoration of rebel activity. The involvement of the French in the Cabanagem is an episode about which little is known and how close a joint campaign against Andréa really came to being formed is a topic for further research. It is possible that rebels did receive munitions and possibly soldiers from the French – all sales of weapons and gunpowder had been banned since Andréa came to Belém. In any case, the French never claimed to be supporting the rebels, though when they left the areas they occupied at the mouth of the Amazon in November 1840, there was evidence that they had been providing a refuge for cabanos escaping persecution.[40]

Aided by the French or not, the regional "meetings" of rebels would have found coordinated action difficult at this time. The major difficulty would have been evading detection by imperial forces. Although naval boats were not numerous, about twenty warships of various sizes and power were patrolling the waterways.[41] Supplies still had to be requisitioned and few risks could be taken. What then were the strategies or aims of the rebels at this time? Why did they carry on, when they knew well that Angelim had been arrested and the repression was in its most lethal phase?

Cabanos used a range of tactics, but not necessarily in a purposefully guided way. For example, in late 1837 the Curuá muster was seemingly playing tricks on the imperial soldiers. From the two thousand people allegedly living there, a couple of score decided to turn themselves in. They were taken to Santarém where they were registered and immediately given a hundred lashes in punishment. They promised then to fight for the

39 Arthur Reis, *Limites e Demarcações na Amazônia Brasileira*. Belém: CEJUP, 1993 [1948]; Peter Rivière, *Absent-minded Imperialism: Britain and the Expansion of Empire in Nineteenth-Century Brazil*, London: Tauris Academic Studies, 1995, 7.
40 Hurley, *Traços Cabanos*, 159. See also Cleary, *Cabanagem: Documentos Ingleses*, 124–125 and 143.
41 Boiteaux, *A Marinha versus a Cabanagem*, 386.

imperial cause. Soon afterwards they were told to destroy their old encampment, assisted by about fifty troops. Making their way to Monte Alegre for supplies, the rebels turned on the soldiers and chopped up more than thirty of them, including their officers. Such occurrences – the surrendering of rebels in order to enmesh themselves with the regulars – were almost commonplace at the time.[42] This so-called insubordination of soldiers was a deliberate attempt to undermine the repression from the inside. These actions complemented the forms of resistance from the outside. Mutiny was a common form of insurgency because men were forced to fight for the imperial army or face almost certain arrest and imprisonment. On hearing about the above episode, Andréa wrote to one of his cabinet ministers "a particular law is needed to end this rebellion which does not require any ceremonies in order to achieve the rebels' extermination."[43] A ceremony, in this sense, meant a trial and due legal process.

By the beginning of 1838 the Maués muster was gaining ground and recruits. In response they came under sustained attack. Maués (Luzea) was located in the middle of a labyrinthine network of streams, lakes, and rivers, and some overland routes to the Tapajós and Madeira rivers. It was a new town formed as a result of the Mundurucu peace settlement at the end of the eighteenth century and had initially resisted the rising tide of the cabano movement. Mura, Maués, and some Mundurucu Indians had been involved in the establishment of the settlement as a rebel stronghold.[44] But "all the chiefs of the Mundurucu on the Canuman and Abacaxi Rivers have presented themselves [to the imperial army] and with their kinsmen have made war on the cabanos."[45] Apparently, only the Mundurucu had the skills to track down the insurgents.[46] A series of operations had been launched with the result that rebel canoes were seized, prisoners taken, and a number of deaths occurred. Even so, Maués was to continue as a rebel position and never be conquered as Ecuipiranga had been. The leader, Gonçalo Jorge de Magalhães, would negotiate amnesty for his followers (little is known about this leader except that he refused to negotiate with the imperial authorities until they promised a general pardon). On the middle stretches of the Tapajós River, rebels still held some villages. Two imperial soldiers at Santa Cruz, the Mundurucu mission, were killed as they stepped down from their boat, though it is conceivable this was in error, since the

---

42 Boiteaux, *A Marinha versus a Cabanagem*, 371–401; and Hurley, *Traços Cabanos*, for instances of surrender.

43 Hurley, *Traços Cabanos*, 40.

44 Captain Antônio Firme Coelho to President of Pará Francisco José Soares d'Andréa, June 6, 1837, on board Pataxo Januário near Santarém, APEP cod. 1052, doc. 238.

45 President of Pará Francisco José Soares d'Andréa to the Imperial Minister of War Sebastião do Rego Barros, Pará [Belém], May 2, 1838, APEP cod. 906, doc. 15.

46 [?] Military commander to Colonel of the Amazonas Expedition Manuel Munis Tavares, August 14, Fort in Alenquer, APEP cod. 1112, doc. 102.

captain of the men refused to take revenge or to negotiate with the villagers (in all likelihood, Mundurucu was defending themselves from all outsiders).

By the end of 1838, rebel activity around the mouth of the Amazon near Breves and Marajó had been terminated. The Curuá meeting of two thousand rebels had also been dispersed and the gardens in which they had "grounded their hopes were completely destroyed." This left the axis between the Tapajós and Madeira rivers as the stamping ground for the remaining cabano forces.

New Policies and the Amnesty

Andréa issued new orders to his commanders on how to proceed in the ending of hostilities in April 1837. These "Instructions" consisted of twenty-nine articles ranging from the conduct of military expeditions to the treatment of women, and were listed in no coherent order. In this way the officers were entrusted with much power and became more locally significant than the justice of the peace and municipal councilors. The former was allowed to deal with unruly women and small infractions but not rebels and their crimes. A war footing was the order of the day. Andréa, first of all, wanted a census to be undertaken to establish exactly who was supposed to be where. All "unknowns" should be dispatched to the capital, probably to be sent to serve in the army in the south of Brazil. Similarly, better-off families should also select a military representative to travel to the capital and report for duty. Both these forms of recruitment anticipate the press-gangings, which allegedly took place around Belém.

Perhaps most significantly, Andréa wanted the commanders to enlist a police guard (*guarda policial*) composed of local "individuals capable of holding arms, and who are between 15 and 50 years of age, choosing those people who are the most wealthy, or of the highest position, and above all the officials of the old militias."[47] A year later, the kind of people to be included was changed from rich to "white men". And "men of color who have property" could also be integrated, so long as they "behave decently, they and their family."[48] It is not really clear why the change: perhaps the lack of rich, white applicants. The police guards were effectively regular soldiers and were required to report to the army barracks on a daily basis when they were not participating in an expedition. Naturally this detracted from their being able to carry on with their commercial interests. But these were exceptional times.

About a year later in 1838, Andréa gave further orders that showed he realized force was not enough in repressing the rebels. The police guard was

---

47 Article 6 in Francisco José Soares d'Andréa, *Instrucçoens Geraes para os Commandantes Militares.*

48 José Soares d'Andréa, *Instruccoens para a Organização dos Corpos de Trabalhadores e Regulamento dos Mesmos Corpos*, Palácio do Governo do Pará, Belém, August 8, 1838, 24 (reprinted in Carlos Moreira Neto, *Índios da Amazônia, de Maioria a Minoria, 1750–1850*, Petrópolis, Vozes, 1985, 273–275).

to be matched by the "workers' corps" (*corpos de trabalhadores*). With both institutions he sought a form of political and economic organization that would fix social relations in a new way. They introduced a crude and two-dimensional social structure of the compulsory labor service (not dissimilar from the Directorate but without any financial stake in production or political role in the running of the village):

All the rest of the population [not included in the police guard] will be enlisted, by district, of all the men of color from the age of 10 years and above. They should be separated into squadrons of more or less the same strength ... The purpose of these corps is above all to avoid vagabonds and loafers, and to organize people for public service work.[49]

Only those owning property and involved in "useful work" (*trabalho util*) would be exempt from this obligatory labor service. "Indians, mestiços, blacks who are not slaves, who do not have establishments on which they work constantly" were to form the ranks of the workers' corps. The possibility that there were people without land or family homes is extremely unlikely, for reasons discussed throughout this book. And if they did not have a secure domestic livelihood, the cause would have been the repression of rebellion, troops burning houses, powerful land owners taking advantage of the absence of neighbors to acquire more territory, and so on. In 1848, 10 years after its founding, the numbers registered in the workers' corps totaled 7,385, about thirty-five percent of men of the adult male population. (The police guard accounted for about forty percent and slaves the other twenty-five percent.) Undoubtedly the numbers in the late 1830s would have been higher.

The workers' corps was hated, and not only by those whom it controlled but also those who wanted to employ Indians, for there was no labor market. The workers were on permanent call and could be requisitioned for any kind of public service work. They had little time off and could not attend to their own household economies; that is, the identical grievances of the late colonial period were continued into the national period. At the end of the 1840s the president of the province was clearly disturbed by the conduct of the captains commanding the labor squadrons. Reports stated the corps had been converted into a means of servitude and private gain. In the presidential addresses of 1848 and 1849 it was noted that they should be abolished, but in the absence of anything better with which to replace it, the president had resolved to maintain the institution. How can we avoid the events of 1835, the president wanted to know, other than giving fruitful employment? How can we control the abuse by officers? How can we force people to work who have all the natural resources they need at an arm's length and "live in the lap of

49 D'Andréa, *Instrucçoens para a Organização dos Corpos de Trabalhadores*, 24–26.

abundance?" Variations on these questions are still asked by the contemporary élite and the same mistakes and misunderstandings being made.[50]

These new institutions were deliberately formed on the basis of race and class, despite never matching onto each other. It would be almost impossible for those in the workers' corps to escape the oppression of their bosses by gaining property and thus buying themselves out of this near slavery. How many "men of color" were included in the police guard is not known and the lists do not give details. The workers' corps formalized a class divide that had been present for the region's past one hundred years, but it was a gap that reformers such as Mendonça Furtado in the 1750s and Francisco de Souza Coutinho in the 1790s had hoped to close. The workers' corps can be understood as a reopening of the fractures of the past, for it legitimized and deepened class and racial distinctions. The workers' corps was enforced until 1855.[51]

One episode would have, however, cheered the rebels as they reinforced their positions in the Lower Amazon. Bararoa and his crew had been focusing their efforts on the destruction of Maués for most of the first half of 1838. Various defensive points were positioned on the lakes and streams, protecting Maués from attack. An estimated thousand rebels occupied the area under the leadership of Jorge de Magalhães. On August 1, 1838, Bararoa arrived in the Lake of the Autazes with one hundred and thirty men in nine canoes. These numbers allowed flexibility in offensive maneuvers and the small boats enabled deeper penetration of small creeks. They launched a large attack on a position in Lake Soares on the Madeira River. But when they did so, their approach was not met by gunfire. Only women and children were found at the site; they were informed that the men had gone to Lake Sampaio. Bararoa

50 For workers' corps figures and commentary, see "Falla dirigida pelo Exm Snr conselheiro Jeronimo Francisco Coelho, presidente da Província do Gram-Pará, á Assembléa Legislativa Provincial na Abertura da sessão ordinaria da sexta legislatura no dia 1 de outubro de 1848," Pará, Typ. de Santos & filhos, 1848, 31. The 1849 free adult population was 39,751; see "Mapa Estastica da População do Pará em 1849," BNRJ I-32, 10–4. William Herndon, *Exploration of the Valley of the Amazon*, Washington: Taylor and Maury, 1854, 256–258, translates the relevant section on the workers' corps from Coelho's 1849 presidential speech.

51 Little has been written on the workers' corps, either by contemporary observers or scholars. Bates, *The Naturalist*, vol. 2, 93, says they had a semimilitary organization and the captains invariably abused "their authority, monopolising the service of the men for their own purposes." Bates' comment comes from the annoyance that he cannot engage the workers to paddle his canoe, missing the point that he might be guilty of the same abuse. See also William Henry Edwards, *A Voyage up the River Amazon, Including a Residence at Pará*, London: John Murray, 1847, 81. For recent discussions Vicente Salles, *O Negro do Pará sob o Regime Escravidão*, Rio de Janeiro: Fundação Getulio Vargas, 1971, 272–277, Itala Bezerra da Silveira, *Cabanagem: Uma Luta Perdida* ..., 147–156 and Barbara Weinstein, *The Amazon Rubber Boom 1850–1920*, Stanford: Stanford University Press, 1985, 42–43, who reckons the workers were mainly employed as rubber tappers on the stands in the Tapajós River area. An interesting task would be to compare the workers' corps *Instructions* with three other key pieces of legislation for the Amazon: (1) the mission regulations (*Regimento das Missões*) in 1693, (2) the Directorate in 1755, and (3) the orders for ending the Directorate in 1798.

moved on and attacked a small rebel point on the lakeside, but this held only six men who opened fire and then ran into the forest. Frustrated but undeterred, Bararoa commanded a scouting party of twelve men that searched the nearby lakes, encountered nothing, and eventually came out to the Madeira River on August 6 and decided to head back to Manaus. Soon he came under attack from seven rebel canoes, apparently belonging to the Muras. They captured him, tortured him to death, and eventually threw his body in the water to be eaten by piranha.[52]

Andréa lamented his death and celebrated his military contribution. With rebel positions still stubbornly in place at the beginning of 1839, Andréa must have been feeling increasingly frustrated. There was one sign of improvement, however, as commercial trade up and down the Amazon was reestablishing itself – likely to have been led by the British and American traders. Still, Andréa continued to face local criticism of his measures and their apparent lack of success. Was the uncompromising repression misjudged? Now was a time for amnesty and to move on, some were arguing. Andréa vehemently resisted any such policy.[53] In such an atmosphere, witch-hunts and accusations feasted on the fear and terror.

In this context, a denunciation was made of Manoel Sanches – the leader of the destruction of Ecuipiranga. He had been in Belém from late 1837 for he was a regionally elected deputy. He also had set himself up as a leading critic of Andréa, to whom some had seen him as a successor.[54] Then he was accused of planning the murder of Andréa and requesting a younger brother to find a suitable assassin. Sanches was arrested on January 23, 1839 and put aboard the infamous prison ship, *Defensora*, on which at least two hundred prisoners had already died.[55] There, he was segregated from other inmates and not allowed visitors. After a relatively speedy trial due to the importance of the case, he was found innocent of all charges. By April 8 he had published a pamphlet saying that he had been the "victim of skullduggery and personal hatred."[56] No records of the trial or the pamphlet seem to have survived. The outcome of the process suggested either a surprising judicial impartiality or a return to the factionalism of the 1820s and early 1830s.

---

52 This account is based on Andréa's letter to the Imperial Minister of War in Rio, October 23, 1838, who in turn derived the information from José Luiz de Souza, commander in Santarém, in Hurley, *Traços Cabanos*, 167–169.

53 Francisco José de Souza Soares d'Andréa, *Falla com que o Exmo. Marechal Francisco Jozé de Souza Soares d'Andréa, Prezidente e Commandante das Armas da Província do Pará encerrou a primeira sessão da Assembléia Legislativa da mesma Província no dia 15 de maio de 1838*, Typographia Restaurada de Santos, e Santos menor, Pará, 1838, 17–18.

54 Commander of the Expeditionary Forces Joaquim José Luiz de Souza President of Pará Francisco José Soares d'Andréa, March 29, 1838, Santarém, APEP cod. 1067, doc. 64.

55 Moreira Neto, *Índios na Amazônia*, 314.

56 Raiol, *Motins Políticos*, 997.

Whatever the reason, the court's judgment can be interpreted as an indication of the turning of the tide against Andréa.

Despite the continuing rebel operations in the Amazonas region, Andréa felt he had maintained the "territorial integrity of the empire." He requested permission from Rio to step down and take on other work; perhaps he also feared for his life after the attempted assassination. He was replaced by a Paraense-born lawyer who did not hide his contempt for the way Andréa had conducted the province in the past few years. Nevertheless, Bernardo de Souza Franco did not reintroduce the constitution and still commanded all units to pacify rebel points. On leaving office, Andréa wrote to his successor that

The province is generally quiet, with the following exceptions: in Amazonas and its districts peace can only be maintained with arms in hand, particularly on the Madeira River, where the Indians are not completely obedient. Rebels have also established themselves at the headwaters of the Tapajós River and continue to cross overland to and threaten Maués ... on the Tapajós forces are still needed to maintain communication with Cuiabá, where the rebels have found some sympathizers.[57]

All other places of recent conflict were tranquil. Though Andréa had not succeeded in ending the rebel movement, he had changed its character. The "threat" it posed was no longer as serious as it had been when he came to Pará, and was contained more or less in the labyrinthine waterways of the Lower Amazon. Souza Franco appeared undaunted by the difficulties that lay ahead but immediately adopted a more conciliatory approach to the situation. By August 1839 he gave his first presidential address to the Provincial Legislative Assembly.

In Amazonas military operations continue, and difficult it will be to continue the war without employing light and conciliatory means, taking into consideration the vastness of the territory which must protected ... In respect to the culprits of the rebellion I have worked incessantly to get to know this important material. I have read all trial records and have calculated that more than half of those involved are deceased, and amongst these most are leaders and assassins. Those not yet arrested are mostly simple individuals who have not committed notable crimes. I have asked the Government of His Imperial Majesty to grant an exceptional amnesty, excluding assassins, to commanders of rebel points, and officials who served Eduardo [Angelim]. I am awaiting a response.[58]

---

57 Raiol, *Motins Políticos*, 995. Further evidence on the Cuiabá link is found in the letter by Commander of the Expeditionary Forces Joaquim [José] Luiz de [Souza] to Justice of the Peace in Santarém Manoel Pereira do Lago, September 5, 1838, Santarém, APEP cod. 1075, doc. 50. Apparently a trader was responsible for trafficking arms and gunpowder.

58 Bernardo de Souza Franco, *Discurso Recitado pelo Exmo Snr Doutor Bernardo de Souza Franco, Prezidente da Provincia do Pará quando abrio a Assemblea Legislativa Provincial no dia 15 de agosto de 1839*, Typographia Restaurada de Santos, e Santos menor, Pará, 1839, 2; also in Raiol, *Motins Políticos*, 998.

The new president recognized that "it will be difficult to conclude a war in which the enemy has so many advantages in terms of number of positions and knowledge of the locale."[59] One of the shocking outcomes of the repression so far was the number of people who had been killed, a fact noticed even by Andréa.[60] Perhaps for these reasons the region needed an amnesty. If political stability was a less burning question, it was the economy that was now a preoccupation for Souza Franco, for with fewer laborers it would be a long time in recovering.[61]

A positive response from the Rio regency regime concerning the partial amnesty came in November 1839. The most significant rebel position in Maués was contacted by the commander, João Miranda Leão. He invited Magalhães, the leader, to come forward and stop hostilities; in turn, there would be no more punitive expeditions. Magalhães, by messenger, asked for proof that Leão would keep his word. In response, Leão sent his firstborn son, accompanied by a group of soldiers in a canoe, to give his word of honor. On March 25, 1840, 980 rebels led by Magalhães came into the bay in front of Maués in their canoes. Subsequently, the rebel chief pledged allegiance to the emperor, Pedro II, and the imperial government; his soldiers handed in their "weapons, and bows and arrows."[62] In an act reminiscent of the factionalism of the independence period, two hundred of the Police Guards in Santarém and Óbidos mutinied, for they disagreed with the amnesty. They left their posts and "congregated in the forests," and demanded that the leader of the Amazonas forces be replaced. The authorities feared an imminent attack but the guards returned to their houses and nothing happened, once Leão went back to Belém.[63] Despite the amnesty, a high state of alert continued.

By this point, Souza Franco had left the presidency to pursue his ambitions in the south, only to return a year later as vice president of Pará. He was replaced by a southerner, João Miranda (unrelated to the commander above), who retained the state of emergency. In spite of the "enjoyment of unalterable calm" in the province, there remained the fear

59 Bernardo de Souza Franco to Imperial Minister of War, Pará [Belém], November 9, 1839, APEP cod. 906, doc. 194.

60 Andréa, *Discurso*, 1838.

61 Raiol, *Motins Políticos*, 1000, subtly makes this suggestion.

62 Araujo Lima, *Amazônia*, 129; President Miranda to Imperial Minister of War, May 10, 1840, [Belém], in Moreira Neto, *Índios na Amazônia*, 318; Antônio de Miranda, *Discurso Recitado pelo Exmo. Snr. Doutor João Antônio de Miranda, Presidente da Província do Pará, na abertura da Assembléia Legislativa Provincial no dia 15 de agosto de 1840*, Typographia Restaurada de Santos, e Santos menor, Pará, 1840; see also Boiteaux, *A Marinha versus a Cabanagem*, 396–397.

63 Bernardo de Souza Franco, *Discurso Recitado pelo Exmo. Snr. Doutor Bernardo de Souza Franco, Vice-Prezidente da Província do Pará na abertura da Assembléa Legislativa Provincial no dia 14 de abril de 1841*. Typographia Restaurada de Santos, e Santos menor, Pará, 1841.

that rebels could easily take up arms any time they wished. Miranda wanted to arrest Magalhães and his officials since they were not included under the terms of the amnesty. If not, these "tapuias, and other stupid people who considered themselves betrayed by their government, will return to the forests and find themselves fugitives again."[64] A few months later, he claimed "the amnesty has produced the best results ... Without this measure so salutary and well employed, they [the rebels who lay down their arms and sought the protection of the government] would have joined up with those who remain outlaws, and continue to remain hidden away in the forests ... and at each moment cause us to be perpetually anxious and fearful."[65] This implied ongoing military expeditions to make sure calm was maintained but also to pursue those who were still considered to be dangerous, and fall outside the amnesty. In August 1840 a pardon was granted to Angelim and Francisco Vinagre, but they were not allowed back to Pará until 1851.

This denouement appears to be a relatively quiet end to the war. Yet the trouble for the people of the interior was far from over. British consul in Belém Augustus Cowper, who had lived through most of the troubles, tells his superior in Rio in May 1840 that:

The president [Miranda], scorning all rules of constitutional government, makes himself absolute, and although in the present state of the country, an absolute government would probably be the most suitable for the general happiness, and the present president is a man well calculated to affect this. Yet it is deeply to be regretted that he allows his officers to perform acts which are the utter ruin of his country's prosperity.

The first act of violence performed, was the forcible transport of the Indian as soldiers to other provinces seized when they were coming from the interior with the produce of the country, this drove many to join the cabanos whilst other hid themselves, and sent their wives and daughters to the city with their produce; not however content with the first unjust act the officer of the different forts [sic], now arrested the canoes upon pretence of government service, and land the poor peasants' stock, who from fear of its perishing by exposure, sell it to these legalized robbers at a little of its value. They then forward it on to their own account in the city.

These acts have rendered produce so scarce in Pará, that it is eagerly bought up at enormous prices and every arrival brings fresh news of losses sustained by its sale in Europe and America, if it were not for this the population, small as it is, could well supply itself with the every luxury, but as it is a stranger is astonished at the enormous sale he is obliged to pay for the commonest necessaries of life, at the moment my lord we are paying 22 pence for a 4 lb loaf ...

64 President Miranda to Imperial Minister of War, May 10, 1840, [Belém], in Moreira Neto, *Índios da Amazônia*, 318.

65 Miranda, *Discurso Recitado*; extracts in Raiol, *Motins Políticos*, 1002.

Property is very insecure, and I believe the occurrences of 1835 might be reached, whenever it pleases the rebels to make the attempt.

Your Lordships will perceive that in the above remarks there is ample cause assigned for the depression of commerce, but with all this the province is quiet.[66]

A few weeks later, Cowper informed Lord Palmerston, then British foreign secretary, that Miranda, a native of Rio de Janeiro, is continuing to relocate people from the interior with drastic consequences for the economy.

My Lord,

I regret to inform your Lordship that his Excellency the President, altho [sic] an energetic reformer of some of the many abuses of this state, and evidently a man desirous for the welfare of the province has adopted the fatal policy of his predecessors, a policy too, so dramatically opposed to every notion of constitutional government, and has commenced kidnapping the peasantry without the distinction of color, for the purpose of transporting them as soldiers to the disturbed province of Maranham; these forcible abductions are at present confined to the Indians and settlers of the Acará [the area where the many of the Belém cabano leaders lived].

The immediate consequences of this step are, at first, undisguised discontent and secondly, a scarcity of provisions by no means likely to allay the excitement. The peasantry refrain from bringing their produce to the city, and farinha, in this country the stuff of life, has risen within a week from one milreis the alqueire, or one halfpenny, to two milreis and a half, or one penny farthing, being a rise of 150 percent in seven days.[67]

The counter-insurgency period was characterized not just by carnage on both sides. There were press-gangings and mutinies, disloyalty and betrayal, executions, and long-term imprisonment. The policy of conscription at gunpoint served the need for recruits to fight wars in other lands and cleanse the region of undesirables. It is difficult to imagine a more systematic attack on the peasantry, as Cowper called them, than the range of measures taken in the late 1830s. For these reasons, we should not be surprised by the relative size proportion of the population enlisted in the workers' corps (thirty-five percent of the total). As we will see below, their numbers were greatly diminished by death, flight, and kidnapping. The rest were imprisoned in their districts (they could not leave them) and by compulsory labor obligations.

A general amnesty, building on the exceptional one, was granted to rebels all over Brazil on August 22, 1840 by Pedro II. His age of majority was proclaimed prematurely in July 1840 when he was fourteen years old and

66 British Consul Augustus Cowper to Right Honourable Lord Viscount Palmerston (via G[eneral] C[onsul in] B[razil]), British Consulate in Pará [Belém], May 27, 1840, NAL FO 13, 165–166, folios 90–92.
67 British Consul Augustus Cowper to Right Honourable Lord Viscount Palmerston (via G[eneral] C[onsul in] B[razil]), British Consulate in Pará [Belém], July 25, 1840, NAL FO 13, 165–166, folios 111–112.

Pedro became emperor of Brazil.[68] Curiously, the first rebel government in mid-January 1835 had said they wanted nothing to do with the Rio government until Pedro reached his majority (though Vinagre recanted this proposal a month later).[69] Whether Pedro's new role as emperor inspired a calmness and greater trust in the South we shall not know: that would imply an unlikely continuity of rebel leadership and objectives over five years. Nevertheless, the coincidence of the ending of all military operations and Pedro's coming of age is remarkable. The amnesty may have marked an end to open hostilities, but the emotional scars, racial and ethnic divisions, and ongoing corruption of social justice persisted. All the hatreds of the past were still present but a political opposition in which poor Indians, blacks, and mestiços were central actors was no longer a possibility. These people were severed from their former hopes and passions and a grieving process began, which for many may have involved a distancing from their losses and their memories.

On the Numbers of Dead

Unsurprisingly, travelers and scientists who went into the interior of Amazon in the decade or so after the Cabanagem remarked on the apparent paucity of people. For example, Prince Adalbert of Prussia, who went down the Xingu River and then to Belém in 1842, wrote, "It will scarcely excite wonder after the occurrences of such events that the number of inhabitants in the province has in the last years diminished rather than increased."[70] Henry Bates bemoaned that in places like Alter do Chão, "there is now scarcely an old or middle aged man in the place."[71] These comments cannot be taken as totally reliable evidence, since the prince and the naturalist were not comparing villages before and after the Cabanagem, though they might have been reporting what others told them.

The absence of people could also be explained by disappearance and relocation, since this is what the laboring classes had been doing (and had been forced to do) for a century or more in any case – retreating into the forest or remote areas, and joining other communities; although the laws introduced by Andréa were deliberately designed to prevent such movement.

One of the great questions arising from the rebellion is how many people really died? The unhappy answer is very many, but it is impossible to know

68 Raiol, *Motins Políticos*, 1001; though there were still naval patrols on going in the Amazonas area in 1841, Souza Franco, *Discurso*, 3.

69 The majority the rebels would have had in mind, though, was Pedro's eighteenth birthday (December 2, 1843).

70 Prince Henry Adalbert, *Travels in the South of Europe and in Brazil with a Voyage up the Amazon and the Xingu*. London, 1849, 155.

71 Bates, *A Naturalist*, vol. 2, 81.

the precise numbers. There are many complicating factors, not least of which are the inaccuracy and unreliability of military reports. For example, death tolls for the same attack often varied wildly. Deaths were caused by military activity on both sides, often in isolated areas, on farms and the river. The true human devastation of the repression was deliberately hidden so questions would not be asked. On the other hand, there were three massacres by rebels: 1) in Belém on January 7, 1835 of about twenty Portuguese merchants, 2) in Vigia in October 1835, where seventy people died, and 3) in Santarém in March 1836, where thirty whites were killed. There may have been others, though probably not on the same scale, for this kind of information would have been widely reported. But less is known about the counter-insurgency operations, where it was not uncommon to read of many scores being killed, especially in Belém in July and August 1835, and May 1836. Additionally, many more may have died in the prisons of each town and aboard the hulks, *Defençora* and *Xin-xin*.[72]

Two commentators, Henrique Handelman and Raiol, both reasonably close in time to the events, offer an estimate of the numbers killed. Neither is clear over what period the deaths occurred, or whether they are referring to the Cabanagem period, January 7, 1835 to the amnesty in 1840 (if so, which one) or to the series of rebellions that characterized the period from 1820 to 1840. Handelman, who does not give his sources but who was a friend of Prince Adalbert (his *History of Brazil* is dedicated to him), reckons that ten to twelve thousand people lost their lives in the fighting and the prisons from lack of food and cruel treatment.[73] Raiol, on the other hand, has a much higher figure, which he is "sure is not an exaggeration." He suggests that "more than thirty thousand were immolated in the demagogic fury and the reaction of the government forces."[74] Both sides suffered equally, he claims, but most deaths went unregistered and were easily ignored.[75] He describes the human misery of the period as a "holocaust," invoking another biblical reference, this time to the Old Testament notion of wholesale human sacrifice.[76]

If the population of Pará was about one hundred and twenty thousand, then Raiol's thirty thousand figure, a quarter of the total, is staggering. Nevertheless, it is likely that the region to have suffered most in the repression was the Lower Amazon, the area between Gurupá and Manaus. The Belém area may have experienced greater deaths among white slave-owning élite, since not only were they more concentrated there, the rebel

---

72 Chasteen, "Cautionary Tale," 116 and see n. 55.

73 Henrique Handelman, *História do Brasil*, Rio de Janeiro: Instituto Histórico e Geográphico Brasileiro, 1931 [1860], 315.

74 Raiol, *Motins Políticos*, 1000.

75 Raiol, *Motins Políticos*, 1001.

76 Raiol, *Motins Políticos*, 1005.

Table 8.1 *Changes in population for towns of the Lower and Upper Amazon before and after the Cabanagem*

	1833	1849	% Change
Santarém	3985	5231	31.27%
Óbidos	2987	5942	98.93%
Alter do Chão	818	913	11.61%
Vila Franca	2736	1983	−27.52%
Monte Alegre	1780	1689	−5.11%
Alenquer	1208	1824	50.99%
Faro	1989	1500	−24.59%
Pinhel	865	2010	132.37%
Boim	708	893	26.13%
Silves	1505	920	−38.87%
Maués	3719	3417	−8.12%
Borba	1740	1075	−38.22%
Vila Nova (Parintins)	3137	3243	3.38%
Manaus	3614	2964	−17.99%
Serpa (Itacoatiara)	547	378	−30.90%
Total	31338	33982	8.44%

furor against them was strongest. Raiol's insistence that equal numbers died on both sides seems somewhat misjudged, although it would suit his general opinion that both the rebels and the repressors were as bad as each other and an alternative needed to both.

Comparing the population figures from 1833 and 1849 in the Lower and Upper Amazon (see Table 8.1), some important observations can be drawn. There was, overall, about an eight percent increase in population. The greatest increase, a doubling, was in the area on Lower Tapajós River, Pinhel, and Boim, which can be explained by the settling of Mundurucus in the villages under imperial control and their use in rubber tapping. Alter do Chão, also on the Tapajós, experienced a twelve percent increase, undermining Bates's claim noted earlier. But Vila Franca, Faro, Silves, Borba, Parintins (Vila Nova), and Manaus underwent significant decreases of between seventeen and thirty-eight percent. In other words, if numbers of resettled Amerindians are subtracted, there is apparently no overall increase or decrease in the region. This does not mean that half the towns in Table 8.1 did not experience a demographic collapse, due to the repression or flight.

Whatever the numbers killed, maimed, deported, or kidnapped, the violence and affliction must have left deep psychological wounds. A generation since 1820 had grown up surrounded by death, conflict, and fear. Few families could have escaped the loss of a kinsperson. How did this generation take forward their memories? How did they deal with death?

The Aftermath of Rebellion

At the declaration of the exceptional amnesty, President Bernardo de Souza Franco wrote pessimistically that the Amazon remained "seething with suffocated passions. The underprivileged and wronged understand one another. They communicate their grievances and rancor to a large number of others. It is easy to find reasons [for such grievances] in the forced labor, exigencies, constraint and oppression that always accompany such dissensions and civil wars."[77] Nothing was resolved. Élites remained anxious that another explosion of popular sentiment could occur at any time.

The following decade of 1840–49 was as wretched as ever: the workers' corps forced men into their new assignments, such as rubber tapping near the Tapajós and Tocantins rivers, and old forms of domination.[78] Food in towns was scarce and money in short supply (some copper counterfeit money remained at this time) and prices were out of control. In a 1845 report on the decadent state of the Upper Amazon, Mattos bemoaned the misery of the region, echoing his earlier comments: "most villages are depopulated of inhabitants and some are without a home, many are hiding in the forests in order to avoid the heavy service of becoming enlisted in the workers' corps."[79] In order to develop the region, he proposed strong leadership and government and the creation of a new province of the Upper Amazon, which eventually occurred in 1850.

The usual explanation for the ferocity and longevity of the Cabanagem follows the accommodating, if patronizing, perspective of Souza Franco cited previously: the simmering tensions between whites and Indians spilled over as more power was given to the provinces in the early 1830s. Outsiders took the long view when commenting on the state of ethnic relations. Before the Cabanagem, Henry Lister Maw was probably the first to empathize with the Indians in 1828 as he reflected on the disorderly path to independence. The search for the motives of such deep hatred was, according to Maw, a waste of time because "as practical facts [they require] little depth of reasoning to trace their causes or effects, for any unprejudiced person can ask himself what is the cause of these evils existing to a greater or lesser extent in proportion to the degree of injustice that has produced them."[80]

After the rebellion, this argument was even more starkly stated as the inevitable product of two centuries of Portuguese exploitation of Indians. Recalling Kidder's earlier comments on the "despised Indian," he also wrote in 1838 that "in no part of Brazil have so great cruelties been practiced against

---

77 Hemming, *Amazon Frontier*, 228.
78 Weinstein, *The Amazon Rubber Boom*, 42–43.
79 Mattos, "Relatório," 146.
80 Maw, *A Passage*, 324.

the Indians; and in no part have they been so fearfully revenged."[81] We must be careful with this view, however. It fits with the diminution of the rebels' political aims to race hate. In the interior of the province, in 1849 Bates met John Hislop in Santarém. Hislop, a Scot resident there of 35 years, told him the place was nothing compared to what it had been – "Santarém suffered greatly."[82] Before the disorders, Santarém was flourishing, trade was much greater; Hislop particularly mentioned the miners from Matto Grosso, who brought their gold and diamonds down the Tapajós to Santarém, seeking to buy European goods. There were also many large proprietors, rich in slaves and cattle, and the production of cacao was larger.[83] Now much of this had gone, though it would come back soon enough, Hislop reckoned. Elsewhere, the élite had yet not returned. Their property had been smashed or stolen and recovery was impossible.[84]

Bates characterized the rebels as "scoundrels and mistaken patriots," and the rebellion as "a political squabble between whites [that is, Brazilian and Portuguese], which began the troubles and ended, in this part of the country [the Lower Amazon], in a revolt of the Indians."[85] Tantalizingly, he wrote in a throw-away comment: "much more can be said on the matter" but he thought "the details would serve no useful purpose."[86] When Bates left Santarém, he moved upstream to Manaus and then up the Solimões River. After a further five years upriver, he returned downstream and was overcome by the change in the Lower Amazon towns. They were cleaner and better looking, with a more vibrant commercial life. There was a clear improvement in the economic aspect, which he noticed too in Belém despite the yellow fever outbreak, which had hit the city in the early 1850s. A change in the prosperity of the traders was being translated into new buildings and streets:

81 Kidder, *Sketches*, 313. Kidder also describes the period as one in which "revenge rioted in the blood." James Cooley Fletcher and Daniel Parish Kidder, *Brazil and the Brazilians: Portrayed in Historical and Descriptive Sketches*, Boston: Little, Brown, 1879, 547. Recall the interpretation of the Cabanagem given by Capistrano de Abreu, who blamed it on the Portuguese attitudes and policies concerning Indians in the eighteenth century (see page 106). See also Prince Adalbert traveling in the mid-1840s, who confirmed this opinion: "These disturbances were the fruits of the ceaseless oppression which the white population had from the very first exercised on the poor natives and in no part of Brazil more than here," Adalbert, *Travels*, 154.

82 Bates, *A Naturalist*, vol. 2, 17. For more information on Hislop's life, see Edwards, *A Voyage up the River Amazon*, 101; Herndon, *Exploration of the Valley of the Amazon*, 323; R. Stewart Clough, *The Amazons: a Diary of Twelve Months Journey on a Mission of Inquiry up the River Amazon for the South American Missionary Society*, London, 1879, for an incident in which Hislop was attacked by someone trying to steal from his house.

83 Bates, *A Naturalist*, vol. 2, 17.

84 Edwards, *A Voyage up the River Amazon*, 71, on a Portuguese man called Godinho in Vigia; Bates, *A Naturalist*, vol. 1, 86, on the Scottish trader Archibald Campbell who had estates on Marajó.

85 Bates, *A Naturalist*, vol. 2, 16.

86 Bates, *A Naturalist*, vol. 2, 18.

"for many years the past the provincial government had spent their considerable surplus revenue in beautifying the city."[87]

These sympathetic explanations of the Cabanagem were the liberal humanist reactions of educated men. But they were nevertheless portraying the civil war as one of race hate. This was a convenient simplification, suiting the imperial forces of repression more than the rebels the men were trying to understand. These writers also conveyed a sense of unavoidability of the events.[88] Again, there is little support for this view. Some governors of the Amazon had genuinely sought to merge the differing interests, while others had not. Some Indians colluded with the colonial system and gained materially for doing so, while others resisted and fought it with all their power.

In the mid- to late nineteenth century, anecdotes flourished concerning the revolutionary activities alongside more general reflections. Some were recounted by the laboring and élite classes to the foreign travelers and scientists, indicating the vitality and sensitivity of the memories. These stories originate in firsthand accounts and they suggest a new generation coming to terms with the memories of kinsfolk and neighbors. For example, Bates was told by the residents of one village on the Tapajós River that they had to move from a previous site because the place had been overcome by red fire ants since the Cabanagem. The villagers explained that the ants had sprung up from the blood of slaughtered cabanos.[89] This kind of story speaks to a process of mythologization, perhaps integrating an ancient tale. On a more heroic level, there abounded celebrated accounts from both sides of the conflict. Geologist Herbert Smith, who spent many years in the Lower Amazon in the 1870s, wrote "to this day old men will tell you brave stories of the great rebellion."[90]

Yet there was also reluctance to recount the trauma of the past. Bernardino de Souza, a priest who had extensive experience working in the Amazon in 1860s, made a collection of sketches from the history of the region. In one of them he recounted the memories of an old and respectable lady from Óbidos, who reminisced as she was sitting in a rather morbid setting. A chapel had been built to Our Lord Jesus in thanks for saving the people of Óbidos from the rebels. Unfortunately, it was built too close to the river's edge and erosion had destroyed part

---

87 Bates, *A Naturalist*, vol. 2, 411, says that the revenue almost wholly derives from the high custom house duties. More than half of all the foreign trade in 1858 was with Britain.

88 William Edwards, an American naturalist, also noted the disastrous effect of Cabanagem during his travels on the Amazon in 1846 and early 1847. He reckoned the region would maintain the peace if the provincial government acted with "sufficient discretion," thus implying they had not in the past. Edwards, *A Voyage up the River Amazon*, 10.

89 Bates, *The Naturalist*, vol. 2, 97.

90 Herbert Smith, *Brazil: The Amazons and The Coast*, New York: Scribner, 1879, 75.

of the cemetery. As a result, human bones were sticking out where the ground had given way.[91]

I was still a child [at the time of the Cabanagem]. We do not really talk about it anymore, it is almost only the business of bygone times. How we all suffered because of the men who wanted something that no one knew, not even they themselves! The Cabanagem was a scourge sent by God to punish us. It was a plague that ravaged the land where I was born. Everyone suffered from it. It even seemed that time went by sadly.[92]

It is impossible to corroborate this woman's feelings with other sources. Yet it would not take much imagination to suppose they were shared by others at the time. To talk of loved ones who endured pain or were killed at the hands of enemies, perhaps through torture, would have been distressing. Indeed, the woman goes further and decries the futility of the rebellion. Such losses did not even serve a purpose, she says. This view may be a gendered one, given the dearth of men in some places.

The ambivalence of these oral histories helps explain why no memorial was dedicated to those who died. We know nothing of the private or local ways of remembering the dead. Each town had its own general burial ground, as did hamlets and villages. During the rebellion, attackers threw many bodies into the river as a means of efficient disposal. Few names were given to those who lost their lives; no list exists except the prison records. Public memorialization of Cabanagem has only taken place very recently to mark the 150th anniversary of the 1835 uprising. Even this monument does not make clear who is being commemorated. In the nineteenth century such a memorial may have stood for a reconciliation of the social and ethnic differences. But this kind of monument was a later phenomenon starting in Brazil with the war against Paraguay in the 1850s. In any case, the belief in racial divisions prevented a common commemoration.

As the second half of the nineteenth century wore on, what might be called old Pará – the people and ways of life marked by the late colonial period – was displaced. A new Pará was taking over as the profits from rubber were invested in public and private infrastructure and immigrants came in search of work. With distance, the ideological significance of Pará's rebellion of the 1830s became less threatening. It was incorporated into various kinds of reflections, mostly hegemonic, on the region. Raiol completed his five-volume study of the period in 1890. Naturalist writer Inglês de Souza, who was born in Óbidos, penned stories about the Lower Amazon

---

91 The sight of human bones is confirmed by Barrington Brown and William Lidstone, *Fifteen Thousand Miles on the Amazon and Its Tributaries*, London: Edward Stanford, 1878, 194–195.

92 Francisco Bernardino de Souza, *Lembranças e Curiosidades do Valle do Amazonas*. Pará, Typ. do Futuro, 1873, 113–114; also appears in the same form in his *Commissão do Madeira, Pará e Amazonas*, Rio de Janeiro: Typographia Nacional parte 3, 1874–1875, 12–13.

set during or shortly after the Cabanagem. References abound as to the suffering experienced. Portuguese novelist Francisco de Gomes Amorim set a romance called *The wild ones* (Os selvagens) in the Tapajós region during the 1830s with characters from Mundurucu and Mura Indians. Like Inglês de Souza, Amorim had spent a good part of his childhood in Pará and soaked up stories of earlier times. These examples are extended treatments of either oral or textual sources. They are part of a legitimization, if not a demoralization, of a particular way of understanding the troubles. The study of this process is beyond the present concern except to indicate the shifting meanings at the end of the nineteenth century in a new context. The uprising's legitimization created a hegemonic version that suited the old and new ruling classes alike.[93]

One of the major outcomes of the repression was the affirmation of Pará as part of imperial Brazil. Politically, the dominant classes were forced to conform to the aspirations of the empire. The workers' corps connected the laboring classes to this emerging sense of national identity by putting them under the hierarchical control of municipal authorities who were in turn answerable to the province's president, nominated and dependent on the Rio regime. It would take another change of attitude to disband the workers' corps, as did happen with the general amelioration of conditions in the province in the mid-1850s. These workers reestablished themselves as a semiautonomous peasantry, though by then the most desired lands had all been taken by cacao planters and raisers of livestock. The centrality the peasants had assumed in the first few decades of the century was broken and they were pushed into the interstices of the agrarian and extractive sectors, which were never developed enough to innovate their forms of production. Peasants were left more or less in control of their labor, their desire to work autonomously, and the natural resources of the region. This transformation provided the conditions – a mobile, environmentally knowledgeable labor force – though no one could have known it at the time, for the next conquest of the Amazon in the second half of the nineteenth century by a new élite hungry for rubber. The late 1850s saw the riverways opened up to foreign commercial vessels. Exports and imports accelerated at a pace unknown for almost the whole of Brazil. The region that Capistrano de Abreu described as being less populated and further away from civilization than ever in the 1840s was becoming the envy of the American world. In the space of fifty years it had moved from a peripheral colonial region written off by the Portuguese through a bloody and ambivalent independence, a rebellion on a magnificent scale, to an exporter of rubber to a world market and arena of conspicuous consumption.

93 The fact that these "memorials" are books is significant; books can be hidden away and are aimed at the literate.

CONCLUSION

The Making of the Brazilian Amazon

The decision to grant Pedro II his majority at the age of 14 may have coincided with the quieting of spirits in Pará. It did not, however, herald peace in the other agitated provinces. Rio Grande do Sul's Farroupilha revolt and Maranhão's Balaiada continued in those regions' countryside. There would be other liberal eruptions in São Paulo (1842), Minas Gerais (1842), and Pernambuco (1848). The rural insurgency on the Alagoas and Pernambuco border, the Cabanada, had simmered for three years (1832–1835). Though not liberal in origin, it challenged the control of land by new landowners. The Muslim slave rebellion in the city of Salvador in January 1835 had threatened to overthrow the regional leaders, but the plot was discovered before it got under way. The Sabinada in that province had also been put down in March 1838, four months after it began. The challenge to the new nation and its leaders, popular exclusion from the political process, land confiscation, capitalist transformation, and slavery had been vigorous yet they were put down robustly. Each rebellion played a fundamental part in the constitution of modern Brazil. The reprisal allowed centralized authority to be reimposed on the regions. In Pará, this forced a reconfiguration of local patron/client relations and the local ruling class to find common interest and become dependent on national rulers.

Two questions present themselves in understanding the historical significance of the far north's rebellion in the set of political and social revolutions in the Brazilian provinces. The first is, How can we interpret the events in Pará within the context of early nineteenth century upheavals in Brazil. A brief comparison will afford a general overview of the extraordinary revolutionary wave rolling over Brazil in the 1830s. The second question is to ask about the place of the rebellion in the context of Amazonian development.

The two concerns are in fact intimately connected. Following the 1830s the Amazon became a more convincing part of the new nation. The fear of the potential fragmentation of Brazil sounded the death bell of democratic liberalism. The rest of the nineteenth century in the Amazon, with rubber extraction dominating, would not have been possible without the political

"Brazilianization" of Pará more or less achieved in 1840. The problem was not obstructive missionaries, lazy natives or corrupt colonials, as the Portuguese had supposed, rather the political ideas themselves. While the élites in Pará resigned themselves to central domination, the popular will remained defiant and suspicious of those in positions of authority, and the region itself stubbornly difficult to colonize.

Comparing the Cabanagem with the Regency Rebellions

Conventionally, studies of the regency in Brazilian historiography have attended to the political intrigues between various factions, the rise and demise of the radical liberals, the transformation in their own thinking, and the conservative comeback (*regresso*). The rebellions are an important aspect of this narrative, but they are seen as essentially derivative of the liberal reforms that gave more power to the provinces. Decentralization produced an escalation of conflict on a local level, because the regions were unprepared for the transfer of power. In this view, the rebellions were basically illegitimate. The historical judgment is that the reforms were wrongheaded and irresponsible. In other words, the repression of each rebellion was thoroughly necessary, for Brazilian unity was made possible. The liberal or republican experiment, as the regency is sometimes known, was a vital, if disastrous, phase since it provided a wake-up call to national leaders for the need for strong central control.

Recently there have been more sophisticated and less patronizing revisions of this argument. For example, Emilia Viotti da Costa has underscored the resistance national élites had to triumph to establish their hegemony. While framing the 1831–1840 rebellions in liberal discourse, she also notes that most people did not participate for ideological purposes but "were moved by more immediate and concrete concerns."[1] There were, she explains, a variety of fault lines: Portuguese/Brazilian, black/white, natives/foreigners, rich/poor, foreign commercial agents/local merchants and artisans, soldiers/officers, and so on.[2] Thus individuals had multiple identifications and acted pragmatically rather than out of conviction for a single set of new ideas. There is nevertheless in this view an implicitly negative characterization of mass participation in the rebellions. Like Caio Prado, it is assumed that the popular classes did not articulate liberal demands. But the fact is, many of them did, as is clear in the previous pages and from work by scholars like Jeffrey Mosher who studied the period

---

1 Emilia Viotti da Costa, *The Brazilian Empire: Myths and Histories*. Chapel Hill: University of North Carolina Press, 2000, 68.
2 Viotti da Costa, *The Brazilian Empire*, 68–69.

in Pernambuco.[3] Rebels of all kinds did frame their goals in the same constitutional language that defined national politics. It is difficult to understand the call for a removal of a nominated official – or the call by the townspeople of Alter do Chão in Chapter 6 for the appointment of a native-born assessor of taxes – as not both concrete and ideological.

Another point of contention is the importance historians have accorded each regional uprising. This lack of consensus can, in part, be put down to their different theoretical persuasions. For Prado, writing from a materialist perspective, the Cabanagem was the most significant because it was fought on the largest scale and achieved the most. Still, he also condemned it as the most vague in political terms because it was led by Indians and mestiços who had been duped into the factional infighting by unscrupulous élites. Roderick Barman, examining the forging of modern Brazil, perceives the most threatening as the Farroupilha of Rio Grande do Sul. It was the only one to demand secession and took the longest to repress; though he concedes it was not taken as seriously as the northern rebellions, perhaps because of the lack of peasant participation. Leslie Bethell takes a chronological view and avoids comparing one with the other. He understands the Cabanagem as a "popular movement but not of the people the liberals had in mind."[4] This characterization gets to the heart of the issue for understanding how to compare the Cabanagem with other rebellions and its place on the imperial stage. It is precisely with the expression of the interests of the "popular movement" that this study has grappled.

Generally, the assumption has been that the regency rebellions can be seen together in spite of their local characters. In a recent essay John Chasteen has criticized this collective understanding and especially the thesis that they resulted from too much power being conceded to the regions. For him, this interpretation is offered "without evidence, enthusiasm or elaboration."[5] In the last twenty years, such dissatisfaction has led some scholars to study in more depth the regional contexts in which the rebellions took place. Attention has been directed to the formation of the local groups, their struggles and alliances, and their appeal to popular participation in conflicts. Topics such as race, class, and popular culture have been an integral part of these studies.

---

3 Jeffrey Mosher, *Political Struggle, Ideology, and State Building: Pernambuco and the Construction of Brazil, 1817–1850*, Lincoln: University of Nebraska Press, 2008.

4 Leslie Bethell and José Murilho de Carvalho, "Brazil from Independence to the Mid-Nineteenth Century," in Leslie Bethell (ed.), *The Cambridge History of Latin America. Vol.3, From Independence to c. 1870*, Cambridge: Cambridge University Press, 1985, 704.

5 John Chasteen, "Cautionary Tale: A Radical Priest, Nativist Agitation, and the Origin of Brazilian Civil Wars," in Rebbeca Earle (ed.), *Rumours of Wars: Civil Conflict in Nineteenth-Century Latin America*. London: Institute of Latin American Studies, 2000, 104.

This recent scholarship on the northern rebellions agree they defy casting in national terms. The revolts were composed of diverse leaders and participants, and some groups were not under the central control of the rebels. Side switching was commonplace, less as an ideological change than a shifting of alliances. It would seem the more the provincial level is researched, the more difficult generalization becomes. The fact that these revolts are complex entities is an expression of the social legacy of Portuguese colonial rule in those places.

Although the political, environmental, and economic history and culture of each province was dissimilar, the north of Brazil shared common characteristics in the independence and regency periods. They had roughly cotemporaneous cycles of rebellion in the post-independence period, as democratic liberalism became the main language of insurrection; they shared calls for reform of the political order and constitutional entitlement. Slave revolts in the late colonial period also fed into local disputes for power in Bahia and Pernambuco, influencing the course of provincial politics.[6] They each had a bloody path to independence with local battles between Brazilian patriots and Portuguese troops; they challenged the right of Rio administrations to impose presidents; they enjoyed calls for greater inclusion of all people in the political process; and each place had a heterogeneous population. As mentioned above, various fault lines crossed the diverse ethnic categories and few of them were predictable. However, the struggle over independence, including the resistance of Portuguese troops and the presence of British mercenaries in the north, produced new alliances. Local Brazilian leaders had to tune into popular cultures of resistance. In particular, priests and military officers played a special role in forming alliances across classes, though journalists, artisans, and others also acted as leaders and crucial supporters. The alliances introduced a new political world with new expectations, and consciousness shifted. For example, the foiled attack on Belém, planned for the end of 1834, came out of a long-held coalition of journalists, priests, landowners, and the urban and rural free poor. An example from Maranhão can be seen below. These coexistences opened up communal dialogues between those who were opposed to hegemonic forces in much the same way as elsewhere in Latin America during the same period. Jeffrey Mosher, in the context of Pernambuco, argues that these spaces created real political and ideological differences between partisan positions.

---

6 See João José Reis, *Slave Rebellion in Brazil: The Muslim Uprising of 1835 in Bahia*. Baltimore: John Hopkins University Press, 1995; and Marcus Carvalho, "O Outro Lado da Independência: Quilombos, Negros, Pardos em Pernambuco, (Brasil), 1817–1823," *Luso-Brazilian Review*, 2006, 43, 1, 1–30.

In mid-1823, the governments of all northern provinces were replaced following the threat of violence. Though Pará and Bahia had pro-Portuguese constitutionalists in government, Maranhão had a radical liberal ruling. Matthias Assunção points to the importance of this brief period of rule in the province: it made way for the involvement of popular classes in regional politics and alliances with liberal patrons. Its president from July 1823 to November 1824 pursued an anti-Portuguese policy. When the Portuguese and their Brazilian sympathizers tried to overthrow him, the president opened the prisons to raise a popular army. Moreover, the council of São Luís around this time opened its doors to a wider range of representatives in order to express the general will of the people (as also happened in Belém in January 1835). The revolutionary meetings were seen as a kind of citizen council, in which all men had equal rights and the power to make decisions.[7] These actions marked a new phase in the political history of Maranhão and Pará. The élite could struggle for power between themselves, but they would need the help of the lower classes. Yet Assunção writes the masses were previously "unpoliticized" in Maranhão.[8] This may be so in terms of national politics. But it implies popular classes were passive before independence and their mobilization by élites.

My argument for Pará has been that a tradition of popular resistance guided opposition to colonial rule. This tradition was based in a mobile way of life tied to the rivers and based in diverse economic activities, and dependent on the autonomy of labor power and an extended family linked to a farmstead or hamlet. A threat to any of these aspects could lead to local conflict. This included controls on movement, land grabbing, and obligatory labor activities. In the independence period, this popular culture of opposition was fused with a liberal language concerning order, fairness, and equality in law. For example, a key perception that the law was not being implemented fairly often acted as a spur to revolt, as happened in Santarém at the end of 1835.

Assunção argues that the Balaiada was "first and foremost a peasant war against recruitment [to the army]."[9] Maranhão was predominantly a plantation economy based on slave labor, but there were significant numbers of small holders and cattle farmers who produced for local markets. The failure to recognize the "legitimacy of their aspirations" led to the rebellion of a diverse set of people in the interior of Maranhão.[10] The alliance of peasants

7 Matthias Röhrig Assunção, "Élite Politics and Popular Rebellion in the Construction of Post-Colonial Order: The Case of Maranhão, Brazil, 1820–1841," *Journal of Latin American Studies*, 1999, 31, 17 and 14. For Belém, see the signatories to the "Acta do Conselho Extraordinária de Cidadaos Reunidos na Salla do Conselho do Governo," January 7, 1835, Coleção Cabanagem: Revolução de Vinagre, BNRJ II, 32, 4, 17.
8 Assunção, "Élite Politics and Popular Rebellion," 16.
9 Assunção, 3.
10 Assunção, 6.

and ranchers with slaves and runaway slaves in 1838 provided the main rebel force for the next four years. In Pará, the movement bridged urban and rural districts, yet its peasant base was as strong as in Maranhão, though there is no evidence that recruitment to the army was a particular or new focus in the Cabanagem. Forced labor had been policy throughout the colonial era (missionaries had to supply workers on a rotation basis and Pombaline policy followed this practice).

In northern provinces generally there was a greater shift towards larger scale enterprises in the late colonial period, which undermined peasant livelihoods. Despite the different economic and social profiles of Maranhão and Pará, their peasantries acted to defend their interests using the new ideologies in circulation. It is also apparent from Assunção's argument that the various rebel groups while employing liberal language were more antioligarchical than lusophobic in particular.

According to Assunção, the Balaiada had two different expressions, one in the east and the other in the south of Maranhão. The eastern part of the province was predominantly a subsistence-oriented region; while in the south more prosperous plantation owners and ranchers were in control. These differences in social structure made for a break between the people who had initially congregated under a single leadership. This rupture also freed the poorer participants from their patron client networks, occasioning the split between élite and popular liberalism. This same development can be seen in Pará at the outbreak in January 1835. The initial phase was marked by a wide alliance between all opposed to the president. Élite liberals took over the administration and elected their own president. When he was killed a few weeks later by former supporters, control of provincial government came under popular control. Very quickly the rebellion spread to the interior and sought to involve lower-class participants from the inside, as it were.

A crucial difference between Maranhão and Pará was the nature of alliances between élites in the interior and the provincial capital. The southern expression of Balaiada was fueled by élites who felt they were being marginalized by those in São Luis. They mobilized support to defend their local interests. By contrast in Pará, bosses upriver of Belém, while fewer in number, had strong links with the capital. The divisions were not between rural and urban but rather ideological, radical, and otherwise. It was precisely the connections between the leaders in different places that allowed the imperial army and navy access to the interior, with personnel to fight against rebels, and knowledge of the environment. Without the alliances between factions of the élite in villages, the capital, and the invading forces, it is unlikely the Cabanagem in the interior would have been defeated as quickly as it was (more than a number of years). It may have run on and on with the occasional explosion, in much the same way Amerindian counter-colonial wars had done in the eighteenth century.

The only other rebellion to take place in the hinterland, involve peasants, and the land they worked is the Cabanada. This insurgency occurred slightly earlier, starting in 1832 and lasting until 1835. It had connections to urban movements in Recife and follows from the revolts of 1817 and 1824. The Cabanada involved alliances between runaway slaves, peasants, Indians, and landlords on the frontier of the provinces of Pernambuco and Alagoas. It started as a barracks revolt that demanded the return of Pedro 1. A group of officers who had been discharged following the abdication of Pedro in 1831 had mobilized a wide cross-section of poor and people from the interior. By the end of 1832 the predominantly urban and military alliance had been crushed but it continued in the countryside where some landowners and peasants retreated and mobilized supporters.

Cabanada rebels also called for the return of Pedro 1. According to Marcus Carvalho, their motivation was not the same as that of the Portuguese conservatives in Recife. Rather, the intention was against the liberal reforms that saw the destruction of peasant livelihoods. They had been evicted from their lands as sugar plantation owners pushed deeper into the interior of the south in search of fertile lands. Previously, peasants had been protected by royal control of public lands. Moreover, the introduction of the justice of the peace in 1827 broke traditional patronage networks. Small holders had to obey the justices and received nothing in return, whereas their traditional patrons had always returned the support clients offered – "clientelism is not a given but a relationship," Carvalho writes.[11] The Jacuipé Indians of the region were also drawn into the conflict. They joined forces with the peasants as they rose up against forced recruitment to fight the rebels. With the growth of the Cabanada, slaves ran away from plantations and became the most faithful of its fighters. The result was a wide, if somewhat fragile, coexistence between different groups under the leadership of Vicente de Paula, the son of a priest. The broad base of the insurgent coalition in Pernambuco was also present in Pará and Maranhão.

Despite surface differences, the Cabanada shares many common features with the Cabanagem. Cacao or sugar planters' search for fertile lands in the interior of each province is evidence of the agricultural intensification that broke durable political and economic arrangements. The fact that rebels in Pernambuco sided with Pedro I has to do with their loss of privileges, not their rejection of liberal values *per se*. We know less about the patronage networks in Pará, but it is likely that similar relations were in place. Like the Jacuipé Indiana, the Mundurucu were drafted to fight for the ruling élite. However, the warrior Indians from Amazonia continued to provide their

11 Marcus Carvalho, "The 'Commander of All Forests' Against the 'Jacobins' of Brazil: The Cabanada, 1832–1835," 3 (AHRC project Rethinking Histories of Resistance in Brazil and Mexico, http://www. llc.manchester.ac.uk/clacs/research/projects/RethinkingHistoriesofResistance/).

services to the imperial army and did not have reason to switch sides. In Pará, Pedro I was generally a hated figure, having been held responsible for the death of 252 soldiers in the hull of the Brig Palhaço. Overall, the rebels from each province did not seek separation from the rest of the nation. Instead, they sought to inject their own values and aspirations into the center ground of political life and thereby ensure their recognition and visibility. Intriguingly, rebels in both provinces dyed their clothes red.

What about the ethnic and class alliances in other regions? The Sabinada revolt began the year before the Balaiada in army barracks. Within hours, mestiço officers and soldiers took charge of the capital and nominated a new president. The initial alliance was between the army and urban intellectuals, including Francisco Sabino Alvares da Rocha Vieira, a journalist and teacher whose name is now used to refer to the revolt. Over time a garrison of armed slaves was created to defend the city from imperial troops. Still, the rebellion never extended to the countryside to include peasants, the peripheral élite, and plantation slaves. The Sabinada featured fewer ethnic alliances than the movements to the north and remained an urban phenomenon. This suggests the stronger presence of élite liberal characteristics in Salvador. The lack of social depth and geographical extension allowed the Sabinada to be repressed relatively quickly. Yet the focus on the nomination of provincial presidents and wanting to break off relations until Pedro II's majority were liberal persuasions present in Pará and Bahia (not Maranhão, for they were never in possession of the capital).

Although the rebellions involved significant participation of slaves, the leaders were also ambivalent about abolition.[12] Many slaves identified with the revolts and sought leaders who would welcome them. In some cases, slaves comprised their own armed groups. In Maranhão, Cosme Bento das Chagas, a freed slave, gathered about two thousand recruits, mostly from runaway communities, to his rebel army. They initially conducted their own war and later formed an alliance with another large rebel camp. The recognition of the racial characteristics of the conflict in all three provinces was of major significance. Ever since independence, slaves had been demanding freedom from their bondage and for the first time, slaves and nonslaves fought side by side, especially in Maranhão and Pará.[13] Nevertheless, the leaders did not countenance ending slavery.

Overall, Assuncão relates that the Balaiada was an intensification of an internal struggle among élites, which marginalized those in the interior (quite different from the Cabanagem but similar to Pernambuco in the early to mid-1830s). The peasantry had their grievance over forced service in

---

12 Hendrik Kraay, "'As Terrifying as Unexpected': The Bahian Sabinada, 1837–1838," *The Hispanic American Historical Review*, 1992, vol. 72, no. 4, 517.
13 Assuncão, 31, 33–34.

the army. This combination of interests took advantage of the weakness of central authority in Rio. Military reforms, according to Kraay, were also at the core of the Sabinada. Officers and people of color who had previously enjoyed serving in the segregated militia could not find an easy transfer to the new National Guard formed in 1831. Earlier, separate regiments existed for whites and people of color. Their amalgamation in 1831 meant that the people of color were excluded and could not use their old commissions since whites did not want to be commanded by nonwhites. Kraay underscores the significant role of the state to influence racial categories through the reforms, bearing similarity with Pará and the Cabanagem's repression and Andréa's labor policies. Discontent with military policies in Pará did not appear to be the significant feature it was in the other provinces, though this needs more research.

Pará was furthest away from the national center of power and least significant economically. Its rebellion lasted the longest, spread widely, installed a provincial government for fifteen months, and had the greatest long-term impact on population levels and economic recuperation. Bahia, the closest of the northern regions to Rio and most important economically, experienced the shortest revolt that made no inroads into the interior. The fact that the racial aspects of each were different reflects the kinds of people in each place rather than fundamentally different dimensions.

I have deliberately omitted from consideration the Farroupilha revolt in the far south on the border with Uruguay and Argentina. Any formal similarity with the northern ones hides the complex and diverse social and economic makeup of Brazil at the time. Rio Grande do Sul may have had about a thirty percent slave population, but according to various accounts they did not play a significant part. Instead, the factionalized and militarized élites who fought among themselves for dominance in regional politics were the instigators. The region had become a predominantly livestock economy and was split between the landowning cattle ranchers of the interior and the meat producers of the coast. The fiscal policies of the central government had caused much disgruntlement among the cattle ranchers, who would lead the uprising. In the end, the provincial president's failure to defend cattle-owning interests led to his deposition and the takeover of the capital Porto Alegre in November 1835. Although the rebels did not remain in control for long, they retreated to the interior and waged war against central government until 1845. The Farroupilha had a significant international dimension, for not only were cattle coming across the border from the south, meat *(charque)* was exported to Uruguay. This complex of economic and political factors was absent in the northern rebellions, as was a section of the élite determined to keep fighting. Furthermore, the ethnic conflict between Portuguese and Brazilian, native and foreigner apparently had no place in Rio Grande do Sul. Nevertheless, all regency rebellions shared the hostility to rule from the center, which brought little benefit to the *patrias* (provincial homelands).

The Cabanagem was the only Brazilian revolt in which the imperial leaders used the ideology of caste or race war. The term comes directly from the wider Latin American context, especially Mexico. The radicalized turn was a complex outcome of the justification for the repression and the effect of radical élites mobilizing the masses through violent means. Yet the written pronouncements from rebels do not contain any evidence that they saw themselves as fighting whites as a single category. Racial hatred was not a significant mobilizing force; lusophobia was never characterized as such. Similarly, Terry Rugeley argues that the caste war in the Yucatan peninsula was not the outcome of a long period of racial antagonism. In the period preceding the war, the most visible political violence was the municipal uprising. These were complex events, revealing "struggles internal to the new and decidedly multiethnic municipalities of independent Mexico."[14] To view these rebellions as preparation for the caste war is misleading. So what was the connection between the violence and the caste war? Like Pará, a variety of motives was in play, including land alienation, labor obligations, tax revenue, and changes in patron-client relations.

The violence in the Yucatan continued to the 1840s, when political identities remained unpolarized around predictable race-like groups. Rather, the uprisings were "in fact a manifestation of crude, embryonic party politics: multiethnic, formed by strands of patron-client relationships that extended from the affluent urban politicians to landless peasants, with innumerable strands of intermediaries connecting the two."[15] These patron client ties became unleashed as peasants lost faith with the mediators and Maya chiefs. In Pará the absenting of the élites and patrons from the rebellion also broke the bonds that had connected the region in chains of alliances. Yet the peasants, organized by a dynamic of local family and long-distance commercial networks, continued their struggle.

As news of the murder of Pará's president in January 1835 and the intended slave revolt in Salvador reached ruling liberals in Rio, a mood change took place. The regent, a priest from São Paulo named Diogo Feijó, had gone from wanting to promote decentralization in the early 1830s to strengthening the new nation in the mid-1830s. That transformation had the revolt in Pará at its core. What made the rebellions in the north so fearful – and different – was the kind of participant. The importance of keeping the nation together was about making sure the right sorts of people were in control in the provinces, and their submission to a renewed central command.

14　Terry Rugeley, "Rural Political Violence and the Origins of the Caste War," *The Americas* 53, no. 4 (1997), 473.
15　Rugeley, "Rural Political Violence," 495.

This book has sought to understand the regional social dynamics of the Cabanagem. Through this picture at the end of the colonial and the beginning of the national eras, the study places the Amazon in the context of Brazilian political history and related peasant movements in Latin America. Far too often the Amazon is, at best, forgotten or at worst excluded from this continental perspective. Its histories and its social complexities are materially and ideologically connected to this wider world. The study of the Cabanagem demands that such linkages be followed and comparisons drawn in common experiences of revolt; if only because the cabano rebels both called into question some connections and intensified others. What was the role of the Cabanagem in the conservative backlash and in the political solution found in the early 1840s? Although I have suggested it figured centrally, this claim requires more research. For in analyzing further the making of the Brazilian Amazon in second half of the nineteenth century the perception of national leaders toward the region will be better known. How these perceptions contribute to a specific kind of understanding of the region as a place apart without history, or at least a particular kind of history that suited the invention of the nation. Other questions arise from this book, including the role of the Church in the fomenting alliances and the formation of élites across urban and rural districts. Still, by rethinking the Cabanagem as a predominantly peasant rebellion amalgamating local interpretations of liberal politics and popular anticolonial histories, this book intends to contribute to the recasting of the history and anthropology of the Brazilian Amazon.

The Cabanagem in the Context of Amazonian Development

The Amazon is a historical place like any other: contested and chaotic.[16] The magnificence of its rivers and the grandeur of its forests – its exotic character – should not distract from the recognition of the social, economic, and political transformations the region has undergone. The people who live there behave much the same as those from very different environments or empires. What, then, is the distinctive historical interest of this place? By offering an answer through the window of a complex transition, the aim has involved establishing the multiple and overlapping contexts within which Pará was made a part of Brazil. I hope I have gone

---

16 This argument echoes David Cleary who writes, in an essay looking at the changing historical visions of the region, "the basic fact [is] that for all its specificity, and uniqueness of its natural environments, the Amazon basin is much like anywhere else in historical terms." David Cleary, "Science and the Representation of Nature in Amazonia: From La Condamine through Da Cunha to Anna Roosevelt," in Ima Vieira, José Maria da Silva, David Oren, Maria Ângela D'Incao (eds), *Diversidade Biológica e Cultural da Amazônia*, Belém: Museu Goeldi, 2001, 293.

some way to investigating how the region in 1835 nearly diverged from the rest of Portuguese-speaking America; and the interests that forced it to converge. The period covered in this study is not just interesting in terms of the rebellion and the jostling for power, but a crux, a historical turning point at which various futures were contemplated. From being a relatively fluid and mobile society, Pará went to a starkly unequal and more controlled one. Nevertheless, Amazonian peasant values would survive and play an important part in provisioning markets with rubber in the second half of the nineteenth century.

The basis of this divergence was a heterogeneous society (arguably one of the most diverse in South America) in which the river and its movements provided the markers for social and commercial life. Pará at the end of the eighteenth century had not developed a well-founded class of plantation owners or oligarchs. The small numbers of the élite, some imported, others local, still considered they were born to rule. Reforms and new legislation had changed only a few aspects of regional existence while others stubbornly remained. For instance, Mendonça Furtado's "Instruction of 1755" that Portuguese be the main language of communication in the villages along the rivers was not to be realized for at least another hundred years.[17] More generally, the imposition of imperial authority on Pará in 1840 was the culmination of official Portuguese policy pursued from the 1750s. The intentions of the Portuguese and Brazilian élites were not quite the same but their effects were: the subordination of a sociologically and historically distinct region to a larger entity paying less attention to local interests. This domestic colonialism has impoverished the development of modern Brazilian Amazonia.

The submission of Pará was a long and cumulative process that started in concerted fashion in 1750 with the arrival of Mendonça Furtado, the marquis of Pombal's brother, and saw the peace declarations of the Mura and the Mundurucu Indians in 1784 and 1795, respectively; the emancipation of village Indians in 1799; the arrival of the royal family in Rio in 1808; Felipe Patroni's talk of adhering to the Portuguese constitutionalist revolution in 1820; Grenfell's overseeing of the death of 252 soldiers in the hull of a prison ship; the abdication of the Portuguese monarch Pedro I; and, perhaps finally, Pedro II's coming of age in 1840. These were just some of the significant events that contributed to the tense inclusion of Pará in Brazil and their associated institutional presences. This gradual assimilation then ran in parallel with the political emancipation of Brazil. One was not possible without the other. In Pará, "Brazilianization" meant marginalizing

---

17 According to my informants from the Lower Amazon, lingua geral was still spoken in the mid-twentieth century. It is now coming back into use in the twenty-first century as communities reclaiming their Indian identity are learning it.

the Indians and their mixed offspring (and the Portuguese). Given the large and central presence of Indians, the importance of their labor, and the persistence of the river-based way of life, this sidelining was always going to be difficult. So the making of the *Brazilian* Amazon was an ongoing process, the subordination of the region never being complete or total. Nevertheless, the people of Pará paid a high price for their political adherence to Brazil. Again, this makes the place as historical as any other: there are continuities and changes, following struggles and conquests.[18]

In other words, some ambiguity remains concerning the identity of the place: hence, the recurring image of the Amazon as almost empty of human society, then as much as now. For example, the great Brazilian writer Euclides da Cunha, despite having traveled widely in the region, wrote in 1909 of the Amazon as a "land without history."[19] It was just not the past he wanted to recognize. Another more recent case of misrecognition is the British government's serious consideration in November 2006 of a proposal to privatize the Amazon in order to reduce global warming. The Secretary of State for the Environment admitted there would be "sovereignty issues involving the government of Brazil," but insisted big problems often required radical plans. Clearly, it is surprise to some that the Amazon has a history and one in which foreign powers played a major role. This view of the Amazon as a global resource and an extraneous society has its origin in the ending of the Cabanagem. The historical slate was wiped clean. Going against all the evidence available, the Amazon was transformed into a region rich in nature, ready to be plundered by outsiders and the people who lived there were made invisible.[20] In effect, the place was turned into "Amazonia."

The particular way in which the Cabanagem was vanquished allowed for a break with a past in which gains had been made by the urban poor and peasants. A practical and ideological shift in social relations had been achieved by the representatives of imperial Brazil. In a sense, the crushing

---

18 One response by the modern élites to this situation is the appropriation of a peasant culture for their own interests. They have promoted a folklorized version of the Amazon's distinctive identity, at once making it unthreatening for wider consumption and exotic enough to retain some fascination. Here I am thinking of tales about the rose-colored dolphin transforming into a handsome man or forest-dwelling monsters such as the *mapinguari*. For analyses of the enchanting beings in Amazonian folklore, see João de Jesus Paes Loureiro, *Cultura Amazônica: Uma Poética do Imaginário*, Belém: Cejup, 1991; Candace Slater, *Dance of the Dolphin: Transformation and Disenchantment in the Amazonian Imagination*, Chicago: Chicago University Press, 1994.

19 Euclides da Cunha, *The Amazon: Land Without History*, Oxford: Oxford University Press, 2006.

20 The Amazon has inevitably come to suffer from these bouts of attention by those who do not always wish it well. The comment from the British Minister is illustrative of the gap between reality and perception. The periodic inclusion in wider debates always misunderstands the socially complex realities and reduces them to an inappropriate level. The problem is compounded by the implementation of development projects that do not derive from an identifiable reality but an imposed prejudice, such as the British Minister's.

of the Cabanagem was a second conquest, some two hundred years after the Portuguese settled in Belém. The creation of the workers' corps was the emblematic expression of peasant exclusion.

Most significantly, the repression changed how racial classifications mapped onto social identities. Originally, racial terminology had developed out of specific terms that refer to a person's parentage and establish his or her legal identity. This knowledge of ancestry was far too specialized for popular usage so, as David Cleary has shown, these terms shifted their everyday meanings during the colonial period "from ancestry to physical appearance."[21] Terms such as *mameluco, cafuz,* and others came to be associated in daily discourse with observable characteristics: high cheek-bones for Indianness, black curly hair for Africanness, and big noses for Portugueseness. The change of racial classification to appearance was intim-idating to the élite, for it questioned their birthright to privilege and status; both were under scrutiny in the early nineteenth century. Andréa's painting of the Cabanagem as a race war was therefore critical to checking the shift as it tried to reach a political conclusion. Even if Andréa and his officers could not eradicate the conflation of race and appearance in popular culture, he could reaffirm the official link between race and class, as he did in setting up the police guards and the workers corps.

The continuities that spread across the colonial and imperial periods were economic and cultural. The peasant way of life consisted of hamlets of kinspeople and close neighbors working on a range of tasks, such as fishing, hunting, raising livestock, collecting forest products, and agriculture. The attachment to a rural dwelling did not preclude spending time in a town, being mobile, or doing military service. The peasantry was composed of Indians, mestiços, freed slaves, and poor whites. Indeed, the economic role and values of this heterogeneous peasantry, to which many numbers have been added, have persisted to the present day. It has been able to adapt to and accommodate new demands in each phase because of its semi-independent existence and ability to exploit a diverse range of freely avail-able resources and environments.

In cultural terms, one enduring feature has been the local adaptation of Catholicism based on the cult of saints. Senhor Raimundo was a "civilized Indian" whom the English naturalist Henry Bates met in 1849. He was married, an esteemed hunter, spoke lingua geral and Portuguese, and lived in a place called Caripí, about 50 miles southwest of Belém. According to Bates, Raimundo "insisted" he was an Indian and had "red skin," but had nothing against the white man, except for his taking land from the Indians without any intention of using it. Raimundo's only wish was to be "left

---

21 David Cleary, "'Lost Altogether to the Civilised World': Race and the Cabanagem in Northern Brazil, 1750 to 1850." *Comparative Studies in Society and History* 40, 1, 1998, 109–135.

alone"; he had been accused of participating in the Cabanagem but denied any involvement. During Bates' mid-January stay with Raimundo, a "religious begging expedition" arrived at the house, playing music and processing with the image of São Tomé (see pages 63–64). The musicians were offered food and hammocks in an outlying open shed. Bates does not say what Raimundo contributed to the expedition apart from hospitality, but he surely would have promised something, perhaps some food for the festival. For the duration of the visit, São Tomé's icon was placed in a small cupboard (*oratório*) next to Raimundo's saint, which was prettily decorated with ribbons, offerings, and candles. Yet before the procession left after breakfast, Raimundo and Bates had already gone to hunt in the forest.[22]

Raimundo and his wife survived the Cabanagem years and continued to speak lingua geral and remain faithful to their saints. São Tomé is significant not just because he is the patron saint of Indians, but because the cult persisted despite its association with the beginning of the rebellion. On the evidence here, and similar encounters, Bates and other scientists relayed in their accounts from the 1840s and 1850s, the lively popular culture emerged from the period relatively unscathed and untransformed. In many ways, Raimundo's presence so close to Belém in 1849 speaks to the small but nontrivial success of the peasant rebellion as a defense of a way of life. As Raimundo said, all he wished was to be unhindered in the pursuit of his life. This same desire was what contributed to slaves and Indians fleeing to their forest refuges, a consistent feature of colonial and imperial Amazonia. The struggle for Amazonia persisted as a body of pragmatic knowledge that allows riverine peasants to survive. The rebellion, which saw both material interest and popular conceptions of liberty and equality come together, had not entirely been defeated. The energies then were not only shaped by everyday experiences of injustice and colonial subjugation, and the revolutionary times. They were directed in important ways by a work ethos, popular culture, religion, family networks, and the central importance of rivers in Amazonian lives.

The comments made by visitors to the region in the 1840s and 1850s serve to illustrate the persistence of a defiant peasant ethos. Bates traveled with his fellow naturalist, Alfred Wallace. Both men were totally reliant on the labor of locals (often those in the workers' corps), not just to move them around and feed them but also to help locate species and give their environmental knowledge. Although the Britons had a humanistic attitude toward their assistants, their patience was constantly tried by the lack of interest locals had in working for money. No amount of cash could persuade some people to work, if they did not want to; if forced by violence, they would escape at

22 Bates, *A Naturalist*, vol. 1, 189–197.

the earliest opportunity.[23] This is a recurring characteristic still observed in the twenty-first century: riverine peasants dislike working for bosses, whatever the level of remuneration. Geographical mobility and an independent spirit are the hard-to-break habits of the riverine-based world.

As well as the achievements of the rebellion, this book has tried to acquaint the reader with the lives of struggle and survival from which the movement grew.[24] How people like Antônio the slave defied the white bosses from Santarém and mocked their religious ceremonies and desired their women; the fugitive from slavery who became a queen of her mocambo; the Indian who said he was "no-one's servant," challenging the authority of a white man to tell him what to do. Or the Mura of the Lower Amazon who accommodated runaways, attacked property, and stole as Robin Hood did to distribute to their poor fellows. These people used their intelligence, passion, courage, and humor to fashion a life. Some creatively sought to make something more of their circumstances instead of passively accepting them. Combined with the thousands of men and women who sought to realize a new society in which they would be justly treated, organize their labor, and choose leaders, we have the story of one of Brazil's greatest rebellions.

23 See, for example, Alfred Russell Wallace, *A Narrative of Travels on the Amazon and Rio Negro with an Account of the Native Tribes and Observations on the Climate, Geology, and Natural History of the Amazon Valley*, London: Reeve, 1853, 160–161. The American naturalist William Edwards who traveled in 1846–1847 in the Amazon wrote: "In the vicinity of Santarém the scarcity of laborers is most severely felt, slaves being few and Indians not only being difficult to catch, but slippery when caught ... Desertion is so common, and so annoying, that it receives no mercy from the authorities." William Edwards, *A Voyage up the River Amazon including a Residence at Pará*, London: John Murray, 1847, 103.

24 I am here alluding to the chapters in David Sweet and Gary Nash's edited collection, *Struggle and Survival in Colonial America*, Berkeley: University of California Press, 1981.

Glossary of Terms in *Portuguese* and <u>English</u>

Aguardente Sugar cane rum, also known as *cachaça*. Though banned as a unit of exchange in the colonial era, its use was widespread.

Aldeia An Indian village controlled by a missionary order or a secular authority.

Alferes Second-lieutenant, standard bearer.

Alqueire Unit of dry measure; regions had different values. In Pará, four quarts was 36.27 liters.

Alvará Royal decree.

Angelim Term for a type of hardwood, like Maparajuba (or massaranduba). Nickname of the most significant leader in the Cabanagem, Eduardo Nogueira.

Arroba Unit of weight equivalent to 32 pounds or 14.75 kilograms.

Auto A written declaration made on oath. There were many types of autos.

Bando Written, public proclamation by an authority.

Barque Sailing vessel with three or more masts: fore and aft rigged on aftermast, square rigged on all others.

Branco Literally, "white person"; as much a term of social status as physical description.

Brigue Brig, two-masted vessel with both masts square rigged.

Cabo de canoa Pilot of a boat, a very important position in the colonial and early imperial periods.

<u>Cacao</u> Sometimes spelled *cocoa*. The seed of a tropical American tree (Theobroma cacao), which is ground into powder for cocoa drink or chocolate.

Cacaul Cacao plantation.

Câmara Municipal council.

Canoa Generic term for a boat that may or may not have had sails and can be large or small in size.

Capitão de mato Individual responsible for the organization of expeditions to fetch escaped slaves. The post was part of a paramilitary troop specialized in the repression of slaves.

Caramuru Conservative party that fought for the return of Pedro 1 to Brazil in the early 1830s.

Carronada Short, front-loading swivel-headed cannon. Designed to fire packed pieces of iron (10 cm in caliber and weighing 2.7 kg) that disperse in the air. The carronada was effective against crowds and in taking out sails of ships at sea.

Carta Régia A royal provision addressed to a person.

Cítio In Brazil, an estate or farmstead; in Portuguese, a place or area (also spelled *sítio*).

Colubrine Long cannon, 30 calibres.

Conto Unit of money worth one thousand mil-reis, 1,000$000.

Côrtes Portuguese congress for elected deputies from the provinces and colonies. It was inactive during the eighteenth century and was revived in 1820 following liberal and constitutionalist demands against absolutism.

Criado Servant or dependent.

Degredado Exiled criminal; a banished person.

Devassa A judicial review or inquiry.

Directorate Legislation governing the administration of Indians in the Brazilian Amazon; also applied to the whole of Brazil from 1758–1798.

Directores Administrators (director) of Indians in the Directorate (*Directório dos Índios*) during the second half of the eighteenth century.

Dízimo A tithe or tax payable to the state, collected on behalf of the Church.

Edital Proclamation, often by a municipal council, informing public of new laws.

Engenho A sugar mill and surrounding plantation.

Escuna Schooner or sailing ship with at least two masts (foremast and mainmast), the mainmast being the taller. The word derives from the term *schoon/scoon*, meaning "to move smoothly and quickly."

Esmeril Small front-loading naval cannon in use during the eighteenth and early nineteenth centuries.

Fazenda A farm normally for livestock raising; the royal or imperial treasury.

Forças dos Brazileiros Reunidos "United Brazilian Forces," the phrase rebels in Lower Amazon used to refer to their movement in the Cabanagem.

Fortaleza A fort, which in Grão Pará was usually a dilapidated guardhouse with a small numbers of soldiers. Sometimes included a prison, *cadeia*.

Gambarra Two-masted cattle barge.

Gentio Literally, *gentile*. Term used to refer to amerindians living outside the colonial world.

Juiz ordinário President of the town council with some powers to judge and sentence in minor cases. No legal training was required. These individuals worked without remuneration for one year.

Juiz de paz Justice of the peace, a new position created by liberal reformers in 1827 to replace the juiz ordinário. Justices were elected by each district.

They dealt with all policing and criminal cases that carried a penalty of less than 100 mil-réis.

Igarité Single- or double-masted vessel of various sizes usually used for transport, with space for rowers on the sides and sometimes strong enough to hold cannon.

Imperial Anything or anybody allied with the administration of the Brazilian empire based in Rio from 1822 onwards. In the documents, *legalistas* is used to indicate those on the side of the empire.

Indians People of amerindian descent and who were rounded up to live in missions or directorate villages. They may or may not have maintained their previous tribal or ethnic identity by various reciprocal ties such as visits and marriages. There was some conflict between Indians with different ethnic affiliations living in colonial villages.

Lavrador Literally, *worker*; also small holders, peasant.

Liberal A person who espoused arguments for constitutional reform, limited monarchy, and equality. The liberal educated elite were divided over a series of issues, such as more regional autonomy, abolition of slavery, and monarchical power. Only in the 1850s was the Liberal Party formed.

Lingua geral Generic Tupi language. Used as the main form of communication from the seventeenth century in the Amazon between Indians, missionaries, and soldiers until the 1750s, but remained current for at least another century.

Mameluco Person of white and amerindian ancestry, considered closer to the white population.

Mocambo Runaway slave community.

Mestiço General term for a person of mixed ancestry.

Memorial Treatise on the conditions of a particular place or facts about a subject.

Montaria Canoe for transport and travel, usually rowed by a handful of people, and in the early nineteenth century adapted for sailing.

Morador Colonist; head of household.

Olária A pottery business that made roof tiles and earthenware. Before 1799 it was under the control of the village director, and after this date it was open to contract awarded by a municipal council.

Pajé Shaman, also called *feiticeiro* (witch doctor) by chroniclers.

Paraense A person from Pará (or Grão Pará to 1823).

Pardo Dark-skinned person, similar to mulatto.

Pelourinho Whipping-post for public punishment in main square, a symbol of royal control, the symbol of a town with a municipal council.

Principal Indian headman in directorate village. Outside of these villages, the term *Tuxáua* is used.

Regatão River trader.

<u>Regency</u> Period of rule between April 1831 and June 1840 when Brazil was ruled by a regent (variously a group of one or three men).

Roça Garden plot of land of subsistence crops.

Sertão Interior, backlands.

Sertanejo Person from the backlands.

Sesmaria A land concession by the Portuguese monarch.

Sesmeiro A holder of a land grant.

Tapuio Polysemic term most often used to refer to detribalized amerindians, who are part of the colonial society. Also meant all nonspeaking Tupi-guarani people in Brazil, such as the Mura. Tupi speakers used the term to refer to their enemies and the people they enslaved. Still used in the Amazon in much the same way as *caboclo*, but is less common.

Termo Municipal district, similarly to *comarca*.

Ubá Dugout canoe.

Várzea Floodplain land.

Vereador Councilor in a câmara.

Key Events

1772   The end of direct control of the Amazon region (Grão-Pará and the Rio Negro) from Lisbon. From this point, the overseas administration of Portuguese America is conducted from Rio de Janeiro.

1784   Peace accord between the Mura and Portuguese Crown.

1791   Slave revolution in San Domingos (Haiti).

1795   Peace accord between the Mundurucu and Maués and the Portuguese Crown.

1799   Francisco de Souza Coutinho, the governor general of the Amazon, terminates the Directorate legislation (the obligation of Indians to work for an export economy). In its place, he creates a new army of light militia. Indians can buy themselves out by earning more than a daily soldier's salary.

1804   Independence of Haiti.

1808   The Portuguese royal family takes up residence in Rio de Janeiro with help of British navy, escaping Junot's invasion of Lisbon.

1808   The invasion of Cayenne by troops from the Amazon in order to prevent French expansionist intentions in the region. Troops remain until 1817. Much traffic of ideas and goods between Pará and Cayenne during this time.

1808   Brazilian ports are opened to vessels of friendly nations to Brazil; Britain leads the trade of imports and exports to the colony.

1815   The end of Napoleonic wars; transatlantic commerce develops. Britain tries to stop slave trafficking from Africa.

1817   Anti-Portuguese uprising in Pernambuco, "the confederation of the Equator."

c. 1819   The establishment of the first British vice-consul in Belém, Henry Dickenson, a trader who sent on goods to Britain. There were at least a handful of other Britons in Pará at the time.

1820   August, liberal rebellion in Porto, Portugal, and call for constitutional monarchy.

1821   January, the Province of Pará declares itself in favor of the O Porto constitutional reforms, the first in Portuguese America.

1821	April 24, the King of Portugal, Dom João VI, departs for his homeland from Brazil after a 13 year absence. He leaves his Portuguese born son Pedro I as prince regent in charge.
1822	March, publication of the first newspaper printed and published in Pará, "*O Paraense.*"
1822	September 7, Pedro I declares Brazil independent from Portugal.
1823	August, Pará adheres to Brazil's independence, forced by British mercenaries, and is the last province to become part of the new Empire.
1823	October 21, death by suffocation of 252 anti-Portuguese soldiers in the hull of the Brig Palhaço, a prison ship moored just outside Belém.
1823	November, radical liberal takeover of Cametá and subsequent bombardment of the town by Imperial forces.
1824	Violent liberal uprisings around Santarém. Alenquer and Monte Alegre accompanied by Portuguese reaction against Independence.
1826	Further violent takeover of council in Cametá.
1827	Establishment of the justice of peace by liberal reformers wishing to distribute centralized powers to local districts.
1831	Pedro I abdicates and leaves for Portugal, and Pedro II, his 5-year-old Brazilian born, son stays behind as emperor in waiting; a regency government is created.
1831	August 7, loyal Portuguese soldiers depose the nominated President of Pará, the Viscount of Goiana, and elected vice-president, João Gonçalves Batista Campos. The soldiers ransack the city of Belém. Batista Campos sent into exile in the interior of Pará but escapes and rallies support in Santarém region.
1831	August, the establishment of the National Guard, which in Pará, unlike the rest of Brazil came to be dominated by Portuguese loyalists.
1832	February, Batista Campos is declared legitimate vice president of the province by the council chambers of towns in the Lower Amazon.
1832	June, uprising in Manaus by radical liberal soldiers, burning of council buildings and loss of the official records.
1833	April 16, Portuguese attacks in Belém resulting in 90 deaths of liberal opponents.
1833	May, return of some towns in the Amazon to native – mission – names. Santarém become Tapajós and Óbidos, Pauxis.
1834	Introduction of new paper currency following circulation of false copper coinage and high inflation.
1834	Last shipment of slaves from Africa arrives in Belém, the slave trade across the Atlantic was abolished by the British.

1834	May, retreat of radical liberals to Acará region (near Belém), where many have land and homes. Plan is hatched to overthrow the president on September 7 independence day.
1834	October, attack on Malcher's farm on Acará River by government forces, houses smashed up, Felix Clemente Malcher arrested, Batista Campos escapes, only to die from an infected wound in December.
1835	January 7, storming of Belém by about 65 rebels, murder of president Lobo de Souza, and his vice president and British mercenary. Malcher released from prison and nominated president and Francisco Pedro Vinagre his vice president.
1835	May 12, failed Imperial troops' attack on Belém led by nominated vice-president Angelo Custodio Côrrea.
1835	June, Francisco Pedro Vinagre, having persuaded his followers to lay down their arms, allows newly nominated president from Rio into the city, Manuel Rodrigues, to take up position.
1835	July, Vinagre arrested and during August Belém experiences nine days of very heavy fighting. Imperial forces retreat to the boats and the declaration of Eduardo Nogueira "Angelim" as president.
1835	October, the murder of all but one of the crew of the British schooner Clio. Its shipment of guns and other products are distributed amongst local families in the vicinity of Salinas.
1836	March, most towns of the interior of Pará declare themselves loyal to the presidency of Angelim. The military encampment at Ecuipiranga is established near Santarém consisting of about 2000 people.
1836	May, Angelim abandons Belém, leaving some soldiers to defend the place, but the forces of General Andréa retake city on May 13.
1836	May 13, legal troops establish control of Belém, and General Soares Andréa is installed as president, whose first act is to lift the constitutional rights of individuals and impose martial law.
1836	September, repression moves up river toward Santarém. Arrest of Angelim and his deportation to the South of Brazil.
1836	October, Imperial troops retake Santarém.
1837	March, failed attack on Santarém by rebels.
1837	July, Imperial troops successfully destroy the fort at Ecuipiranga. Rebels disperse and regroup around Maués.
1838	Creation by General Andréa of the "*Corpos dos trabalhadores*" (workers' corps), forced conscription for all people who are without property.
1839	Bernardo de Souza Franco, a liberal Paraense lawyer, is nominated president of Pará and more reconciliatory stance is adopted toward rebels.
1839	November, amnesty for those in prison awaiting trail.
1840	June, full amnesty for all rebels. Pedro II, at 14 years old, becomes the Emperor of Brazil.

List of Significant People

ANDRÉA, Francisco Jozé de Souza Soares de. A general in the Brazilian army, sympathetic to independence. His mother was Portuguese; his father, Brazilian. He came to Brazil with the royal family fleeing Napoleon's troops as they approached Lisbon in 1807. When he was asked to go to Pará to suppress the Cabanagem, he was in semiretirement due to the amount of complaints and accusations leveled against his military conduct. As president of Grão Pará from May 1836, he suspended the constitution and imposed martial law in order to repress the rebels. He thought there was a "birth pact" among all "people of color" to kill whites in the Amazon.

ANGELIM, Eduardo Nogueira. The third and most important rebel president of Pará (August 1835 to May 1836 when he was barely twenty years old). He was a friend of Batista Campos and came from humble origins in Ceará; his parents migrated to Pará when he was young. He negotiated with the British navy over the future of Pará and secured the safety of Alexander Paton. Angelim is a nickname, meaning a type of tree of extremely hard wood with a mottled yellow and brown complexion, used principally for furniture.

AYRES, Ambrosio Pedro. He was nicknamed *Bararoa*, an infamous mercenary and repressor of rebels in the Lower and Upper Amazon, 1835–1838. His origins are obscure: some said he was German and others said he was an exile from the northeast of Brazil, escaping a crime. He was eventually seized by rebels and horribly executed.

BAENA, Antônio Ladislau Monteiro. Portuguese military officer who came to Pará in 1803 and although he did not support Brazilian independence he remained in the region until his death in 1850. He also signed the first rebel proclamation in January 1835 when Malcher was made president. His lasting contribution is his scholarly work on the history and culture of the region: *The Compendium of the Eras of Pará, 1615–1823* (written in 1830, published in 1838) and *A Chorographical Essay on the Province of Pará* (written in 1833, published in 1839).

BATES, Henry Walter. Naturalist born in Leicester who spent 12 years in the Amazon, traveling along the main rivers. Spoke a little lingua geral and authored arguably the best English-language chronicle on the Amazon.

BATISTA CAMPOS, João Gonçalves. Paraense Brazilian, priest, and owner of a sugar mill with slaves. He was born in Belém in 1782 and died, escaping arrest, on the eve of the Cabanagem rebellion in December 1834 (apparently not under suspicious circumstances). The single most important and most influential liberal figure in the period from 1820 to 1835, imprisoned frequently and well connected to liberals elsewhere in Brazil. His great strength was oratory but he also edited anti-Portuguese newspapers. There is some debate whether he was little more than a self-interested politician who stirred the radical sympathies of his supporters to achieve his aim of being president of Pará.

BERNARDO DE SOUZA, Francisco. Pernambucan Brazilian, in exile for murder; a freed slave and soldier who led the takeover of Manaus in 1836. Shot dead in subsequent fighting.

CORDOVIL, João Pedro. Brazilian military officer, probably from São Paulo, who occupied land near the present-day town of Parintins first in the late 1790s. With a missionary, resettled thousands of Mundurucu and Maués Indians in the early nineteenth century along the Amazon river near Parintins, and created an Indian army that was instrumental in campaigns recovering escaped slaves and against rebels in the 1820–1840 period.

COUTINHO, Francisco de Souza. Governor of Pará (1790–1803) and, like Mendonça Furtado, a great reformer and well connected through his siblings' positions (Rodrigo and Domingos de Souza Coutinho). He ended the Directorate legislation in 1799, partly blaming the white village administrators for stealing the produce of Indians in their care.

FERNANDES DE SOUZA, André. Liberal priest who worked in the Lower and Upper Amazon and Rio Negro in the early nineteenth century. His report on the Indians of the region written for Pedro 1 offers a damning picture of whites' abuse of Indians as well as some important ethnographic content.

FLORENCE, Hercule. French-born artist who was part of the Langsdorff expedition (1825–1829). The only person to travel down the Tapajós River in 1828, leaving some attractive and accurate watercolors and drawings of Indians and colonial life, as well as a diary first published in French in 1875.

FRUCTUOSO, Joaquim. Mundurucu chief who lent support to Imperial army during Cabanagem.

GRENFELL, John Pascoe. British mercenary and Cochrane's deputy during independence. He oversaw the suffocation and death of 252 prisoners in a prison hull in 1823.

HENRIQUE MATTOS, João. Born in Barcellos on the Negro river, the grandson of Henrique João Wilckens, and commissioned military officer. Mattos was active in the repression of rebels in the Lower Amazon.

HISLOP, John. Scottish trader based in Santarém and Óbidos from about 1820 to 1855.

KIDDER, Daniel. A Methodist missionary to Brazil; visited Belém in 1838 and provided a short history of the long-term abuse of Indians and their subsequent rebellion.

MALCHER, Felix Clemente. Born in Monte Alegre, Pará, and lived near Belém, was elected to the government in 1823 and nominated as the first rebel president in January 1835. A few weeks later, he was murdered by an opposing faction of rebels.

MAPARAJUBÁ, Miguel Apolinário. Paraense Brazilian, probably from Santarém, rebel leader in Lower and Upper Amazon, shot dead in Manaus in mid-1836. He was said to have read the Bible avidly and imposed strict discipline on his soldiers. Maparajubá is a nickname, and is a tree of extremely hard, reddish wood used in the construction of boats and houses.

MARCELINO DE SOUZA, Diniz. Paraense Brazilian and commissioned officer; a rebel leader until September 1836, when he was persuaded to fight for the loyalists. He was killed in the final attach of Ecuipiranga in July 1837.

MARTIUS, Karl. Bavarian scientist and historian. Following the marriage of Leopoldina to Pedro I, King Maximilian of Bavaria sent Martius and Spix to Brazil to investigate natural history and the people of the country. They wrote a three-volume scientific narrative on Brazil, the third volume of which stands as the first liberal humanist account of the Amazon with sympathetic studies of the Mundurucu Indians and histories of the exploration of the rivers. Martius also wrote a prize-winning essay in 1838 on the anthropology of Brazil, which founded the idea of the country being composed of Portuguese, Amerindians, and African traditions.

MAW, Henry Lister. British naval officer whose sword was taken from him at Santarém in 1828, causing a diplomatic ruckus.

MENDONÇA FURTADO, Francisco Xavier. Governor of Grão Pará (1752–1759). Drafted a series of new legislation for the region, including the secularization of mission villages, the outlawing of prejudice against Indians, and the establishment of a new state-run company to monopolize trade. He spent a number of years traveling in the Amazon and lived for about a year in Barcellos on the Negro River as part of the boundary commission. He was born in Portugal and the younger brother of Sebastião Carvalho de Mello, Pombal.

PATON, Alexander. Scottish crew member of the gun-carrying Clio schooner in 1835. While his fellow crewmen were being massacred, he escaped with another man. Paton managed to survive a terrible few weeks on the run until he was too ill to continue; his partner drowned while crossing a creek. Paton was eventually delivered to the British navy and wrote a remarkable account of his adventures with the help of the parish vicar in his native Montrose.

PATRONI, Felipe. Paraense educated at Coimbra, where he was influenced by liberal ideas. He introduced the first printing press in 1822 and edited the first newspaper printer in Pará, *O Paraense*. He did not seek political office.

QUEIROZ, João de São José. Benedictine friar who served as bishop of Pará in the early 1760s before a scandal forced him to resign. The chronicles of his two long pastoral visits are among the most learned and astutely observed pieces on late colonial Pará.

RAIOL, Domingos Antônio. Paraense Brazilian born in Vigia in 1830 and died in 1912. After his father was killed by rebels in 1835, Raiol went on to write a history of the political uprisings of 1820 to 1835 in and around Belém, which retains its freshness and insights in the period to this day. Was a liberal monarchist in political temperament and served as provincial presidents in Ceará and Alagoas.

RODRIGUES DE SOUZA, Joaquim. Paraense Brazilian and judge in Santarém in 1835–1836, accused of arbitrary implementation of the law and despotism and hounded out by rebels and liberals.

RODRIGUES FERREIRA, Alexandre. Born in Salvador, Brazil in 1756, trained in natural history at Coimbra University, Portugal. In 1783, despite many misfortunes, he led the first scientific expedition to the Amazon, which lasted until 1792. Ferreira's writings and the watercolors produced by the expedition's artists are an extraordinarily rich source of ethnographic information.

SANCHES DE BRITO, Antônio Manoel. Paraense Brazilian, missionary in Juruti with Mundurucu Indians in 1820s and early 1830s, then justice of the peace in Faro and Óbidos. Unofficial leader of the destruction of Ecuipiranga.

SANCHES DE BRITO, Raimundo. Paraense Brazilian, Indian director in the Lower Amazon in the 1790s, priest in Óbidos from 1820 to 1850s. Brother of Antônio Manoel.

SPIX, Johann. Bavarian scientist who traveled with Martius in the Amazon 1818–1820. His early death prevented him from making as full a contribution as his partner.

TAYLOR, John. British mercenary with the Brazilian navy during the Cabanagem.

VINAGRE, Francisco Pedro. Second rebel president of Pará from February to June 1835. Like Angelim, he came from humble origins and lived near Belém.

References

Archives and Manuscript Collections

AHI   Arquivo Histórico do Itamaraty, Rio de Janeiro
        Arquivo Particular do Barão do Rio Branco
AHU   Arquivo Histórico Ultramarino, Lisbon
        Documentos Manuscritos Avulsos da Capitania do Pará
APEP   Arquivo Público do Estado do Pará, Belém
        Fundo: Catálogo das Sesmarias
        Fundo: Documentação Judiciário
        Fundo: Secretaria da Capitania do Grão Pará, (1616–1823) SCGP
        Fundo: Secretaria da Presidência da Província, SPP (Documentação do Governo 1824–1965)
APOEP   Arquivo de Prelazia de Óbidos, Estado do Pará
        Livro de Baptismos 1805–1816
        Livro de Baptismos 1816–1830
        Livro de Baptismos 1830–1838
APSEP   Arquivo de Prelazia de Santarém, Estado do Pará
        Livro de Termos de Casamentos da Freguesia de Santarém 1764–1798
BIHGB   Biblioteca do Instituto Histórico e Geográphico Brasileiro, Rio de Janeiro
        Coleção Alencar Araripe
        Coleção General Andréa
        Coleção Manuel Barata
BL   British Library
BNRJ   Biblioteca Nacional, Rio de Janeiro
        Fundo Cabanagem: Revolta de Vinagre
NAL   National Archives, London
        FO 13, Foreign Office: Political and Other Departments: General Correspondence before 1906, Brazil
        FO 128, Foreign Office: Embassy and Consulates, Brazil: General Correspondence, 1821–1956

Published Documents

Adonias, Isa. *A Cartografia da Região Amazônica; Catálogo Descriptivo, 1500–1961*. Rio de Janeiro: Conselho Nacional de Pesquisas, Instituto Nacional de Pesquisas da Amazônia, 1963.

Alves Filho, Ivan. *Brasil: 500 Anos em Documentos*. Rio de Janeiro: Mauad Editora, 1999.

Amaral Lapa, José Roberto. ed. *Livro da Visitação do Santo Ofício da Inquisição ao Estado do Grão Pará (1763–1769)*. Petrópolis: Vozes, 1978.

Andrada e Silva, José Bonifácio de. *Projetos para o Brasil.* Edited by Miriam Dolmikoff. São Paulo: Companhia das Letras, 1998.

Barata, Francisco José Rodrigues. "Diário da Viagem que fez à Colônia Holandesa de Surinam, feito pelo Porta Bandeira da Sétima Companhia do Regimento da Cidade do Pará, pelos Sertões e rios deste Estado em Diligência do Real Serviço," RIHGB, 8, 1–53, 1846.

Bettendorff, João Felipe. *Crônica dos Padres da Companhia de Jesus no Estado do Maranhão.* Belém: Cejup, 1990.

Biblioteca e Archivo Público do Pará. "Catálogo Nominal dos Posseiros de Sesmarias," 1904, *ABAPP*, 3, 5–149.

Castello-Branco, Camillo, ed. *Memórias de Fr. João de São José Queiroz (Bispo do Pará).* Porto: Typographia da Livraria Nacional, 1868.

Cleary, David, ed. *Cabanagem: Documentos Ingleses.* Belém: SECULT, Impresa Oficial do Estado, 2003.

Coelho, Jerônimo Francisco. *Falla Dirigida pelo Exmo Snr Conselheiro Jeronimo Francisco Coelho, presidente da Província do Gram-Pará, á Assembléa Legislativa Provincial na Abertura da Sessão Ordinaria da Sexta Legislatura no dia 1 de Outubro de 1848,* Pará:Typ. de Santos & filhos, 1848.

Feijó, Diogo Antônio. *Diogo Antônio Feijó.* Edited by Jorge Caldeira. São Paulo: Editora 34, 1999.

Franco, Bernardo de Souza, *Discurso recitado pelo Exmo Snr Doutor Bernardo de Souza Franco, Prezidente da Provincia do Pará quando abrio a Assemblea Legislativa Provincial no dia 15 de agosto de 1839.* Pará: Impresso na Typographia Restaurada de Santos & Santos menor, 1839.

Inglês, José de Brito. "Memória Sobre a Capitania do Pará," *RIHGB*, 203, 109–154. 1949.

Leal, Felippe, José Pereira. "Memoria Sobre os Acontecimentos Políticos que Tiveram Lugar no Pará 1822–1823," *RIHGB*, 22, 161–200, 1859.

Mattos, João Henrique de "Relatório do Estado da Decadência em que se acha o Alto Amazonas," *RIHGB*, 325, 143–180, 1979 [1845].

Mendonça, Marcos Carneiro. *A Amazônia na era Pombalina: Correspondência Inédita do Governador e Captião-General do Estado do Grão-Pará e Maranhão Francisco Xavier de Mendonça Furtado.* 3 vols. Rio de Janeiro, IHGB, 1963.

Miranda, João Antônio de. *Discurso Recitado pelo Exmo Snr Doutor João Antônio de Miranda, Prezidente da Província do Pará, na Abertura da Assembléia Legislativa Provincial no dia 15 de Agosto de 1840,* Pará: Impresso na Typographia Restaurada de Santos & Santos menor, 1840.

Oliveira, Adélia Engrácia de, ed. *Autos de Devassa Contra os Índios Mura do Rio Madeira e Nações do Rio Tocantins (1738–9).* Manaus: Fundacão Universidade do Amazonas, 1986.

Prazeres, Frei Francisco de Nossa Senhora dos. "Poranduba Maranhense, ou Relação Histórica da Província do Maranhão," *RIHGB*, 54, 185–277, 1891 [1820].

Queirós, João de São José, "Viagem e Visita do Sertão em o Bispado do Gram Pará em 1762 e 1763," *RIHGB*, 9, 43–107, 179–237, 328–375, and 476–527, 1847.

Ramos, Luis de Oliveira, ed. *Diários das Visitas Pastorais no Pará de Caetano Brandão.* Porto: Universidade do Porto, 1991.

Rosário, Manuel da Penha do. "Lingua Vulgar versus Lingua Portuguesa: A Defesa do Padre Manuel da Penha do Rosário Contra a Imposição da Língua Portuguesa aos índios por Meio de Missionários e Párocos," *ABNRJ* 111, 7–62, 1993 [1773].

Soares d'Andréa, Francisco Jozé de Souza. *Falla com que o Exmo Marechal Francisco Jozé de Souza Soares d'Andréa, Prezidente e Commandante das Armas da Província do Pará encerrou a primeira sessão da Assembléia Legislativa da mesma Província no dia 15 de Maio de 1838.* Pará: Impresso na Typographia Restaurada de Santos & Santos menor, 1838.

Instrucçoens Geraes para os Commandantes Militares da Província do Pará, Palácio do Governo do Pará, 04 de abril de 1837. Pará: Impresso na Typographia Restaurada de Santos & Santos menor, 1837.

Discurso com que o Presidente da Província do Pará fez a Abertura do 1a sessão da Assembleia Provincial no dia 2 de Março de 1838. Pará: Impresso na Typographia Restaurada de Santos & Santos menor, 1838.

Souza, André Fernandes de. "Notícias Geográphicas da Capitania do Rio Negro no Grande Rio Amazonas." *RIHGB* 10 (1848): 411–503.

Vergolino-Henry, Anaiza, and Napoleão Figueiredo, eds. *A Presença Africana na Amazônia Colonial: Uma Notícia Histórica.* Belém: Falangola Editora, 1990.

Wilckens, Henrique José. "Muhuraida ou o Triunfo da Fé–1785." *ABNRJ* 109, 79–165, 1989.

Secondary Sources

Abreu, Capistrano de. *Chapters of Brazilian History.* Oxford: Oxford University Press, 1997.

Abreu, Marta. "Popular Culture, Power Relations and Urban Discipline: The Festival of the Holy Spirit in Nineteenth Century Rio de Janeiro." *Bulletin of Latin American Research* 24, no. 2 (2005): 167–180.

Accioli de Cerqueira e Silva, Ignacio. *Corográfia Paraense, ou Descripção Física, Histórica, e Política, da Província do Gram-Pará.* Bahia, 1833.

Acevedo, João Lúcio d'. *Os Jesuitas no Grão Pará: Suas Missões e Colonização.* Belém: Secult, 1991 [1901].

Adalbert, Prince Henry W. *Travels in the South of Europe and in Brazil with a Voyage up the Amazon and the Xingu.* London: 1849.

Alden, Dauril. "Economic Aspects of the Expulsion of the Jesuits from Brazil: A Preliminary Report." In Henry Keith and S. F. Edwards (eds.), *Conflict and Continuity in Brazilian Society.* Columbia: University of South Carolina Press, 1969.

——— "The Significance of Cacao Production in the Amazon Region During the Late Colonial Period: An Essay in Comparative Economic History." *Proceedings of the American Philosophical Society* 120, no. 2 (1976): 103–135.

——— "Late Colonial Brazil, 1750–1808: Demographic, Economic and Political Aspects." In Leslie Bethell (ed.), *Colonial Brazil.* Cambridge: Cambridge University Press, 1991.

Almeida, Rita Heloísa de. *O Diretório dos Índios: Um Projeto de "Civilização" no Brasil do Século XVIII.* Brasília: Editora Universidade de Brasília, 1997.

Amoroso, Marta. "Corsários no Caminho Fluvial: Os Mura do Rio Madeira." In Manuela Carneiro da Cunha (ed.), *História dos Índios do Brasil.* São Paulo: Companhia das Letras, 1992.

——— "The Portrayal of Indians in the Colonial Epic." In Bernard MacQuirk and Solange Ribeiro de Oliveira (eds.), *Brazil and the Discovery of America: Narrative, History, Fiction, 1492–1992,* 113–124. Lewiston: Edward Mellon Press, 1996.

——— and Nadia Farage, eds. *Relatos da Fronteira Amazônica no Século XVIII. Documentos de Henrique João Wilckens e Alexandre Rodrigues Ferreira.* São Paulo: NHII/USP, FAPESP, 1994.

Anderson, Robin. "Following Curupira: Colonization and Migration in Pará 1758–1930 as a Study in Settlement of the Humid Tropics." Ph.D. dissertation, California, 1976.

——— "The Caboclo as Revolutionary." In Eugene Parker (ed.), *The Amazon Caboclo: Historical and Contemporary Perspectives, Studies in Third World Societies,* 32 (1985): 51–87.

Andréa, José. *O Marechal Andreia nos Relevos da História do Brasil.* Rio de Janeiro: Biblioteca do Exercito, 1977.

Appadurai, Arjun. "Disjuncture and Difference in the Global Cultural Economy." In Michael Featherstone (ed.), *Global Culture: Nationalism, Globalization and Modernity.* London: Sage, 1990.

Araujó e Amazonas, Lourenço de. *Dicionário Topográfico, Histórico, Descritivo da Comarca do Alto-Amazonas*. Recife: Typografia Comercial de Meira Henriques, 1852.

Armitage, John. *The History of Brazil*. London; 1836.

Assunção, Matthias Röhrig. *A Guerra dos Bem-te-vis, a Balaiada na Memória Oral*. São Luís: SIOGE, 1988.

"Élite Politics and Popular Rebellion in the Construction of Post-Colonial Order: The Case of Maranhão, Brazil, 1820–1841." *Journal of Latin American Studies* 31, no. 1 (1999): 1–38.

"Cabanos contra os Bem-te-vis." In Mary Del Priore and Flávio dos Santos Gomes (eds.), *Os Senhores dos Rios: Amazônia, Margens e Histórias*. Rio de Janeiro: Elsevier, 2003.

Baena, Antônio Ladislau Monteiro. *Compêndio das Eras do Pará*. Belém: Universidade Federal do Pará, 1969 [1838].

Ensaio Corographico Sobre a Província do Pará. Brasilia: Senado Federal, 2004 [1839].

Barata, Manoel Cardoso. *Formação Histórica do Pará*. Belém: Universidade Federal do Pará, 1973 [1915].

Barata, Mario. *Poder e Independência no Grão-Pará*. Belém: Conselho Estadual da Cultura, 1975.

Barman, Roderick. *Brazil: The Forging of a Nation, 1798–1852*. Stanford: Stanford University Press, 1988.

Barros, Maria Cândida, and Antônio Luis Salim Lessa. "Um Dicionário Tupi de 1771 como Crônica da Situação Linguística na Amazônia Pombalina." *Anais do Seminário Landi e o Século XVIII na Amazônia* (2003). http://www.filologia.org.br/soletras/8sup/4.htm

Bates, Henry Walter. *The Naturalist on the River Amazons*, 2 vols. London: John Murray, 1863. *The Naturalist on the River Amazons*. Vol. abridged. London: Everyman, 1969.

Bernardes, Dênis de Antônio Mendonça. "Pernambuco e sua Área de Influência: Um Território em Transformação (1780–1824)." In Istvan Janscó (ed.), *Independência: História e Historiografia*. São Paulo: Hucitec, 2005.

Bernardino de Souza, Francisco de. *Lembranças e Curiosidades do Valle do Amazonas*. Pará: Typ. do Futuro, 1873.

Commissão do Madeira, Pará e Amazonas, Rio de Janeiro: Typographia Nacional, 1874–1875.

Bethell, Leslie. *The Abolition of the Brazilian Slave Trade: Britain, Brazil and the Slave Question 1807–1869*. Cambridge: Cambridge University Press, 1970.

and José Murilo de Carvalho. "Brazil from Independence to the Mid-Nineteenth Century." In Leslie Bethell (ed.), *The Cambridge History of Latin America*. Cambridge: Cambridge University Press, 1985.

"1822–1850." In Leslie Bethell (ed.), *Brazil: Empire and Republic, 1822–1930*. Cambridge: Cambridge University Press, 1989.

Bezerra Neto, José Maia. *Escravidão Negra no Grão Pará*. Belém: Editora Paka-Tatu, 2000.

and Décio Guzmán, eds. *Terra Matura: Historiografia e História Social na Amazônia*. Belém: Editora Paka-Tatu, 2002.

Boehrer, George. "Variant Versions of José Bonifácio's "Plan for the Civilization of the Brazilian Indians." *The Americas* 14, no. 3 (1958): 301–312.

Boiteaux, Lucas Alexandre. *A Marinha Imperial versus a Cabanagem*. Rio de Janeiro: Imprensa Naval, 1943.

Botelho, Angela Vianna and Liana Maria Reis. *Dicionário Histórico Brasil: Colônia e Império*. Belo Horizonte: Autêntica Editora, 2003.

Bouysse-Cassagne, Thérèse. "In Praise of Bastards: The Uncertainties of Mestizo Identity in the Sixteenth and Seventeenth Century Andes." In Olivia Harris (ed.), *Inside and Outside the Law*. London: Routledge, 1996.

Boxer, Charles. *The Golden Age of Brazil, 1695–1750: Growing Pains of a Colonial Society*. Berkeley: University of California Press, 1962.

Portuguese Society in the Tropics: The Municipal Councils of Goa, Macao, Bahia, and Luanda, 1510–1800. Madison: University of Wisconsin, 1965.

Brown, Barrington and William Lidstone. *Fifteen Thousand Miles on the Amazon and its Tributaries*. London: Edward Stanford, 1878.

Burns, Bradford E. *Nationalism in Brazil: A Historical Survey*. New York: Praeger, 1968.

Cabral, João de Pina and Susana Matos Viegas, eds. "Outros Nomes, Histórias Cruzados: Os Nomes de Pessoa em Português," *Etnográfica*, 12, 1, 2008.

Cardoso, Ciro Flammarion. *Economia e Sociedade em Áreas Coloniais Periféricas: Guiana Francesa e Pará (1750–1817)*. Rio de Janeiro: Graal, 1984.

Cardoso, Fernando Henrique, ed. *O Brasil Monárquico, Dispersão e Unidade.*. Vol. 4. Rio de Janeiro: Bertrand Brasil, 2004.

Carelli, Mario. *Les Carnets du Naturaliste Hercule Florence*. Paris: Gallimard, 1992.

Carneiro da Cunha, Manuela, ed. *História dos Índios do Brasil*. São Paulo: Companhia das Letras, 1992.

and Eduardo Viveiros de Castro, eds. *Amazônia: Etnologia and História Indígena*. São Paulo: FAPESP, 1993.

Carvalho, Marcus. "O Outro Lado da Independência: Quilombos, Negros, Pardos em Pernambuco, (Brasil) 1817–1823." *Luso-Brazilian Review* 43, no. 1 (2006): 1–30.

"The 'Commander of All Forests' against the 'Jacobins' of Brazil: The Cabanada, 1832–1835." In *Rethinking Histories of Resistance in Brazil and Mexico (AHRC project)*. Manchester, UK, 2008. http://www.llc.manchester.ac.uk/clacs/research/projects/RethinkingHistoriesofResistance.html

Charlet, Ronaldo Braga. "Construção da Hierarquia Militar no Pará: Contestações e Negociações dentro da Ordem, 1808–1822." Master's thesis, Federal University of Pará, 2000.

Chasteen, John. "Cautionary Tale: A Radical Priest, Nativist Agitation, and the Origin of Brazilian Civil Wars." In Rebecca Earle (ed.), *Rumours of Wars: Civil Conflict in Nineteenth-Century Latin America*. London: Institute of Latin American Studies, 2000.

Chiavenato, José Júlio. *Cabanagem: O Povo no Poder*. São Paulo: Brasiliense, 1984.

Cleary, David. "'Lost Altogether to the Civilised World': Race and the Cabanagem in Northern Brazil, 1750 to 1850." *Comparative Studies in Society and History* 40, no. 1 (1998): 109–135.

"Science and the Representation of Nature in Amazonia: From La Condamine through da Cunha to Anna Roosevelt'," in Ima Célia Guimarães Vieira, José Maria Cardoso da Silva, David Conway Oren, Maria Ângela D'Incao (eds.), *Diversidade Biológica e Cultural da Amazônia*. Belém: Museu Goeldi, 2001.

Clough, R. Stewart. *The Amazons: A Diary of Twelve Months Journey on a Mission of Inquiry up the River Amazon for the South American Missionary Society*. London, 1879.

Coatsworth, John. "Patterns of Rural Rebellion in Latin America: Mexico in Comparative Perspective." In Friederich Katz (ed.), *Riot, Rebellion and Revolution: Rural Social Conflict in Mexico*. Princeton: Princeton University Press, 1988.

Cochrane, Thomas. *The Autobiography of a Seaman*. 2 vols. London: Constable, 1996.

Coelho, Geraldo Mártires. *Anarquistas, Demagogos e Dissidentes: A Imprensa Liberal no Pará de 1822*. Belém: CEJUP, 1993.

Uma Crônica do Marivilhoso: Legenda, Tempo e Memória no Culto da Virgem de Nazaré. Belém: Imprensa Oficial do Estado, 1998.

Cointe, Paul Le. *L'Amazonie Brésilienne*. 2 vols. Paris: Editeur Augustin Challamel, 1922.

"As Pedras Verdes das Amazonas." *Revista do Instituto Histórico e Geográphico do Pará* 7 (1932): 170–172.

Collingwood, Robin George. *The Idea of History*. Oxford: Oxford University Press, 1994.

Corrêa, Antônio Eutalio. *A Fragata Leopoldina e a Missão Grenfell no Pará*. Belém: UNAMAZ, 2003.

Costa, Emilia Viotti da. *The Brazilian Empire: Myths and Histories*. Chapel Hill: University of North Carolina Press, 2000.

Cruz, Ernesto. *História do Pará*. 2 vols. Belém: Editora da Universidade Federal do Pará, 1963.

Cunha, Antônia Geraldo da. *Dicionário Histórico das Palavras Portugueses de Origem Tupi*. São Paulo: Melhoramentos, 1999.

Cunha, Euclides da. *Rebellion in the Backlands*. Chicago: Chicago University Press, 1944.

The Amazon: Land without History. Oxford: Oxford University Press, 2006.

Daniel, João. *O Tesouro Descoberto no Máximo Rio Amazonas*. 2 vols. Rio de Janeiro: Editora Contrapunto, 2003.

Davidson, David Michael. "Rivers and Empire: The Madeira Route and the Incorporation of the Brazilian Far West, 1737–1808." Ph.D. dissertation, Yale University, 1970.

"How the Brazilian West was won: Freelance and State on the Mato Grosso Frontier." In Dauril Alden (ed.), *Colonial Roots of Modern Brazil*. Berkeley: University of California, 1973.

Dean, Warren. *Brazil and the Struggle for Rubber: A Study in Environmental History*. Cambridge: Cambridge University Press, 1987.

Delson, Roberta Marx. "Inland Navigation in Colonial Brazil: Using Canoes on the Amazon." *The International Journal of Maritime History* 7, no. 1 (1995): 1–28.

"The Beginnings of Professionalization in the Brazilian Military: The Eighteenth Century Corps of Engineers." *The Americas* 51, no. 4 (1995): 555–574.

Dias, Manuel Nunes. *Fomento e Mercantilismo: A Companhia Geral do Grão Para e Maranhao (1755–1778)*. 2 vols. Belém: Universidade Federal do Pará, 1970.

Domingues, Ângela Maria Vieira. "A Educação dos Meninos Índios do Norte do Brasil na Segunda Metade do Século XVIII." In Maria Beatriz Nizza da Silva (ed.), *A Cultura Portuguesa na Terra da Santa Cruz*. Lisboa: Editorial Estampa, 1995.

Quando os Índios eram Vassalos: Colonização e Relações de Poder no Norte do Brasil na Segunda Metade do Século XVIII. Lisbon: Commisão Nacional para as Comerações dos Descobrimentos Portugueses, 2000.

"Fámilias Portugueses na Colonização do Norte Brasileiro." In Maria Beatriz Nizza da Silva (ed.), *Sexualidade, Familia e Religião na Colonização do Brasil*. Lisboa: Livros Horizonte, 2001.

Edwards, William. *A Voyage up the River Amazon Including a Residence at Pará*. London: John Murray, 1847.

Farage, Nadia. *As Muralhas do Sertões: Os Povos Indígenas no Rio Branco e a Colonização*. Rio de Janeiro: Paz e Terra, 1991.

Fausto, Boris. *História Concisa do Brasil*. São Paulo: EDUSP, 2001.

Fausto, Carlos. *Inimigos Fiéis: História, Guerra e Xamanismo na Amazônia*. São Paulo: EDUSP, 2001.

Figueiredo, Lúcio. *Rebeliões no Brasil Colônia*. Rio de Janeiro: Jorge Zahar, 2005.

Fletcher, James Cooley and Daniel Parish Kidder. *Brazil and the Brazilians. Portrayed in Historical and Descriptive Sketches*. Boston: Little, Brown, 1879.

Flory, Thomas. *Judge and Jury in Imperial Brazil: 1808–1871: Social Control, and Political Stability in the New State*. Austin: University of Texas Press, 1981.

Freire, José Bessa. "Da 'Fala Boa' ao Português na Amazônia Brasileira." *Amerindia* (Paris) 8 (1983): 39–84.

Fritz, Samuel. *Journal of the Travels of Father Samuel Fritz*. London: Haklyut Society, 1922.

Funes, Euripides. "Nasci nas Matas, Nunca tive Sehnhor: História e Memória dos Mocambos do Baixo Amazonas." In João José Reis and Flávio dos Santos Gomes (eds.), *Liberdade por um Fio: História dos Quilombos no Brasil*. São Paulo: Companhia das Letras, 1999.

"Mocambos do Trombetas: História, Memória e Identidade." In *Estudos Afroamericanas Virtual*, Universidade Federal do Ceará, 2004. www.ub.es/afroamerica/EAV2/gomes_d.pdf

Furtado, Lourdes. *Pescadores do Rio Amazonas: Um Estudo Antropológico da Pesca Ribeirinha numa Área Amazônica*. Belém: MPEG, CNPq, 1993.

Gomes, Flávio dos Santos *Histórias de Quilombolas: Mocambos e Comunidades de Senzalas no Rio de Janeiro, Século XIX*. Rio de Janeiro: Arquivo Nacional, 1995.

"A 'Safe Haven': Runaway Slaves, Mocambos, and Borders in Colonial Amazonia, Brazil." *Hispanic American Historical Review* 82, no. 3 (2002): 469–498.

"Etnicidade e Fronteiras Cruzadas nas Guianas (secs xviii-xx)," *Estudos Afroamericanos Virtual*, May 2004, 30–59.

Goulding, Michael, Nigel Smith, and Dennis Mahar. *Floods of Fortune: Ecology and Economy Along the Amazon*. New York: Columbia University Press, 2000.

Guardino, Peter. *Peasants, Politics and the Formation of Mexico's National State: Guerrero 1800–1857*. Stanford: Stanford University Press, 1996.

The Time of Liberty: Popular Political Culture in Oaxaca, 1750–1850. Durham: Duke University Press, 2005.

Gudeman, Stephen. "Compadrazgo as a Reflection of the Natural and Spiritual Person." *Proceedings of the Royal Anthropological Institute* (1971): 45–71.

Gudeman, Stephen with Alberto Rivera. *Conversations in Colombia: The Domestic Economy in Life and Context*. Cambridge: Cambridge University Press, 1991.

Guimarães, Lucia Maria Bastos Paschoal, and Maria Emilia Prado, eds. *O Liberalismo no Brasil Imperial: Origens, Conceitos e Prática*. Rio de Janeiro: Editora Raven, 2001.

Handelmann, Henrique. *História do Brasil*. Trans. By L. F. Lahmeyer. Rio de Janeiro: Instituto Histórico e Geográphico Brasileiro, 1931 [1860].

Haring, Clarence. *Empire in Brazil*. Cambridge: Harvard University Press, 1958.

Harris, Mark. "The Brazilian Floodplains: Where Cholera does not kill Caboclos." In Sophie Day, Akis Papataxiarchis, and Michael Stewart (eds.), *Lilies of the Field: How Marginal People live for the Moment*. Boulder: Westview Press, 1999.

Life on the Amazon: The Anthropology of a Brazilian Peasant Village. Oxford: British Academy, Oxford University Press, 2000.

"Uma História dos Nomes: A Alcunha, o Primeiro Nome, e o Apelido no Pará, Norte do Brasil," *Etnográfica (Lisbon)*, 12, 1 (2008): 215–236.

Hartt, Charles. "Notes on the Lingoa Geral or Modern Tupi of the Amazonas." *Transactions of the American Philological Association* 3 (1872): 58–76.

Hemming, John. *Red Gold: The Conquest of the Brazilian Indians*. London: Macmillan, 1978.

Amazon Frontier: The Defeat of the Brazilian Indians. London: Macmillan, 1987.

Henderson, James. *A History of the Brazil: Comprising its Geography, Commerce, Colonization and Aboriginal Inhabitants*. London: Longman, Hurst, Rees, 1821.

Herndon, William. *Exploration of the Valley of the Amazon*. Washington: Taylor and Maury, 1854.

Hobsbawm, Eric. *The Age of Revolution, 1789–1840*. London: Abacus, 1977.

Hooneart, Eduardo, ed. *História da Igreja na Amazônia*. Petropolis: Vozes, 1991.

Humphreys, R. A., and John Lynch, eds. *The Origins of Latin American Revolutions 1808–1826*. New York: Alfred Knopf, 1965.

Hurley, Jorge. *A Cabanagem*. Belém: Livraria Clássica, 1936.

Traços Cabanos. Belém: Oficina Gráfica do Instituto Lauro Sodré, 1936.

James, C. L. R. *The Black Jacobins*. Harmondsworth: Penguin, 2005.

Jancsó, István. ed. *Brasil: Formação do Estado e de Nação*. São Paulo: Hucitec, 2003.

ed. *Independência História e Historiografia*. São Paulo: Hucitec, 2005.

Joseph, Gilbert, and Daniel Nugent, eds. *Everyday Forms of State Formation: Revolution and the Negotiation of Rule in Mexico*. Durham: Duke University Press, 1994.

Katz, Friederich. *Riot, Rebellion and Revolution: Rural Social Conflict in Mexico.* Princeton: Princeton University Press, 1989.

Kelly, Arlene. "Family, Church and Crown: A Social and Demographic History of the Lower Xingu Valley and the Municipality of Gurupá, 1623–1889." Ph.D dissertation, University of Florida, 1984.

Kidder, Daniel Parish. *Sketches of Residence and Travels in Brazil.* 2 vols. Philadelphia: Sorin & Ball, 1845.

Kiemen, Matthias. *The Indian Policy of Portugal in the Amazon Region, 1614–1693.* New York: Octagon, 1973.

Kraay, Hendrik. "'As Terrifying as Unexpected': The Bahian Sabinada, 1837–1838." *Hispanic American Historical Review* 72, no. 4 (1992): 501–528.

———. *Race, State and the Armed Forces in Independence-Era Brazil: Bahia, 1790s-1840s.* Stanford: Stanford University Press, 2001.

Kuznesof, Elizabeth. "Sexual Politics, Race and Bastard Bearing in Nineteenth Century Brazil: A Question of Culture or Power," *Journal of Family History* 16, no. 3 (2005): 241–260.

Ladurie, Emmanuel Le Roy. *Carnival: A People's Uprising at Romans 1579–1580.* London: Scholar Press, 1980.

Langfur, Hal. *The Forbidden Lands: Colonial Identity, Frontier Violence, and the Persistence of Brazil's Eastern Indians,* Stanford: Stanford University Press, 2006.

Leacock, Seth. "The Economic Life of the Maués Indians." *Boletim do Museu Emilio Goeldi (Série Antropologia)* 19 (1964): 1–30.

Leal, Felippe José Pereira. *Correções e Ampliações ao que Sobre a Revolução que Arrebantou na Cidade do Pará em Janeiro de 1835 Publicou o Conselheiro João Manoel Pereira da Silva.* Bahia, 1879.

Leite, Serafim. *História da Companhia de Jesus no Brasil.* Vol. 3 and 4. Rio de Janeiro: Instituto Nacional do Livro, 1943.

Leonardi, Victor. *Os Historiadores e os Rios.* Brasilia: Editora Universidade de Brasilia, 1999.

Lessnoff, Michael. *The Social Contract.* London: Macmillan, 1986.

Lévi-Strauss, Claude. "The Social Use of Kin Terms." In Paul Bohannon and John Middleton (eds.), *Marriage, Family and Residence.* New York: The Natural History Press, 1968.

Levine, Robert. *Vale of Tears: Revisiting the Canudos Massacre in Northeastern Brazil, 1893–1897.* Berkeley: University of California Press, 1995.

Lewin, Linda. *Surprise Heirs: Illegitimacy, Patrimonial Rights, and Legal Nationalism in Luso-Brazilian Inheritance, 1750–1821.* Stanford: Stanford University Press, 2003.

Lima, Araújo. *A Amazônia: A Terra e o Homen.* São Paulo: Companhia Editora Nacional, 1975.

Lima, Ivan Stolze. *Cores, Marcas e Falas: Sentidos da Mestiçagem no Império do Brasil.* Rio de Janeiro: Arquivo Nacional, 2003.

Lima, Leandro Mahalem de. "Rios Vermelhos, Perspectivas e Posições de Sujeito em Torno da Noção de Cabano na Amazônia em Meados de 1835." Master's thesis, São Paulo, 2008.

Lima-Ayres, Deborah. "The Social Category Caboclo: History, Social Organization, Identity and Outsider's Social Classification of the Rural Population of an Amazonian Region (the Middle Solimões)." Ph. D. dissertation, University of Cambridge, 1992.

Loureiro, João de Jesus Paes. *Cultura Amazônica: Uma Poética do Imaginário.* Belém: Cejup, 1991.

Lustosa, Antônio de Almeida. *Dom Macedo Costa, Bispo do Pará.* Belém: Cruzada da Boa Imprensa, 1993.

Machado, André. "A Quebra Mola Real das Sociedades: A Crise Política do Antigo Regime Português na Provincia do Grão-Pará (1821–1825)." Ph.D. dissertation, University of São Paulo, 2006.

Maclachlan, Colin. "The Indian Directorate: Forced Acculturation in Portuguese America (1757–1799)." *The Americas* 28, no. 4 (1972): 357–387.

"The Indian Labor Structure in the Portuguese Amazon." In Dauril Alden (ed.) *Colonial Roots of Modern Brazil.* Berkeley: University of California, 1973.

"African Slave Trade and Economic Development in Amazonia, 1700–1800." In Robert Brent Toplin (ed.), *Slavery and Race Relations in Latin America.* Westport: Greenwood Press, 1974.

Magalhaes, Basílio de. "A Cabanagem." *RIHGB* 171 (1936): 278–305.

Magalhães, José Vieira Couto de. *O Selvagem.* São Paulo: Companhia Editora Nacional, [1876] 1935.

Mallon, Florencia. *Peasant and Nation: The Making of Postcolonial Mexico and Peru.* Berkeley: University of California Press, 1995.

Marcoy, Paul. *A Journey across South America, from the Pacific Ocean to the Atlantic Ocean.* Translated by E. Rich. 2 vols. London, 1873.

Marin, Rosa Acevedo. "A Influência da Revolução Francesa no Grão-Pará." In José Carlos da Cunha (ed.), *Ecologia, Desenvolvimento e Cooperação na Amazônia.* Belém: UNAMAZ, UFPA, 1992.

Martins, José de Souza. "The State and the Militarization of the Agrarian Question in Brazil." In Marianne Schmink and Charles Wood (eds.), *Frontier Expansion in Amazonia.* Gainesville: University of Florida Press, 1984.

Martius, Karl. "How the History of Brazil Should Be Written." In Bradford E. Burns (ed.), *Perspectives on Brazilian History.* New York: Columbia University Press, 1967.

Maués, Raymundo Heraldo. *Pajés, Padres, Festas e Santos: Catolicismo Popular e Controle Eclesiástico, Um Estudo Antropológico numa Área do Interior da Amazônia.* Belém: Cejup, 1995.

Maw, Henry Lister. *Journal of a Passage from the Pacific to the Atlantic, Crossing the Andes in the Northern Provinces of Peru, and Descending the River Marañon, or Amazon.* London, 1829.

Maxwell, Kenneth. "The Generation of the 1790s and the Idea of a Luso-Brazilian Empire," in Dauril Alden (ed.), *The Colonial Roots of Modern Brazil.* Berkeley: University of California Press, 1973.

Pombal: Paradox of the Enlightenment. New York: Cambridge University Press, 1995.

"The Spark: Pombal, the Amazon and the Jesuits." *Portuguese Studies* 17, no. 1 (2001): 168–183.

Naked Tropics: Essays on Empire and Other Rogues. New York: Routledge, 2003.

Conflicts and Conspiracies: Brazil and Portugal 1750–1808. London: Routledge, 2004.

Medina, José Toribio, ed. *The Discovery of the Amazon.* New York: Constable, 1988.

Mello e Souza, Laura de. *Desclassificados de Ouro: A Pobreza Mineira no Século XVIII.* Rio de Janeiro: Graal, 1983.

The Devil and the Land of the Holy Cross: Witchcraft, Slavery, and Popular Religion in Colonial Brazil. Translated by Diane Grosklaus Whitty. Austin: University of Texas, 2003.

Menendez, Miguel. "A Área Madeira-Tapajós: Situação de Contato e Relações entre o Colonizador e Indígena." In Manuela Carneiro da Cunha (ed.), *História dos Índios do Brasil.* São Paulo: Companhia das Letras, 1992.

Metcalf, Alida. *Family and Frontier in Colonial Brazil: Santana de Parnaiba, 1580–1822.* Berkeley: University of California Press, 1992.

Midosi, Paulo. *Portugal, or Who is the Lawful Successor to the Throne?* London: John Richardson, 1828.

Millet de Saint-Adolphe, J. C. R. *Diccionário Geográphico, Histórico e Descriptivo do Império do Brazil.* Translated by G. Lopes de Moura. Paris, 1845.

Mintz, Sidney, and Eric Wolf. "An Analysis of Ritual Co-Parenthood (Compadrazgo)." *South Western Journal of Anthropology* 6, no. 4 (1950): 341–368.

Monteiro, John. "Escravidão Indígena e Despovoamento na América Portuguesa." In Francisco Faria Paulino (ed.), *Brasil: Nas Vesperas do Mundo Moderno*. Lisboa: Commisão Nacional, 1992.

Negros da Terra: Índios e Bandeirantes nas Origens de São Paulo. São Paulo: Companhia das Letras, 1994.

"The Heathen Castes of Sixteenth-Century Portuguese America: Unity, Diversity, and the Invention of the Brazilian Indians." *Hispanic American Historical Review* 80, no. 4 (2000): 697–719.

Moore, Denis, Sidney Facundes, and Nadia Pires. "Nheengatu, (Lingua Geral Amazônica)." *Proceedings of The Meeting of The Society for the Study of the Indigenous Languages*, no. July (1993): 93–118.

Morais, Francisco. "Estudantes Brasileiros na Universidade de Coimbra (1772–1872)." *ABNRJ*, 62 (1940): 137–335.

Moreira Neto, Carlos de Araújo. "Henrique João Wilkens e os Índios Mura." *ABNRJ*, 109 (1989): 227–301.

Moreira Neto, Carlos de Araújo. *Índios da Amazônia, de Maioria a Minoria, 1750–1850*. Petropolis: Vozes, 1985.

Mosher, Jeffrey. "Political Mobilization, Party Ideology, and Lusophobia in Nineteenth-Century Brazil: Pernambuco, 1822–1850." *Hispanic American Historical Review* 80, no. 4 (2000): 881–912.

"The Struggle for the State: Partisan Conflict and the Origins of the Praiera Revolt in Imperial Brazil." *Luso-Brazilian Review* 42, no. 2 (2005): 40–65.

Political Struggle, Ideology, and State Building: Pernambuco and the Construction of Brazil, 1817–1850. Lincoln: University of Nebraska Press, 2008.

Mota, Carlos Guilherme, ed. *1822: Dimensões*. São Paulo: Perspectiva, 1972.

Moura, Clovis. *Quilombos: Resistência ao Escravismo*. São Paulo: Ática, 1989.

Muniz, João de Palma. "Limites Municipais do Estado do Pará." *ABAPP* 9 (1916).

Adesão do Grão-Pará a Independência. Belém: Conselho Estadual da Cultura, 1973.

Nazarri, Muriel. "Concubinage in Colonial Brazil." *Journal of Family History* 21, no. 2 (1996): 107–118.

Needell, Jeffrey. *The Party of Order: The Conservatives, the State, and Slavery in the Brazilian Monarchy, 1831–1871*. Stanford: Stanford University Press, 2006.

Nimuendaju, Curt. "The Mura and the Piraha." In Julian Steward (ed.), *Handbook of South American Indians, 255–266*. Bulletin 143: Bureau of American Ethnology, 1948.

Nugent, Stephen. *Amazonian Caboclo Society: An Essay in Peasant Economy and Invisibility*. Oxford: Berg, 1993.

and Mark Harris, eds. *Some Other Amazonians: Modern Peasantries in History*. London: Institute for the Study of the Americas, 2005.

Paolo, Pasquale di. *Cabanagem: A Revolução Popular da Amazônia*. Belém: Conselho de Cultura, 1985.

Parker, Eugene, ed. "The Amazon Caboclo: Historical and Contemporary Perspectives." *Studies in Third World Societies*, 32 (1985).

Paton, Alexander. *Narrative of the Loss of the Schooner Clio of Montrose*. Montrose, 1879 [1837].

Pereira, Nunes. *Os Índios Maués*. Manaus: Editora Valer, 2003 [1954].

Platt, Tristan. "The Andean Experience of Bolivian Liberalism." In Steve Stern (ed.), *Resistance, Rebellion and Consciousness in the Andean Peasant World, 18th to 20th Centuries*. Madison: University of Wisconsin Press, 1987.

with Pablo Quisbert. "Knowing Silence and Merging Horizons: The Case of the Great Potosí Cover-Up." In Mark Harris (ed.), *Ways of Knowing: New Approaches in the Anthropology of Knowledge and Learning*. Oxford: Berghahn Books, 2007.

Porro, Antônio. *As Crônicas do Rio Amazonas.* Petrópolis: Vozes, 1993.
Os Povos das Aguas: Ensaios de Etno-História Amazônica. Petropolis, São Paulo: Vozes, Edusp, 1996.
Dicionário Etnohistórico da Amazônia Colonial. São Paulo: Cadernos do Instituto dos Estudos Brasileiros, 2007.
Prado, Caio. *The Colonial Background of Modern Brazil.* Berkeley: University of California Press, 1969.
Evolução Política do Brasil. São Paulo: Editora Brasiliense, 1976 [1933].
Priore Mary Del and Flávio dos Santos Gomes, eds. *Os Senhores dos Rios: Amazônia, Margens e Histórias.* Rio de Janeiro: Elsevier, 2003.
Queiroz, Jonas and Flávio dos Santos Gomes. "Amazônia, Fronteiras e Identidades: Reconfigurações Coloniais e Pos-coloniais (Guianas- Séculos XVIII-XIX)." *Lusotopie* 1 (2002): 25–49.
Raffles, Hugh. *In Amazonia: A Natural History.* Princeton: Princeton University Press, 2002.
Raiol, Domingos Antônio. "A Catequese dos Índios do Pará." *ABAPP*, no. 2 (1902): 117–183.
"O Brasil Político." In *Obras de Domingos Antônio Raiol, Barão de Guajará.* Belém, Pará: Conselho Estadual de Cultura, 1970 [1858].
Motins Politicos, ou Historia dos Principais Acontecimentos Políticos da Província do Pará, desde oano de 1821 até 1835. 3 vols. Belém: Universidade Federal do Pará, 1970 [1865–1890].
Ramos, Alcida. *Indigenism: Ethnic Politics in Brazil.* Madison: University of Wisconsin Press, 1998.
Reis, Arthur C. F. "A Explosão Cívica em 1832." *Revista do Instituto Geográphico e Histórico do Amazonas* 2, nos 1 and 2 (1932): 45–63.
Dom Romualdo Coelho de Souza. Belém, 1941.
A Amazônia que os Portugueses Revelaram. Rio de Janeiro: Ministério da Educação e Cultura, Serviço de Documentação, 1957.
História de Óbidos. Rio de Janeiro: Editora Civilização Brasileira, 1979.
Historia de Santarém: Seu Desenvolvimento Histórico. Rio de Janeiro: Editora Civilização Brasileira, 1979.
História do Amazonas. Belo Horizonte: Editora Itatiaia, 1989.
A Política de Portugal no Valle Amazônico. Belém: Secult, 1993.
Limites e Demarcações na Amazônia Brasileira. Belém: CEJUP, 1993 [1948].
"A Ocupação de Caiena." In Sergio Buarque de Holanda (ed.), *O Brasil Monarquico, História Geral da Civilização Brasileira, Tomo 2, Vol. 3.* Rio de Janeiro: Bertrand Brasil, 2003.
"O Grão Para e Maranhão." In Fernando Henrique Cardoso (ed.), *O Brasil Monarquico, Part 4, Dispersão e Unidade, História da Civilisação Brasileira.* Rio de Janeiro: Bertrand Brasil, 2004.
Reis, João José. *Slave Rebellion in Brazil: The Muslim Uprising of 1835 in Bahia.* Baltimore: John Hopkins University Press, 1995.
Death is a Festival: Funeral Rites and Rebellion in Nineteenth-Century Brazil: University of North Carolina Press, 2006.
Restall, Matthew, ed. *Beyond Black and Red: African-Native Relations in Colonial Latin America.* Albuquerque: University of New Mexico Press, 2005.
Ribeiro, Gladys Sabina. *A Liberdade em Construção: Identidade Nacional e Conflitos Antilusitanos no Primeiro Reinado.* Rio de Janeiro: Relume-Dumará, 2002.
Ricci, Magda. "Do Sentido aos Significados da Cabanagem: Percursos Historiográficos." *Anais da Arquivo Publico do Pará* 4, no. 2 (2001): 241–271.
"O Fim do Grão-Pará e o Nascimento do Brasil: Movimentos Sociais, Levantes e Deserções no Alvorecer do novo Império, 1808–1840." In Mary Del Priore, and

Flávio dos Santos Gomes (eds.), *Os Senhores dos Rios: Amazônia, Margens e Histórias.* Rio de Janeiro: Elsevier, 2003.

"Cabanagem, Cidadania e Identidade Revolucionária: O Problema do Patriotismo na Amazônia Entre 1835 e 1840." *Tempo (Niterói)*, 2007, 11, 22, 5–30.

Rivière, Peter. *Absent-Minded Imperialism: Britain, and the Expansion of Empire in Nineteenth-Century Brazil.* London: Tauris Academic Studies, 1995.

Rocque, Carlos. *Grande Enciclopédia da Amazônia.* Belém: Amazônia Editora, 1968.

Rodrigues, Aryon Dall'Igna. "As Linguas Gerais Sul-Americanas," 1996. http://vsites.unb.br/il/lablind/lingerais.htm

Rodrigues Ferreira, Alexandre. *Viagem Filosófica: Memórias, Antropologia.* Rio de Janeiro: Conselho Federal da Cultura, 1974.

Rodrigues, Isabel Vieira. "A Política de Francisco Xavier Mendonça Furtado no Norte do Brasil (1751–1759)'." *Oceanos* 40, October/November (1999): 94–111.

Rodrigues, José Honorio. *Independência: Revolução e Contra Revolução: As Forças Armadas. Vol. 3.* Rio de Janeiro: Livraria Francisco Alves Editora, 1975.

Roller, Heather Flynn. "Colonial Collecting Expeditions and the Pursuit of Opportunities in the Amazonian Sertão, c. 1750–1800," *The Americas*, 66, 4, 2010, 435–467.

Roosevelt, Anna, ed. *Amazonian Indians from Prehistory to Present.* Tucson: University of Arizona Press, 1994.

Rugeley, Terry. *Yucatan Maya Peasantry and the Origins of the Caste War.* Austin: University of Texas Press, 1996.

"Rural Political Violence and the Origins of the Caste War." *The Americas* 53, no. 4 (1997): 469–496.

Russell-Wood, Alfred. "Women and Society in Colonial Brazil." *Journal of Latin American Studies* 9, no. 1 (1977): 1–34.

Society and Government in Colonial Brazil 1500–1822. Aldershot: Variorum, 1992.

"Centers and Peripheries in the Luso-Brazilian World 1500–1808." In Christine Daniels, and Michael Kennedy (eds.), *Negotiated Empires: Centers and Peripheries in the Americas, 1500–1820.* New York: Routledge, 2002.

Salles, Vicente. *O Negro no Pará sob o Regime da Escravidão.* Rio de Janeiro: Fundação Getulio Vargas, 1971.

Memorial da Cabanagem. Belém: CEJUP, 1992.

Vocabulário Crioulo: Contribuição do Negro ao Falar Regional Amazônico. Belém: Instituto das Artes do Pará, 2003.

O Negro na Formação da Sociedade Paraense. Belém: Editora Paka-Tatu, 2004.

Santos, Francisco Jorge dos. "Dossiê Mundurucu: Uma Contribução para História Indígena da Amazônia Colonial." *Boletim Informativo do Museu Amazônico* 5, no. 8 (1995).

Além da Conquista: Guerras e Rebeliões Indígenas na Amazônia Pombalina. Manaus: Editora da Universidade do Amazonas, 2002.

Santos, João. *Cabanagem em Santarém.* Santarém: Livraria Atica, 1986.

Santos, Paulo Rodrigues dos. *Tupaiulândia.* Santarém: ICBS/ACN, 2000.

Santos, Roberto. *História Econômica da Amazônia (1800–1920).* São Paulo: Editora Queiroz, 1982.

Sargen, Ian. *Our Men in Brazil: The Hesketh Brothers Abroad.* Lancaster: Scotforth Books, 2009.

Schwartz, Stuart. *Slaves, Peasants and Rebels: Reconsidering Brazilian Slavery.* Champaign-Urbana: University of Illinois Press, 1992.

Schwartz, Stuart, and Frank Salomon. "New Peoples and New Kinds of People: Adaptation, Readjustment, and Ethnogenesis in South American Indigenous Societies (Colonial Era)." In Frank Salomon and Stuart Schwartz (eds.), *The Cambridge History of the*

Native Peoples of the Americas, vol. 3, Part 2: South America. Cambridge: Cambridge University Press, 1996.

Schwarz, Roberto. "Misplaced Ideas: Essays on Literature and Society in Late Nineteenth-century Brazil," in *Misplaced Ideas: Essays on Brazilian Culture.* London: Verso, 1992.

Scott, James. *Weapons of the Weak: Everyday Forms of Peasant Resistance.* New Haven: Yale University Press, 1985.

Seckinger, Ron. "The Politics of Nativism: Ethnic Prejudice and Political Power in Mato Grosso, 1831–1834," *The Americas* 32, no. 4, (1975): 393–416.

Serrão, Joel, ed. *Dicionário de História do Portugal.* Lisboa: Iniciativas, 1963–71.

Serulnikov, Sergio. *Subverting Colonial Authority: Challenges to Spanish Rule in Eighteenth-Century Southern Andes.* Durham: Duke University Press, 2003.

Silva, João Manoel Pereira da. *História do Brazil na Menoridade do Pedro 2.* Rio de Janeiro: Havre, 1888.

Silva, Maria Beatriz Nizza da. "Apêndice: Política Externa de D. João VI no Respeitante a Definição Territorial do Brasil." In Maria Beatriz Nizza da Silva (ed.), *O Império Luso-Brasileiro 1750–1822.* Lisboa: Editorial Estampa, 1986.

ed. *Dicionário da História da Colonização Portuguesa no Brasil.* São Paulo: Verbo, 1994.

ed. *História da Família no Brasil Colonial.* Rio de Janeiro: Editora Nova Fronteira, 1998.

Silveira, Itala Bezerra da. *Cabanagem, A Luta Perdida . . . ,* Belém: Secretaria de Estado da Cultura, 1994.

Slater, Candace. *Dance of the Dolphin: Transformation and Disenchantment in the Amazonian Imagination.* Chicago: University of Chicago Press, 1994.

Smith, Herbert. *Brazil: The Amazons and The Coast,* New York: Scribner, 1879.

Smith, Nigel. *Man, Fishes, and the Amazon.* Gainesville: Florida University Press, 1982.

The Amazon River Forest: A Natural History of Plants, Animals and People. Oxford: Oxford University Press, 1999.

Smyth, William. "Account of the Rivers Amazon and Negro, from Recent Observations," *Journal of the Royal Geographical Society,* 1835, 11–23.

and Frederick Lowe. *Narrative of a Journey from Lima to Pará.* London, 1836.

Sommer, Barbara. "Negotiated Settlements: Native Amazonians and Portuguese Policy in Pará, Brazil, 1758–1798." Ph.D. dissertation, University of New Mexico, 2000.

"Cupid on the Amazon: Sexual Witchcraft and Society in Late Colonial Pará, Brazil." *Colonial Latin American Historical Review* 12, no. 4 (2003): 415–446.

"Colony of the Sertão: Amazonian Expeditions and the Indian Slave Trade." *The Americas* 61, no. 3 (2004): 401–428.

"'Cracking Down on the Cunhamenas: Renegade Amazonian Traders under Pombaline Reform." *Journal of Latin American Studies* 38, no. 4 (2006): 767–791.

Souza, Inglês de. *Contos Amazônicos.* Rio de Janeiro: Presença Edições, 1988.

O Cacaulista. Belem: UFPa, 2003.

Souza, Márcio. *A Paixão de Ajuricaba.* Manaus: Editora Valer, 2005.

Spix, Johann Baptist von and Karl Martius. *Viagem pelo Brasil, 1817–1820.* Belo Horizonte: Editora Itatiaia, 1981.

Spruce, Richard. *Notes of a Botanist on the Amazon and Andes.* London: Macmillan, 1908.

Stern, Steve, ed. *Resistance, Rebellion and Consciousness in the Andean Peasant World, 18th to 20th Centuries.* Madison: University of Wisconsin Press, 1987.

Sweet, David Graham. "A Rich Realm of Nature Destroyed: The Middle Amazon Valley, 1640–1750." Ph.D. dissertation, University of Wisconsin, 1974.

"Francisca: Indian Slave," in David Graham Sweet and Gary Nash (eds.), *Struggle and Survival in Colonial America.* Berkeley: University of California Press, 1981.

"Native Resistance in Eighteenth-Century Amazonia: The 'Abominable Muras' in War and Peace." *Radical History Review,* no. 53 (1992): 49–80.

and Gary Nash (eds.), *Struggle and Survival in Colonial America*. Berkeley: University of California Press, 1981.

Tavares Bastos, A. C. *O Valle do Amazonas*. São Paulo: Companhia Editorial National, 1937.

Thompson, Edward P. "Patrician Society, Plebian Culture." *Journal of Social History* 7, no. 4 (1974): 382–405.

Thomson, Sinclair. *We Alone Will Rule: Native Andean Politics in the Age of Insurgency*. Madison: University of Wisconsin Press, 2002.

Thorlby, Thiago. *A Cabanagem na Fala do Povo*. São Paulo: Paulinas, 1987.

Treece, David. *Exiles, Allies, Rebels: Brazil's Indianist Movement, Indigenist Politics, and the Imperial Nation-State*. Westport: Greenwood Press, 2000.

Tutino, John. *From Insurrection to Revolution in Mexico: Social Bases of Agrarian Violence, 1750–1940*. Princeton: Princeton University Press, 1986.

Vainfas, Ronaldo, ed. *Dicionário do Brasil Colonial (1500–1808)*. Rio de Janeiro: Editora Objectiva, 2000.

——— ed. *Dicionário do Brasil Imperial (1822–1889)*. Rio de Janeiro: Objetiva, 2002.

Vale, Brian. *Independence or Death!: British Sailors and Brazilian Independence, 1822–25*. London: Tauris Academic, 1996.

Velho, Otávio. *Frentes de Expansão e Estrutura Agrária*. Rio de Janeiro: Zahar Editores, 1972.

Veríssimo, José. *A Pesca na Amazonia*. Belém: Editora da Universidade Federal do Pará, 1970.

——— "As Populações Indígenas e Mestiças na Amazônia, Linguagem, Crenças e Costumes." *RIHGB*, no. 50 (1887): 295–390.

——— "As Populações Indígenas e Mestiças da Amazônia: Sua Língua, suas Crenças, seus Costumes." In José Veríssimo (ed.), *Estudos Amazônicos*. Belém: Editora da Universidade Federal do Pará, 1970 [1878].

Vianna, Arthur. "As Festas Populares." *ABAPP*, no. 3 (1968): 225–261.

Vidal, Laurent. *Mazagão, La Ville qui Traversa L'Atlantique: Du Maroc a L'Amazonie, (1769–1783)*. Paris: Aubier, 2005.

Vilaça, Aparecida. *Quem Somos Nós: Os Wari Encontram os Brancos*. Rio de Janeiro: Editora da UFRJ, 2006.

Viveiros de Castro, Eduardo. *From the Enemy's Point of View: Humanity and Divinity in an Amazonian Society*. Chicago: University of Chicago Press, 1992.

Wagley, Charles. *Amazon Town*. New York: Macmillan, 1976.

Wallace, Alfred Russell. *A Narrative of Travels on the Amazon and Rio Negro with an Account of the Native Tribes and Observations on the Climate, Geology, and Natural History of the Amazon Valley*. London: Reeve, 1853.

Weinstein, Barbara. *The Amazon Rubber Boom 1850–1920*. Stanford: Stanford University Press, 1985.

——— "Persistence of Caboclo Culture in the Amazon: The Impact of the Rubber Trade, 1850–1920." In Eugene Parker (ed.), "The Amazon Caboclo: Historical and Contemporary Perspectives," *Studies in Third World Societies*, 32 (1985): 89–113.

Whitehead, Neil. *The Lords of the Tiger Spirit: A History of the Caribs in Colonial Venezuela and Guyana, 1498–1820*. Dordrecht: Foris Publications, 1988.

Wilcken, Patrick. *Empire Adrift: The Portuguese Court in Rio*. London: Bloomsbury, 2004.

Wright, Robin and Manuela Carneiro de Cunha, "Destruction, resistance and transformation: Southern, Coastal and Northern Brazil, 1580–1890," Salomon and Schwartz (eds.), *The Cambridge History of the Native Peoples of the Americas, vol. 3, Part 2: South America*. Cambridge: Cambridge University Press, 1996.

Index

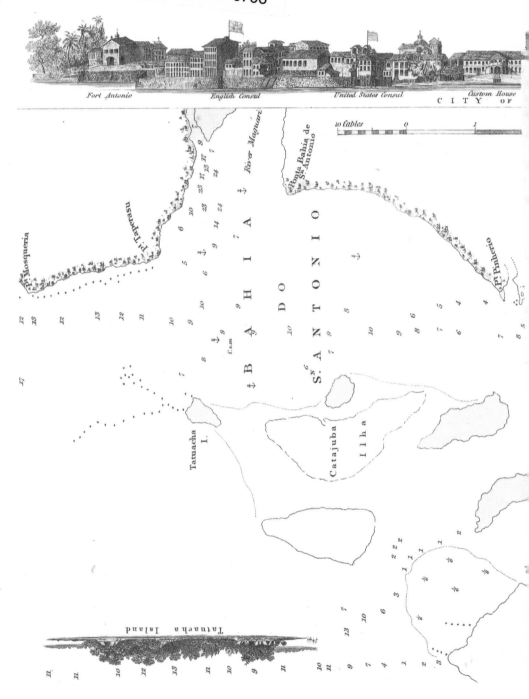

Fort Antonio   English Consul   United States Consul   Custom House

C I T Y   O F

10 Cables   0   1

P.ᵗ Mosqueria

P.ᵗ Taperasu

River Maguari

Ponta Bahia de Sᵗ Antonio

P.ᵗ Pinherio

B A H I A   D O   Sᵗ A N T O N I O

Tatuacha I.

Catajuba Ilha

Tatuacha Island